NATO

AND AMERICAN SECURITY

OTHER BOOKS FROM
THE CENTER OF INTERNATIONAL STUDIES
PRINCETON UNIVERSITY

NATO

AND

AMERICAN SECURITY

EDITED BY KLAUS KNORR

PRINCETON, NEW JERSEY

PRINCETON UNIVERSITY PRESS

1959

Printed in the United States of America
by Princeton University Press
Princeton, New Jersey

PREFACE

As EXPLAINED in Chapter 1, this book is the product of a joint enterprise. All authors are indebted to co-authors and to the participants in a Princeton conference on problems of NATO strategy. My own indebtedness is special since my responsibility is special. For making helpful comments on the report reproduced in the Appendix, I am grateful to Arthur Burns, Bernard Cohen, Frederick S. Dunn, Daniel Ellsberg, Herman Kahn, Gardner Patterson, and Glenn Snyder. In the more difficult task of writing Chapter 12, I was greatly assisted by the critical comments of Arthur Burns, Daniel Ellsberg, Herman Kahn, and Glenn Snyder.

My gratitude is especially great to Jean MacLachlan, who edited the entire book with accustomed accomplishment.

KLAUS KNORR

Princeton
March 25, 1959

CONTENTS

CONTENTS

PART I

STRATEGIC BACKGROUND

CHAPTER 1

THE STRAINED ALLIANCE

BY KLAUS KNORR

IN 1958, it is fair to say, the North Atlantic Treaty Organization began to be seriously strained by a profound crisis of confidence. Little seemed to be amiss according to official announcements from SHAPE and member governments. Nor did the general public in the NATO countries show much concern, except over local issues such as Cyprus. But parliamentary records, newspaper reports, articles, books, lectures, and conversations told a different story. Increasingly the question was put: Can NATO, with its present forces and strategy, still be expected to defend the West against possible aggression and aggressive threats—indeed, to deter military aggression? Is the alliance still able to fulfill its central function?

I

Down the record of history, alliances have come and gone, some short-lived, some lasting over long stretches of time. We cannot predict whether NATO, only about ten years old, will prove relatively durable or not. To be sure, it is normal for even solid alliances to experience strains and stresses. From its inception, NATO has been subject to centrifugal pulls—such as French dissatisfaction over lack of NATO support in Algeria, the Franco-British invasion of Egypt in 1956, the three-cornered conflict of Britain, Greece, and Turkey over Cyprus, the fisheries dispute between Iceland and Britain—without losing fundamental cohesion.[1] These many but minor pulls only reflect the fact that the allied nations have different interests regarding many foreign policy issues and view the external world in more or less different ways; they do not prove disruptive so long as the advantages of alliance are felt to outweigh the disadvantages.

It is also true that, by historical standards, NATO is no ordinary alliance. Strictly speaking, it is not a defense community, as it is sometimes called, for a community has common central institutions, and NATO is a compact among sovereign states. The members have only bound themselves to exercise their sovereign powers in prescribed ways,

---

[1] For an introduction to NATO's history and also an excellent analysis of its problems, see Ben T. Moore, *NATO and the Future of Europe*, New York, 1958.

when any other member is under attack. The compact is revocable at the will of each member; decisions are made on the unanimity principle and are carried out at the will of each government.

And yet, as an alliance, NATO can claim to be in some ways unique. Outwardly, this uniqueness is expressed by a profusion of common military institutions and elaborate machinery for consultation. Before the Korean War, NATO was, as a wag put it, like the Venus of Milo— all SHAPE and no arms. Thereafter, however, arms were provided and NATO developed a network of common commands and coordinated forces, and a degree of consultation, which—though not satisfying all its proponents—go far beyond what any other alliance of free nations has achieved in peacetime, and which could not be pushed *radically* further without transforming the alliance into a community with supranational organs.

To some extent, no doubt, this proliferation of joint military institutions and forces reflects the recognition that, owing to the technological revolution in weapons, defense and deterrence of attack demand forces that are fully mobilized in time of peace. But this recognition alone would have failed to bring forth the noted results without more fundamental conditions: a similarity and compatibility of basic political orientations and the firm expectation that, among these countries, internal conflict would not be resolved by resort to military power.

Indeed, though nobody can call it a federation or confederation of states, NATO is sometimes claimed to be more than a military alliance. But if it is, it is so only to the most inchoate extent. Surely the alliance as a whole, and especially the United States and the United Kingdom, are unprepared to adopt the integrative measures with which the Community of Six is experimenting in the European Economic Community, the Atomic Energy Community, and the Coal and Steel Community; and, despite repeated attempts, it has even proved impossible to breathe life into Article II of the North Atlantic Treaty, which exhorts the members to promote close economic collaboration. In no other field of interest are the allies as united as in their interest in withstanding Soviet military moves against themselves. In its present form, NATO is primarily a defense alliance against possible Soviet aggression *in Europe*. And it is as such a defense alliance that, over the near future at least, it will wane or prosper.

Despite impressive military collaboration, NATO as a defense alliance has from its beginning suffered not only from minor pulls of divergent interests, but also from basic defects which now, during the current crisis of confidence, are coming more sharply to the fore.

First, although the military power of Soviet Russia has been menacingly great and growing rapidly, the military effort of the NATO allies as a whole has tended to be parsimonious. Though Russia has been and remains decidedly inferior to the NATO allies in population and economic resources, it has diverted to the military sector a larger proportion of its national product than they of theirs; and this, in addition to efficient use of these resources, has permitted Russia over the past ten years to gain greatly and ominously, relative to the NATO combine, in over-all military strength. This defect of not devoting to defense enough manpower and other resources varies from ally to ally. But even the United States and Britain, the two allies which during these years allocated the largest proportion of their national product to defense, have shown a disposition to place "economy before defense," as many critics put it.

Second, short of a supranational solution requiring a merging of national sovereign powers, it is inevitably difficult for a large group of countries to develop a common and efficient strategy and balanced military forces. The main difficulty is, of course, that the military interests of the coalition partners are not sufficiently convergent and that, in the absence of federation, mutual trust in the dependability of allies is necessarily incomplete and naturally subject to doubt and corrosion. It is a weakness of the alliance that this difficulty has not been mitigated by closer cooperation. And the first defect, it should be noted, aggravates the second, for the smaller the total defense effort of the alliance, the greater is the need for agreement on the most effective strategy and for the economies of complementary and interdependent forces.

In part, but only in part, the United States is perhaps especially responsible for the second defect. American predominance in decision-making in NATO and at SHAPE and the retention of SAC—overwhelmingly the mainstay of Western deterrence—as a national, rather than as part of a joint, military instrument are easy to understand and easy to justify. The United States is by far the most powerful of the allies; it has important military interests and obligations outside Western Europe; and the inherent difficulties of joint decisions over the use of SAC, or part of it, would have made it a far less efficient instrument. Nevertheless, the limits which the United States set to its sharing of military strategy and capability have tended to reinforce the independent reluctance of its partners to share the defense effort to a greater extent than they have done.

II

These two defects of NATO have contributed, and are contributing, to the current crisis which threatens to undermine the solidarity of the NATO allies. This crisis, however, is the direct result of Russia's swift gain in strategic nuclear capability and, more recently, of her lead in the development of ballistic missiles. With Western Europe no longer protected by the umbrella of SAC's superior thermonuclear power, it is now commonly assumed in Europe that both the USSR and the United States are capable of inflicting unacceptable damage on the other and that, in fact, the American striking force is vulnerable to a Russian surprise attack, while the advantage of a surprise attack on Russia is denied to the United States because of political and moral constraints. If the Russians should add to their lead in missile development by substantially outproducing the United States in ICBM's—a contingency which is being widely anticipated by American critics of their country's defense posture—the opening "missile gap" would lend increasing substance to Moscow's claim of having achieved a decisive thermonuclear superiority over the United States.

Under these circumstances, it is not surprising that the existence of at least a strategic nuclear stand-off between the two big antagonists has cast doubt on America's readiness to protect its allies by the threat of massive retaliation, which is now viewed as a threat to commit national suicide. It is this diminished credibility of America's capability for massive deterrence which is the crux of the present crisis. Whether *in fact* the United States will be less ready in the future than it was in the past to use SAC for the protection of its allies is only one aspect of the problem and probably not the most important. How Russia and the Western Europeans assess the American potential of response may be decisive. The premise underlying the new doubt is that nations are unlikely to accept the risk of nuclear warfare except in direct self-defense.

What chiefly causes anxiety in Western Europe is not a Russian thermonuclear threat to the entire alliance, which would mean a *direct* threat to the United States itself. From this the Russians are still felt at present to be deterred by SAC—although the "missile gap," if it develops in significant dimension or is believed to have so developed, should in time prompt the additional fear of the possibility of American defeat and consequent Soviet military mastery over the entire West. The main anxiety at present is over a Soviet strategic threat or a limited ground attack on one or more of the European members of the alliance

—anxiety over a Russian move, in other words, which the threat of American strategic reprisal may no longer deter. In the light of these fears, a European ally, without thermonuclear weapons of its own, would seem to be helpless in the face of a strategic bomb threat from the Soviet Union. And the possibility of a surface attack by Russian forces has raised sharp fears because of the numerical superiority of Soviet forces over NATO's shield; the destruction which Europe might suffer, especially if tactical nuclear arms were employed; and the assumption, in some allied countries at least, that what would be limited war for the United States and perhaps the United Kingdom would be total war for themselves.

Whether objectively justified or not, the diminished credibility of American massive reprisal is thus bringing out and hardening the divergent patterns of risk and interest within the alliance. Several possible consequences are foreshadowed. Certainly France will and other allies may follow the British example of wanting strategic nuclear deterrent power *of their own.* The bid for such independent capabilities will not only confront the United States with a host of problems, including demands for American weapons; it is also possible, if not probable, that the alliance will crumble once independent strategic nuclear forces are diffused among the NATO countries. For, in that event, with too many fingers on too many independent triggers, the increased risks of alliance might well outweigh its diminished benefits. The benefits might appear to have declined because independent deterrents were available, and the risks to have been enlarged because an incautious ally could involve its partners in crises and war.

At the same time, a sharpened sense of insecurity in Western Europe, no doubt spurred by Soviet propaganda, may arise and engender, in some European countries at least, strong public pressures toward an escape from the horrible threat of destruction by seeking disarmament, arms control, and political accommodation with the Communist world. Such pressures would not only put Western governments in a feeble bargaining position vis-à-vis the USSR, possibly resulting in arrangements extremely risky to the West; they might also generate dissent and conflict among as well as within the NATO countries. Alternatively, acute feelings of insecurity may produce apathy and despair on a scale so large that the national will to stand up against aggression is broken, and Soviet inroads become feasible by means of forceful threats and diplomatic guile.

III

To recognize the current crisis in NATO, to worry about it, and to concede that this crisis is loosing forces which may disrupt the coalition is not the same as predicting that NATO as a going concern is about to fall apart. There is a great deal of momentum and vitality in the NATO compact, and disruptive forces will provoke remedial reactions. But successful adaptation to new circumstances depends on these circumstances being honestly faced and appraised, on constructive criticism and innovation.

Indeed, some readers may be disturbed by the frankness with which the weaknesses of NATO are admitted and discussed in this book. Is it not harmful, they might ask, to bring these problems into the open and thus perhaps fan the discontent already abroad in Western Europe? But such arguments would be fallacious. It would amount to self-deception to assume that the difficulties under discussion can be swept under the rug and kept hidden there; and to talk frankly about NATO weaknesses is surely the prerequisite of constructive planning.

Since NATO is primarily a defense alliance, and since the present crisis of confidence results from a shift in the military balance between the West and the Soviet world, the maintenance of NATO as an effective arrangement calls for a defense strategy and force composition capable of lessening current feelings of insecurity. At this point, we do not know whether there is a grand strategy, better than the prevailing one, which would be both feasible and effective in deterring the Soviet Union, and which Western Europeans would believe to be feasible and effective. What is certainly required is a thorough assessment and comparison of all possible solutions.

This book is intended to make a contribution to the search for solutions. It does not claim to have found a solution or solutions that are complete and acceptable. Abstract reasoning can do no more than prepare the way for solutions of strategy problems. When it comes to the crucial test of feasibility, the number of variable factors to be taken into account ranges beyond the technical military complex. Above all, what people and governments *think* the facts to be is as important as the facts themselves. The modest plan of this book, then, is to discuss important elements of possible solutions, for at this point the need is for far-ranging analysis, disciplined by available knowledge but unrestrained by any premature attempt at establishing consensus. In fact, though the authors are agreed on many basic conditions and important consequences, they are in disagreement on others. This is healthy, since, at this time, we need a lively competition of ideas. It was for this reason that multiple authorship seemed to hold the promise of richer content than the work of a single author.

In Part I, *Hilsman's* chapter provides the essential historical context; it discusses the main changes in NATO strategy since its inception, and shows how we arrived at the present parlous state of NATO affairs. The chapter by *Black* and *Yeager* informs the reader succinctly of what is known, and can be inferred, about Soviet reactions to NATO, thus clarifying the basic problem with which the alliance must grapple. In Part II, the chapters by *Rathjens, Hoag*, and *Kaplan* analyze the general strategic problems of all-out and limited war and their deterrence. The chapter by *Burns* is addressed to the question of whether or not the United States should share its nuclear weapons more widely with its allies, provided certain conditions are given. *Schelling's* chapter presents an analysis of some major problems in the control of armaments and surprise attack. *Healey's* chapter describes how British strategic thinking developed during the past history of NATO and specifically explains why the United Kingdom decided to join the nuclear club. The chapter by *Craig* gives an account of German attitudes and thinking about NATO and its strategy, of German reactions which are inevitably affected by the country's proximity to the Soviet Army, its desire for reunification with East Germany, and its special concern over disengagement in Central Europe. *Nitze's* chapter, finally, examines various alternatives to NATO as it is now constituted. The last chapter is the editor's evaluation of the chief problems and proposals presented in the book. The Appendix contains the report of a conference on problems of NATO strategy, commenting on and adding to the ideas discussed in the preceding chapters.

IV

A few more introductory remarks remain to be made.

This book is not concerned with all aspects of NATO. It concentrates deliberately on problems of military strategy which, however— as observed in the foregoing—touch on the heart of NATO's problem. It is conceivable that, in the course of time, the coalition will discover new and important issues of common concern, and make these a major and perhaps the governing purpose of NATO. But such a development is not now in sight. Neither, as already mentioned, does this book emphasize the problems involved in the politics of military strategy. At this time, it was felt, concentration on one aspect of the problem would have its special rewards.

Concentration on the military problem is sometimes questioned on the ground that the chief Communist threat is not in fact military, but diplomatic, propagandist, subversive, and economic. This may well be true. But our knowledge of Soviet intentions now and in the future is far too imperfect to permit us safely to exclude or minimize the military threat. Moreover, if the less likely threat should materialize, its consequences might be of a sudden and horrible finality. Lastly, the probability, however low or high, that the East-West struggle may be fought out by military means can be greatly diminished, and possibly removed, if our strategy of deterrence remains effective.

Exactly the same counterarguments hold when it is contended that a military explosion is least likely in Europe. We cannot be sure of this assumption; disaster would be absolute if the military explosion did occur there; and the better prepared NATO is militarily, the less likely a destructive war in Europe will be. Without adequate defense in Europe, be it noted furthermore, Soviet influence might indeed grow by non-military means, and do so to such an extent that the independence of our European allies would be in grave jeopardy.

CHAPTER 2

NATO: THE DEVELOPING
STRATEGIC CONTEXT

BY ROGER HILSMAN

IT is by now a commonplace that both the mode and the structure
of the international relations of our day will be set largely by the
revolution in military strategy arising from the development of nuclear
weapons and missiles. And if Western statesmen are ever inclined to
forget it, the deepening crisis in NATO, the key alliance in Western
defenses, will serve to remind them. The dilemma is clearly one of
strategy. Badly outnumbered on the ground, the NATO forces have
only a doubtful choice. Faced with aggression, even though it is limited,
they can call for nuclear and thermonuclear weapons to be used in a
strike on the Soviet homeland. Or they can use "battlefield" atomic
weapons against the Soviet armies while refraining from the ultimate
act of a strike on the Soviet Union.

Massive retaliation on Soviet cities would undoubtedly bring about
a counter-retaliation, with death and destruction to both the United
States and Western Europe that seem beyond effective comprehension.
The cost would be so high that both the Europeans and the Russians
must wonder whether the United States could bring itself to choose
a course of action that seems to amount to suicide, except to meet an
aggression that threatens the survival of the United States itself. On
the other hand, the Europeans, at least, must also wonder about the
alternative of using only "battlefield" atomic weapons. In the first
place, would there be any meaning in a defense by such violent and
destructive means? The Europeans do not need to be reminded that
in Exercise *Carte Blanche*, a NATO maneuver in which 335 simulated
atomic bombs were dropped in 48 hours, the umpires concluded that
over one and a half million Germans would have been killed and
three and a half million wounded.

This dilemma will probably become sharper still when missiles
replace the manned bomber. If the submarine-based Polaris missile and
the intercontinental ballistic missile (ICBM) fulfill expectations,
Europe's importance for the defense of at least the continental United
States will diminish sharply. It must be expected that there will be,
if not a revival of isolationist sentiment in the United States, at least

weakened support for maintaining American ground forces in Europe and even greater obstacles to be overcome in a decision to order nuclear reprisal in the event of a limited or ambiguous aggression against a European member of NATO. In the circumstances, the doubts of Europeans about whether the United States will actually come to their defense can also be expected to grow. As the mass of the European population comes to understand still better the nature of the strategic dilemma facing NATO, the pressures on the European governments will increase. In some future crisis, when the Soviet Union threatens punitive action or engages in missile intimidation as it did at the time of the Suez crisis, demand in the European countries for a separate deal with the Soviets may be very strong.

The question is whether a strategy can be found for NATO that will permit it to serve the political and military objectives of the European members of the alliance, as the present choice of all or nothing could hardly do. One can conceive of several possibilities. For example, rather than being solved, the NATO dilemma might simply be eliminated by the neutralization and demilitarization of Europe in a negotiated agreement along the lines suggested by George Kennan. In this same vein, it is also conceivable that the Europeans, under certain conditions, might decide to adopt neutrality as their policy and so attempt to put themselves outside the arena of the Cold War. As for military alternatives, there are probably only two. One of these is to strengthen the coalition force—for example, as proposed by its Commander, General Norstad, in his pleas for 30 standing divisions. The other is to help the European members of NATO build independent strength, which would necessarily require them to have nuclear weapons of their own.[1]

From one of these alternatives or some combination of them NATO must develop a new strategy that will better serve the political and military goals of its members. But the problem is not as stark as this statement implies, and the choices are not as free and open. NATO is an organization that has existed for some years. As with all organizations, it has acquired rigidities along with structure. Decisions have been taken that have closed certain paths of action with finality. And expectations have been created in the minds of people in the member states that cannot be disappointed without political cost. NATO, in a word, has a history—a history that sets a context within which present

[1] For an exploration of these four possibilities, see my article, "On NATO Strategy," in *Military Policy Papers*, Washington, D.C., Washington Center for Foreign Policy Research, December 1958.

and future decisions must be made and which, for good or evil, will bear upon those decisions. It is the task here to attempt to relate that part of this history that is concerned with military strategy—to attempt to identify the major shifts and turns of NATO's strategic decisions, the factors bearing on these shifts and turns, and, if possible, something of the bounds, as well as the expectations, that they have created.

The task is not an easy one. The documents are all very highly classified, and since they are "combined"—that is, controlled by more than one nation—the procedures for getting them downgraded are enormously complicated. One must therefore depend on published sources, newspaper accounts, the rumors and gossip reported by the columnists, and, finally, on what participants in the events remember and feel free to relate in interviews.[2] These materials contain extraordinarily accurate information, especially if the person using them has had inside experience himself and therefore some feeling for what is both probable and legitimate. But even so, because they are incomplete, one cannot be definitive or even certain of having avoided gross misinterpretations. The best that one can hope to do is to reconstruct the larger outlines of the strategic situation facing NATO in each particular time period and to deduce the probable strategic response, checking with the sources wherever possible in the hope of obtaining encouragement, if not confirmation. The exercise is not so much one in narrative history-writing as in historical war-gaming. But it may still be useful as a background for thinking about the future.

I

In the early days of NATO, military planning was done by a hierarchy of international committees with headquarters in Belgrave Square

[2] Two of the most useful sources are official publications: Lord Ismay's *NATO: The First Five Years*, Paris, 1955, and the *NATO Letter*. Other major sources are J. D. Warne, *NATO and Its Prospects*, New York, 1954; Colonel Andrew J. Goodpaster, "The Development of SHAPE: 1950-1953," *International Organization*, ix, No. 2 (May 1955), pp. 257-62; Ben T. Moore, *NATO and the Future of Europe*, New York, 1958; Gardner Patterson and Edgar S. Furniss, Jr., *NATO: A Critical Appraisal*, Princeton, N.J., 1957; Drew Middleton, *The Defense of Western Europe*, New York, 1952; Theodore H. White, *Fire in the Ashes*, New York, 1953; Howard K. Smith, *The State of Europe*, New York, 1949; Arthur C. Turner, *Bulwark of the West*, Toronto, 1953; Royal Institute of International Affairs, *Defence in the Cold War*, London, 1950; *idem, Atlantic Alliance: NATO's Role in the Free World*, London, 1952; and various hearings before committees of the United States Congress. I have also relied heavily on interviews.

For help in locating sources and for criticisms and suggestions on the manuscript, I am indebted to the following: Bernard C. Cohen, Malcolm W. Hoag, Louis Morton, Roy Lamson, Colonel Charles H. Donnelly, Colonel George A. Lincoln, Colonel Edward L. Rowny, Klaus Knorr, and Lt. Colonel Joseph Rockis.

in London. The United Kingdom and most of the European members of NATO had previously entered into their own agreement for collective self-defense, the Brussels Pact. Under this Pact there had been established the Western Union Defense Organization, with delegations of military planners from all the signatories and an observer group from the United States (Delegation to Western Union, or DelWU) that was authorized to participate actively "as appropriate." When the North Atlantic Treaty was signed, these delegations were expanded and set immediately to work.[3]

The results of their planning efforts were three distinct plans—the Short-Term Defense Plan, the Medium-Term Plan, and the Long-Term, so-called "requirements" Plan. The Short-Term Plan was apparently simplicity itself. It was an emergency plan, and its purpose was principally to save as many of the troops as possible in the event of war. It amounted to little more than assignments to withdrawal routes, the authority to commandeer ships in British and Allied ports to be used for evacuation, and perhaps a desperate hope—which was never expressed—that Franco might let the Allied troops pass through Spain or even stand with them in an attempt to hold at the Pyrenees. This was the plan for the immediate future, the period of the oft-repeated and undoubtedly apocryphal remark of the NATO staff officer whose reply to a question as to what the Soviet troops needed to reach the Pyrenees was, simply, "Shoes." This plan was apparently ignored by SHAPE when it was established in 1951, though it undoubtedly remained available for a while in the files of some of the national contingents.

The Medium-Term Defense Plan was a battle plan, looking forward to the day when the allies would have some portion of the troops they needed and, more importantly, when they would have the logistical back-up to permit deployment as a fighting force. Before the attack on South Korea in 1950, NATO had only twelve divisions, 400 airplanes, and a very small number of naval vessels.[4] Most of these troops were poorly equipped and trained. They were deployed not for defense, but for occupation. The British and Americans were scattered in penny packets in Northern and Southern Germany, respectively, and the French were far to the rear, in the Rhineland and the Black Forest. They had little armor or the supply, engineer, and heavy artillery troops that give an army its punch and mobility. There

[3] The American delegation was redesignated the Joint American Military Advisory Group (JAMAG).

[4] Lord Ismay, *op.cit.*

were few prepared positions and not enough ammunition in the whole theater to last more than a few weeks. Supply lines, finally, for both the British and the Americans ran not perpendicular to the front, but parallel to it, from Hamburg and Bremerhaven on the extreme left. In many places these supply lines were within a few miles of Soviet armor.

The first task was therefore to shift these supply lines, build new airfields in the proper tactical positions, establish supply dumps and hospitals, and flesh out the corps and army supporting troops. When these steps had been taken, the NATO forces could be redeployed to positions from which they could move to battle and put up some kind of creditable fight even before they reached full strength. It was for this situation that the Medium-Term Plan was designed. What it apparently contemplated was a withdrawal behind a screen of mechanized cavalry units (the American unit was the so-called constabulary force) to positions behind the Rhine.

It might also be noted that during the discussions that took place as the build-up proceeded about which of the Allied nations was to get which sector of the front, one idea was paramount, though never openly expressed. This was that, try as they might, the allies had only a slim chance of holding at the Rhine if war came during this interim period. Each of the participants, in consequence, wanted a sector that would permit retreat. This was not cowardice, but merely prudence. In a sector permitting maneuver, one could hope to live to fight another day. The southern position, in Bavaria, was the bad one; for the force there would very likely be pinned against the Alps. The center position was the best; the force here could retreat into France and perhaps make a stand farther back—if necessary, at the Pyrenees.

The Long-Term Plan was not a battle plan, but one of requirements, an analysis of the forces needed to defend Europe in a major war. In such a war, the main Soviet thrust would have to come as all attacks on Western Europe had come—across the North German plain. A secondary attack could be expected on Italy, in the Brenner-Trieste area, as well as on Scandinavia. But the war would be won or lost on the old, familiar Western Front, extending from Basle to the mouth of the Rhine-Ijssel.

The planners apparently assumed that atomic weapons would not soon become available in large quantities, and the war they visualized was therefore only slightly different from World War II in its later stages. Thus, as the planners saw it, there were three different requirements to be considered. The first need was for forces to cover the major approaches—the North German plain, the Fulda and Belfort gaps, and so on. For these approaches, the calculations were based on established rules of thumb for division fronts. Second, there had to be forces to screen the intervening areas between approaches, but here positions could be manned more lightly. Finally, a reserve had to be provided of roughly one-third the total force. For the old Western Front, the total came to between 80 and 85 divisions. To this had to be added about ten more divisions for the Brenner-Trieste area and about five for the Scandinavian area, making a grand total of about 100 divisions.

An attacker needs at least a three-to-one superiority to dislodge a force that is adequate to the terrain it is defending, with its flanks anchored on natural obstacles and a reserve to seal off a penetration or stop a turning movement. And even if the attacker has this order of superiority, the battle may still go either way, depending on skill, morale, luck, and the other intangibles of war. But it would take more than either skill or luck to save an outnumbered force that is also inadequate to its terrain. In the kind of war the planners visualized, a NATO force of only 60 or 70 divisions would have had to choose between cutting the defenses in the major approaches or scaling down the reserves to a force too small to make its intervention felt. Disaster would have probably been inevitable. But with a force of about 100 divisions, NATO could hope to hold off an enemy two or even three times as large.

This requirements plan was the touchstone that the NATO military used in recommending force goals to the member governments, beginning in 1950 or even earlier. But, as we shall see, the military recommendations were not approved by the member nations until much later, at the Lisbon meeting of the North Atlantic Council in 1952.

II

Developing these plans was not difficult; what took time was the so-called "closing-the-gap" exercise. The "gap," of course, was the hiatus between the roughly 100 divisions required and the total of what the member nations were willing to put up. Apparently there was in this exercise some paring of the forces required, especially supporting forces. There was also, apparently, some reshuffling of D-day, D+15, and D+30 requirements. But the main effort of the allies was in trying to persuade each other to increase the size of their contributions in terms of troops.

In their attempts to close the gap, the planners went over the same ground many times. Of course, the results were not divisions, but only promises to build divisions in the future. Even so, the gap remained large. One gathers that the French may have made some unrealistic promises at one stage and that the United States earmarked at least one Marine division for post-D-day assignment to Europe. The exercise also seems to have resulted in agreements to improve the readiness of some of the divisions manned by reservists. But there was no sense of urgency, prior to Korea, and the gap remained.

There is reason to believe, however, that the planners of all the member states very early came to have their own ideas of how and when the gap was going to be filled, though they never spelled it out for the record. Soviet intransigence and aggressiveness had led us to form the alliance, which was by itself a powerful deterrent, especially since it was reinforced by the United States near-monopoly of atomic weapons. It was understandable that the NATO members were reluctant to make any more sacrifices until there was some clear sign that the Soviets had decided to shift from cold to hot war in spite of our declarations. One has the impression that the planners had long known that, when and if that sign came, the "gap" would be closed rather quickly, and in two ways. First, it was expected that the members would increase their pledges—once the shooting started, as Lord Montgomery is supposed to have said. But the second and final increment was expected to come in only one way—by rearming the Germans. It was not that the military were insisting on German rearmament out of professional admiration for the Germans or addiction to a plan that demanded German rather than some other kind of soldier. On the contrary, the military apparently felt that if the governments wanted to make the sacrifice, the 100 divisions could come entirely from the original members of NATO. After all, France alone had fielded over 100 divisions at the start of World War II (although this may also illustrate that mere numbers are not enough). The major considerations in rearming the Germans were military, in that the allies needed troops. But it was political considerations that were really determining. The first of these, of course, was the unwillingness of the original members of NATO to carry the burden by themselves. But there was also a conviction that it would be wiser and more just to help in restoring an energetic people's independence and strength than to attempt to sit on them forever.

What provided the urgency—the sign that was interpreted to mean a shift in Soviet intentions—was the Communist attack on South

Korea. And what made this sign even more convincing was the fact that it had been preceded by a change in Soviet capabilities: it was late in 1949 that the Soviets exploded their first atomic bomb. These two events—the Soviet success in atomic weaponry, followed quickly by the Communist attack on South Korea—combined to produce a remarkable unanimity among the NATO allies. There was little discussion, but everyone seemed to be agreed that the Soviets had shifted back from political means for achieving their ambitions to military ones.[5]

It was at the very next meeting of the North Atlantic Council following the Korean invasion, in September of 1950 in New York, that it was decided to rearm the Germans. The proposal was put forward by Mr. Acheson on behalf of the United States and, although the French and Belgians voiced some objections, the United States carried the day.[6]

It was also at the New York meeting that the term "forward strategy" seems first to have been used. "Forward strategy" is what is technically called a "strategic concept," which sometimes serves as a goal but more usually as a guide line for war planning. Just what the "forward strategy" concept means and what influence it has had on Allied strategy have been the subject of much confusion. There has been some suspicion that just as the Schlieffen Plan came to dictate German policy in the period before World War I, so the concept of "forward strategy" came to dictate American and Allied policy. The notion is that it was the military's addiction to "forward strategy" and their pressure for both the real estate and the forces to give them the capacity to execute it that brought about the rearmament of Germany. Put this way, the suspicion has little foundation in fact. Indeed, a case can be made for the opposite proposition that "forward strategy" was something the civilians imposed upon the military. At the time of the New York meeting, most of the military were apparently assuming that, when and if they got the 100 divisions they needed, they would defend at the Rhine. But one of the points made at New York was that the Germans would have little incentive to rearm if the most they could expect to save from destruction and occupation was the western fragment of their country. The term "forward strategy" as it was first used in just those words was apparently a promise to the Germans, as

---

[5] See, for example, the testimony of General Omar Bradley, Chairman of the Joint Chiefs of Staff, at the MacArthur hearings. *Military Situation in the Far East*, Hearings Before the Committees on Armed Services and Foreign Relations, U.S. Senate, 82nd Congress, 1st Session, Washington, D.C., 1951, pp. 731-32.

[6] Lord Ismay, *op.cit.*, p. 32.

well as to the Dutch and Danes, to try to defend east of the Rhine rather than on it. The strongest support for the proposition that "forward strategy" was a promise to the more exposed members of NATO is the mild dismay on the part of the working-level planners in London (this was still before the days of SHAPE) who undertook the task of developing a plan to implement it, and the fact that the best they could apparently come up with was a plan for a counter-attack from the Rhine line at the southern and possibly northern flanks of what was assumed would be the Soviet thrust.

In fact, the genesis of "forward strategy" was much more compli-cated than either of these propositions would indicate. To military men, one of the very first conclusions to be drawn from the effective-ness of the atomic bomb dropped on Hiroshima was that large-scale landings on a small beachhead were no longer possible.[7] Operations like that at Normandy would be out of the question if the enemy had even two or three atomic bombs. If United States power were ever needed on the European Continent in a future war, the enemy invasion would have to be stopped short of complete occupation. In addition to this purely "military" reason for rejecting a strategy that relied on liberating Europe was the European attitude toward occupation. It was perfectly clear to all concerned that the Europeans would not have the incentive to rearm if the most they could hope for was occupation and eventual liberation. For all these reasons, a defense along the Rhine was the minimum acceptable strategy.

For even this purpose men were needed and room to maneuver—real estate in which to delay the enemy as the Allied forces took up their positions along the Rhine and readied themselves. It was certainly within the capabilities of the allies, as suggested above, to furnish the 100 divisions needed without German help, and they already had the real estate by virtue of their occupation of Germany. But neither the Danes nor the Dutch, much less the Germans, were satisfied with a defense that abandoned much of their countries at the outset. And it was very clear to all concerned that the allies were not prepared to make the sacrifices necessary to build a force of 100 divisions by

[7] For example, General Omar Bradley, testifying before the Armed Services Com-mittee of the House of Representatives, said that ". . . large-scale amphibious opera-tions, such as those in Sicily and Normandy, will never occur again." Elaborating this statement, he also said that ". . . appraising the power of the atomic bomb, I am wondering whether we shall ever have another large-scale amphibious operation. Frankly, the atomic bomb, properly delivered, almost precludes such a possibility." See mimeographed copy, "Statement of General Omar N. Bradley, Chairman, Joint Chiefs of Staff, Before the Armed Services Committee of the House of Representa-tives," September 26, 1950, Library of Congress (LC call number UA 23874).

themselves. As a result, the military became early advocates of German rearmament and were willing to try to develop a strategy that would make German rearmament politically feasible. But there were apparently few among the military who had much confidence that a stand forward of the Rhine was possible until several years later, after the shift to atomic weapons. "Forward strategy," in sum, is still another illustration that strategic decisions are very rarely attributable to purely "military" motives or pressures.

It might be well to mention one other decision about which there has been almost as much confusion as about "forward strategy." This is the "year of maximum danger" toward which NATO preparations were geared. Much has been made of the lack of realism in the notion that anyone could predict that one particular year would be more dangerous than any other, and when the Republican Administration took office in 1953, it was decided that preparations would be pointed not toward a particular year but toward the "long haul." The genesis of the idea of the "year of maximum danger" is obscure, but it seems to have appeared first in NSC 68 as an estimate of the date—1954—by which the Soviet Union could build a significant stockpile of nuclear weapons.[8] In this instance, the "year of maximum danger" was an evaluation of Soviet capabilities, and some of the participants in the rearmament effort may well have come to regard it literally, as the year in which the United States would have to be prepared to meet a Soviet onslaught. But for the most part the "year of maximum danger" had a more prosaic function. It takes two years and longer to recruit and train a division; it may take five or six years to design and begin producing a new tank. On the other hand, uniforms can be manufactured and transported to the place of use in a few months. The problem is one of phasing: there is no point in having the uniforms ready before the troops are ready to wear them or in having troops without weapons. The "year of maximum danger" was less a target date than a guide line for planning. It was, in fact, "stretched out" as the build-up proceeded.

The decision in September 1950 to rearm the Germans was only one of the steps taken by the allies in response to the attack on Korea. Another was to establish a unified command structure for NATO— the Supreme Headquarters, Allied Powers Europe (SHAPE)—and to appoint a Supreme Commander. Early in 1951, General Eisenhower

[8] NSC 68 was a National Security Council paper that reappraised U.S. military policy following the explosion of the first Soviet atomic bomb in 1949.

took up the post of Supreme Allied Commander, Europe (SACEur), and his first task was to make the Command operational.

What was needed was not only troops for war, but also what came to be known as "infrastructure." This was a French railroad term denoting all the construction work that was required before track could be laid—the bridges, embankments, tunnels, and so on. In NATO, it came to be used as a generic term for the facilities that stand behind a modern army—headquarters installations, communication networks, airfields, supply dumps, fuel pipelines, radar stations, port facilities, and so on.

As these efforts went forward, the NATO military continued to press for the force goals laid down in the old requirements plan. Finally, in 1952, the North Atlantic Council at its meeting in Lisbon approved a goal of 96 divisions.[9]

There were undoubtedly those among both the military and the civilian leaders of the Allied nations who did not believe that the members of NATO would ever achieve a full 96-division force or that there was any real need to. The long-range bomber force armed with nuclear weapons was a potent deterrent, and it was far from clear at the time of the Lisbon meeting that the Soviet Union would so quickly overtake us. Then, too, improvements in both weapons and transport were making the new divisions much more powerful and versatile than their World War II counterparts. The new divisions might therefore cover wider fronts than contemplated under the old rules of thumb. Finally, there was undoubtedly some feeling that a modest increase in forces plus steps to put our logistical and support facilities on a war basis would be sufficient to operate as an effective deterrent. Once we had a force that could deny the Soviets the opportunity of taking us by surprise, we would have at least the strength to buy time in which to improvise. One might argue that the Lisbon goals were approved as a matter of principle and declaratory policy, but that the member states did not intend even then to implement them. On the whole such a view seems extreme, but in any case the process of scaling down the goals and stretching them out in time began almost immediately after the Lisbon meeting had closed.

It might be well to emphasize that the total of 96 divisions called for at Lisbon was apparently for D+30. From the information available, one gets the impression that the force to be on the line at all times—the screen—was to consist of about 35 or 40 divisions. This

[9] *Department of State Bulletin*, xxvi, No. 663 (March 10, 1952); and Lord Ismay, *op.cit.*, pp. 47, 151.

would mean a force of from seven to nine divisions in the Brenner-Trieste area, another two or three divisions in the Scandinavian area, and about 25 on the central front. The remainder of the 96 divisions were apparently to be units manned principally by reservists which could be mobilized by D+15 to D+30, with two or three divisions coming from the central reserves in the United Kingdom and the United States.

The logic in this phasing is fairly obvious. With a screen of about 25 divisions on the central front, the allies could have denied the Soviets any hope of succeeding with a surprise attack. The Soviets would have had to bring up additional divisions from their reserves in the Soviet Union itself, and thus would have given the allies ample warning in which to mobilize their full strength. The proper size for the screen, in other words, depended on what the Soviets maintained in Eastern Germany.

III

By the end of 1953, much had been accomplished in both the troop build-up and infrastructure. From the Swiss border to the mouth of the Ijssel, there were about 15 Allied divisions with appropriate supporting forces—tanks, artillery, and tactical air power—which themselves marked a vast increase in NATO's strength.[10] Italy was by that time able to furnish from seven to nine divisions and Denmark and Norway one or two. Ten more divisions of good quality could have been mobilized at intervals from D+3 to D+30, and from 30 to 40 others of rather doubtful quality could also have been mobilized by D+90.

A complicating factor in the meantime had been the accession of Greece and Turkey to NATO.[11] This added from 20 to 25 new divisions to NATO's strength, but it also extended the defense perimeter to a whole new area that was peculiarly difficult to defend. Indeed, it seems doubtful whether the forces there could have held against a major onslaught. They would have been useful against a limited aggres-

[10] Divisions without supporting air power and corps and army troops could not exert much power. When the number of divisions is used as a measure of the relative power of two forces or of any increase of power of one force over time (as is the common practice), the term "x divisions" should be regarded as a form of shorthand for "x divisions with appropriate supporting aircraft, tanks, artillery, engineer, and supply troops."

[11] See "Protocol to the North Atlantic Treaty on the Accession of Greece and Turkey, October 17, 1951," in Department of State, *American Foreign Policy, 1950-1955, Basic Documents,* Vol. 1, Washington, D.C., U.S. Government Printing Office, p. 853.

sion and as a diversion in all-out war, drawing off Soviet strength, but the security of the southeastern area depended more on the deterrent value of being linked to the main NATO area than on the forces actually stationed there.

In infrastructure, the achievement was impressive. When SHAPE was first established, there were only 15 airfields available for use; by the end of 1953, there were well over 100.[12] In addition, construction had begun on others that would bring the total to 165 by 1955. An extensive communication network had been established or was under construction—a total of 16,000 kilometers of land lines, 10,000 kilometers of radio relay circuits, and 1,700 kilometers of submarine cables. The construction of fuel pipelines, storage tanks, and pumping stations for the support of both tanks and jet aircraft had been begun. Hospitals, supply dumps, headquarters installations, port facilities, all were established or in process.

Finally, there had been the essential practice in teamwork: joint and combined maneuvers had been held and detailed war plans worked out.

By the end of 1953, in sum, NATO had been transformed from a traditional alliance, implying little more than a commitment to stand together, to an integrated coalition army. The idea of a European Defense Community, in which German troops were to be combined with those of the other Continental members of NATO into an international army, was proving to be a dead end (it was not until the autumn of 1954 that EDC failed in the French Assembly and Germany was admitted to NATO). But even without the German contribution, NATO's strength was impressive. The NATO army, it is true, was still too weak to face the Soviet Union confidently. But it had at least enough strength to eliminate one possibility that had caused peculiar anxieties. This was surprise on the ground. Throughout the early days of SHAPE, the United States strategic air power and superior atomic stockpile were the only deterrent. The Soviet forces in Eastern Germany, without reinforcement, could have overwhelmed the Allied ground forces that could have been brought against them. Each autumn the Soviet forces held maneuvers; at any time, they needed only to change direction to reach the Pyrenees. But this had now changed. The 15 Allied divisions, backed up as they were with a proper infrastructure and supporting troops of all kinds, including reservist divisions, could have put up a creditable fight. It seemed unlikely that the Soviets would take them on with just 22

[12] Lord Ismay, op.cit.

divisions, and any attempt to reinforce would have constituted a warning and given the allies time in which to improvise.

If a war had come in 1953, it would in all probability have followed the pattern outlined in the old Medium-Term Plan. The principal weapon would have been the American Strategic Air Command. The Allied forces in Germany would have dropped back to positions on the Rhine without attempting to fight anything but skirmishes, using the mechanized cavalry screen. On the Rhine, they would have offered battle. If this and the air war went well, they could have hoped to counterattack. But the hope was slim.

IV

It is ironic that no sooner had NATO completed its transformation from a traditional alliance to a new form of coalition army than the strategic situation changed so radically as to cast doubt on its utility. The sources of this change were four, all concerned with nuclear weapons. In the first place, the Soviets not only discovered how to make atomic and thermonuclear bombs, as they were bound to, but they also built a long-range air force of their own, much more rapidly than had been expected. In the second place, they very early began to work on and equip their ground forces with a whole range of atomic weapons suitable for use on the battlefield.[13] The third factor was the growing public understanding of the implications of atomic weapons—the growing doubt among Europeans whether the NATO coalition army could defend them without calling down the very destruction that defense forces are intended to guard against. The fourth was the policy decision, on the part of the United States and Britain, to rely more heavily on nuclear weapons, the "new look" decision to emphasize nuclear air power in defense preparations at the expense of ground and naval power.

The Soviet Union had developed its nuclear technology at an amazing rate after its first atomic explosion in 1949. The United States exploded a hydrogen or thermonuclear "device" in November of 1952 (although there are hints that another may have been exploded somewhat earlier), but did not explode a workable bomb until March 1954.

---

[13] Some forces in the field had these weapons in 1954 or even earlier. See the announcement of General William M. Hoge, Commander in Chief, U.S. Army, Europe, as reported in the *New York Times*, January 16, 1955. Notice also that "battlefield" atomic weapons are not necessarily small weapons. See Bernard Brodie, "Nuclear Weapons: Strategic or Tactical?" *Foreign Affairs*, xxxii, No. 2 (January 1954), pp. 217-29.

The Soviets, on the other hand, set off their first workable H-bomb in August 1953.

In regard to "battlefield" atomic weapons, it is more difficult to be exact. But in 1954, and perhaps earlier, the Soviet forces in Eastern Germany began to have a range of such weapons. What is more, the Soviet ground forces had been undergoing an almost continuous modernization ever since the end of World War II.[14] Although the number of Soviet divisions (175, of which 22 are in Eastern Germany) has remained relatively constant, their nature has changed radically. These divisions today are much more highly mechanized, are apparently equipped with rockets and missiles, and have a higher proportion of air-transportable equipment. Almost the whole force is now equipped with atomic firepower. By any standard, the Soviet army is a formidable force.

Parenthetically, it might be well to ask just what purposes such a large atomic army might serve. Contemplating the awesome destructiveness of nuclear weapons and the range and speed of missiles or even jet bombers, one finds it difficult to believe that ground armies will have the central role in all-out war, or, indeed, that they will have any role at all beyond mopping up and occupation. The Soviets, of course, may have their eye on limited atomic wars, but it seems doubtful that so many divisions would be needed in a limited engagement. They may also be preparing for war limited to conventional weapons. But, again, so many divisions would imply a very large war, large enough in fact to encompass the whole of Europe; and one wonders how either side could refrain from using the ultimate weapons if all of Europe were at stake. The Soviet motive in maintaining such large ground forces may be nothing more than military conservatism and a hedge against revolt. But there remains one possible utility for such a large force, whether or not the Soviets are consciously providing for it. Although the notion stretches the imagination, it is at least conceivable that a breakthrough in tactical doctrine might enable ground armies to learn to live in an atomic battlefield after all. If this did happen, some sort of "broken-backed" war in which ground armies played a central role would again become possible. This does not, of course, mean that the Soviets have thought the problem through and devised such a doctrine. The disquieting thought is only that they have been right for the wrong reasons before. The Soviets built over 400 submarines in what was apparently an imitation of German sea strat-

[14] See Raymond L. Garthoff, *Soviet Strategy in the Nuclear Age*, New York, 1958.

egy, which hardly seems appropriate for contemporary war. But the development of the Polaris-type missile is suddenly giving their submarines a new relevance, since a proportion can be adapted to carry at least one missile. And those that cannot can still be used as hunter-killers.

The third source of change, growing European uneasiness about the implications of nuclear weapons, has been described above. Exercise *Carte Blanche* was probably the greatest single shock to European opinion, but the facts of the NATO strategic dilemma seem to be increasingly understood.

The fourth source of change, the "new look" decisions to rely principally on nuclear weapons, had their beginnings in the United Kingdom.[15] The idea of relying principally on the deterrent effect of nuclear weapons was first considered late in 1951 and early 1952, in the first months of Sir Winston Churchill's prime-ministership. Churchill sent Air Marshal Sir John Slessor to the United States to sound out the American Joint Chiefs of Staff on the idea, but without success.

The new Eisenhower Administration was more receptive. There had been indications of the new line of thought during the 1952 election campaign and even further development of it in the meetings of Admiral Radford, Charles E. Wilson as Secretary of Defense designate, and President-elect Eisenhower in the Pacific after the election, but before the new Administration took office. The first official sign of a new policy apparently came in NSC 162/2, a National Security Council document that seems to have reached the conclusion that the major threat to be met was "total" war.[16] It apparently laid down the policy that the Services could plan on using nuclear weapons wherever needed, which may have been Admiral Radford's condition for giving his support to the "new look" decisions.

Essentially, the new policy was to rely not so much on nuclear weapons as on air power armed with nuclear weapons, or, more accurately, to rely on its deterrent value. As first enunciated by Secretary Dulles in his "massive retaliation" speech in January 1954, the implication was that the United States would no longer meet a local aggression with a defense confined to the local area but would retaliate with

[15] See Charles J. V. Murphy, "A New Strategy for NATO," *Fortune*, January 1953. The "new look" decisions are also being studied by Glenn Snyder. See his forthcoming case study in the series sponsored by the Institute of War and Peace Studies, Columbia University.

[16] See Alsop, "New Look: Secret History," *New York Herald Tribune*, February 22, 1954; and Charles J. V. Murphy, "Defense and Strategy," *Fortune*, December 1953.

atomic bombs against the originators of the aggression—that we would "retaliate, instantly, by means and at places of our choosing." This policy, Secretary Dulles said, "permits of a selection of military means instead of a multiplication of means. As a result, it is now possible to get, and share, more basic security at less cost."[17]

In the ensuing debate, Secretary Dulles denied that the original interpretation of his policy was correct and appeared to bow to the criticisms of it. It seemed clear that in such a policy there was danger of starting a spiral into all-out nuclear war. It also seemed likely that the very reluctance that any American President would feel at taking such risks, for the sake of what would seem to be a relatively small bit of territory on the Free World perimeter, might encourage local attacks rather than deter them. In a series of speeches and articles, Mr. Dulles seemed to retreat steadily. But, even so, the decision to emphasize nuclear air power at the expense of ground and naval power still stood. It was clear to all concerned that the United States was embarking on a phased reduction of its ground strength: instead of a build-up to the goal of 24 divisions, the process was to be put in reverse, aiming at a total of 14 divisions.

These developments had an immediate effect on NATO. What worried the military commanders was the obvious danger of falling between two stools. The civilian authorities were using the increased firepower of nuclear weapons as a justification for cutting down on the numbers of troops. But at the same time the weapons were slow in coming and, even more importantly, no one had made an unequivocal decision about the circumstances in which the weapons were to be used. The nightmare that haunted the old German General Staff was a two-front war: for the NATO commanders, the nightmare was that after preparing for a war in which atomic firepower was to substitute for manpower, they would have to fight without either. Their fear was that, if the Soviets did attack with their massive ground armies, the member governments of NATO would for political reasons delay giving permission to use nuclear weapons until after the initial battle had been lost and the NATO forces were too crippled and disorganized to use the weapons effectively. In a sense, the military were merely insisting that the consequences of the "new look" decisions to rely on atomic air power be faced squarely. By and large they were successful. In December 1954, the North Atlantic Council granted the military permission to base their war plans on the use of atomic weapons

[17] John Foster Dulles, "The Evolution of Foreign Policy," *Department of State Bulletin*, xxx, No. 761 (January 25, 1954), p. 108.

from the outset of hostilities.[18] The Council specified that the decision
did not include permission to use the weapons until final approval
was given, when and if war came. But, having gone so far, the NATO
Council would find it difficult to turn back in the midst of crisis.
As a practical matter, it seems unlikely that final approval could be
denied.

The United States decision to rely principally on nuclear weapons
also had its effect on Britain's defense effort. Although the British began increasing their own strategic air force and atomic capability early,
it was not until 1957 that they made the full shift. In their 1957 White
Paper on defense policy, the British government announced its decision
to reduce its forces from 690,000 to 375,000 by 1962, and to equip the
remainder with "atomic rocket artillery."[19] The British Army of the
Rhine was cut from 77,000 to 64,000 men immediately, with further
reductions to follow.

One of the ironies in NATO is that only since the decision to base
NATO strategy on nuclear weapons have the allies had any real hope
of carrying out "forward strategy," in its political sense of a stand at
or near the Iron Curtain.

The reasoning behind this hopefulness is worth discussing. Many
of today's commanders seem to think that in a nuclear war the preferred pattern of a defensive battle on the ground might still be the
classic one—along the lines, for example, of the Battle of the Bulge
in World War II. In this kind of battle, forces opposite the point of
the enemy salient give way, keeping themselves intact and maintaining contact with adjacent units if possible. The units on the shoulders
of the salient, however, must hold at the first opportunity they get,
and a portion of the reserves must be used to help them hold. By these
tactics, the enemy is led to expend his force straight forward, his lines
of communication are extended, and he has increasing difficulty in
keeping up the momentum of his attack. Then, when the attacker has
spent his force and his lines are stretched thin, the defender commits
his reserves in attacks on the enemy's flanks, at or near the shoulders
of the salient, to cut him off entirely. Throughout, air power is used
to interdict supply lines and to slow down or prevent withdrawal. In
nuclear war, the same basic defensive pattern might be followed, or
even preferred, since the enemy's concentration during the breakthrough, and through the narrow neck created by the retreat of the

[18] See *Department of State Bulletin*, xxxii, No. 810 (January 3, 1955), p. 10, for
the text of the communiqué.
[19] See the British White Paper on Defense, April 4, 1957.

defending forces, would offer such lucrative targets for atomic weapons that one could hope to break the enemy's strength for once and all.

But nuclear weapons also offer the possibility of following a more forward strategy of holding at or near the border. If enough resistance can be offered at the forward line to force the enemy to concentrate, then nuclear weapons used in quantity might break up the attack before it could fully develop. Whatever penetration the enemy did effect could then be mopped up with a rather small force of highly mobile reserves. The validity of this concept is open to argument, as will be discussed below, but it obviously has merit enough to have been the basis for both new plans in NATO and also an entirely new set of force goals.

V

NATO's new force goals are no secret. As described by General Lauris Norstad, the present Supreme Allied Commander,[20] they call for a standing force of 30 divisions, in place on the forward line and ready to fight with either conventional or atomic weapons. These divisions will apparently be backed up by other divisions manned by reservists that can be mobilized within three or four weeks, but there would be fewer of these than under the Lisbon goal of 96 divisions and less emphasis is placed on them, since it is assumed that a nuclear war would have to be fought with the forces on hand when it began.

The main function of this force of 30 divisions is to fulfill the commitment to "forward strategy" in all-out war. It is assumed that the Strategic Air Command would require no more than 30 days in which to do its work, and for this period of time it is believed that a 30-division force, fully supplied with atomic weapons and battlefield missile systems, could hold very near the eastern border.

But holding in an all-out war is obviously not the only purpose a 30-division force might serve. In Norstad's mind, a second purpose would be to give NATO the means for dealing firmly with a probing action to achieve a political advantage or with a short, swift movement designed to face the West with a *fait accompli*. His reasoning has two stages. The first point is that 30 divisions could by themselves deal with a minor aggression. The second is directed toward the *fait accompli*. If NATO had 30 divisions on the line, the minimum Soviet bid would have to be so high that nuclear reprisal might be the most appropriate response. By making it impossible for the Soviets to gain

[20] *NATO Letter*, v, No. 12 (December 1957).

anything with a small force, the 30 divisions act as a deterrent to a whole range of aggressions.

The third purpose that Norstad describes for the 30-division force seems to be merely another aspect of the second—a partial answer to the need for an intermediate response between nuclear reprisal, on the one hand, and a skirmish to meet a border incident, on the other. In Norstad's words, "Should we fail to maintain reasonable Shield strength on the NATO frontier, then massive retaliation could be our only response to an aggression, regardless of its nature. There is real danger that inability to deal decisively with limited or local attacks could lead to our piecemeal defeat or bring on a general war. If, on the other hand, we have means to meet less-than-ultimate threats with a decisive, but less-than-ultimate response, the very possession of this ability would discourage the threat, and would thereby provide us with essential political and military manoeuverability."[21]

It is important to emphasize that Norstad has denied that this force would give him the capability of fighting a limited war in Europe against the Soviets.[22] What he apparently has in mind is a force that could deal with attacks by the satellites, with probing actions by the Soviets, and with accidental outbreaks of violence between Soviet and Allied forces. With the 30-division force, NATO could put up enough resistance to force the Soviets to make their intentions perfectly clear, and the West could thereby avoid resorting to nuclear reprisal prematurely. All of these contingencies would seem to fall into the category of "limited war," and Norstad's denial may be motivated principally by the fact that the Soviets hear his public pronouncements on NATO strategy just as clearly as Westerners do. As Norstad argues for a goal of 30 divisions, he cannot forget that he has only from 16 to 18 divisions on hand. This is not sufficient strength to fight a limited war involving the Soviets, and he must be careful to put them on notice that at the moment even a limited action may bring down nuclear reprisal. Even if NATO had all the troops it wanted, finally, a statement that a limited war was possible might be a temptation for the Soviets to try one.

This concern for Soviet reactions would presumably be reason enough for Norstad to deny the possibility of limited war in Europe, but it is apparently not the only concern. Although the SHAPE planners plead for the kind of strength that will enable them to make an "intermediate" response, they seem to distinguish between different levels

[21] *Ibid.*
[22] *New York Times,* July 21, 1958.

of limited war. They speak of "probing actions" for political purposes, of short, swift movements designed to seize a position and so face the West with a *fait accompli,* and of "local" attacks. But they seem to regard a "big" limited war like that in Korea—a Soviet attempt, for example, to unify Germany by force—as something entirely different. Although the point is debatable, as will be discussed below, in general they seem to be convinced that if the Soviets ever decide to try a large-scale war in Europe, even though it is limited geographically to Europe alone and in weapons to conventional types, then the West would have no alternative to nuclear reprisal even if NATO had the full 30 divisions plus reservists that Norstad is asking for.

The Norstad goal of 30 divisions seems a radical departure from the Lisbon goal of 96, but it is not really as radical as the juxtaposition of 30 and 96 might imply. The 30-division force is the standing screen for the central region—that is, the area from Switzerland to the Baltic. For this same area, the Lisbon goal actually contemplated a smaller standing force, about 25 divisions. Although the Norstad goal puts greater emphasis on the standing force, it still calls for reservist divisions, too. To compare the Norstad and Lisbon goals, one must therefore add, first, these reservist divisions; second, the forces for the Brenner-Trieste and Scandinavian areas; and, third, the divisions that under certain circumstances might be brought from the central reserves in the United States and the United Kingdom. The grand total probably comes to something like 70 or 75 divisions, and this is not very different from the Lisbon goal of 96 when improvements in firepower and mobility are considered. The major difference is that the ready force on the line at all times—the 30-division force—is a higher percentage of the total under the Norstad goal.

The choice of 30 as the number of divisions in the ready force seems to be based on two considerations. The first of these is the assumption, already noted, that all-out nuclear war would be short and that, since mobilization would be extremely difficult or impossible, NATO would have to fight with the forces on hand when the war began. The second consideration is probably the size of the force the Soviets maintain in Eastern Germany. The Soviets could add a few divisions to the 22 they now have without attracting attention, but any substantial increase would hardly go unnoticed. Thus, so long as the Soviets maintain their force in Eastern Germany at its present level, a 30-division NATO force would serve the purposes Norstad has described. But if the Soviets increase their forces on the forward line, the NATO forces would also have to be increased.

There are two final observations that must be made about the Norstad goal. The first concerns the conclusion, on which the goal seems to be based, that battlefield nuclear weapons might finally make it feasible to pursue the "forward strategy," in its political sense of defending at the Iron Curtain. The hope is that atomic weapons could break up forces massing for an attack before the attack could begin. This may well be feasible, but atomic weapons could also break up a defense designed to hold a static line, and the net advantage is likely to be with the attack rather than the defense. No one can be certain, but it seems prudent to assume that in atomic war both the offense and the defense must be mobile. If so, the "line" between the opposing forces would be defined not by fortified positions but by active patrolling, and a breach of the "line" would be met by a series of delaying skirmishes, followed by a counterattack from highly mobile reserves. If these indications are correct, it seems reasonable to suppose that there would be no particular advantage to the defense in atomic war and that numerical superiority would continue to give an important edge to the side that had it. For all these reasons, ground atomic warfare would presumably be unusually fluid and far-ranging, as well as destructive, and one wonders whether it is realistic to hope that the battle could be confined to the border areas.

The second observation concerns the conviction that, even with the full complement of forces that General Norstad has requested, it would still be necessary to respond to a major attack confined solely to Europe with nuclear strikes on the Soviet homeland. A coordinated Soviet assault, whether conventional or nuclear, on the whole of Europe but confined solely to Europe, is probably the least likely contingency now facing the West. The incorporation of Europe into the Soviet bloc would so shift the balance of world power that the United States would be obliged to regard the loss of Europe as tantamount to final defeat. The Soviets must recognize this, and it seems unlikely that they would launch such an attack without forestalling United States reprisal by a strike on SAC bases and the continental United States. But the coming of missiles will sharply reduce the strategic significance of Europe for the defense of the continental United States, and the Soviets may not regard the high psychological stake the United States has in Europe's continued freedom as sufficient motive for transforming a purely European war into the ultimate one. The time may come, in sum, when the Soviets begin to think of an attack on Europe as a worthwhile gamble. There are several ways in which this particular threat might be met;[23] the point to be made here is only that it may be premature to decide that the Norstad proposal is not one of them. So long as the ready forces on the two sides of the line are roughly equal, the Soviets could not hope to launch a successful attack without bringing up reinforcements. The logistics problem is formidable, and it seems unlikely that the Soviets could bring more than from 30 to 40 divisions across Poland in the first 30 days. Such a large movement of troops could not be hidden, and NATO would have about three weeks in which to mobilize. If the United States also added to its capabilities in long-range transport, troops might even be brought from the central reserves in the United States and the United Kingdom. Thus, with skill and luck, the total force that NATO could muster might well be able to cope with a Soviet attack in precisely the terms in which it was made.

However, an important qualification must immediately be lodged. NATO must lay its plans in terms of the least, not the most, favorable contingency. Since the Soviet forces are equipped with nuclear weapons of all kinds, they have the option of using nuclear weapons at the outset, and NATO plans must account for this possibility as the first priority. But preparing for nuclear war makes it more difficult to retain the capacity for fighting a conventional one. This does not mean that a nuclear army cannot fight conventionally upon occasion. Men will continue to carry rifles for a long time to come, machine guns and mortars will continue to be standard equipment, and missiles can carry TNT warheads as well as nuclear ones. But there is some question as to how far a war can go without becoming nuclear when nuclear weapons are present. The dangers are two. The first is that one side's deployment for conventional war might present such a lucrative target for atomic weapons that the other side would see in it either an opportunity for a quick victory or the last chance of avoiding certain defeat. The second danger is that, in preparing for nuclear war, conventional forces may be so neglected as to leave no alternative to nuclear weapons. The expense of a dual capability is great, and the tendency is to drop the conventional weapons that have no role in nuclear war, as we have tended to junk artillery as missiles became available. Missiles can fire conventional warheads, but there is a point at which their great cost can be justified only by the greater effectiveness of the nuclear, rather than conventional, warhead.

On the other hand, if one can judge from the very recent past, the attitude of nations toward nuclear weapons is entirely different from the attitudes toward even the most radical of earlier technological in-

[23] For a discussion of these, see my "On NATO Strategy," *loc.cit.*

novations. It may be that in future crises both sides will go to extraordinary lengths to avoid either using nuclear weapons themselves or putting the enemy in a position where he feels compelled to use them. If this is so, a decision to prepare for and force the enemy to fight only one kind of war may no longer be a realistic choice. For example, it has been argued that a failure to make the proper preparations for limited war may restrict our future choices to either accepting defeat in a conventional war or transforming it into a nuclear one. But if it is widely accepted that initiating the use of nuclear weapons is unforgivable, then the one consequence—being forced to accept defeat—may be even more likely than the other.

As a result of these opposing pressures—on the one hand, the difficulty of maintaining a dual capability and, on the other, the risks of nuclear war—there may be fewer limited wars than we have supposed. And those that do occur may also be smaller than we have supposed: if the restrictions on using nuclear weapons mount in step with the difficulties of maintaining both nuclear and conventional forces, then the incentive to keep outbreaks of violence under tight control will also increase.

VI

Looking back over the development of NATO's strategy, one is struck by the similarity, which so many have remarked upon, between our present situation and that of the period ending in 1914. There were two great power blocs then, as now. There was then, as now, a long series of recurring crises, each bringing the world to the brink of war, with the final crisis hardly distinguishable from any of the others that had been met and passed. In those days, too, technology had had a revolutionary impact on weapons that was not thoroughly understood or digested. Machine guns were to change the whole character of war, just as nuclear weapons and missiles are doing today. The difference may be that the very extensiveness of the changes today are making us more aware of their significance. There is also a remarkable similarity between the mobilization plans of 1914—especially the Schlieffen Plan, which provided for an intermeshing of mobilization with battle—and the high state of readiness required of the two strategic air forces today. Both sides, presumably, now have the "fail safe" procedures followed by the United States Strategic Air Command that enable us to turn our forces back before they cross the enemy's borders. In this ability to "fail safe," our war plans are similar to the World War I mobilization plans of the French, the British, and even the

Russians. But with the coming of missiles, "fail safe" procedures will be more difficult to work out, and the situation will more nearly correspond to that created by the German Schlieffen Plan, which could not be halted without running what were regarded as prohibitive risks. As with the Schlieffen Plan, there is already an unusual advantage in being the first to strike, carrying the same implication that the risks of giving an enemy even an opportunity to seize the initiative may be greater than those of war.

Of course, an analogy such as this can be pushed too far or misinterpreted. Just as the analogy between the Schlieffen Plan and forward strategy fails to consider the role of political pressures, so may the analogy here. There came a point at which the rigid requirements of the Schlieffen Plan began to dictate Germany's moves in the events leading to World War I, but it must not be forgotten that the plan was in the first instance a consequence of foreign policy, not a cause. Germany's ambitions imposed on her military the requirement of devising a plan for fighting a two-front war. This plan, in its turn, imposed requirements on foreign policy, but the original impetus was in the other direction. Even Schlieffen himself regarded his plan as a "gamble that is beyond our strength."

Thus it is the political and diplomatic, rather than military, posture that originally sets the tenor of events. But the two periods are also similar in this. As A. J. P. Taylor has remarked, there was then, as now, the same preoccupation with being "firm" and with the deterrence of all-out war itself. On both sides, statesmen believed that if they made their threats strong and determined, peace would be preserved and they would also get their way. Each new crisis successfully met and passed seemed to confirm the theory. Having bullied their way through one crisis, they were more than ever tempted to bully their way through the next.

But, in this context, military preparations that put premiums on a high state of readiness restricted the choices open to diplomats still more. The rigidity of mobilization plans tended to make the statesmen even more dependent on deterrence by threats of all-out war than they might otherwise have been. If Germany's only alternatives, once mobilization had begun, were all or nothing, her statesmen had no choice but to threaten all. Any tendency, even in the small powers such as Serbia, to use the delicate balance as an umbrella for adventure had to be quashed immediately.

In NATO today, the West is equally dependent on deterrence by threat of all-out war and suffers in the same way from its corollaries.

There is no assurance that even the Norstad goals will be achieved, and the NATO planners seem to be agreed that if their present force of from 16 to 18 divisions is challenged, it must be supported by full-scale nuclear reprisal. Of all the past decisions in NATO, in fact, it is this decision to rely on nuclear weapons that has been most influential in shaping the strategic context in which future policy must be made. It would be well if this commitment were more fully understood. Present NATO policy does not allow for a conventional response to even a limited aggression. And this policy means exactly what it says, principally because the means for any other policy are not available. In the words of Field Marshal Montgomery, the decision has been made that, if we are "subjected to a major attack we would use the nuclear deterrent *as a weapon* to help in our defence—even if nuclear weapons were not used against us in the first instance."[24]

"And that," Montgomery concludes, "is how we stand today."

[24] Field Marshal the Viscount Montgomery of Alamein, "The Present State of the Game in the Contest Between East and West, and the Future Outlook," *Journal of the Royal United Services Institution*, November 1958. Montgomery's emphasis.

CHAPTER 3

THE USSR AND NATO

BY CYRIL E. BLACK AND FREDERICK J. YEAGER

I. The Assumptions of Soviet Policy

THE policy of the USSR toward NATO, to be fully appreciated, must be examined in the light of the evolving Soviet image of the process by which the Soviet form of socialism will eventually prevail throughout the world. The inevitability of the ultimate achievement of a world socialist state has never been questioned by the Soviet leaders, but their view of the circumstances and tempo of this evolution has undergone a significant change in the period since the formation of NATO.

Since the Second World War, Soviet official thinking on the course of international relations has passed through two broad phases. In the immediate postwar period, Soviet policy was preoccupied with exploiting the opportunities inherent in the strategic position of the USSR in Eastern Europe and in the revolutionary unrest in Asia—areas which were on the periphery of Western influence. At the end of the war, the Soviet leaders still regarded their system as on the defensive, and threatened by "capitalist encirclement." Even after the establishment of ideologically friendly states on the European and Asian borders of the USSR, and with the announcement by Zhdanov in 1947 that an "anti-imperialist and democratic camp" now existed side by side with the "imperialist and anti-democratic camp," the tone of Soviet official statements still conveyed the impression that "capitalism" was a dominant force in world affairs. The geographical encirclement might have been broken, but not the political and economic. This attitude was also reflected in some measure in the traditional Soviet theory of the "inevitability of war" between the two systems, which implied that the rival system was strong enough to challenge Soviet socialism decisively in the realm of military power.

In recent years the Soviet outlook has undergone a striking change. Discussion of "capitalist encirclement" is no longer heard, and the sense of isolation and defiance which inspired that doctrine has given way to a spirit of unprecedented self-confidence. Recent statements by party leaders have stressed the view that encirclement is a thing of the past. In its place, as they see it, something like a balance has been established, with the "socialist system of states" embracing no less than one-third of the world's population. The increasing opportunities for promoting communism in the uncommitted countries are also emphasized, and the prospect of encircling capitalism is anticipated in the foreseeable future. This surge of self-confidence has also led to the abandonment of the doctrine of the "inevitability of war." In declaring in 1956 that war between the two systems was "not a fatalistic inevitability," Khrushchev was not merely stressing the horrors of nuclear war. He was also asserting that the USSR was so well equipped with modern arms that it could deter any opponent from contemplating a major armed conflict.

While it is clear enough that a striking change has occurred in the Soviet outlook, it is difficult to designate a precise turning point between weakness and strength, caution and boldness. Many indications of the new confidence were present before Stalin's death, and some of these may be traced back to 1947. It was nevertheless not until the USSR developed strategic nuclear capabilities comparable to those at NATO's disposal that the new confidence found its full expression. Perhaps the Twentieth Party Congress in February 1956 may be taken as the crucial turning point in the development of the Soviet outlook. Since that date Soviet policy has had important setbacks as well as significant successes, but in balance there has been a continuing growth in the various components of national prestige. The forceful speeches of Khrushchev and of Marshal Malinovsky, his Minister of Defense, at the Twenty-first Party Congress in late January and early February 1959 clearly reflected the extent and nature of the prevailing spirit of optimism.

In evaluating these changes in outlook, one is always inclined to question whether official statements of the Soviet leaders can be taken at face value. Is it not possible that the new boldness is a propaganda line designed to win support at home and gain prestige abroad, or simply a reflection of Khrushchev's ebullient personality? There are, after all, many reasons for the Soviet leaders to view the world with concern. The revolutions in Poland and Hungary represented a major challenge to the Soviet system, and the doctrines of Gomulka, Tito, and Mao continue to threaten the ideological unity of the Soviet orbit. Moreover, China is beginning to loom as a rival force, and within a generation it may have a billion well-organized workers and peasants bordering the sparsely settled Asian provinces of the USSR. At the same time, the Soviet leaders have seen the remarkable political and economic resurgence of Western Europe, and especially West Germany, as well as the initial steps leading to the establishment of intermediate-range nuclear weapons on the Continent. Despite all these reasons for caution and concern, it seems more likely than not that the confident attitude reflected in the public statements of the Soviet leaders is genuine. There are many elements of distortion in official statements issuing from the USSR, and indeed much of Soviet prestige abroad is based on a systematic misrepresentation of the Soviet scene. When it is a question of the major policy declarations of the Soviet leaders, however, there is good reason to believe that these correctly express their understanding of the situation. Soviet Marxism is a set of assumptions and a general outlook rather than a specific plan of action, and it is these assumptions and this outlook that have undergone such a significant change in the past decade.

Associated with this growing confidence in the international position of the USSR on the part of the Soviet leaders has been their assertion that the "general crisis of capitalism" has been sharpening. They believe that this crisis originates in the contraction of the areas formerly controlled by the "capitalists" as the Soviet orbit expands, and in the consequent pressures on "capitalist" production. From the Soviet point of view, this is bound in the long run to result in greater state controls, increasing exploitation by the monopolies, and more intense rivalry among the "capitalist" states. The latter, for their part, are trying to stave off defeat by consolidating their positions. They have joined forces in an unbalanced coalition of strong and weak states in an effort to overcome their inherent rivalries. They also support policies of militarism and imperialism with a view to bolstering their shrinking economies.

To the Soviet way of thinking, NATO represents the principal weapon of the "capitalist system of states" in its effort to combat the socialist tide. As the Soviet leaders see it, NATO is an instrument for the domination of the weaker allies by the United States, and to a lesser extent by the United Kingdom. NATO also provides the justification for the large military expenditures by which the "capitalists" are trying to stabilize their economies. Without these military expenditures, according to the Soviet theorists, they would be plagued by a decline in production accompanied by unemployment, which would hasten the contraction and ultimate collapse of their system. The Soviets recognize that their own policy is to some extent responsible for the existence of NATO, insofar as its formation was a reply to the aggressive Soviet actions in Europe and Asia after the Second World War. From their point of view the expansion of the Soviet orbit was a part of the inexorable course of history, and NATO was a foreseeable part of the price.

Once the gains of postwar expansion were consolidated, the main Soviet effort was directed toward convincing the members of NATO that the USSR wished to live with the rest of the world in a spirit of "peaceful coexistence." Coexistence does not mean that the expansion of socialism and the contraction of "capitalism" will cease, for Soviet Marxism regards human society as normally in transition to socialism. It means rather that socialism will continue to expand primarily by peaceful and gradual means rather than through explosive revolutions. The new confidence in foreign policy was accompanied in the mid-1950's by assurances that Soviet heavy industry had finally reached a level of growth that would henceforth permit the simultaneous rapid development of light industry and agriculture. When the new Seven-Year Plan (1959-1965) was announced late in 1958, it was cited as evidence that the period of coexistence would be one of rapid gains for the Soviet form of socialism.

A comprehensive treatment of Soviet policy toward NATO would have to deal with the entire world, since the front in the struggle between socialism and "capitalism" is everywhere. For the purposes of this chapter, a narrower approach has been adopted. The primary focus is on NATO in the strict sense of the term, and on the strategic nuclear capabilities of the United States which are not under NATO command but form an essential part of its defensive strategy. Limitations of purpose and of space permit no more than peripheral attention to Soviet policy in those areas of the world which are not of primary importance to the European members of NATO.

Any evaluation of Soviet policies in the field of strategy and security is seriously hampered by the critical shortcomings of the sources, which are limited very largely to published statements of military specialists and political leaders. The available military publications do not necessarily reflect the innermost thoughts of the Soviet high command, and they frequently lag considerably behind technical developments. The Soviet political leaders, on the other hand, have tended to use the related issues of security requirements and heavy industry as political shillelaghs in intra-party struggles. Both military and political leaders, naturally enough, are inclined to conceal problems and doubts that might affect Soviet prestige—and likewise to overstate achievements in cases where political gains might result.

These various distortions may be reduced to a considerable degree by taking into consideration official estimates of Soviet military capabilities by members of NATO, and by falling back on our general knowledge as to how the Soviet system works. If the stated policies of the Communist Party are evaluated in the light of the prevailing military doctrine and of what is known of actual military capabilities, the probable courses of Soviet action can be estimated within a reasonable range of certainty. In some fields of policy, military doctrine is so comprehensive and capabilities are so varied as to give political leaders a wide freedom of choice. In others, doctrine, capabilities, and policy exert a mutually restraining influence. In speculating on the relationship and interaction of these three elements, insofar as they can be isolated from each other, the rapid evolution which each has been undergoing in recent years requires the exercise of particular caution.[1]

II. The Soviet Critique of NATO Strategy

NATO strategy is discussed in the USSR only as a plan for aggression. This may be explained in part by theoretical considerations for, according to Soviet Marxism, "capitalism" must by definition resort to aggressive measures. The Soviet approach has a further basis in traditional military doctrine, according to which a defensive strategy for NATO would rely primarily on powerful ground forces in Europe. Primary reliance on strategic nuclear weapons, as seen from this viewpoint, does not look like a defensive policy. The construction of a network of American bases around the Soviet Union has caused great apprehension in that country, and has stimulated a massive effort to find a counterweight to American strategic power. In reacting to this challenge, Soviet leaders are doubtless inclined to ignore or overlook the early postwar years when American and West European military forces were very largely demobilized and when the United States was prepared to offer a plan for the international control of atomic energy. The Soviet leaders also face the practical consideration that they cannot very well discuss NATO strategy as a plan for defense, as this

[1] Students of this subject are indebted to the pioneering contributions of Raymond L. Garthoff's *Soviet Strategy in the Nuclear Age* (New York, 1958), which presents a comprehensive summary and analysis of recent Soviet military writings, and of Herbert S. Dinerstein's *War and the Soviet Union* (New York, 1959), which concentrates particularly on questions of policy. Mention should also be made of N. Galay, "New Trends in Soviet Military Doctrine," *Bulletin of the Institute for the Study of the USSR* (Munich), III (June 1956), pp. 3-12; J. M. M., "Changing Military Thought in the Soviet Union," *World Today* (London), XIII (December 1957), pp. 517-28; and Herbert S. Dinerstein, "The Revolution in Soviet Strategic Thinking," *Foreign Affairs*, XXXVI, No. 2 (January 1958), pp. 241-52. These articles first brought to the attention of the Western public the significant evolution of Soviet military thought.

would involve implicit recognition of the possibility of aggression by the USSR.

Strategic Nuclear Weapons

It is generally assumed in the USSR that the central feature of NATO strategy is the use of strategic nuclear weapons, although such a strategy is alien to traditional Soviet military doctrine, which stresses the coordinated employment of all branches of the armed forces. Moreover, Soviet commentators had some difficulty in following the rapid evolution of American military policy. They understood the discussion of "balanced forces," but when the "new look" came they found it difficult to believe that the ground and naval forces would actually be subordinated in such a marked degree to air power. In the end, with some hesitance and questioning disbelief, they finally reached the conclusion that NATO strategy was, in fact, predicated on the assumption that strategic nuclear weapons would suffice to win any general war. At about the same time that the American debate was in progress, Soviet strategy also began to move toward greater reliance on strategic nuclear weapons.

The central feature of the Soviet critique of NATO strategy is that primary reliance on strategic nuclear weapons is a fallacy. Strategic striking power alone, according to Soviet military theory, cannot be decisive. Strategic nuclear weapons can wreak massive destruction, they maintain, but cannot seize and hold enemy territory. A strategy of relying primarily upon strategic nuclear weapons is in their view "adventuristic." In seeking to explain to themselves why the United States should have arrived at this fallacious view, Soviet commentators have fallen back largely on theoretical arguments. "Capitalist" states, they say, cannot trust the working class and are therefore fearful of arming them. Moreover, the "capitalists" engaged in the manufacture of aircraft and missiles have gained a dominant influence in the government, and do not wish to see their profits reduced by the diversion of the military budget to other forms of armament. Finally, social and economic contradictions are driving the "capitalists" to seek a shortcut to victory. When all of these various arguments are reduced to their essence, it is simply that it takes all branches of the armed forces to win a war. If anyone seeks a shortcut, his good judgment must be warped by non-military considerations.[2]

[2] Garthoff, *op.cit.*, pp. 118-45, presents a well-documented summary of Soviet views of American and NATO strategy.

Surprise Attack

In the Soviet view, the factors which lead NATO to place its preponderant hopes on strategic nuclear weapons will also tend to incline it toward a surprise attack on the USSR. Although emphasizing that final victory in modern war through surprise attack alone is impossible, the Soviets recognize that surprise does give great advantages to those who employ it. While surprise has always been very tempting to aggressors, the Soviets point out, it is even more so now in view of the development of nuclear weapons and strategic delivery systems.

Soviet commentators have always construed the development of the United States air bases around the periphery of the USSR as an indication that the United States and NATO in general count heavily on surprise attack. These bases, the Soviets maintain, can be quickly neutralized in war by Soviet strategic retaliation and many of them rapidly overrun by Soviet ground forces. They consequently reason that these bases could be of only limited use in the prolonged type of war which they envisage. Therefore, they conclude, these bases are designed with only one purpose in mind—a surprise attack on the USSR.

Finally, the Soviets also view surprise attack as a weapon of last resort for "capitalists." This view of NATO is based primarily on theoretical considerations. The decline of "capitalism" is inevitable, as the Soviets see it, and in their desperation "capitalists" will do everything in their power to avoid defeat. The American doctrine of "massive retaliation," announced in 1954, is frequently cited in support of this view. Khrushchev and other Soviet leaders have on a number of occasions given the very strong impression that they believe that a surprise attack by NATO may well occur at some future time when a Soviet victory by peaceful means appears to be inevitable.[3]

European Members of NATO

The role of the European members of NATO in a general war, as Soviet commentators see it, is not only to grant air and missile bases to the United States but also to supply the bulk of the manpower for the NATO army and to bear the brunt of the ground fighting. In the initial phase, the task of the European allies, supported by tactical nuclear weapons, is to hold in check the Soviet armies while the United States concentrates on strategic nuclear strikes. A few years

[3] See especially Walter Lippmann's report of his interview with Khrushchev in October 1958 in *The Communist World and Ours*, Boston, 1958, pp. 21-24.

ago the Soviets envisaged the role of the European members of NATO as one of fighting a delaying action until American ground forces in significant numbers could be landed on the Continent. Now the Soviets assign the principal ground role to the European allies, and especially to the West Germans, with American forces deployed from across the ocean for use as reinforcements rather than as the main ground fighting force. Soviet discussion of the role of the European members of NATO is accompanied by a good deal of propaganda about the United States utilizing the manpower of its allies for its own purposes.

Before the development of missiles, a major Soviet criticism of NATO strategy was that the advanced air bases were vulnerable to Soviet air attack and that most of them could be rapidly overrun by Soviet ground forces. With the development and deployment of their intermediate-range missiles, the Soviets claimed that airfields in Europe, North Africa, and Asia Minor had lost their significance. Ironically, the development in intermediate-range missiles, which seemed to eliminate the danger posed to the USSR by the NATO bases, has become a threat of much greater proportions as a result of the NATO decision of December 1957 to establish missile sites in Europe. The Soviets still consider, however, that NATO ground forces are insufficient in strength to hold back a concerted Soviet drive designed to overrun both air bases and missile sites.

The employment of tactical nuclear weapons, the Soviets believe, is a two-edged sword. Although recognizing advantages to defensive forces, they also point out advantages in offensive operations. Furthermore, the Soviets are perplexed by the trend toward decreasing NATO ground forces, in view of the stated intention to use tactical nuclear weapons. In the Soviet view the use of these weapons, with their anticipated casualty and disruptive effects, calls for more rather than fewer ground forces to compensate for expected losses.

United States Ground and Naval Forces

Soviet military commentators do not attribute a very significant role to the United States ground and naval forces in a general war. The army, in their view, would arrive on the scene in force only after the initial exchange of nuclear strikes and after the main encounter between the Russian ground forces and those of the European members of NATO. The Russians tend to picture American strategists as believing that American ground forces could be moved in by air to play a decisive role in securing control over enemy territory following the initial exchange on land and in the air.

The Russians argue that the American ground forces are not being maintained in sufficient strength to support such a strategy. Moreover, such forces as exist could not be brought to the scene of action very rapidly. As one Soviet military commentator has put it: "Modern states are still a long way from setting up 'flying armies.' Railways, roads, and shipping lanes, their junctions and ports, are the arteries without which a modern army cannot get along."[4] For these reasons they tend to discount the role of American ground forces in general war.

As to the navy, Soviet strategists emphasize in particular its role as an auxiliary to the strategic air force in launching nuclear strikes, and in guarding the American sea lanes to Europe. The Soviets see future American naval policy as concentrating on the building of nuclear submarines, in contrast to the present reliance on aircraft carriers. They envisage United States aircraft carriers as giving only temporary assistance to a strategic air force. They argue that aircraft carriers within effective range of the USSR can be rapidly located by air reconnaissance, and destroyed by Soviet aircraft, submarines, and land-based missiles.

Moreover, guarding American sea lanes to Europe is viewed as extremely difficult because of the modern weapons, including submarines, available to the USSR. Soviet commentators often mention the difficulties faced by Great Britain in two world wars in keeping her supply routes open. The implication is that in a future war these difficulties would be practically insurmountable.

Tactical Nuclear Weapons

Soviet official spokesmen attribute NATO's decision to employ tactical nuclear weapons in support of ground operations to the desire of the United States to restrict and divert the devastation of war to Europe and thereby to escape the consequences to the American continent of a strategic nuclear exchange. Soviet military doctrine has, in general, denied that a valid distinction can be made between the strategic and the tactical use of nuclear weapons. It is argued that most tactical targets are in populated areas, and that under these circumstances the use of tactical nuclear weapons would be as destructive to the centers of population as to the tactical targets. They would in effect be weapons of mass destruction, and use of such weapons would inevitably lead to the use of all types of nuclear weapons in view of the

[4] Major General N. Talensky, "Prevention of Surprise Attack," *International Affairs* (Moscow), No. 8 (August 1958), p. 54.

consequences for either adversary of being hit first by an all-out nuclear attack.

NATO as a Deterrent

While Soviet spokesmen persist in discussing NATO strategy as a plan of aggression, it is not difficult to derive from Soviet policies and comments an idea as to how they evaluate the strength of NATO as a deterrent to the use of their own military power. There can be no doubt, for instance, that the Russians have a healthy respect for American air power. In recent years very substantial resources and authority have been assigned to their Air Defense Forces, which embrace under one command all the elements of their air defense system. This is supplemented by an intensive civil defense training program. The incessant campaign for the liquidation of the advance bases which are so essential to NATO's deterrent power, and the great restraint with which Russia's preponderant strength in ground forces has been used for political bargaining on the European continent, also reflect the success of NATO strategy as a deterrent. Only in very recent years, as Soviet strategic nuclear strength has achieved approximate parity with that of NATO, has the USSR begun to issue warnings and undertake policies reflecting a greater confidence in its own strength.

At the same time, Soviet spokesmen see three developing weaknesses in NATO's defenses. First, the advance air bases and missile sites on the periphery of Russia are too vulnerable to be of sustained value. The Russians maintained this before the advent of intermediate-range missiles, and naturally feel even more positive about it today. Second, the Russians maintain that American society, being "capitalist" and hence by definition rent by contradictions, is less able than the Soviet to withstand the strain of atomic war. As a Soviet military commentator has put it: "The use of atomic weapons against the unstable rear of the aggressor will lead to incomparably greater consequences than the use of these weapons against a strong monolithic rear. . . ."[5] Finally, the Soviets are naturally aware of the limitations of NATO ground forces in Europe. Even if they were willing to admit the weakness of the Soviet position implicit in the unreliable armies of its allies in Eastern Europe, the Soviet leaders would maintain that they can keep them under control and still have ample resources left to deal with NATO.

[5] Major General G. Pokrovsky, in *Marksizm-leninizm o voine, armii, i voennoi nauke* [Marxism-Leninism on war, the army, and military science], Moscow, 1955, p. 169; cited in Garthoff, *op.cit.*, p. 138.

III. Soviet Strategy and NATO

The element of ideology is much less prevalent in Soviet writing about the military strategy of the USSR than in that about NATO. There is a long tradition of Soviet military doctrine which antedates NATO, and which is in many respects more closely related to the military thought of Continental Europe and of pre-revolutionary Russia than it is to Soviet Marxism. The main outlines of Soviet military strategy with regard to the challenge represented by NATO may therefore be set forth with some assurance.

The central aim of Communist policy is the modernization of Russia, with special emphasis at this stage on heavy industry. The expansion of the Soviet system to an eventual world socialist state is taken for granted as the ultimate theoretical goal of Soviet policy, although in the allocation of resources and risks this goal necessarily assumes a secondary place today. The problem confronting Soviet strategy is how to protect the security and interests of the Soviet-led coalition of states, and how to enlarge this coalition as opportunity permits, without risking the large-scale destruction of the Russian people, cities, and industry which a major war would entail so long as NATO retains its present relative strength.

Strategic Nuclear Weapons

One theme that underlies all of Soviet military thinking is that the aim of war is to destroy the enemy's armed forces and that this can be achieved only by the combined use of the air, ground, and naval forces employing the entire range of weapons made available by modern technology. In discussing in recent years their approach to strategy, Soviet commentators have constantly contrasted their own belief in a balanced use of forces with the special emphasis on strategic bombing in American strategy. In stressing this contrast, the Soviet authorities do not take into consideration the differences in the respective strategic positions of the United States and the USSR, or the fact that American strategy has only deterrent aims.

The discussion of military theory since Stalin's death has in general confirmed the traditional view that wars can be won only by the combined use of all branches of the armed forces. In this view, nuclear weapons represent a significant increase in the destructive capabilities of all branches of the armed forces, but do not call for revision of the basic strategic doctrine. At the same time, there has been since 1953 an extensive exploration of the military problems created by the

new technology, and there can be no question that the Soviet authorities have been greatly impressed by the destructiveness of nuclear
weapons. They constantly refer to the fact that nuclear warfare will
have disastrous consequences for all participants, and, as is well known,
their primary attention in recent years has been devoted to the development of new weapons.[6]

Soviet strategy assumes that a general war will start with an exchange of strategic nuclear strikes, and every effort has been made
to prepare the USSR for a full share in this activity. Emphasis was
initially placed on destroying American bases on the periphery of the
USSR, and it can now be assumed that Russia has a supply of intermediate-range missiles adequate for this purpose. Since 1956 the use
of missiles against the European members of NATO has on several
occasions been intimated, and Soviet-based intermediate-range missiles
can now reach most of Europe. The USSR has also developed a strategic air force which has the mission of neutralizing its American
counterpart, and long-range missiles are in production.[7] This very
active interest in strategic nuclear weapons has nevertheless not altered
the Soviet view that only by the coordinated employment of all branches
of the armed forces can victory be assured, and consequently that any
general war would tend to be prolonged despite the great destructiveness of the initial strikes.

Surprise Attack

While Stalin was in power, published discussion of strategy did not
depart from the accepted Soviet doctrine which held that "permanently operating factors," consisting of the stability of the home front
and the morale, size, equipment, and leadership of the armed forces,
determined the outcome of a war regardless of such initial advantages
as one side might gain from surprise. This doctrine was promulgated
by Stalin in February 1942 to meet the crisis of the German attack, and
it remained in force until 1955. The decisive turning point in Soviet
thinking in this regard, following a prolonged controversy in military
circles, was the publication of an article by Marshal Rotmistrov which
recognized that with the advent of nuclear weapons surprise could be
decisive. "In certain cases," he wrote, "surprise attack with the massive
employment of the new weapons can provoke the quick collapse of

[6] Dinerstein, op.cit., pp. 91-166, discusses the domestic political implications of the
Soviet debate on the destructiveness of nuclear war.

[7] Asher Lee, ed., Soviet Air and Rocket Forces, New York, 1959, offers a comprehensive evaluation of Soviet capabilities in this field. See also F. J. Krieger, ed., Behind
the Sputniks: A Survey of Soviet Space Science, Washington, D.C., 1958, pp. 205-34.

a state whose capability for resistance is low as a result of basic failures of its social and economic structure, and also of an unfavorable geographical location."[8]

In applying this new doctrine to the Russian situation, Marshal Rotmistrov assumed that the strategic air power at the disposal of NATO would be used for a surprise attack on the USSR in a preventive war. He therefore advocated a policy of pre-emptive attacks by the USSR in order to forestall such a surprise, and went on to make an important distinction between preventive and pre-emptive attacks. The former are unprovoked attacks undertaken by "imperialist" states attempting "to compensate for their internal organic weakness,"[9] whereas the latter represent an attempt "to seize and hold the strategic initiative" at a time when the enemy is preparing to launch a preventive attack.[10]

Since this initial formulation the distinction between preventive and pre-emptive attacks has been frequently restated by authoritative sources. Official denials that the USSR contemplated pre-emptive attacks were forthcoming when this change in doctrine was noted in the Western press, but the tone and content of Soviet military writings lead to the conclusion that the new doctrine is in fact an element of Soviet policy. It should also be noted that, as applied to the USSR, this recognition of the importance of surprise has modified but has not replaced the doctrine of the permanently operating factors. Soviet theorists maintain that, in view of the size and military strength of the USSR, nuclear surprise would be a disaster but not a catastrophe. Everything possible should be done to forestall such a disaster, but, if it came, the Soviet Union would survive to win in the end.[11]

The question of surprise, whether preventive or pre-emptive, provides an interesting example of the interrelationship of doctrine, capabilities, and policy. Doctrine now makes provision for an initial Soviet nuclear strike, defined as pre-emptive, in the event that an enemy appears to be on the point of launching an attack, defined as preventive. Capabilities, now that the USSR has a lead in long-range missiles that are already in production, appear for an indeterminate period to give initial Soviet striking power an advantage over that at the disposal of NATO. In determining policy, Soviet political leaders

---

[8] Marshal of Tank Troops P. Rotmistrov, "O roli vnezapnosti v sovremennoi voine" [On the role of surprise in contemporary war], *Voennaia Mysl'*, No. 2 (February 1955), p. 19.

[9] *Ibid.*, p. 20.   [10] *Ibid.*, p. 21.

[11] Some implications of this doctrine are discussed in Garthoff, *op.cit.*, pp. 84-87, and Dinerstein, *op.cit.*, pp. 167-214.

thus have an increasing range of choice. The distinction between preventive and pre-emptive attacks, while logical in essence, depends entirely on one's decision as to when an enemy is about to strike. This
decision is up to the Soviet leaders, and will be made on the basis of
their own preconceptions and justified after the event. The consistent
Soviet presentation of the Korean attack of June 1950 as defensive,
although under circumstances vastly different from those of a nuclear
exchange, is suggestive as to the Soviet attitude. Capabilities do not
give Soviet policy-makers such a wide range of choice as does doctrine,
and so long as deterrence is reasonably mutual they will no doubt
exercise the greatest caution in evaluating the enemy's intentions. What
is significant is that within the USSR the political leaders have the
final choice in the matter of surprise, and military doctrine and capabilities must be regarded as conditioning and limiting factors.

Soviet Ground and Naval Forces

While recognizing the importance of strategic power, the USSR
assumes the full employment of ground and naval forces and envisages
a long war in which the entire resources of the nation would be involved. To this end it maintains very large ground forces, reorganized
and extensively modernized since World War II. These forces are
presumably capable of fighting with either nuclear or conventional
weapons. In the event of a general war, it would no doubt expect to
occupy such strategic points as the entrances to the Baltic Sea and
Black Sea and perhaps to overrun the whole Continent. In other situations, the Soviets may also be able to draw upon their ground forces,
backed by a large number of trained reserves, to supply manpower as
"volunteers," as was threatened during the Suez crisis. Further, the
Soviets have a strong capability for providing material support both
for Soviet allies engaged in limited wars, and for insurrectionists in
areas accessible from the territory of the USSR and its allies.

The Soviet submarine fleet, comprising some 500 submarines, of
which about half are long-range, would be used not only to protect
Soviet coastal waters from encroachment by NATO fleets, but also
to sever sea communications between the United States and its European allies as well as to supplement strategic nuclear attacks against
the United States. The submarine fleet might well be deployed in
advance of a conflict, and it could be refueled from mobile bases. The
surface warships, supported by shore-based navy planes and missiles,
would be used to deny close access to Soviet shores by NATO fleets

and to conduct harassing and amphibious operations in the Black Sea, the Baltic Sea, and the North Atlantic.[12]

While this chapter is primarily concerned with NATO in the narrow sense of the term, a comprehensive view of the implications of a general war would have to give due consideration to the Asian aspect of such a conflict. The USSR has important naval and air bases in the Pacific area, it has in China a military ally with great resources, and it also has the capability of reaching the Indian Ocean with relative ease by land routes. One must assume that, in a prolonged conflict following initial nuclear strikes, military operations would engulf the entire area from the Caucasus to the Bering Straits. Neither side could hope for ultimate victory unless it had the ability to impose military control over this vast area.

East European Members of WTO

The Soviet alliance system antedates NATO, and is based on mutual assistance treaties concluded with the government-in-exile of Czechoslovakia in 1943 and with Yugoslavia and Poland in 1945. To these were added in 1948 a series of bilateral twenty-year mutual assistance treaties with all of the states in the Soviet orbit in Eastern Europe. The Warsaw Pact of May 1955—embracing Albania, Bulgaria, Czechoslovakia, East Germany, Hungary, Poland, Rumania, and the USSR—although heralded as a reply to the inclusion of West Germany in NATO, was in essence no more than the reformulation of existing treaty relationships.

The Warsaw Treaty Organization provides a somewhat less complex organization than NATO, with more loosely integrated forces. Whereas a Soviet marshal is the supreme commander of the alliance's military forces, the treaty stipulates that the deputy commanders will be the defense ministers or other military leaders of the signatory states, and that these deputies will be in command of the forces allocated by their governments to the joint command. WTO provides for three organs: a joint command, a joint command staff, composed of representatives of the general staffs of the member states, and a political consultative committee made up of representatives of the signatory governments. Although not officially a member of WTO, China has pledged its full support to that organization. The WTO countries meet from time to time and have evolved a common policy on European problems which in no way differs from that of the USSR.

[12] There are valuable discussions of Soviet strategy in M. G. Saunders, ed., *The Soviet Navy*, New York, 1958, especially pp. 168-86 and 243-58.

The weaknesses of WTO are well known. Loyalty of the Polish and Hungarian armies to Soviet leadership is demonstrably lacking and one may well question that of the other states, which have never publicly defied Soviet authority. It therefore seems likely that the USSR does not plan to use these armies for the occupation of Europe during a general war, but it may well envisage a military role for them. One can conceive of circumstances under which Polish and Czech forces could be used against the Germans, Hungarian, Rumanian, and Bulgarian against the Yugoslavs, and Bulgarian against the Greeks or the Turks.

Limited War

Limited war may be defined as armed conflict between two or more states that is limited as to objectives, area, or weapons—as distinct from indirect aggression, in which armed conflict is restricted to the territory of a single state.[13] It is significant that Soviet military writers have not devoted a great deal of attention to limited war. Available expressions of opinion constantly reiterate the belief that it is becoming increasingly difficult to limit wars, regardless of whether they are conducted by tactical nuclear weapons or by conventional weapons. The Soviets maintain that the existence of two opposing alliance systems, each embracing many countries located in different parts of the world, makes it likely that a limited war starting in Europe, where the major forces of the two alliance systems are located, would inevitably develop into a major war. It is a matter of regret that detailed Soviet comment is not available on the many variants of limited war, such as wars conducted by the armed forces of the USSR or by those of its allies, and wars conducted in areas of primary importance to NATO members as distinct from those in areas more removed from NATO interests.[14]

While the Soviets have a clear interest in maintaining that wars can no longer be limited, in order to restrain the United States from giving military assistance to unstable governments, it is nevertheless significant that in the period of NATO's preponderance (1949-1956) the USSR did not as a matter of deliberate policy resort to limited war

[13] This is a rather strict definition of "limited war." A much broader definition, proposed by Secretary of the Army Wilber M. Brucker, includes all forms of civil strife. Under this definition, there have been eighteen limited wars since 1945. See the *New York Times*, January 23, 1959, p. 7.

[14] Colonel A. Kononenko, "Lokal'nye voiny v politike i strategii SShA" [Local wars in the policy and strategy of the USA], *Mirovaia Ekonomika i Mezhdunarodnye Otnosheniia*, No. 10 (October 1958), pp. 16-25, is a typical recent statement. See also Garthoff, *op.cit.*, pp. 97-117.

directly or through third states in areas of primary interest to NATO members. In the case of Korea, which was in many respects a typical limited war, it seems more likely than not that the conflict was initiated in an effort to consolidate local gains and came to involve NATO members owing to a miscalculation of American intentions.

This appears to be a case where extensive capabilities have been held in check by a narrow doctrine. Now that a rough parity with NATO has been achieved in strategic nuclear weapons, it is likely that Soviet political leaders will be less cautious in regard to limited war, especially if initiated by an ally in an area remote from NATO interests. It is significant that the USSR itself has retained its full capability for waging limited war with conventional weapons. In this regard it has a great preponderance over NATO, and where such preponderance exists, the possibility of its being used should not be overlooked.

Indirect Aggression

On the borderline between war and peace is indirect aggression: the fomenting of civil strife in another state through the arming of bands, propaganda, and other forms of subversion. Like limited war, indirect aggression can often be carried out through third parties. The manner in which the Greek Communists were aided in the period 1944-1949, with provision of material assistance by Albania, Bulgaria, and Yugoslavia, and through propaganda and diplomacy by the USSR, may be regarded as a typical case of indirect aggression. Of a somewhat similar character was the assistance given by the USSR to the Communists in China in the period 1945-1949, and in Czechoslovakia in the period preceding the coup of 1948. Indirect aggression has long been a Soviet specialty, although it is not referred to as such by the USSR.

Indirect aggression is less provocative than limited war, in that it does not involve the armed forces of two states and consequently is more capable of being isolated from the arena of international politics. The possibilities of its use are also more restricted, in that it requires a situation in which a substantial proportion of the victim's population is already disloyal to the state. One can nevertheless imagine cases in areas of interest to NATO in which the USSR could employ indirect aggression.[15]

[15] United Nations General Assembly, *Question of Defining Aggression* (A/2211, 3 October 1952), pp. 55-58, contains a useful review of the problems raised by indirect aggression.

IV. The Politics of Coexistence

A major objective of Soviet foreign policy is to reduce the relative strength of the "capitalist system of states," and in recent years NATO has been the central target of this campaign and "peaceful coexistence" the principal stratagem. Assuming an inevitable "transition to socialism" throughout the world, the Soviets anticipate that a policy of coexistence will yield a variety of results. It will provide opportunities to exploit differences of opinion within the rival alliance system, and occasionally to extract concessions. It will encourage the members of NATO to relax their defenses and to reduce their military budgets. The reduction of military expenditures, according to Soviet Marxism, will serve to sharpen the "general crisis of capitalism" and promote forces that will hasten its collapse. At the same time, the socialist system will be making domestic gains and winning new converts in the uncommitted countries.

While waging peace, the Soviet leaders never ignore the possibility of using more forceful methods when this seems expedient. Even in a period of peaceful coexistence, warnings, threats, and subversion are frequently employed. The Soviets estimate that by nibbling away at areas of secondary interest to NATO members, and by supporting their allies in limited wars and indirect aggression where this is feasible, they can expand their system by means short of general war. A significant factor in the ability of the USSR to conduct a successful policy of peaceful coexistence is its relative military strength. Hence the problems confronting NATO strategy relate not only to the prevention of general war, but also to all other levels of competition, including especially the complex forces that come into play when political negotiations are undertaken.

Propaganda

NATO has been the priority target for Soviet propaganda in Europe since the spring of 1949. The Soviet case against NATO has maintained that the United States is waging an aggressive policy as part of a plan for world hegemony, that NATO is an American device to enslave Western Europe, that NATO undermines the United Nations and fosters a revival of German militarism, and hence that it is a threat to the security of Europe and to general peace.

These themes are developed in a wide variety of forms, of which the radio and press are only the most obvious. The extensive "peace campaign" has achieved some success in creating the impression that the USSR is a champion of international cooperation whose efforts are being thwarted by the West. The USSR also has the assistance of national Communist parties in the NATO countries and of Communist-sponsored international front organizations which operate as fifth columns within the NATO countries. It likewise makes good use of the opportunities presented by the United Nations and other international bodies and conferences to state in a wide variety of ways its case against NATO.[16]

Pressure on NATO Members

In addition to propaganda on a wide front, the USSR has not hesitated to employ more forceful methods. One of these has been the use of various forms of pressure against the European members of NATO. In an exchange of correspondence early in 1949, for instance, the Soviet government warned Norway of the danger of becoming involved in the "aggressive aims of a definite grouping of powers" not of its own choosing. It also rejected the assurance that no foreign bases would be granted on Norwegian territory unless Norway was attacked or threatened with attack, on the ground that the aggressors could easily fabricate a threat to Norway as a means of obtaining agreement to the manning of Norwegian bases by other NATO forces. The USSR offered to conclude a non-aggression pact "to dispel any doubts of the Norwegian Government that a threat of attack could supposedly emanate from the Soviet Union." Despite this offer, Norway went ahead and joined NATO, recalling perhaps the history of the Soviet non-aggression pacts with the Baltic states and with other neighbors of the USSR.[17] Similar pressure was exerted on the other European members of NATO, but without the accompanying offer of a non-aggression pact.

Later, when the USSR achieved parity with NATO in strategic nuclear weapons, the Soviet leaders indulged in more direct warnings as to the consequences to the European members of NATO of the employment of nuclear weapons. On numerous occasions they have pointed out that the USSR was less vulnerable to nuclear weapons than the European members of NATO, by virtue of the more concentrated population and resources of the latter. The most dramatic of these reminders was the series of notes sent by the USSR during

[16] Evron M. Kirkpatrick's *Target: The World* (New York, 1956) and *Year of Crisis* (New York, 1957) provide a comprehensive summary of Communist propaganda activities in 1955 and 1956, respectively.

[17] *Current Digest of the Soviet Press* (New York), 1 (March 1, 1949), p. 23; 1 (March 8, 1949), p. 27.

the Middle East crisis in 1956 to Great Britain, France, and the United States. While these notes differed somewhat as to detail, in substance they served as a reminder that the USSR possessed a full range of nuclear missiles. The notes to Great Britain and France were widely interpreted as a formal threat, although technically they were no more than a forceful gesture asserting the right of the USSR to be consulted in the decisions being taken in regard to the Middle East.[18]

Since the Middle East crisis, Khrushchev has on a number of occasions warned NATO members that they would be subjected to bombardment with nuclear weapons in the event of war. For instance, on December 21, 1957, he asserted before the Supreme Soviet that "crushing retaliatory blows will be struck both at countries on whose territory NATO military bases have been set up and at countries which themselves have set up these bases for aggressive purposes."[19] More recently, in an interview with a Greek publisher, Khrushchev warned that "the existence of atomic bases on Greek territory could, in the event of an armed conflict, lay the country open to atomic retaliation with all its attendant tragic consequences."[20]

Continuous pressure on the European members of NATO has also been exerted through the Communist parties in those countries where they were influential. Through their press, which in some cases had a wide circulation, the Communists gave full support to the Soviet propaganda line. In national parliaments, they have vigorously opposed all measures in support of armaments and European integration. In a few significant instances, the Communist bloc of votes has been crucial in defeating measures vital to the strength of NATO. The Communist parties, and associated subversive organizations, have also been widely used in some NATO countries to promote strikes in industry and transportation which directly affected the supply of arms to NATO. Whenever possible, subversion and espionage have also been resorted to. While the Communists have not succeeded in gaining membership in government coalitions in NATO countries, they have in a number of cases been able to exert significant pressure as a result of their extensive influence and connections.

Disengagement

The political and economic resurgence of Western Europe in recent years, and the growing strength of the NATO coalition in Europe,

[18] Hans Speier, "Soviet Atomic Blackmail and the North Atlantic Alliance," *World Politics*, IX, No. 3 (April 1957), pp. 307-28.
[19] *Current Digest of the Soviet Press*, X (February 12, 1958), p. 7.
[20] *Ibid.*, X (June 11, 1958), pp. 19-21.

represent a challenge of major proportions to the Soviet system. The prosperity of the German Federal Republic and the poverty of the German Democratic Republic, as well as the continuing symbol of a thriving West Berlin in the heart of the Eastern zone, provide a striking contrast and a constant source of disquiet to the peoples under Communist rule. It is clear that the USSR has a strong interest in the withdrawal of American and British forces from Europe and the dissolution of NATO.

The question is, what terms is the Soviet government prepared to offer? To the objective observer, it would seem reasonable that the Soviet Union would be prepared to withdraw its forces from Eastern Europe to achieve this result. If such terms were accepted, the Soviet forces would remain within easy striking distance of Eastern Europe, whereas the return of British and American forces would be much more difficult and the blow to NATO's morale might be decisive. There are serious considerations, however, which make such a sweeping Russian offer unlikely. It would represent a retreat from gains made since the war, and this runs against the current trend of Soviet policy. Quite the contrary, there is much more likelihood that in their present mood of confidence the Soviets hope to achieve their aims without such extensive concessions. Moreover, the question of German unification is the heart of the disengagement problem, and on this issue the Russians have thus far been particularly uncompromising.

Current Soviet policy includes both the exertion of direct pressure on the occupying powers along the lines of Khrushchev's recent proposals, and support for the Rapacki Plan. This plan, in its present form, calls for the prohibition of the production, stationing, and employment of nuclear weapons in the two Germanies, in Poland, and in Czechoslovakia, and the limitation of conventional forces stationed in this zone. Reflecting the new Soviet outlook is the official attitude regarding these proposals that, in view of the terrors of nuclear warfare, both parties should be ready for a "reasonable" settlement without resort to threats of war.

The effect of these proposals would be to curtail seriously NATO's defensive capability. It would make West Germany virtually defenseless in view of the preponderance of Soviet conventional forces. The position of American, British, and French forces in West Germany would be greatly weakened, if denied the support of tactical nuclear weapons. In West Germany a spirit of neutralism would be fostered, and serious consideration of complete demilitarization as a price for reunification would be encouraged.

The ultimate Soviet purpose is no doubt to unite Germany on Soviet terms. Relying on a strong German desire for peace and unity, and on the preponderance of Soviet military strength in Europe, the USSR hopes in the course of time to checkmate NATO on this issue. Khrushchev has recently referred to the Nazi-Soviet pact of 1939 as a significant precedent.[21] Within the context of a Soviet victory on the German issue, a more general "disengagement" would be an anticlimax.

It is always possible that the Soviet viewpoint as expressed in a variety of public statements represents no more than a bargaining position, and that if formal negotiations were undertaken very extensive concessions would be made. This possibility cannot readily be evaluated until Soviet terms are given a decisive test. From the available evidence, however, the Soviet government would appear to be confident that it can create a situation in which West Germany would be attracted by Soviet terms. A decisive feature of this confidence is the Soviet belief that NATO's military position, whatever its strength as a deterrent to a general war, is no longer a vital restraint to the USSR in situations that call for the exertion in Europe of pressures short of a threat of general war.

Disarmament

As in the case of disengagement, the USSR has a strong interest in the general reduction in expenditures on armaments. Here again, however, the available evidence tends to indicate that Soviet leaders hope to achieve this in a form that would be to the advantage of the Soviet bloc. The initial aim of Soviet policy on disarmament is to achieve a complete ban on nuclear weapons at a minimum cost to the USSR in international inspection and controls, which it considers a form of intrusion in its internal affairs. The slogan "Ban the Bomb" formed the basis of the Soviet peace campaign designed to convince public opinion in the NATO countries, as well as in the uncommitted areas, of the peaceful nature of Soviet intentions. In negotiations, however, the Soviets have consistently demanded that weapons of mass destruction must first be unconditionally prohibited before practical measures of control can be fruitfully discussed and agreed upon.

As one technique of achieving its goal, the USSR has proposed that the nuclear powers, as a first step, should solemnly pledge not to employ these weapons. It has insisted that control and inspection of such a pledge are not technically feasible or politically desirable. A

---

[21] Lippmann, op.cit., pp. 16-18.

simple moral pledge by states not to use these weapons is therefore regarded as the most feasible course of action. An acceptance of this position without comparable restrictions on other forms of armament would place an unwarranted reliance on a Soviet pledge and would remove the basis of NATO's deterrent power while leaving unimpaired the Soviet bloc's superiority in conventional warfare.[22]

As an intermediate step, the USSR has given priority in recent years to the cessation of nuclear tests. It is the Soviet contention that the question of cessation of nuclear tests must be dealt with independently of other disarmament and political issues. The ban must be applied to all states, including those on the threshold of becoming nuclear powers, and must be controlled with an absolute minimum of international inspection teams on Soviet territory. The Soviet expectation is that such a ban on nuclear tests will provide a suitable psychological environment in which to press subsequently for the complete banning of nuclear weapons on Soviet terms.

Similarly, in the case of surprise attack, the Soviet government has shown no inclination to discuss inspection and control of missile sites and air bases. Its view is that once nuclear weapons have been banned by mutual consent and regulated unilaterally in a spirit of mutual confidence, means of inspection can be worked out to safeguard against surprise attack by conventional weapons.[23] The Soviet leaders appear to be confident that, in the event such a program were accepted, the Soviet system could achieve its ultimate goals by means short of war.

V. IMPLICATIONS OF SOVIET POLICY

In the years ahead, two main problems confront NATO in its relations with the Soviet alliance system. One is the danger of war by miscalculation. The other is the employment by the USSR of methods short of general war for the achievement of its general objectives.

It has been noted that one of the central features of Soviet military thought in recent years has been the recognition that surprise, if not decisive, gives the aggressor far greater advantages than at any previous time in the history of warfare. The Soviet leaders also believe that the "capitalists" may as a last resort be driven to aggression to avoid defeat. In any event, the USSR is in all likelihood as sensitive as is

[22] A. V. Topchiev, "Disarmament and International Tension," *Bulletin of the Atomic Scientists*, xiv, No. 10 (December 1958), pp. 405-8, is a characteristic statement of the Soviet position. The author is secretary-general of the Academy of Sciences of the USSR.

[23] Lippmann, *op.cit.*, pp. 27-30; Talensky, *loc.cit.*, pp. 53-55.

NATO to the possibilities of surprise. In this atmosphere the chances of miscalculation are obvious, and are likely to increase. This danger is diminished in some degree only by the acute awareness by both parties of the risks inherent in the situation, as reflected in the negotiations concerning measures for guarding against surprise.

The second problem, that of the employment by the USSR of methods short of general war, is a great deal more complex and in the long run even more difficult of solution. Military power as a threat, according to Soviet doctrine, is more important than its actual employment for the achievement of the ultimate objective—the "transition from capitalism to socialism" throughout the world. Had it not been for the reassertion of American military power after 1947, the USSR would probably have been able by means of threats and subversion alone to make significant gains. Indeed, resort to war is not normally necessary if one state possesses overwhelming military power. During the period from 1949 to 1955, in which NATO had a clear preponderance in strategic nuclear weapons, Soviet actions in Europe were limited almost exclusively to propaganda stressing the desire for peace. It seems fair to say that, as concerns the areas of primary interest to NATO members in this period, the strategic nuclear weapons available to NATO deterred not only the strategic capabilities of the USSR but also its capabilities in the realm of limited war, indirect aggression, political subversion, and threats and warnings which could be used in political bargaining. Even in areas of secondary importance to NATO members, with the problematic exception of Korea, limited wars were not initiated.

Now that an approximate parity in nuclear weapons has been achieved between the two alliance systems, the strategic nuclear weapons available to NATO no longer deter such a wide range of Soviet capabilities. Indeed, in all probability they deter only Soviet strategic nuclear capabilities and limited war in Europe or in other areas of major concern to NATO members. In the event that successful measures are agreed to for the prevention of surprise attacks, or when widely dispersed and relatively invulnerable solid-fuel missiles become available, it seems likely that something resembling a nuclear stalemate will result. It is likely that Soviet leaders already believe such a stalemate to have been achieved. In this situation, the range of Soviet courses of action short of nuclear war—limited war with conventional weapons in areas of secondary importance to NATO members, especially if the initiative is taken by third states, as well as indirect aggression and political subversion in areas of primary importance to NATO members—will become increasingly undeterred by the strategic nuclear capability available to NATO.

To meet this Soviet challenge, NATO not only needs a capacity to conduct limited war with conventional weapons in distant areas, and to protect its members and their friends from indirect aggression and political subversion. It must also evolve a political program of modernization suited to the needs of the times and adaptable to conditions in societies at widely different stages of development. In the Soviet way of thinking, war is secondary to political action in the implementation of policy. To compete successfully with the USSR, NATO members must be able not merely to wage war but also to prosecute a systematic policy designed to achieve nothing less than the modernization of the entire world by methods which give due recognition to the welfare and dignity of the individual.

PART II

PROBLEMS AND POLICIES

CHAPTER 4

NATO STRATEGY: TOTAL WAR*

BY GEORGE W. RATHJENS, JR.

FOR the last decade the keystone of Western strategy with respect to Europe has been reliance on United States strategic bombing capabilities as the ultimate deterrent to Soviet aggression in Europe. The credibility of that policy is being questioned; that is the crux of the NATO dilemma today. A few years ago limited war was thought to be possible elsewhere, but not in Western Europe. There were questions about the possible outcome of a major war in Europe—about how long and what measures would be required to defeat the USSR, and what levels of damage Europe might sustain in the course of the conflict; but it was generally believed that a major conflict there would be fought not merely with the objective of containing Soviet power, but with that of causing its collapse. Total war in which the Soviets would almost surely be the losers was thought to be the almost certain consequence of any overt aggression by them in Europe. This prospect was a credible deterrent. With the growth of Soviet nuclear capabilities, the situation is rapidly changing, and increasingly it is asked whether an American president would order an all-out attack against the Soviet Union in response to seizure or strangulation of West Berlin, for example, or invasion of eastern Turkey—or, for that matter, of all of Europe—knowing full well that this would be followed by the destruction of a number of American cities, and many millions of Americans.

A frequent reply is that even though the United States might not launch SAC as a response, the Soviets could not afford to take the chance that we would. With respect to a Soviet onslaught against Europe as a whole, this is probably still true, but clearly the trend is running in such a way that the risk to the Soviet Union is decreasing

---

* Unless otherwise qualified, the terms "total war," "all-out war," and "unlimited war" refer here to conflict in which the United States and the Soviet Union are so engaged that they attack each other and each other's allies with nuclear weapons to the extent that they can. Certainly, to a large part of the world, such a war would seem "total." Lesser conflicts might seem total to one or more participants, but would have much less widespread catastrophic effects; for present purposes, they will generally be regarded as limited.

I am indebted to many of the participants in the Princeton Conference of 1959 on NATO, and also to Joseph H. Lewis and Karl Kreilkamp, for helpful discussions and criticism.

with time. Risks that may be unacceptable today may be taken tomorrow, unless there is a radical change in the Western military posture.

Today, then, NATO must face such questions as these: (1) To what Soviet moves is the prospect of a thermonuclear exchange likely to serve as an effective deterrent? (2) Can the spectrum of such possibilities be kept broad without at the same time producing an unacceptable risk of accidental total war? (3) What courses of action and force postures will be required for all-out war? (4) And what will the requirements be for situations with respect to which a thermonuclear exchange is not a credible deterrent?

This chapter addresses itself primarily to these questions, although the possibilities implied in the second make it clear that limited war cannot be ignored entirely, since questions of general and of limited war cannot be treated in isolation.

I. On the Distinction Between Limited and Total War

The distinction between the objectives, strategies, and weapon-system requirements for the two types of conflicts is much sharper today than it has been in the past. Even in the last few years, arguments were often heard to the effect that we need not concern ourselves with the limited-war problem because preparation for total war would automatically provide what was required for any limited conflict, especially if the limited conflict were in Europe (when the possibility of limited war there was acknowledged at all). Paradoxically, varying arguments by the most extreme advocates of air power, on the one hand, and by Army and Navy protagonists, on the other, led to this same conclusion. And for a very few years there was probably much validity to both arguments.

Air power advocates could argue that, in the event of a small limited war, some of the relatively small number of aircraft designed primarily for nuclear delivery could, if necessary, deliver conventional ordnance (or small atomic weapons); and that they could deter larger limited conflict with their nuclear capability or, if necessary, use it to affect the outcome decisively. For example, in 1958 General White, Chief of Staff of the Air Force, said: "The real deterrent to significant local conflict is nuclear firepower. The whole of this firepower is our general war deterrent. That portion of this firepower, up to the total necessary to achieve resolution, is the adequate force for local warfare. . . . Air Force requirements in any likely local war situation can be met with forces provided for general war purposes under existing conditions."[1]

[1] In *Air Force*, XLI, No. 1 (January 1958), pp. 49, 51.

And General Gerhart, in an Air Force presentation before Congress, said simply, "The Air Force capability to meet local war situations is contained within its general war forces."[2]

Army and Navy advocates argued the case of the "broken-backed" total conflict. They acknowledged that strategic bombing with nuclear weapons would produce great damage, but maintained that the crippled adversaries would continue the conflict, and that to bring it to a successful conclusion would require operations with armies and navies during and after the nuclear exchange. In 1958 this view was still held at the highest levels in the Department of Defense; for example, Secretary of Defense McElroy stated that, along with retaliatory forces, others were necessary in general war for such purposes as keeping open sea lines of communication and conducting operations on land.[3]

Moreover, since NATO's inception there has been an argument to the effect that ground and tactical air "shield" forces were necessary to keep Soviet armies out of Western Europe until the effects of strategic attacks against the Soviet Union could make themselves felt. In 1958 this concept was enunciated by General Maxwell Taylor, Chief of Staff of the United States Army,[4] and also in the British White Paper on defense policy.[5]

Perhaps more to silence critics who were concerned about the possibility of having to fight limited wars than to give added weight to the need for conventional forces, it was held that needs for the unpopular limited conflicts could be met by the same forces as were required for general war. See, for example, the statement of General White above, and one by Secretary of the Army Brucker: "I wish to emphasize that the Army's pentomic divisions retain a significant nonatomic capability so that flexibility is retained. Thus, they are combat-ready for both limited and general war."[6]

In their time, and it was surely less than a decade ago, both the concept of a "broken-backed" war and the need for a strong holding capability in Europe had validity, but, though these arguments have been stated as United States policy fairly recently, it is increasingly recognized that the above-stated role for the "shield" forces and the

[2] *Department of Defense Appropriations for 1959, Department of the Air Force,* Hearings Before the Subcommittee of the Committee on Appropriations, House of Representatives, 85th Congress, 2nd Session, Washington, D.C., 1958, p. 21 (referred to hereafter as *Defense Appropriations for 1959*).

[3] *Ibid., Overall Policy Statements,* p. 6.

[4] "Strategy of Sword and Shield," *Signal,* xii, No. 8 (April 1958), p. 5.

[5] *Report on Defence, Britain's Contribution to Peace and Security,* Cmd. 363, London, HMSO, February 1958, p. 2.

[6] *Defense Appropriations for 1959, Overall Policy Statements,* p. 240.

"broken-backed" war concept are clearly outmoded; fortunately they have lost some of their advocates.[7] The White Paper of 1957 on defense policy[8] made it fairly clear that, by that time, the British government was inclined to the view that British policy should be based on the assumption that a thermonuclear exchange would be decisive in itself.[9] The main arguments for NATO ground forces now seem to be to deter and, if necessary, to handle limited incursions, most probably by satellite nations; and to force any Soviet attempt at major aggression in Europe to be so obvious that ambiguity with respect to Soviet intentions will be negligible. And, with respect to total war, interest is flagging in planning for contingencies subsequent to a thermonuclear exchange. It is increasingly recognized that a thermonuclear attack would produce such damage that any recipient might have little interest in, or capability for, continuing the conflict. For example, Dean Acheson has remarked that ". . . successful nuclear attack on the United States could result, on conservative estimates, in death or injury to a third of our population. The destruction and disruption of our highly specialized and interdependent society could be so great that the nation, as an operating entity, would either cease to function, or be forced to devote all its efforts to the survival of the living."[10]

When the expected damage to each side is of this order, and there is little reason to believe that the capabilities of each side to inflict

[7] In an excellent discussion of Soviet strategic thinking (*Soviet Strategy in the Nuclear Age*, New York, 1958), Raymond Garthoff shows that the Soviets are apparently even more firmly wedded to the concept of the "broken-backed" war. This view is, of course, almost inevitable in the light of the Soviet thesis that communism must eventually triumph; it is also perhaps a reflection of the very dominant role of army, as contrasted with air force, officers in the Soviet defense establishment. There does not appear to be any evidence of responsible Soviet strategists admitting the possibility that a thermonuclear exchange might destroy Soviet society, or even that it might be decisive in all-out war. Indeed, only within the last few years do they appear to have recognized that the use of nuclear weapons in the counterforce role might be such an important factor that there would be considerable advantage in a surprise attack.

[8] *Defence, Outline of Future Policy*, Cmd. 124, London, HMSO, 1957.

[9] There is an interesting critique of the 1957 White Paper by Sir John Slessor in *The Great Deterrent*, New York, 1957, p. 301. He points out that while the over-all tone of the paper is one of recognition of the decisive nature of a thermonuclear exchange, the authors nevertheless refused to face squarely the implications of this fact. Thus, there is a vestige of the older strategic thinking in the paper: an argument for forces which would not be very useful if the thermonuclear phase of the war were decisive, and which would be woefully inadequate for the "broken-backed" war if it were not.

[10] *Power and Diplomacy*, Cambridge, Mass., 1958, p. 37. Higher casualty figures have been estimated in an FCDA study which predicts that, by the 60th day after attack, 48 per cent of the population would have died and another 14 per cent would have been injured. (Reported in National Planning Association, *1970 Without Arms Control*, Washington, D.C., 1958.)

damage on its adversary will do other than increase, then it becomes very difficult to believe that forces of a tactical type, be they army, navy, or air, could have a significant role in an all-out war. In particular, it is hard to see how the existence of "shield" forces in Europe could significantly affect the outcome. In the event of all-out war, it is likely that Europe would sustain damage comparable to that inflicted on the United States and on the Soviet Union; if so, it would scarcely be an asset to anyone. (On the contrary, it would be a liability, as is a wounded soldier compared with a dead one.) Conventional forces there might have a role in maintaining order, just as they would in the United States or the USSR, but this is hardly the role envisaged for them in NATO planning.

On the other hand, strategic weapons are not likely to be used in limited conflicts. Our reluctance to use such weapons, which has been so clearly demonstrated in Korea and Indo-China, can only be reinforced by the recognition that it has and will become increasingly dangerous to attempt such solutions, in view of the growing possibility of the adversary's responding in kind. It seems clear, in short, that the types of forces required for all-out and limited war will in the future have little in common.

Even more useless and unsuitable in thinking about the thermonuclear war are the traditional concepts of victory. Just as there are differences in weapons requirements for the two kinds of war, so must there be differences in objectives. A nation might hope to win a limited war in the sense of emerging from it with an actual increase in "net worth," as did the United States from the Mexican and Spanish-American Wars. Though victory in this sense is certainly not now a reasonable prospect with respect to total war, there has in the past been the prospect of some sort of "victory" with respect to major general wars. In such wars as World Wars I and II, there was at least the expectation, presumably held by each side, that continuation of the conflict to the point where the adversary collapsed or surrendered would bring with it conditions superior to those that might have obtained if the challenge of war had not been accepted, or if surrender had occurred at a stage when the war was still limited. It is important to note that the idea of "winning" a general war—presumably in this sense—is, or at least recently was, still popular in United States military circles. For example, in testimony given in 1958, General Irvine, speaking for the Air Force, and Admiral Burke, speaking for the Navy, both stated that our retaliatory capabilities must be such that they would permit us to "win" a general war if we should engage in one.[11] Such statements no longer make much sense.[12] I am inclined to the view, shared by many others, particularly outside military circles, that neither side can "win" an all-out war. Certainly, if descriptions such as that by Mr. Acheson, quoted above, with regard to the consequences of such a war, are anywhere near correct, it would be stretching the imagination to say that, on emerging from such a conflict, we would have had much of a "victory." There may be much in the argument that the survival or renaissance of the values we cherish would be less probable following a future unlimited conflict than if we simply surrendered to Soviet demands.

Some may infer that acceptance of this argument must necessarily lead to advocacy of a policy of surrender as a rational choice. But this does not follow at all, for the USSR would presumably be comparably damaged in an all-out war, and will be no more eager to engage in one than are we. By accepting the possibility of something worse than surrender we can hope to avoid both. The threat of mutual destruction can be effective as a deterrent, *but only provided that there is a basis for Soviet expectation that such war will be the consequence of the aggression which we desire to deter.* Limited aggression by the Soviet bloc against, for example, Formosa could be deterred by the threat of all-out war, but for such deterrence to be credible there would have to be an expectation that such war would be the consequence of the aggression. Clearly, *after* the fact of a Communist invasion of that island, all-out war would not be in the American interest. It would not save Formosa, but only ensure destruction of the United States. Thus, for the threat of all-out war to be effective in such a circumstance, there must be a mechanism which can make it reasonably probable that the holocaust cannot be prevented once a certain line is crossed; the need is for an automatic, veto-proof response. In principle, it is, of course, possible to counter all threats with this deterrent, but to provide a credible mechanism for ensuring automaticity of response to lesser threats may be very difficult. Moreover, there may be an unacceptable concomitant increase in the probability of accidental all-out war if the attempt is made to cover too broad a spectrum of threats with the counterthreat of all-out war. Minimizing the need for limited-war capability, therefore, increases the probability of accidental all-out war.

[11] *Defense Appropriations for 1959, Department of the Air Force,* p. 374; *ibid., Over-* and *Policy Statements,* p. 449.

[12] I have discussed this point in some detail in "Notes on the Military Problems of Europe," *World Politics,* x, No. 2 (January 1958), p. 182.

Another conflict of objectives calls for clarification. Most of those who believe it possible to "win" an all-out war recognize that the damage will be so great that avoidance of the conflict must take priority over "winning" as an objective. But so long as they accord *any importance whatever* to "winning," they do not escape the dilemma, because most, if not all, measures taken to improve the probability of "winning" will also make the accidental triggering of war more probable. Nor does one escape it even by renouncing the objective of "winning," if one still clings to the belief that it is desirable to try to reduce damage to oneself in the event of war. For example, a counterforce strategy which tried to minimize damage to us by destroying as much enemy capability on the ground as possible is also a strategy which requires quick reaction—reaction to some degree based on equivocal information about enemy intentions. It is not, then, a policy entailing a minimum risk of accidents—a point which is developed further subsequently.

Of course, there are other measures, such as those of passive air defense, which could conceivably reduce damage without concomitant increase in the risk of war. For example, Mr. Acheson has speculated: "If by these measures [that is, a civil defense shelter program] casualties could be reduced to one-third or one-fifth of what they would be under present circumstances, this could well save the whole national structure from collapse. . . ."[13] This observation I believe to be unduly optimistic. I have written elsewhere that in the near future it is likely that offensive possibilities may be such that any attempt to reduce possible damage in a thermonuclear exchange can, and will, be negated at a lesser cost to the adversary by expansion of his offensive capabilities; that, in short, there may be nothing in defense, active or passive; and that, further, offensive capabilities may be made quite invulnerable to attack.[14] We may well be nearing the point where the capabilities of the major powers to wreak destruction will seem almost infinite compared with their finite resources capable of being allocated to defense.

There is one other problem area that needs exploration—namely, the difference in policy and objectives as between deterrence by the

---

[13] *Op.cit.*, p. 46.

[14] "Deterrence and Defense," *Bulletin of the Atomic Scientists*, xiv, No. 6 (June 1958), p. 225. Quite different conclusions must be drawn from a recent study by The RAND Corporation reported by Herman Kahn: "How Many Can Be Saved?" *ibid.*, xv, No. 1 (January 1959), p. 30. He suggests that at least for some years there would be a very considerable payoff, for the side striking first, from a relatively inexpensive civil defense program.

threat of massive retaliation, on the one hand, and graduated deterrence, on the other. With respect to the former, it is clearly the *threat* of retaliation that is all-important, not the actual carrying-out of retaliation. At least against all lesser threats—that is, all those other than direct attack against the United States—launching an all-out retaliatory blow *after* the fact of aggression would be completely irrational if the launching could be prevented. If the threat of *unlimited* war is to be effective as a deterrent, it must be clear that there can be no possibility of choice after the aggression. At that stage, there can be no room for ambiguity in the retaliatory system, at least not for ambiguity dependent on rational decision.

The situation is quite different with respect to *limited* war or *limited* retaliation. During the Quemoy crisis in the fall of 1958, President Eisenhower and Secretary Dulles could reasonably expect that the Chinese would be deterred from attack by our, at first, quite ambiguous statements about our intentions, since it was clear that, subsequent to a Chinese attack, we might (or might not) decide that our interests would best be served by armed intervention. Thus, it is clear that ambiguity may be very important when the threat is a limited one. If the limits beyond which an aggressor can go are poorly defined, then he will presumably stop short of what he regards as unduly risky. Bluffing has a payoff in that one will succeed in deterring aggression in some situations where one would choose not to fight if the aggression actually occurred. It would not, of course, have been in our interest to bring about a global war in the event of the loss of Quemoy. Had this been the only alternative available to us, it seems to me extremely improbable that the Chinese would have been deterred, for they would probably have felt sufficiently confident that the fact that we would still have a choice after the aggression could lead us to but one decision, that of restraint.

Besides the possibility of our direct limited intervention, there was the possibility of a threat of limited retaliation in the cited instance. A stated or implied threat to bomb a specific limited number of Chinese cities in the event of an invasion would have been a credible deterrent, provided it was reasonably obvious that such bombing would not lead to all-out war. This could have been a reasonable course for us; though it would not directly aid in the recapture of the island in question, it would lend credence to any similar attempts at deterrence by us. A worthwhile lesson would have been taught. It would be quite otherwise if our response were all-out war. In such a case, the only lesson would be that the United States chose all-out war—a worthless lesson, since one could have little confidence in predicting that a United States which had been heavily damaged in such a war would repeat the decision in any similar future circumstance. The precedents of the past would scarcely be relevant; indeed, it would be likely that all-out war would then be repudiated as a response to aggression. (Witness the pacifist attitudes prevalent in Japan.) In sum, the threat of massive retaliation is different in kind from the threat of limited retaliation or limited war.

II. The Distinction Between Requirements for Retaliatory and Counterforce Missions

It has been common usage to refer to United States strategic bombing capability as our retaliatory system. However, during most of the last decade, Air Force doctrine played down the importance of pure retaliation, and emphasized the importance of blunting the Soviet offensive. The theory was that, in the event of war, the Soviets would try to mount several strikes, so that even if they struck first, damage to the United States could be held down by a rapid SAC response. The fact that there was ambiguity with respect to terminology and objectives in the past may not have mattered a great deal. Until recently we really had only one weapon system—the manned bomber—for both the retaliatory and the counterforce role (though perhaps we might have pushed other systems harder, had the distinction between the two objectives been clearly spelled out and objectives specified). Today, however, we have in prospect delivery systems with radically different capabilities. Some will be almost completely ineffective in one role or the other; others will be useful for both. The distinction between missions must therefore be taken into account. The priority given to development and procurement of different systems must depend on a clear understanding of objectives.[15]

Requirements for the purely retaliatory role are almost certainly

[15] It is interesting to note that some confusion exists also in Soviet military thinking as to the importance of, and requirements for, the two different missions—see Garthoff, *op.cit.* He points out that the Russians' strategic thinking has emphasized the counterforce mission, as might be expected in the light of their experiences in World War II and their preoccupation with the idea of a long war eventually to be decided by destruction of the enemy's military forces. Yet, in the development of thermonuclear capabilities, the idea of deterrence has apparently been of great importance in Soviet thinking. Thus, ". . . there are cogent reasons for believing that the Soviet Union believes its greatest advantage would be served by avoiding a thermonuclear war and using her growing nuclear striking power to stalemate American deterrent power, and then to take advantage of this neutralization for purposes of gradual and probably indirect aggrandizement" (*ibid.*, p. 103).

rather small. The United States (or any other nation) must have a capability for destroying enough Soviet assets so that anything Russia might gain by attack would be more than offset by her losses. At least in the absence of an effective civil defense program, the most easily destroyed assets are, of course, people. Thus, the minimum retaliatory capability needed by us would be one enabling us to destroy a fairly substantial fraction of Soviet population. For this purpose, there is no requirement for rapidity of response; but retaliation must, of course, be reasonably probable if the deterrent is to be effective.[16]

A system which the enemy cannot locate and attack with sufficient precision, and destroy, will be preferable to one which relies on quick response for effectiveness. With more time available for deciding on enemy intentions, there will be less chance of deciding that the enemy is making an all-out attack when, in fact, he may not be. With respect to deterrence of limited aggression, it must, of course, be clear that the time available for decision-making cannot be used to decide against retaliation after the enemy has, in fact, committed the act the system is supposed to deter. This makes difficult the development of a massive retaliatory system that is both a credible deterrent to limited aggression and, at the same time, unlikely to be launched accidentally. However, when the question is one of direct attack against the United States, this may not be a problem. In such a case it is doubtful that the Soviets would ever mount the attack in the expectation that the response time available to us, however long, would be used to decide against retaliation. It is true that, once we are attacked, retaliation might avail us little, if anything; perhaps it would only cause us more misery, particularly if the enemy retained unexpended nuclear capabilities. However, regardless of our retaliatory posture, human nature being what it is, it would probably be extremely unwise for the Soviets to assume that we would not retaliate to whatever degree we could under such circumstances. The remainder of this chapter is based on the premise that the Russians would assume retaliation.

The size of the force required for pure retaliation will depend on the estimate of the number of casualties that the Soviets may deem unacceptable and on the fraction of the force that might be expected to survive an enemy's first strike and then penetrate enemy defenses.

---

[16] The contrary argument—that retaliation must be rapid—is often offered by military spokesmen, and Henry A. Kissinger so argues in an excellent article, "Missiles and the Western Alliance" (Foreign Affairs, xxxvi, No. 3, April 1958), in which he says: "The retaliatory force for all-out war must be able to inflict the greatest amount of devastation in a minimum of time" (p. 392). He also states, contrary to the view expressed here, that there is a need for great accuracy in a deterrent force (p. 393).

It will also depend on the accuracy of our delivery system; but in no event will there be much of a premium on extreme accuracy. If there is a high probability of landing a weapon anywhere within Moscow, force requirements would not be greatly higher than if accuracy were such that weapons could be dropped very close to specified points. Even if accuracy were so poor that one had to rely on fallout alone as the casualty-producing agent, about fifty weapons of the size exploded in the United States test of March 1, 1954, might be expected to kill about 20 per cent of the Soviet population.[17] Many more, of course, might be required in the event that the enemy had a civil defense program; on the other hand, the number might be somewhat less, and the required yields for many weapons might be smaller, if delivery accuracy were such that cities could be attacked without possibility of failure. In any case, a substantial number of additional deaths might result from indirect causes—disruption of food distribution, and so on.

For the counterforce role, requirements are qualitatively and quantitatively different. First, there is need for a Western intelligence effort sufficient to locate Soviet bases and missile sites, and to keep any mobile systems under surveillance. Speed of reaction and shortness of flight time must have high priority, and accuracy requirements may be much more severe. If the enemy's attack force consisted of bombers exposed on conventional bases or surface-based missiles, delivery within about four miles of the target would be required for weapons in the megaton range.[18] If it were desired to destroy runways, underground hangars, or underground missile sites, it might be necessary to locate the weapon so precisely that the lip of the crater created by the explosion would overlap the target; thus for a one-megaton warhead, delivery within about one-quarter of a mile of a point target might be required.[19] If delivery accuracies were poorer than this, several weapons would be required for each target in order to have a reasonable assurance of its destruction. A counterforce strategy would also entail the prospect of an

[17] Estimation of force requirements for a fallout campaign cannot be very precise because of uncertainties in natural shielding, behavior of inhabitants after the attack, and particularly uncertainties about winds that prevail at the time of attack. The above estimate is a crude one based on the assumption of random delivery within the Ukraine. It is further assumed that each weapon would have an effective lethal area of 3,500 square miles. This is just half the figure mentioned in *The Effects of Nuclear Weapons*, ed. by Samuel Glasstone, Washington, D.C., 1957, p. 423. This reduction is, of course, very arbitrary, but probably not unreasonable considering uncertainties resulting from shielding, overkilling in some areas, etc.

[18] This is based on an assumed required overpressure of 4 psi and a weapon yield of one megaton. These figures were arrived at from a consideration of those in *ibid.*, pp. 111, 175, 237.

[19] Based on information in *ibid.*, pp. 210, 213.

unlimited arms race. In the event that the production and support capabilities of the two sides were about the same, a counterforce strategy could indeed be ruinous economically, if accuracy were so poor that several missiles were required to destroy each missile that the adversary might add to his inventory.

III. Delivery System Capabilities

Much has been said and written recently—particularly by critics of the Republican Administration—about the missile gap, that is, the alleged Soviet lead in missile technology, and about its strategic implications. Albert Wohlstetter[20] and General Thomas R. Phillips[21] have argued that we may have difficulty in maintaining a retaliatory capability sufficient to prevent a Soviet first strike. To determine whether the Soviet lead is as great as some critics contend obviously requires access to classified intelligence. However, it seems clear that, at least in some degree, the United States will be dependent on manned aircraft as the bulwark of its strategic delivery capability for a longer period than the Soviet Union. Before examining the implications of a possible asymmetry in capabilities, it may be well to consider the advantages and disadvantages of the various delivery systems now available and in prospect.

The manned bomber has two important advantages over other systems—great accuracy of delivery and the ability to carry weapons of large yield. With these capabilities, the bomber has a reasonable probability of being able to include any enemy point target which it attacks within the crater or crater lip of the weapon it delivers. Thus, if the threat to a missile site were only from manned bombers, putting it underground would be expected to have a small payoff (except insofar as it might make determination of the missiles' location more difficult). Of course, the bomber is very vulnerable to attack itself, on the ground and in the air. Vulnerability on the ground can be reduced by dispersal over large numbers of bases, putting the bombers in underground hangars, and keeping some airborne at all times. These are all expensive measures, and bombers are very expensive anyway. Chances of their surviving long enough to fly several missions in all-out war may be small. Only the first mission (if that) can be expected to have much payoff in the counterforce role[22]—the role which capital-

---

[20] "The Delicate Balance of Terror," *Foreign Affairs*, xxxvii, No. 2 (January 1959), p. 211.

[21] "The Growing Missile Gap," *The Reporter*, xx, No. 1 (January 8, 1959), p. 10.

[22] It is interesting, however, to note an Air Force argument in support of manned aircraft as contrasted with missiles: "We would get quite a few missions out of each

izes on the bomber's great accuracy of delivery. The longer-range aircraft are, of course, particularly costly; and they can also be expected to be less effective in a counterforce strike than those which are based so that the flight time to target is minimized. But in buying long-range aircraft, such as the B-52's, we have accepted this disadvantage in order to have at least part of our force less vulnerable to surprise attack.

Aerodynamic, as distinct from ballistic, missiles are like bombers in that they are slow; and they are also relatively inaccurate. Thus, they are particularly poorly suited to the counterforce role. However, they may be very useful as a complement to bombers because they are relatively cheap. Large numbers can be used with bombers as decoys to confuse enemy defenses. They can also be very useful in a purely retaliatory role. Cheapness may to a large extent make up for their high vulnerability to enemy active defenses. Mobility and wide dispersal, together with cheapness and consequently the possibility of having large numbers of them, may make such missiles a difficult counterforce target for the enemy.

Difficulty of interception is the one great advantage that ballistic missiles will have over other delivery systems. Even when some intercept capability is available, the problem will be formidable because of the possibility of sending along with the warhead, at little extra cost, large numbers of decoys which may look the same to a radar. This possibility will probably preclude interception except in the very last part of the trajectory—that is, after the warhead has returned to the atmosphere, where discrimination between loaded missiles and lightweight decoys will be possible. It may also be possible, in the future, to increase terminal velocities and produce not-quite-ballistic trajectories. This would further compound the interception problem. But their low vulnerability to interception may be about the only advantage, other than psychological, which the first generation of ballistic missiles will have. It may be that their accuracy, at first, will be so poor that they will have little value in a counterforce role;[23] thus, their short time of flight will have no payoff (except for defying interception). And the first United States missiles of any range—Jupiter, Thor, and

aircraft, which is unlike a missile" (General Coupland, *Defense Appropriations for 1959, Department of the Air Force*, p. 352).

[23] It is interesting in this connection to consider the very great emphasis that the Russians place on missiles. Are we to infer from this that their strategy is primarily a retaliatory rather than a counterforce one? Apparently not, according to Garthoff, *op.cit.* Yet he makes the point (p. 222) that missiles may play a special role in Soviet strategy as a purely deterrent weapon-system and as a blackmail threat rather than as counterforce weapons.

Atlas—will be based aboveground so that they will be very vulnerable to blast from enemy weapons. They, and Titan, will all require liquid oxygen, which is likely to make reaction relatively slow (compared with bombers or later-generation, solid-fueled missiles); and mobility will be impossible for them, or very difficult. (Indeed, no attempt is being made to give mobility to any ICBM;[24] and the most that is claimed for the first-generation IRBM's is "movability."[25]) Finally, with respect to the European-based IRBM's, agreements with host nations regarding conditions of use may further lengthen response times.

However, there is room for great improvement. A later ICBM, the Minuteman, will be based underground and hence be much less vulnerable to attack; and it will be solid-fueled, permitting quicker reaction. The Polaris submarine-ballistic missile system will be completely mobile and certainly very difficult for the enemy to attack successfully, and its use will require no consultation with allies. Accuracies will improve, though how much so would probably be difficult to estimate even with access to classified information. But it would seem to be a fair guess that in the not too distant future the IRBM's (and later the ICBM's) will be a dangerous counterforce threat to exposed targets of known location—conventional air bases and surface-based missiles. The time may come when the combination of yield and accuracy will make even relatively hard-point installations attractive targets.[26] Capabilities of ballistic missiles will vary considerably, and it is particularly relevant here to compare the effectiveness of IRBM's and ICBM's in the counterforce role. Because of their shorter range, the 1,500-mile missiles should have only about one-fourth the delivery error of a 5,500-mile missile, owing to the fact that, at least for early ballistic missiles, all guidance will presumably be during the powered portion of the flight, and thereafter errors will increase linearly with distance. Suppose that the accuracy of the shorter-range missile is such that there is a 90 per cent probability of destroying the target with a single missile. It can be shown that the probability of destruction with a single longer-range missile, with four times the delivery error, will be about 13 per cent,

[24] General Irvine, *Defense Appropriations for 1959, Department of the Air Force,* p. 331.

[25] Colonel Page, *ibid.,* p. 332.

[26] In 1958 Secretary of the Army Brucker said: "When the power of atomics and accuracy of missiles capable of delivering them are considered, it must be assumed that any fixed target can be destroyed if its location is known to the enemy" (*ibid., Overall Policy Statements,* p. 240). His statement is, of course, literally quite true. But, at least for the first-generation missiles, the numbers required for some types of targets may be prohibitively large. If they are not, we may be wasting money putting Minuteman underground.

assuming the same firing reliability, and about 16 weapons per target will be required to give a 90 per cent probability of destruction. Moreover, it is estimated that the cost of IRBM's will be only about $735,000 per missile,[27] compared with $1,600,999 per ICBM.[28] Thus, on a cost basis, a 1,500-mile missile may well be on the order of 35 times as effective as an ICBM against hard-point targets. So long, then, as United States military planning includes destruction of point targets within the USSR as an objective, IRBM's based around the periphery may be much preferred to ICBM's based in the United States. They will also have advantages over sea-based missiles because of lesser cost and the fact that their accuracy will not be degraded because of navigation errors. And they will, of course, be much superior to manned aircraft or aerodynamic missiles because their flight time will be so much less, because they will be less vulnerable to interception, and because they will be cheaper than most manned aircraft.

Thus, really accurate IRBM's would seem to be the almost ideal counterforce weapon. However, it cannot be emphasized too strongly that the closeness of their bases to the Iron Curtain would make them appallingly vulnerable unless they were extremely mobile.[29] An accurate, fixed-base IRBM system would be highly provocative, since its effectiveness would be critically dependent on who fired first. However, it does not necessarily follow from this that they are undesirable. Whether or not we have an IRBM counterforce capability, we must assume that the enemy will find it necessary and possible to maintain what he regards as a sufficient deterrent capability. But our possession of IRBM's (or, for that matter, of European-based manned bombers) makes the maintenance of a sufficient deterrent by him more difficult and costly; and in the event that *we* should strike first, damage to us might be less than if we did not have such capabilities. While we may not be able to rely on such vulnerable European-based systems for retaliation, there might then be an advantage in having such a counterforce capability. However, even if such an advantage could be demonstrated, it would still have to be weighed against the cost of the in-

[27] *Ibid., Department of the Air Force*, p. 315.
[28] *Ibid.*, p. 311.
[29] A comparison of the vulnerability of IRBM and ICBM bases may be illuminating. If Soviet missiles had an accuracy such that the probability of destroying an IRBM base with a single missile was 90 per cent, the probability of destroying an ICBM base would be from 2 to 5 per cent (assuming comparable vulnerability to blast damage; and warheads of equal size and error proportional to range for Soviet missiles). From 50 to 100 larger, more expensive Soviet missiles would be required per ICBM base to get the same 90 per cent expectation of destruction. The threat from aircraft is, of course, also much greater for IRBM bases.

creased probability of accidental war, and against the possibility that we might force the adversary to develop a posture such that if he struck first, damage to Europe might be greater than if we had not had this capability, and this without necessarily reducing damage to the United States.

To return to the implications of a possible missile gap, it would seem clear that, if the Soviets develop a substantial ICBM capability before the United States, this would pose a new hazard for SAC—provided, but only provided, a fairly large number of these missiles can be launched in a very short period of time, and provided they have good accuracy, so that only a reasonable number will be required for a high expectation of crippling the aircraft on SAC bases. From the foregoing discussion, it would seem that a delivery accuracy of several miles would probably suffice. If these conditions can be met, then there may be much less—for a time perhaps, none—of the advanced warning which SAC has heretofore been able to expect; for some time hence, there would be none of the degradation of the enemy attack by our active defenses. Supplementing the SAC capability with surface-based ICBM's and IRBM's would scarcely help much, for they will presumably be as vulnerable as manned aircraft based in the United States and Europe. But even if these accuracy conditions are not met by Soviet missiles, a Soviet lead may put the United States at a considerable disadvantage relative to the past few years because of the increasing effectiveness of Soviet active defenses against manned aircraft. Thus, if the critics of the Administration are right in their dire prognostications about Soviet missile superiority, we may indeed face a period when our ability to retaliate effectively can be questioned. And even if we can be assured of a sufficient retaliatory capability, the period will be one during which the advantage to the side delivering the first strike will be as great or greater than has recently been the case. Thus there will be, as there has been in the recent past, a mutually reinforcing incentive to beat the adversary to the punch, or at least to get in one's licks before all his are delivered.

However, if we can look beyond the period when we are forced to rely on such vulnerable delivery systems as manned bombers and surface-based ballistic missiles, the vulnerability of each side's forces to attack by the adversary may become so slight that the outcome of conflict will be much less dependent on who fires first. Surely, this would be a more stable situation, and one toward which we should strive with great vigor—in my view, even at the expense of renouncing a counterforce strategy as an objective. Thus, the Minuteman and Polaris programs, and any other mobile systems, would seem preferable to continued reliance on manned aircraft, surface-based ICBM's, or any fixed-base IRBM's.

IV. How War Might Start

Before further discussion of possible strategic postures and their implications, it seems appropriate to summarize the possible contingencies with which the West must deal. This will be done here largely in the framework of present capabilities and with special reference to NATO.

The possibility which has had the most profound effect on United States strategy during the last few years is that of a sudden massive nuclear attack against the United States and its allies by the Soviet Union.[30] It is not often argued that this is the most likely way for a war with Russia to begin, but it has been generally acknowledged that it would be the most catastrophic for us. That it has not seemed very likely to happen may in large measure be a consequence of the enormous efforts made to ensure that there would be no reasonable prospect of the Soviets delivering such a blow without suffering damage incommensurate with any possible gain they might achieve. Great efforts have been made to disperse SAC, to defend its bases, to keep substantial portions airborne and ready for very rapid response, and to provide as much warning as possible of Soviet attack. But these efforts do not necessarily ensure that there will be no sudden Soviet attack, for there is always the possibility of error—the chance that in a period of great tension, the Soviets may, on the basis of intelligence errors, decide that they are about to be attacked and had better strike first. By so doing they might, of course, substantially reduce damage to themselves, for it is clear that, for a few years at least, American offensive capability will be much greater prior to an attack than subsequent to one. Faced with such a prospect, the Soviets would have to make the awful choice between certain catastrophic damage if they attacked, and even more damage if they did not and their intelligence assessment turned out to be correct. In a completely rational world they would probably not attack, for they would be forced to draw the conclusion that their intelligence was in error because there was no

[30] It does not follow that the approach of nuclear parity has increased the possibility of an accidental triggering of all-out war above what prevailed a few years ago. On the contrary, the existence of Soviet capability for very substantially damaging the United States must make us less apt to initiate a thermonuclear exchange as a response to lesser aggression than heretofore, and the Soviets, knowing this, have less incentive to attempt a pre-emptive strike, even though they might now assess their chances of success as improved.

rational basis for a United States massive attack—this, even if their radars indicated very large numbers of unknown aircraft over the Soviet Union, or even if there were some nuclear explosions. In the reverse situation, the United States would be forced to the same conclusion. However, it seems doubtful that either side would trust the rationality of its adversary to that degree. Even in a rational world, technological breakthrough, such as the opening of a truly dangerous missile gap, might make a massive surprise attack attractive to one side; or the other might infer this possibility. But it is to be hoped that, in the future, the strategic delivery forces of the two sides may be made much less vulnerable to attack. If, in the example cited above, there were no possibility of the Soviets materially reducing American retaliatory capability by a prompt strike, there would be every incentive for them to discount the intelligence indicators and withhold attack until there was no doubt of United States intentions.

Another possibility—frequently discounted with a remark to the effect that the best we can hope to do is to cope with rational behavior—is that the man or men in control in the Kremlin may order the attack, in desperation, perhaps more out of a conviction of impending personal doom, resulting from internal stresses within the regime, than from any belief in the hopelessness of the struggle against capitalism. And then there is always the specter of the mad man, in control of a single aircraft or missile, who might trigger the catastrophe.

Next to Soviet surprise attack, the contingency that has done most to shape American, and particularly NATO, defense policy has been that of a major Soviet advance in Europe. We are probably still in a period when a massive United States response would follow such an attack, unless possibly the Soviets were able to achieve the conquest almost overnight—so quickly that we would be confronted with a *fait accompli*; the prevention of this, of course, is one of the roles in which NATO forces in Europe can have a part. In an effort to bolster NATO, and to prolong the effectiveness of the massive deterrent, we are repeatedly warned that the Soviets must not be allowed to doubt the certainty of our response.[31] But it must be seriously doubted that repeated reassurances can increase the credibility that we will use the deterrent force in the event of attack. The very fact that it is so frequently necessary to make such a statement causes it to be suspect. If there were no reason for doubt, there would be no need for reassurance.

What is needed is more tangible evidence of our determination, for

[31] See, for example, the British White Paper of 1958, *op.cit.*, p. 2.

what evidence there is, is equivocal. On the one hand, Britain is providing herself with a strategic nuclear capability with our help. Would there be any need for this if there were not doubts about the effectiveness of our SAC as a deterrent? Some have argued that Britain must have her own thermonuclear capability to maintain an adequate voice in world affairs, but what kind of a voice can this give her? Such a force can hardly be helpful in preventing total war, though it might be useful in starting one under conditions when the United States would not otherwise see fit to employ its strategic capabilities. But it might be a reasonable inference that the British (and presumably others) wish thermonuclear capabilities of their own because they are beginning to feel that they cannot rely on the United States. On the other hand, the very lack of evidence of capability or preparation for any *other* response to major aggression in Europe does lend credibility to the threat of thermonuclear reprisal. Reinforcement of the capability for a lesser scale of conflict would clearly detract from the credibility of the big deterrent. However, in spite of the inadequate conventional capability of the West, doubts continue to be raised about our willingness to unleash the thermonuclear holocaust. For example, in a particularly biting criticism of the British White Paper of 1958, the *New Statesman* said: "And once this monumental bluff of the Great Deterrent were called [by the Russians' employment of their massive conventional capability], the West would have no alternatives but to accept a last-minute Munich settlement, giving the Russians all they asked for, or to transport to the imperilled area a conventional army of sufficient strength to hold the Soviet attack. But it is perfectly clear from the White Paper that we do not possess the means to do this, and that we are making no effort to acquire them. Hence the political consequence of Mr. Sandys's defence policy is a foreign policy based on appeasement."[32]

Of course, there are other ways in which the Soviets can threaten Europe—subversion and blackmail. But it is unlikely that all-out war would be contemplated as a response to Soviet successes by subversion. The subversion threat is primarily a problem of internal security or, at most, of very limited war (though, as will be apparent subsequently, there seems to be a possible mechanism for invoking the threat of all-out war in order to deter subversion).

The blackmail threat raises different problems. What would be the responses of the several powers concerned if the Soviets threatened

[32] "The Logic of Annihilation," *New Statesman*, LV, No. 1406 (February 22, 1958), p. 1.

nuclear attack against one of the NATO countries in an effort to influence events outside of Europe or perhaps in the NATO country
itself? We have already seen such an attempt on the occasion of the
British-French intervention in Egypt in 1956. In this instance, the
threats were probably recognized as a bluff, and the decision to withdraw made on other grounds. However, this is not the only instance
of blackmail within Europe's memory. Hitler's efforts to capture Austria and Czechoslovakia stand out as all too successful. Is it not conceivable that, faced with a threat of Soviet nuclear attack, some European governments might collapse like those of Beneš and Schuschnigg;
or might they not withdraw from a commitment in a region such as
Asia, even though supported by the United States? Would the United
States launch SAC when the threat was made, or after it had succeeded,
or not at all? Particularly, would we initiate a global war if the small
state in question made it plain that it preferred to yield to Soviet pressure rather than see the world embroiled in such conflict? Five years
ago, or even two years ago, such Soviet threats might have been recognized as bluff, but will they be so regarded tomorrow—by the United
States and by the small states? Clearly, such Soviet moves might be
"brinkmanship" at its most dangerous; but over the last few years it
has become far less dangerous, from the Soviet point of view, as has
an overt attack against Europe.

It is usually assumed that the Russians' conviction about the eventual
triumph of communism would make nuclear brinkmanship relatively
unattractive to them and any *Götterdämmerung* finish something they
would very much prefer to avoid. Soviet strategic thinking appears to
be replete with warnings against, and criticism of, "adventurism"—
measures involving undue risk of major war.[33] Recently, however, there
has been a suggestion of a somewhat less cautious attitude on the part
of Russia's Chinese friends. If this persists as the relative importance
and strength of Peking increase in relation to Moscow, it is conceivable
that bloc policy—especially in East Asia—will become increasingly
reckless. The specter of a reversal in Soviet strategy is thus raised. Heretofore, because the Soviets lacked a potent retaliatory capability to
match ours, we have been able to rely on our counterthreat to deter
aggression, at least presumably in Europe. However, increasing Soviet
bloc recklessness, coupled with increasing caution on the part of the
West, might not only negate the usefulness of our retaliatory capability
as a deterrent to lesser aggression, but might permit the bloc to use

---

[33] See Garthoff, *op.cit., passim.*

the threat of general war to achieve lesser objectives without actual conflict.

Finally, there is the question of the satellites. Formerly, we worried about attacks by them against NATO countries or neutrals, and it has been argued that NATO forces are important to deter such attacks or, if necessary, to defeat them without resort to all-out war. After the East German riots of 1953, the Hungarian revolt of 1956, and the measure of independence achieved by Poland in the last few years, this threat is largely discounted, only to be replaced by the fear that all-out war may be triggered by satellite revolt. It would surely be most difficult for us and particularly for the West Germans to remain aloof, as in the case of Hungary, if the Soviets found it necessary to crush rebellion in either East Germany or Poland. Yet, what could we do?[34] Our actual response to the Hungarian revolt proved the bankruptcy of United States policy with respect to much of what might happen in Europe. It demonstrated not only that United States and NATO policy was impotent, but that our fear of expanded conflict forced us more or less to accept Communist hegemony over Eastern Europe by stating that we would do nothing in the way of intervention. Can a policy based on massive retaliation be effective at all in furthering our interests in Eastern Europe, the one area in the world where there would seem to be the most hope—based on local popular sentiment—of making inroads against communism, and where the charge of imperialism can have no validity with respect to us, but only with respect to the Russians? With the force postures of the two sides as they are today, it would seem that we must look elsewhere for means of promoting our interest in this part of Europe—perhaps by dealing with the problem in the context of limited war or graduated deterrence, or by some sort of disengagement. I see no means of modifying our posture for all-out war in such a way as to restore to it effectiveness in deterring the Soviets from intervention in satellite or nearby neutral states.

V. Force Requirements and Postures for Alternative Objectives

It will be apparent from the discussion of delivery-system characteristics that our weapons requirements will be very sensitive to the degree

[34] In a very interesting press conference on September 30, 1958 (*New York Times,* October 1, 1958), Secretary Dulles made the point that, had we had a Western-oriented Hungarian free state adjacent to Hungary, as Taiwan is to China, the Hungarian situation might have developed differently.

of importance attached to the counterforce mission. And varying force postures may be preferred, depending on the aggressions to which the threat of all-out war may be expected to serve as a deterrent. At the one extreme, we might seek to make the threat of all-out war a credible deterrent against as broad a spectrum of aggression as possible; this is especially attractive in that it offers the prospect of a defense policy "on the cheap," minimizing the size of conventional forces and the frequency of their commitment in unpopular limited conflict. At the other extreme, we might place reliance on the threat of massive retaliation as a deterrent only to a massive attack against us.

In the following discussion, it is first assumed that *all* the Western powers adopt a purely retaliatory strategy; then, that the United States alone attempts to maintain a counterforce posture; and, finally, that in addition to the United States, other NATO powers also attempt a counterforce strategy.

Assuming that we will give no weight to the counterforce role, and that the only objective is deterrence of all-out attack against the United States, a retaliatory force based on a concept such as the submarine-ballistic missile system would seem ideal. Mobile missiles, either aerodynamic or ballistic, and land-based in North America, would also meet the need since a relatively modest air defense capability could serve to make enemy reconnaissance almost impossible (except perhaps with earth satellites), and without such reconnaissance there would, of course, be little chance of a successful counterforce blow. With either system there would be a lessened chance of accidental war because (1) there would be no incentive for the Soviets to attempt a surprise attack, and (2) there would be no advantage for us in quick retaliation because low accuracy would preclude our destroying many of their weapons not already launched.

Suppose our purely retaliatory system were based on one, or a combination of, the weapon types specified above. It would surely be adequate as a deterrent to direct attack against the United States. But would it be adequate with respect to lesser threats to NATO, such as limited war or blackmail? Clearly not, if the implication were use of the entire system in an all-out war. As has been pointed out above, such a threat would simply not be a credible deterrent to lesser aggression. The alternative for dealing with these threats would be to do so in the context of limited war or graduated deterrence. Let me pass over these possibilities, only pointing out that the weapon systems under discussion would be especially suitable for the graduated deterrent role since their relatively low accuracy would constitute no

threat to the Soviet retaliatory capability, and thus would make it unnecessary for the enemy to launch an all-out attack if one or two missiles were fired at him as a limited response.[35] Since his delivery force
would not be imperiled—and this would be especially true if his force
were also a mobile one—he could afford to wait and see if the intent
was to fire only a few missiles, or if the missiles were the precursors of
an all-out attack. The ballistic missile will be especially desirable for
the graduated deterrent role, at least for some time, because there will
probably be no need for saturation of enemy defenses, as there is with
aerodynamic delivery vehicles. Thus, only a few such missiles would
be required, whereas, if reliance were put on bombers, the requirement
would be for a capability of paying the same "price of admission"—
that is, being able to saturate enemy defenses in order to get a few
bombers through—that would have to be paid if an all-out attack
were being delivered. This would be especially important if the strategy
were one of entrusting to each small state its own graduated deterrent
capability.

Turning to means of invoking the threat of all-out war as an effective deterrent to lesser threats, again assuming a United States posture
that discounts a counterforce role, there seem to be three possibilities
that require discussion. First, there is the development of a more
cohesive union of NATO. For example, if responsibility for deciding
on the issue of war could be vested in a strong, centralized NATO
executive authority, one might hope that the Soviets would regard
nuclear capabilities under the control of that executive as a credible
deterrent to blackmail or other aggression against any part of NATO.
But, at best, the great deterrent would be effective only against a major
attack on the union itself. It could hardly be effective against lesser
threats elsewhere—say, Soviet intervention in satellite revolts or in the
Middle East. Moreover, it would be hard to believe that the strong
executive would unleash the retaliatory capability in response to what
might be considered limited aggression against the union itself; for
example, in response to a seizure of West Berlin, or Finmark in Norway. The need for a graduated deterrent or for "shield" forces to cope
with all lesser aggression is thus apparent. But if reliance were to be
placed on the latter, how large would such shield forces have to be?
They would certainly have to be able to cope with either a land invasion or a sea blockade that threatened any of the European members

[35] Kissinger ("Missiles and the Western Alliance," *loc.cit.*, p. 393) has also argued
that the fact that missiles controlled by the West could not destroy Soviet retaliatory
capabilities guarantees their defensive intent. But it is hard to square this with his
arguments for the need for accuracy in missiles.

of NATO. Thus, the shield forces would clearly have to be able to match any tactical capabilities of the bloc. But even the combination of such forces and the great deterrent might not be able to cope with all threats. Even with a strong federation, it might be doubted that the threat of all-out war could be an effective deterrent of nuclear blackmail threats against a part of the union. The threat of limited or graduated retaliation would again seem a more credible deterrent in the years ahead. Apart from the political difficulties—and it is hard to imagine such surrender of sovereignty—a NATO with a strong central executive would seem to offer little promise of extending the utility of the great deterrent.

An alternative solution involves widespread dissemination of nuclear capabilities. An example is the development by the United Kingdom of a strategic capability. This could, of course, provide a credible means of defending that country against direct attack by the USSR. One argument is that possession of thermonuclear weapons might make it possible for a possessor nation to trigger an all-out nuclear exchange which would eventually involve the United States and the USSR, and presumably their allies. Thus, the necessary mechanism for assuring all-out war would be provided and such possession would then be a credible deterrent.[36] However, there is the alternative possibility that independent nuclear capabilities in the hands of the small powers would provide an effective limited-war or graduated-deterrent capability. Such a capability, therefore, might not necessarily imply all-out war between East and West as a response to, say, Soviet nuclear attack against the possessor nation. Instead, it might represent a response by the small state alone in a war which it regarded as total, but which the Soviets could regard as limited, and in which the United States and other nations possessing nuclear weapons would not be directly involved. Whether the use of nuclear capabilities by the small states in response to aggression would imply limited or all-out conflict would be highly dependent on the nature of their capabilities. If they were of a purely retaliatory type, and hence could not reduce Soviet nuclear capabilities, there would be every reason for the Soviets to treat their use as a limited threat. If it were certain, or even probable, that the small state retained unexpended nuclear strength after a reprisal action, the Soviets would have a strong incentive to seek some reasonable settlement of differences rather than to risk further damage from a demonstrably determined adversary. Of course, if all, or nearly all, of

[36] This argument is developed by J. A. Rafferty in an as yet unpublished paper which I have been privileged to read.

the small state's nuclear capabilities had clearly been expended or destroyed, the Soviets would presumably be motivated to crush it ruthlessly in the hope that other victims would yield more graciously to future pressure. But, regardless of whether the small state retained nuclear capabilities, the Soviets would have every reason to avoid expanding the conflict to include the United States and other nuclear powers—a course which would inevitably bring catastrophic damage to Russia. She would have nothing to gain thereby, and everything to lose—particularly if the damage inflicted by the small state had been moderate. Thus, possession of limited retaliatory capabilities by small states might deter Soviet aggression by posing the threat of conflict which would be limited, from the Soviet point of view at least, and certainly from that of non-participating states. Such a solution to the problem of European defense I have discussed in some detail elsewhere.[37] (There is the additional possibility of the small states having counterforce capabilities, but as indicated earlier, this possibility will be treated only in the context of the United States also having such capability.)

We now come to the third alternative. Suppose, for the sake of the argument, that all of the United States'—indeed, all of the West's—purely retaliatory capability were located in Europe. This might ensure Europe against any blackmail or attack—nuclear or conventional—or even against a coup which might result in the loss of our retaliatory capability, for once it was lost we would be forced to accede to *any and all* Soviet demands—the alternative being Soviet nuclear attack, to which, of course, there would be no deterrent. The consequence of the loss of our retaliatory capability would therefore be either nuclear destruction of the United States or its complete subjugation to Soviet will. For this reason, a threat to our retaliatory capability in Europe would then hardly be less grave than a threat of direct nuclear attack against the United States proper; as a result, we might be expected to respond accordingly if it were about to be lost. Under this assumption there would, of course, be no deterrent to attacks on states outside Europe.

Such a strategy would require a sharp reversal in American policy, since for the strategy to be effective, any capability based in the United States would have to be very small. This, of course, is quite the antithesis of the trend in our strategy to get away from overseas basing.[38]

---

[37] "Notes on the Military Problems of Europe," *loc.cit.*

[38] In this trend away from overseas basing, there are the seeds of a "Fortress America" philosophy; as ICBM's and the Polaris-missile system develop we must expect to see pressures exerted to return to such a policy. It must be obvious, though perhaps not

It is hard to imagine public acceptance of a strategy whose stated objective would be to keep United States-based offensive capabilities so weak that, if we lost our overseas bases, we would be helpless. But it is hardly less believable than the other strategy discussed above— that based on the strong central executive—or a strategy based on a counterforce capability for each small state, discussed below. I am forced to conclude that if American strategic policy were primarily a retaliatory one, there would be almost no hope of deterring limited aggression by the threat of all-out war. The threat cannot be made credible.

Can one draw a different conclusion if one makes the second assumption: that the American strategy is to maintain a counterforce capability, but that the smaller nations will not do so? A different conclusion emerges only if our strategic posture is such that some of the counterforce capability would be lost as a result of limited aggression by the Soviet bloc. And for the deterrent to be credible, the reduction in capability would probably have to be substantial. Thus, as in the case of a retaliatory posture, we might deter limited aggression in Europe by locating our nuclear delivery capabilities there. What fraction of our total force would have to be risked in this way would depend on Soviet estimates of our belief in the counterforce strategy as against one of pure retaliation. Only if the Soviets thought it reasonably probable that we would prefer the holocaust of all-out war to a reduction in our capabilities to the point where they became essentially retaliatory could the counterforce posture avail us anything in deterring limited aggression. I doubt that a few years hence the Soviets will find this very credible.

Finally, we must consider the possibility that not only the United States, but also the European NATO members, collectively or individually, will attempt to maintain a counterforce posture. The question is then raised as to whether this could be effective as a means of invoking the threat of all-out war as a deterrent to lesser aggression. Suppose the aggression occurred, and the small state or states in question launched their strategic capabilities. It can hardly be doubted that this would trigger all-out war, *provided* the counterforce capabilities of the small states were sufficiently great. But it would seem that they would have to be very great, indeed—great enough so that the Soviets would face the prospect of being rendered impotent by their use. Under such

---

explicitly recognized, that this trend also amounts to a shift in emphasis from a counterforce to a retaliation strategy in view of the lesser effectiveness of United States-based and sea-based systems in the counterforce role.

circumstances it would seem reasonable that the Soviets would not wait to have this happen to them, but rather would deliver as many weapons as they could, as quickly as possible, distributed among all their adversaries. Thus, the widespread dissemination of nuclear capabilities as a mechanism for ensuring that all-out war will follow limited aggression implies the procurement by the small states of highly accurate, quick-responding, nuclear delivery vehicles in very large numbers. IRBM's located in Europe under European control would seem to meet the need very well in this respect, *if* there were sufficient numbers of them, *if* they were accurate enough, and *if* they were not so vulnerable that the Soviets could destroy all of a nation's retaliatory capability in a single blow. This is obviously a very hazardous solution to the problem of limited threats; it puts in the hands of many the possibility of triggering a general thermonuclear exchange. It would also be very expensive, almost certainly prohibitively so, since each small state would have to have a capability of seriously reducing Soviet offensive capabilities. This possibility could be made very difficult of attainment, if not impossible, if the Soviets were to rely primarily on relatively invulnerable, mobile delivery systems, or if they were able to maintain a number of fixed sites whose locations were unknown to the West.

Thus, it seems that there is very little real prospect of preventing a further diminution in the effectiveness of the threat of all-out war as a deterrent to lesser aggression. In particular, it would appear that we must face the fact that the problems of European security cannot be solved by posing this threat. Does this sound the death knell for NATO as a military alliance? By no means; but it does mean that, from the military point of view, the alliance can be of value to the European members only insofar as it can be a mechanism for developing limited-war and graduated-deterrence capabilities. It must be recognized that the tactical "shield" forces cannot merely *complement* the massive deterrent capability, but rather *must*, along with graduated-deterrent capabilities, *supplant* the all-out war strategy as the means for European defense. European-based nuclear delivery systems, whether controlled by the United States, Europeans, or NATO as a whole, which could neither deter limited aggression nor be of use in fighting limited war, would be a liability to Europe, because their presence in Europe would serve only to increase the damage that the Continent would sustain in event of war, without reducing the probability that war would occur.

But NATO may still have a role in the all-out war problem. Through it, the members which have an all-out war capability—so far, only the

United States—might obtain facilities useful in the event of such war, like radar sites and, particularly, missile and air bases. This will be especially important if we continue to accord high priority to the counterforce objective. However, if we emphasize the importance of American-controlled nuclear capabilities based in Europe for fighting all-out war, then we must expect Europeans to be reluctant to have them there. Either we must convince them that our weapons based in Europe can also be important as a graduated-deterrent capability or in fighting limited wars, or else we must expect to make compensating concessions to Europeans for the risks they incur in having these facilities on their soil. Thus, through NATO or otherwise, we might expect to be asked for help in building shelters, for continued commitment of United States forces in support of a limited-war capability, for strategic nuclear weapons to cope with threats which we may regard as limited but which will be total from the Europeans' point of view, and, finally, for plain economic assistance.

VI. Major War Without Strategic Bombing

While this chapter is primarily concerned with the problems of NATO and all-out war, perhaps it is not going too far afield to consider briefly the possibility of a war between NATO and the Soviet bloc in which the only limitation would be with respect to employment of nuclear weapons. One might assume that they would not be used at all, or that the only constraint might be that they would not be used against the homelands of the great nuclear powers.

In this connection, it must be pointed out that when the smaller nations control strategic nuclear capabilities, then—insofar as we are concerned with this constraint on their use—these nations must be treated as great powers. For example, with the United Kingdom having such capabilities, the use by the Soviets of nuclear weapons against bases, ports, and so forth in England would presumably be deterred, since it must be assumed that once such weapons were delivered, the war would appear to be very much all-out from the English point of view. And it would have to be inferred that, under such circumstances, there would be a high probability of British retaliation against Moscow to whatever degree was possible.

Let us assume, therefore, that a major war occurs in which strategic nuclear weapons are not used against the homelands of the United States, the Soviet Union, or the United Kingdom. Even though the Soviets might not be able to count on their satellite divisions and, indeed, might be forced to maintain considerable forces in the satellite countries, they would still have a great military superiority in the European theater, except possibly in nuclear weapons available for tactical use.

Now, it is often argued that, under such circumstances, NATO's defense would have to be based on lavish use of tactical nuclear weapons (assuming, as we have, that strategic nuclear weapons are not used). The bases for such arguments are usually that nuclear firepower can make up for deficiency in manpower, and that, in tactical operations, use of nuclear weapons may be relatively advantageous to the defense. Often it is simply stated that we could not win without use of tactical nuclear weapons and that our defense must therefore be based on them. (Too often arguments showing that we could win with them are weak, or are not presented at all.) However, there are persuasive arguments to the effect that it would be disadvantageous to us for tactical nuclear weapons to be used, considering that in the future the Soviet bloc will also have very substantial tactical nuclear capabilities. First, such use may enhance the need for manpower that is quickly available as replacements, a contingency for which the Soviets are better prepared than is NATO. Second, in view of its dependence on ports, NATO's logistic system may be far more vulnerable to interdiction by tactical nuclear weapons than that of the Soviet bloc; this may be especially so because most of the Soviet lines of communication will run through the satellites, where use of nuclear weapons by NATO against many of the most attractive interdiction targets would serve to alienate what might otherwise be potential support from the satellite peoples. Finally, NATO is not really at a disadvantage in terms of available manpower and, so far at least, has a great advantage in industrial productivity. But to realize such an advantage and to make manpower available require lengthy mobilization, and the time required for this is far more likely to be available in a conventional than in a tactical nuclear war.

Of course, it would not do to rely on a conventional defense posture even if it were preferable from our point of view, because the Soviet bloc could always introduce the use of tactical nuclear weapons if it were advantageous to do so. But it probably does not make much sense either to assume that a tactical nuclear posture is the only reasonable one for us. Even if limitation to conventional weapons were disadvantageous to one side, it might prefer to accept such limitation rather than to expand the scale of the conflict with the concomitant risk that the scale might become unacceptable. After all, nuclear weapons were not used in Korea. The European members of NATO may be particularly interested in seeing them not used in Europe.

It is argued that a major war between NATO and the Soviet bloc in which the chief centers of strength of the two sides remain unscathed is completely unreasonable. But is all-out war any more reasonable? If not, we must either be prepared to fight a major war without strategic bombing, or else rely on some means of graduated deterrence to prevent it. The two possibilities are not wholly unrelated. Placing strategic retaliation capabilities in the hands of our NATO allies may go a long way toward deterring any aggression in Europe, and even if aggression does occur, control of nuclear capabilities by European NATO members may well preclude Soviet attacks with nuclear weapons against major ports, bases, and supply installations—perhaps the most vulnerable links in any NATO defense based on the use of tactical nuclear weapons.

VII. Arms Control

Before concluding, a few remarks may be made on the questions of arms control and all-out war.

First, there is the question of a cessation of nuclear tests. Perhaps the most frequent argument offered in this connection is that it is important to limit the nations possessing nuclear capabilities to as small a number as possible, on the grounds that the greater the number, the greater the probability of accidentally triggering all-out war. Of course, this purpose of test suspension could be circumvented if the great nuclear powers were to give nuclear weapons to the smaller states. Let us assume, however, that this would not happen if an agreement on test cessation were successfully negotiated. There would remain the possibility of posing the threat of limited war, or limited nuclear retaliation by those Western nations already having nuclear capabilities, in order to deter limited aggression. But the development of what would otherwise probably be the strongest deterrent to Soviet aggression against small states, particularly nuclear attack or blackmail, would have been precluded—that is, possession by the small states themselves of their own deterrent capabilities. And, as has been pointed out in the previous discussion, this would greatly lessen NATO's chances of victory in a war with the Soviet Union in which strategic bombing of the real centers of strength of the two sides did not occur. For these reasons—and this is a bit paradoxical—the importance of prolonging the credibility of the threat of all-out war as a means of dealing with limited threats would be enhanced if an agreement were reached which had the effect of greatly limiting membership in the nuclear club.

Perhaps more clearly to our advantage, and to that of the Russians, too, would be any measures which might be negotiated or, indeed, which might be taken unilaterally, that would reduce the probability of nuclear surprise attack. But it must be borne in mind that such measures are precisely those which make a successful counterforce strike difficult of attainment. Thus, for each side there is a fundamental incompatibility between accepting measures which will reduce the possibility of staging a surprise attack on its adversary, on the one hand, and of trying to develop or maintain a capability for a successful counterforce strike, on the other. For example, any measures to which the Soviets might agree which would give us better warning of an impending attack would make it easier for us to launch SAC, and thus harder for the enemy to deliver a successful counterforce blow. So long as both sides cling to the counterforce concept, negotiations in this area must amount to a reciprocal surrender of the capability to implement that concept. But these are by no means the only kinds of measures which might diminish the probability of surprise attack. Indeed, the measures which probably offer the greatest prospect of reducing both the chance of effective surprise and the probability of accidental all-out war are those which can be taken unilaterally and which we have previously discussed: reliance on less vulnerable, less accurate delivery means as the keystones of the deterrent capabilities of both sides.

This brings us to the third principal area of arms control that is being considered today, that pertaining to the control of outer space. Since it is hard to see how outer space would be used in war, statements about the advantage or disadvantage of agreements with respect thereto seem premature. Some people, though, seem to have assumed that ballistic missiles, especially the longer-range ICBM's, ought to be considered in such negotiations, even though these are hardly true outer-space weapons. However, even if such a central agreement were possible —and it is clearly a bit late to make one—would the interests of peace be served by negotiating such weapons out of existence? As has been pointed out above, missiles are precisely the weapons which, for some time at least, will have principally a deterrent and not a counterforce capability, at least against a reasonably hardened or mobile retaliatory system. Once we get through the missile gap, if indeed we do, they might be among the least likely of delivery systems to provoke accidental all-out war. *If* we could negotiate an end to improvement in ballistic missile accuracy, it might be particularly desirable to do so, since such a measure would tend to perpetuate the deterrent-only role of the missiles. But would it be wise to eliminate the missiles entirely if the alternative were continued reliance on weapons whose effectiveness is more dependent on who strikes first?

VIII. SUMMARY

The requirements for deterring an all-out Soviet nuclear attack against all of NATO, or just the United States, or any other nuclear power are now, and will probably continue to be, rather small. This will be true despite Soviet adherence to a counterforce war strategy, since there appears to be little reason to believe that the Soviets would be prepared to accept the risks implied in all-out war even if their adversaries had only a moderate nuclear capability. So long as the West has such capability, by far the most probable cause of Soviet massive attack would be a conviction on the part of the Russians that they were about to be attacked. As they become increasingly aware of the damage threat of nuclear weapons, and increasingly incredulous about the West's delivering a nuclear attack in response to lesser aggression, the chances of their launching the first blow will correspondingly decrease.

On the other hand, requirements for a counterforce posture will be very much greater than what would be required for a retaliatory posture. Indeed, adherence to a counterforce strategy may pose the possibility of a ruinous arms race. If we persist in such a strategy, bases around the periphery of the Communist bloc will represent an enormous advantage in terms of delivery vehicle costs, flight times and, for some delivery systems, accuracy. Thus, NATO could continue to play an important role in all-out strategy by facilitating basing near the Iron Curtain. It must be borne in mind, however, that adherence to a counterforce strategy carries with it a far higher probability of all-out war than does reliance on a purely retaliatory strategy. There is also a fundamental incompatibility between reliance on a counterforce strategy and arms control measures which might reduce the probability of effective surprise attack or of accidental war.

It would seem to be time that we think seriously about what our objectives should be. In particular, we must ask whether we should continue to hold to the counterforce strategy and the idea of a massive response to lesser threats—measures which both increase the probability of accidental total war—or whether we should abandon these concepts, and squarely face the necessity for providing greatly increased means of dealing with limited threats.

None of the possibilities for increasing the credibility of the threat of all-out war in order to deter future aggression in Europe appears very promising. A strong centralized NATO executive is probably politically infeasible, and besides unlikely to provide a very credible mechanism. Placing the bulk of American retaliatory capabilities in Europe might make the all-out war threat effective as a deterrent, but such a course is almost certainly not feasible politically. Providing each of the NATO countries with a sufficient offensive capability so that it could trigger all-out war if attacked is probably technically impossible and certainly very risky, perhaps unacceptably so. None of these measures, even if possible and successful as a means of invoking the threat of all-out war in Europe, would be of any avail for deterring lesser aggression outside the area in which the nuclear weapons were based. In particular, the threat of all-out war could not be made credible as a deterrent to Communist aggression in the neutral and uncommitted areas that are of interest to NATO, or as a deterrent to Soviet intervention in satellite revolts. One is forced to the conclusion that the threat of all-out war as a deterrent to lesser aggression is a possibility of rapidly diminishing credibility, and the trend is unlikely to be reversed.

Thus, it is time to recognize that the European members of NATO can no longer be expected to have much interest in perpetuating the alliance primarily as an instrument for deterring or, if necessary, fighting all-out war. To the extent that we feel we must use NATO as a means of maintaining a suitable all-out war posture, we must be prepared to offer Europeans something in return for the risks they thereby incur. We must, through NATO or otherwise (and this regardless of whether we are interested in NATO's value to us in maintaining a satisfactory all-out war posture), seriously explore possibilities for dealing with lesser threats. Either increased limited-war capabilities or increased reliance on graduated-deterrent capability, or a combination thereof, will probably be required.

CHAPTER 5

THE PLACE OF LIMITED WAR IN NATO STRATEGY

BY MALCOLM W. HOAG*

I

TO judge by the public record, a change in the official NATO policy toward limited war occurred sometime during 1957. When General Norstad spoke at the end of January of "NATO: Deterrent and Shield,"[1] he drew a distinction between the strategic airpower forces that served as the main deterrent to Soviet aggression, and the land and supporting sea and air forces in Europe that served as the shield. He mentioned two broad, total-war functions of the shield forces. They were to strengthen the deterrent by making it clearer that the main retaliatory forces would be used in the event of aggression. And if, nevertheless, the enemy was not deterred, the shield forces were to keep Russian troops out of Western Europe, and to hold forward air bases which our retaliatory forces could continue to use. These objectives were reiterated in a later speech in 1957 in which, significantly, a limited-war function was added:

> The functions of the NATO Shield are three. The Russian menace having compelled the organization of NATO, it is essential that we present concrete evidence of our determination, and of our ability, to defend NATO territories. This, then, is the Shield's first function. Our forces are not meant to engage in great campaigns in the traditional sense; rather, they are defensive. Their mission is to hold our frontier until the total effort of the Alliance becomes effective. How long this would take, no one knows, but we believe the time would be short. Accordingly, the need to mobilize men and industry may be less than in the past. How the forces are balanced, their organization and composition, is being governed by this first function.

> The second function of the Shield directly supports our primary purpose, the prevention of war, and is of the greatest interest and importance. The might of our strategic retaliatory forces vastly reduces the danger of a general war. The aggressor knows that to start such a war would invite

---

* I am indebted to many colleagues for helpful discussion, especially to two whose recent publications are directly pertinent: W. W. Kaufmann, "The Crisis in Military Affairs," *World Politics*, x, No. 4 (July 1958), pp. 579-603; and A. J. Wohlstetter, "The Delicate Balance of Terror," *Foreign Affairs*, xxxvii, No. 2 (January 1959), pp. 221-34.

[1] *NATO Letter*, February 1, 1957, pp. 27-30.

his own destruction. However, there remains the risk of a war by accident, by miscalculation. A probing operation to achieve political advantage—a border incident, negligible in itself—might flare out of control. And here lies the value of the Shield Force, deployed along NATO's frontier—a frontier which is not an imaginary line, a mere geographical concept like the Tropic of Capricorn. It is an actual, physical line that runs for more than 4,000 miles through the villages, forests and the farms of Europe. If this critical line, which the 15 NATO nations have vowed to defend, is held with reasonable force, then force must be used to breach it. The decision to apply that force would be terrible in its implications. It must consider not only the stout Shield in immediate defence, but the sharp sword of our strategic retaliation. The Shield Force thus serves to complete the deterrent, to integrate all the elements that compose its strength. This is the second function.

The third function is closely related to the second, but is important enough to be discussed separately. In an era of nuclear plenty and of delivery means adequate in number and in effectiveness, the NATO Shield provides us with an option more useful than the simple choice between all or nothing. Should we fail to maintain reasonable Shield strength on the NATO frontier, then massive retaliation could be our only response to an aggression, regardless of its nature. There is real danger that inability to deal decisively with limited or local attacks could lead to our piecemeal defeat or bring on a general war. If, on the other hand, we have means to meet less-than-ultimate threats with a decisive, but less-than-ultimate response, the very possession of this ability would discourage the threat, and would thereby provide us with essential political and military manoeuverability.

Here, then, is the central military meaning of the NATO Alliance: to deepen the deterrent to another great aggression that could wreck civilization; and also, by means of the covering Shield, to save civilization from being whittled away by forays and incursions which otherwise could be halted only by invoking our full apparatus of destruction.[2]

This statement supplies an admirably succinct statement of NATO's strategic goals. It also may be interpreted in terms of the fundamental questions that are bound to be raised about a limited-war capability: (1) Why have a limited-war capability? (2) What kind of a capability? (3) How much? (4) Under what circumstances is it to be used? (5) How is it to be used?

It is too much to ask of any brief statement that it answer these questions, but such broad answers as were implied by General Norstad's statement are obviously worth critical scrutiny. Adding a limited-war function for the shield forces constituted some acceptance of a criticism that had formerly been resisted. The earlier rigid identification of

[2] *Ibid.*, December 1957, p. 27.

NATO forces with a total-war strategy is now abandoned. Shield forces no longer merely supplement the deterrent, but may be used independently of it. Of course, national forces nominally assigned to the shield have been so used in limited engagements—notably, French forces in Algeria. But General Norstad referred to possible collective use by NATO in Europe, and such use would be novel.

In very general terms, the answer supplied by General Norstad to the question, "Why have a limited-war capability?" is a familiar one. In his phrases, a limited-war capability "provides us with an option more useful than the simple choice between all or nothing." By possessing this option, we may ". . . save civilization from being whittled away by forays and incursions which otherwise could be halted only by invoking our full apparatus of destruction." His implied answer to "What kind and how much of a capability?" is more specific: "How the forces are balanced, their organization and composition, is being governed by the first function"—that of defending NATO territory in total war. This answer is the vital one for military planners, because it outlines policy that governs military requirements. There are multiple functions for the shield forces, but the requirements for implementing the one function are dominant. The other functions are therefore by-products, generating no supplemental requirements of their own.

At least two implications follow: First, the limited-war function has ostensibly been added without any additional cost. Neither larger forces nor differently composed forces are required, and presumably different equipment is not required either. Second, because the trend in fulfilling the first function of shield forces—defense in total war— has been definitely toward reliance upon "tactical" nuclear weapons, the likelihood is enhanced—although by no means made certain— that nuclear weapons would be used whenever these forces were used. Thus the statement sheds some light upon the question, "How is the limited-war capability to be used?"

II

This brief overview shows how a limited-war capability fits into official military planning in NATO. It can also serve to show why any discussion of NATO strategy is necessarily complicated. Why, someone may ask, cannot a limited-war capability be appraised by itself in terms of what it contributes and what it costs? The answer is that it cannot because neither its utility nor its cost is independent of other

NATO capabilities; the differing functions of NATO forces are vitally interrelated.

Thus, if the addition of a limited-war capability were truly costless, even some of those who find little merit in it might regard it with indulgence. But the costlessness can be challenged on several grounds. There is no added cost because the limited-war capability is regarded as a by-product of shield forces. Remove the primary defensive function of these forces in total war, and the by-product economies in the supply of a limited-war capability disappear. Or, even if the primary function remains, the kind of a limited-war capability that is desired may require supplemental equipment, supplies, or even manpower, and the by-product economies are reduced. Consequently, the estimation of the true cost of a limited-war capability cannot be separated from the question of what other sorts of capabilities are desired.

Similarly, the utility of a limited-war capability vitally affects the utility of other military preparations. It may reinforce them or interfere with them. That it may do either is worth emphasizing. The reinforcing or complementary aspects of various preparations are naturally stressed in any justification of a military program—all is in harmony, all is "balanced." But often the interfering or competing aspects go unrecognized or are unduly minimized. Different preparations compete for resources, and this obvious conflict is recognized. But more subtle competition is neglected. There are some understandable reasons for the neglect—notably, the presumption that complementary aspects in military performance will usually be dominant. But competitive aspects cannot be neglected, and may even dominate complementary ones in some cases.

We face the fact that any limited-war strategy for NATO was long resisted. Some maintained that it was not worth adding even if it were free. This view, with which I want to quarrel but to which in fairness I must try to do full justice, logically comes first. For if we are opposed to adding a limited-war capability in NATO when it is free, *a fortiori* we should be opposed to adding it at considerable cost. Therefore, unless we can counter this view or at least cast doubt upon it, there is no point in going on to consider more involved questions about limited-war preparations.

The view in question, of course, supports massive retaliation as the exclusive deterrent to Soviet aggression in Europe. The topic of massive retaliation has been so much debated that we can certainly be terse about it here. Probably most people would agree with the following statement because it is cast in the language of relatives rather than

absolutes: The threat of massive retaliation is more appropriately invoked, and more effective because more credible, the more vital to
our interests the territory in question and the more likely that any
aggression against it would have to take the form of a clear and flagrant
provocation. What and how "vital" our interest is, and what would be
a "clear and flagrant provocation," are always open and demanding
questions—which allows those who place differing reliance upon the
threat of massive retaliation to agree with this general statement of its
applicability.

Having admitted this deliberate vagueness, probably only one aspect
of the statement need be amplified. Why go beyond "vital interest"
to add the second condition at all? Why does not our degree of interest determine the flagrancy of any provocation? The answer is perhaps best perceived in terms of a hypothetical example. Suppose the
Soviets occupy an Alaskan island that is uninhabited and from which
we draw nothing of value. In one sense, our interest in the island is
not vital; it is practically non-existent. Yet our juridical claim to the
area is clear, has been sanctioned by years of tradition, and the geographical line is obvious to all. Moreover, the attacked territory is
ours, not that of an ally. Not to respond with punishment more than
proportionate to the provocation is to invite future aggression, especially aggression less naked in its challenge but involving territory more
vital to us.

The proponent of massive retaliation stresses this bleak prospect as
the likely one if we are not firm. And given this example, which is
tailored to his desires, he can doubly refute the common objection that
the threat to retaliate massively will not serve as a deterrent because
the enemy believes that we would not be so irrational as to commit
"suicide" by attacking massively. First, in his view, to retaliate may
not be to commit "suicide." Being the first to strike massively confers
enormous advantages. Our strategic forces are intact prior to striking,
their attack can be well coordinated and planned to disrupt enemy defenses, and our defenses against air attack can be fully alerted and
prepared. For all these reasons, our power to blunt enemy counter-
retaliation should limit damage to us. Some may estimate that damage
even so limited is still enormous and amounts to "suicide." But the
second argument of the proponent of massive retaliation still applies.
It may be perfectly rational to commit yourself to a response which,
if the enemy commits certain actions, does amount to mutual homi-
cide. The "if" makes all the difference in the argument, because the
probability of his taking these actions may be driven very low by this

policy, compared with alternative policies open to us. Where the "if" is occupation of an Alaskan island, our threat does not in the least mean that we value the island more than our life. It only means that since we believe the enemy values it much less than he does his life, for all practical purposes our threat will serve to reduce to zero the probability of his occupying the island. Hence our threat is not irrational.

This is the simple logic of a massive retaliation policy. But its simplicity vanishes, and its appeal is diminished, when its proponents concede that the probability of all provocations cannot be driven to zero. It is easy to think of provocations that would be far less clear and flagrant than our hypothetical Alaskan invasion. A territory may be in juridical dispute. The line that separates our interests from enemy interests may be fuzzy in various respects. Who provoked whom may be an open issue. And, a factor that we cannot neglect in discussing coalition matters, the territory in question will in all probability be that of an ally rather than our own, or of a nation whose neutral status we want to preserve. Any of these factors can bring the credibility of our retaliating into question. Perhaps more important, they can create bargaining situations in which threats and counterthreats of massive retaliation are brought directly into question. With or without premeditated design by either side, situations can arise in which the key question is, Who will back down first? That there would be mutual gain in both backing down is by no means a sufficient condition for realizing such gain. How to achieve a neat simultaneity in face-saving withdrawals is obviously a very demanding task for diplomacy.

Because of these considerations, a policy of limited war has great appeal. Limited war offers an alternative to unacceptable extremes of violence or appeasement, and gives warfare a truly political function that we sorely need. It promises a series of "cooling off" stages between levels of violence. The pace of hostilities may be slow enough to enable diplomacy to be brought to bear at several stages before all-out war is reached.

NATO, however, poses a severe test for those who espouse limited-war preparations. Their argument is stronger when applied to territories where our interest is less vital, and where provocations are perhaps both more likely and less flagrant and clear-cut than similar incidents would be in Europe. Consequently, we find some who argue for limited-war preparations elsewhere in the world, but who prefer not to compromise the power of the main deterrent by declarations of policy that make it less likely that we would retaliate massively against any attack in Europe. There is much to be said for this view. It would be compelling if only the issues in Europe were absolutely clear-cut. Suppose, for example, there were an agreed boundary line between East and West, with the problem of German reunification amicably resolved, and no prospect of indigenous upheaval on either side of the Iron Curtain. Then potential conflict in Europe might be so unlikely and its sources so clear that a policy of massive retaliation linked to specific territories and to specific acts might be attractive compared with alternative policies. But where the issues are not that clear, such a policy is questionable even for Europe. Therefore, it is a dubious view that would dismiss a limited-war capability for NATO as worthless, and it does seem pertinent to inquire about the cost of such a capability as well as its worth.

III

The official case for the costlessness of a limited-war capability is based upon securing it as a by-product of other functions of the shield forces. But these other functions must be brought into question. The shield forces are supposed to complement the retaliatory forces both in deterring aggression by the threat of total war and in fighting total war should deterrence fail. On balance, however, are they more competitive than complementary?

The main argument for complementarity in deterring aggression is that the presence of troops in Europe will help to define the line which the enemy cannot cross without knowing that he is precipitating total war. Hence the risk of war by accident or miscalculation is supposed to be reduced. Yet, along with this argument, it is claimed that the line in question is "a frontier which is not an imaginary line. . . . It is an actual, physical line. . . ."[3] This view may be disputed, but we need here look only at the internal consistency of the official argument. If the line is so well defined, then the enemy will know when he is crossing it. The real question is what he expects you to do when he does cross it.

On the one hand, he will expect a stronger and perhaps unlimited reaction in the event that his crossing immediately leads to fighting with loss of life to the troops of many NATO countries, especially those of the United States. But against this argument we must pose another. What is the enemy to think if we put sizable numbers of troops along the line? Will he view them as an alternative to the main deterrent rather than as complements to it? Our action in put-

[3] General Norstad, *ibid.*

ting many troops there would tend to indicate that we regard them as an alternative, especially when we announce that we are adding a limited-war function for these troops. The same forces cannot serve as an unfailing "trip wire" for massive retaliation and simultaneously as an alternative to it. In any case, the main impact of our actions and announcements upon enemy estimates is likely to be achieved, so far as the "trip wire" function is concerned, by only a few troops. If we have only a few, he cannot seriously regard them as an alternative to massive retaliation; and to the extent that troop casualties serve as a political triggering mechanism, a few are almost as good as many. If we provide troops in large numbers, we probably strengthen the impression that they are designed primarily as an alternative to massive retaliation, and so impair the credibility of the deterrent about as much as we enhance it. As one contrasting example, suppose we were to put the resources into civil defense in the United States rather than into added troops in Europe. Would this not better strengthen the credibility of massive retaliation?

The "trip wire" concept must be examined still more critically. The troops for this purpose represent incompatible expectations on our part. Presumably we want the enemy to believe that the "trip wire" would function. Else why talk about it? Yet we must notice what a functioning "trip wire" implies about the intelligence of the enemy. If the Soviets believe that there is an appreciable probability that massive retaliation will be triggered by invasion in Europe, there is only one sensible attacking strategy for them. That strategy is not to lessen in any way the surprise of their initiating strategic air blows by preparations in Europe, let alone by actual invasion in Europe. The overriding objective for them must be to damage Western retaliatory power. Getting in the first strategic air blow in a total war obviously confers an enormous advantage upon the aggressor. He can expect to damage our retaliatory air forces, and will hope to cripple them. Thus he reduces the size of the forces that may fly against him. Second, by attacking first he disrupts the planning and coordination of retaliatory air strikes, which also hampers their effectiveness. Third, the diminution in size and the lessened coordination of retaliatory strikes greatly enhance the efficacy of the aggressor's air defenses. And, fourth, enemy defenses can capitalize upon the advance warning that they will receive by virtue of being struck second. All their shooting defenses can be fully alerted, and precious time will be gained for moving their matériel and people into whatever shelters may have been provided. In combination, these advantages are enormous. To forego them by taking preparatory action in Europe that the enemy will recognize, and which he has warned will result in massive retaliation, is sheer madness. The "trip wire" action of our shield forces is the more unlikely to occur, the more likely it is that the enemy will believe our pronouncements about it.[4]

There remain some arguments to the effect that shield forces would complement the main retaliatory forces in actually fighting a total war, and these are obviously linked to deterrence. If the shield forces were so strong that they could counterattack deep into Russia in the event of war, one would have to concede them great total-war value. But certainly no one ever seriously proposed shield forces big enough, and well-defended and mobile enough, to counterattack quickly and deeply. Probably the most ambitious of our objectives for the shield forces was the much more modest one of preserving a base from which such an attack might ultimately be launched, and even this objective has been de-emphasized: "Our forces are not meant to engage in great campaigns in the traditional sense; rather, they are defensive. Their mission is to hold our frontier until the total effort of the Alliance becomes effective. How long this would take, no one knows, but we believe the time would be short."[5] Clearly, no World War II-like notions of a long war culminated by a sweeping ground invasion of the enemy form a part of the current view of the Supreme Allied Commander, Europe, whatever their place in past planning.

Another function of shield forces in total war is that of protecting the air bases from which our retaliatory forces are to operate. The Western advantage in possessing air bases close to the Soviet Union is clear. But it is equally clear that this advantage has become less valuable over

---

[4] There is one other deterrent function claimed for the shield forces that may briefly be dismissed. It has been claimed that, in their absence, the Russians would regard occupation of Europe as a good trade for a devastated Russia, and the big deterrent would accordingly not prevent invasion, even if it were credible as a threat. About all that one can reply to this argument is: Trade to whom? What Russians are supposed to survive to inherit the riches? Even if confident of their own ability to survive, are they assumed to be callously indifferent to the millions of their countrymen who will not? Are they confident of their ability to maintain control in Europe without a functioning home economy and military effort behind them? I think the answers to these questions are, in broad outline, sufficiently evident to indicate that few would regard the trade as ever having been an attractive one in Russian eyes. And if the argument of a "good trade" ever was relevant, it is less so now. In the crassest material terms, the "prize" of the Western European economy has been getting steadily richer on the order of only some 3 or 4 per cent per year, the Russian economy has been growing faster, and our power to devastate Russia in a first strike has probably been growing at a far greater rate. What the Soviets would give up in the "trade" has been growing at a vastly greater pace than what they might gain.

[5] General Norstad, op.cit. (December 1957).

time. Overseas bases represent an enormous one-sided advantage when intercontinental air strikes are infeasible, or when many repeated air strikes are required for airpower to be effective. But in situations where the operating life of a strategic air force is expected to be numbered in days rather than months, and where every sortie can be a sortie with nuclear weapons, it is at most a very few strikes that are decisive. Consequently, retaining overseas air bases long after total war has begun is no longer very important. Moreover, the attack that would greatly interfere with our planned use of overseas bases has to be so quick an attack that, almost by definition, it has to come via missiles or bombers or by sabotage. The holding of a front line many miles distant from our overseas SAC bases is now so tenuously related to the efficacy of our air operations in total war that it may be neglected.

Having so depreciated the utility of shield forces in complementing the big deterrent, we are left with the question whether they have any utility beyond fighting limited wars. For an answer we are reduced to the defense value of shield forces, in the narrowest sense of the word "defense." In the event of total war they may still, if adequate in power, implement the celebrated "forward strategy" by stopping the Soviet invasion. Thus they could prevent the feared sequence of fighting on Western European territory, Soviet occupation, and then perhaps fighting again. Preventing this sequence of events was foremost during early NATO planning, when memories of World War II were fresh. And, understandably, it remains a prominent and highly valued objective. To mitigate disaster is obviously important if you have failed to avert it by a policy of deterrence.

But, as always, the relevant question remains: How desirable is this objective compared with alternatives that might use the resources required to implement the forward strategy? As we have already seen, there is a reasonable presumption that reducing shield forces would have little effect either in encouraging total war or in reducing our power to fight it. Consequently, a reallocation of military resources away from land defenses is indicated unless either (1) the prime objective is changed—that is, the policy of deterring aggression by threatening total war is modified; or (2) the subsidiary objective of protection against land invasion, once war starts, is deemed so valuable that it outweighs the net loss of deterrent power involved in diverting resources to shield forces. It is this second possibility that must now be examined. Is there a case for diverting resources to land defenses in order to mitigate disaster?

Suppose NATO land forces were adequate to contain a Soviet invasion. Such forces in 1948 would have been enough to protect West Europeans from any catastrophic damage. But today the power of the air offense has grown so formidable that nothing approaching such protection is possible. If the Soviets now initiate total war against NATO countries by massive air assault, how can immediate casualties be held below the tens of millions in either the United States or Europe? Anything less catastrophic is highly unlikely today because of the limited efficacy of Western defenses against air attack. The Soviet air threat is steadily growing. Consequently, no assured protection against catastrophe in NATO countries is possible, however strong the defensive ground shield. If the Soviets initiate total war, therefore, what would the defense land shield accomplish? Who then would worry about occupation? The old slogan used in emphasizing the desirability of a "forward strategy" was that there was no point in "liberating a corpse." Today one must consider that there is no more point in defending a corpse than there is in liberating it.

Our European allies are now nakedly vulnerable to Soviet air attack. They are still developing the integrated radar network and interceptor missiles noted as deficiencies by General Gruenther nearly three years ago.[6] Much more important, most of them are within IRBM range and are but minutes of jet flying-time away from the Soviet threat, and any effort to build a high-attrition defense system is bound to be expensive and may be futile. Passive defense, an alternative form of protection, has always been neglected by NATO members. Nowhere in the West have we created anything approaching the hardened and dispersed underground civilizations required for protection against thermonuclear weapons. Realism demands that we face the fact of great vulnerability squarely.

Still, though invulnerability cannot be achieved, some reductions in vulnerability may be purchased at reasonable cost. The very greatness of our deficiencies suggests that there may be some first-order things to do that promise sizable payoffs for modest investments. Providing shelters for civilian populations is one prominent example. Are such things worth doing even though they promise at best only to mitigate disaster, not to eliminate it?

The proponent of large shield forces often argues that resources should not be diverted on any sizable scale to such purely defensive purposes. But if he denies the usefulness of purely defensive measures, then the value of land forces as protectors against occupation is like-

[6] *NATO Letter*, April 1, 1956, p. 12.

wise small. In the context of total war, such forces also promise only to alleviate one kind of enormous damage. The reason that rejects the one purely defensive set of measures serves also to reject the other. And if, on the other hand, the army proponent concedes the usefulness of purely defensive measures, the case for remedying the most glaring deficiencies against air attack becomes strong.

One recourse of the shield proponent is to stress the advantages of a blend while minimizing its disadvantages: "True, dollar for dollar we contribute less to the main deterrent than strategic airpower, but we offer a shield against invasion that it cannot provide. True, some measures to defend against air attack might do more to alleviate destruction—again, dollar for dollar—than we can promise to do, but we contribute to the deterrent more than do such purely defense measures." This is the logical position of the shield proponent who clings to a total-war premise. The great weakness of his argument is that its persuasiveness naturally declines as the spectacular growth of Soviet atomic airpower increases vastly the prospects of bomb damage in the West if war occurs. As the terrors of bomb devastation loom steadily larger relative to those of occupation, the land shield loses its relative appeal as a mitigator of disaster.

Thus, the argument for spending less on the army shield and more on alternative means to relieve disaster becomes steadily stronger in preparing for total war. To make a bad situation worse for shield advocates, he who would spend more on protection against air attack can claim that his measures also contribute to the main deterrent beyond protecting our air striking forces. Their contribution is that of "backbone stiffening." How much the enemy is deterred from truly all-out air assault depends presumably upon his assessment of the security and power of our retaliatory forces and upon little else. But for aggression short of all-out air assault, his assessment is compounded by an additional factor: What is the probability that we would retaliate massively? In seeking an answer to this question, he necessarily assesses the resoluteness of our political leaders, who must authorize retaliation. The risk attached to his contemplated provocation will obviously depend upon how resolute we appear to him, a matter of attitude, and how prepared in fact we are to limit resultant retaliatory damage to us, which should be reflected in our attitude. If we could increase the Soviet assessment of the risk of retaliation even a little by toughening our air defenses, thus appearing more resolute, it would be a productive investment for us. How much we can in this way increase his assessment of the risk is exceedingly difficult to quantify, but arguments for complementary strengthening of the main deterrent are no more loose when referring to more air defense than when referring to a stronger land shield.

IV

These specific arguments that disparage old objectives of NATO planning are derived from two general considerations, both of which reflect the enormous growth in Soviet power in recent years. First, this growth in Soviet military power makes a dollar buy far less security for us than was formerly the case. Because security is relative, the growth in enemy power makes us "poorer." Second, new defense alternatives—air defenses, above all—have become urgent competitors for our defense resources. Formerly almost invulnerable to direct assault, even America is now obviously and terribly vulnerable. Formerly we did not need to spend much even upon the paramount objective of protecting SAC, and the air defense of civilians could be even more neglected. These two effects bear jointly and acutely upon the assessment of the continuing worth of the "forward strategy" in Europe. In a sense, this objective has always been a luxury. We wanted both to deter and yet to ensure against enemy occupation should deterrence fail. As we become relatively "poorer," we may question whether the luxury can any longer be afforded. And as other alternatives become more demanding, we may be inclined to substitute them for the "forward strategy."

That we should do so is also suggested, incidentally, by one special consideration. In early NATO planning the issue of differential exposure to risk was especially prominent. The military risk was particularly great for those in close proximity to the Soviet Union. Now there has been an evening of the burden of direct risk, perhaps even a reversal. Given the overriding importance that the Soviets must attach to the threat of SAC, it becomes their first target in total war. Americans may once have been predisposed to favor a "forward strategy" in order to make less invidious the comparison of European with American risk, but we need be so disposed no longer.

Our conclusion about the utility of shield forces in total war is thus a decidedly negative one. Yet the growth in Soviet nuclear power that casts doubt upon the utility of shield forces is the very same growth that casts doubt upon the simple alternative to them. This alternative, advocated by some at the outset of NATO planning, is to rely upon SAC to deter aggression in Europe and forego any sizable collective military effort. The deficiencies of this alternative are apparent. From an American point of view, it risks total war for us in the event of *any* Soviet provocation in Europe. A European doubts that America will continue to assume such a risk as American vulnerability increases. He very much fears that the credibility of American retaliation is declining in Soviet eyes. For a time, Europeans might view a declining credibility as more than offset by the growing power of SAC. A heavier retaliatory blow, even if less certain, might have been regarded as an unimpaired deterrent. But in a situation where the layman is all too inclined to think that the ultimate in retaliatory power has been or soon will be reached, this offsetting influence appears insufficient.

It is for these reasons—the declining relevance of old arguments for the shield forces, and growing worry about the credibility of the main retaliatory threat—that one finds so many current discussions couched in terms of "the dilemma of NATO strategy," "agonizing reappraisal," and so on. Such discussion has been especially stimulated by trends in Western military preparations that are increasingly at variance with the avowed objectives of NATO strategy. The failure of many NATO countries to meet the goals of the military planners for force contributions is well known. Some of these failures have been explicitly defended in terms of a new rationale that would remove or sharply impair a shield capability in Europe. The Defense Statements of the United Kingdom, coupled with reduction of British conventional forces, are the prominent cases in point.

The drift within the alliance toward a lower and less collective military effort has been noticeable. Yet there is another effect—with contrary implications—of our growing relative poverty induced by growth in Russian strength. We are driven not only to question some of our particular defense objectives as luxuries, but to question national military independence in the same terms. The original driving force for any collective military effort was the perception that the resources of one small nation were grossly inadequate for defense. And one way to get more defense out of our resources is by taking advantage of an economic division of military labor among allies, one that would capitalize upon their special capabilities. For this reason, the word "interdependence" has come again into increasing prominence, side by side with trends that are incompatible with it.

This is the general prospect that enjoins a new consideration of military alternatives. One alternative that we have already in part discussed is straightforward reliance upon SAC. A European who views this alternative with understandable apprehension has at least the consolation that it rationalizes a meager defense effort in Europe. He can divert the resources released from the shield toward limited-war capabilities in other theaters or toward air defense in Europe; and the number of civilian alternatives that could use the released resources is, of course, legion. We need merely repeat the central drawback of such a policy for the protection of Europe, and note the extent to which it might be exacerbated by a more explicit adoption of the policy. If a European member raises only such conventional military forces as are required to take care of its own colonial and other "brush fire" requirements, it would be making no contribution to collective defense. Would not its evident failure to contribute cast further doubt upon the credibility of a SAC response to aggression in Europe?

V

The growing unattractiveness of the old simple alternatives has, of course, stimulated interest in inventing new ones. One sharply different policy, especially attractive to those who assign a very low credibility to threats of SAC response to provocations in Europe, is the creation of nuclear retaliatory forces that are under the control of European governments. The development of intermediate-range ballistic missiles has greatly strengthened the appeal of this alternative. To some, the combination of the IRBM and a thermonuclear warhead seems to solve the problems that formerly precluded self-defense. Formerly no feasible response by a small power could inflict any grievous harm upon a large one. An ability to deliver even a few thermonuclear weapons upon urban centers obviously changes this prospect. Formerly large and expensive forces were required in order to have a reasonably high confidence of delivering even a few warheads. Only a large power might plan to overwhelm the air defenses of other powers by sheer force of penetrating numbers, if not by guile or trickery. But the prospect of weapons like the IRBM that might penetrate enemy defenses much more by virtue of phenomenal speed than by weight of sheer numbers greatly mitigates this problem as well. So the combination of the IRBM and the thermonuclear warhead offers a radical prospect for eliminating the main need for collective defense. To a European enthusiast it may appear to offer a retaliatory power that is large enough, that is within his country's means, and whose response is not wholly dependent upon American decision.

There are several disadvantages, however, that appear when these views are examined more critically. The first is the vulnerability of European-based retaliatory forces. Bringing retaliatory power so close to the Soviets obviously makes it easier for them to strike at these forces with little or no warning. Of special significance, such surprise attacks can be launched by aircraft as well as by ballistic missiles. European-based forces are but minutes of jet flying-time away from Soviet medium as well as heavy bombers. These bombers can carry large bombs that can be more accurately delivered than warheads delivered by missiles. For these reasons, they can be effective even against targets that might be dispersed and hardened enough to be well protected from enemy missiles. If we are interested in creating retaliatory forces—forces that are capable of striking back *after* the enemy has hit directly at them—then the simple addition of soft and vulnerable missile installations close to Soviet bases would seem a poor and losing game for us.

There are many possibilities for reducing the vulnerability of missile bases. We can harden and disperse our missile sites. However, the degree of such hardening and dispersal would have to be greater for bases close to the Soviet Union, because they are exposed to heavier and more accurate attacks. Hence, if such protection is feasible, it will be considerably more expensive than comparable protection for bases that are located deep within the United States. This greater expense for comparable protection, if comparable protection is feasible, must be balanced against the economies of close-in basing that are made possible by smaller missiles for comparable destructive ability.

There are other methods of protection that can be exploited in combination with hardening and dispersal. We can make the retaliatory forces mobile, hoping that the enemy would be so uncertain about their location at any one period of time that he could not hope to eliminate them in surprise attack. Mobility, like other means of protection, can be expensive. Beyond this, it raises some acute political problems. If we speak of mobility on land, how do we expect the people of Europe to respond to the continuous moving-about of nuclear warheads? For one thing, there is the risk of accidents, a risk that would be unduly magnified in popular estimation. And revulsion against such schemes is likely to be heightened, the more people realize that one promising enemy tactic against mobile missiles on the surface is to cover large areas with blast overpressures sufficient to disrupt the functioning of any fragile missiles caught within the areas. These apparent defects of some mobility schemes have stimulated great interest in proposals for mobile systems that would be well hidden away from population centers in order to minimize these risks. The obvious case in point is the Polaris missile to be fired from submarines, a very promising weapon system which, however, raises problems of its own. The submarines are expensive, and they raise a special political problem. If in the interests of security of the retaliatory forces the submarines are kept far at sea, and many countries have them, who knows what nation fired what retaliatory shot?

Given these acute problems of protecting little retaliatory forces in Europe, why, one may well ask, do the Soviets claim to be so deeply troubled about them? The answer, I think, is simple. Our objections refer to the capability of such forces to strike *after* they have been hit first. The Soviets' apprehensions are concerned with the capability of such forces if the West strikes first. Beyond question, IRBM's could cause great damage in the Soviet Union. We in the West realize that there is small likelihood of their being fired before we have been bombed. Given the current control arrangements over the IRBM's, we know that there is no reasonable possibility that the United States and the host nation could agree quickly and secretly on the most fateful of all decisions—the decision to initiate all-out war by firing unrecallable missiles before the Soviets have launched a comparable assault. But the suspicious Soviets cannot be expected to share our expectation. Why, they will ask, would we build obviously vulnerable installations unless we expect them to be used before their vulnerability becomes a problem? In short, our adoption of a scheme that appears to be physically designed for initiating attack is a provocative move from the point of view of the Soviets. And we can hardly expect to convince them and their propaganda audience that our political objectives are inconsistent with our physical designs.

The vulnerability problem should be paramount in any appraisal of IRBM's. But if this problem is surmounted, there remains another difficulty to trouble those who find the IRBM the answer to a declining faith in protection by SAC. Though the growth in European power to retaliate tends to reduce the probability of Soviet provocations in Europe, an offsetting influence in Soviet eyes is the declining credibility of the threat of retaliation by SAC. A growth in independent retaliatory power gives the United States a better reason not to risk her own civilization by responding to provocations against Europe with massive retaliation. And even a small reduction in the Soviet estimate of the likelihood of American reaction may be enough, given the great power of American retaliatory forces, to offset the growth in independent European retaliatory power.[7] The credibility of a Euro-

[7] An arithmetical example may clarify this point. Suppose the Soviets calculate, *before* the European powers have IRBM's, that a given provocation in Europe has

pean response with IRBM's to a flagrant provocation is, after all, not
unity either. When directly faced with the horrible implications of
such drastic action, European countries might give in to atomic blackmail. Again there is a vital difference between American and European
military assessment of such a frightening situation. Should we strike
in full power in response to Soviet provocation, we may hope to disrupt
greatly any subsequent Soviet atomic retaliation. Our targets can be
air bases and missile sites. In brief, we may have some grounds for
believing that our air offense is a main defense against enemy attack.
Those who argue for small retaliatory forces in Europe can have no
such hope. They rely solely upon punitive damage exacted after great
Soviet provocation. Because of small force sizes, they can have little
hope of limiting subsequent damage to themselves.

On balance, it is far from clear that Europeans would gain greater
protection from a proliferation of independent retaliatory forces. And
certainly they are likely to lose if, added to any small decline in the
credibility of American response that is linked to the creation of such
forces, the IRBM's in fact do not have a reliable retaliatory capability
because they are vulnerable. Despite the bleakness of this prospect from
a European point of view, there is still of course the possibility that
we Americans might find such forces attractive as a means of "contracting out" of an alliance obligation without leaving our friends defenseless. Whether we should do so, even if we could, raises great
moral and political problems. But they are probably academic problems, because it is unlikely that we can really disengage from our allies
in this way. For one thing, the total cost of such forces is small only
because the heavy and presumably continuing expenses of missile development have been met by the United States. We are supplying the
missiles even if we should prefer not to be the ones to fire them. And
if the protection of such missiles requires the extreme concealment
typified by the Polaris-carrying submarine, how could we hope to
escape responsibility for any missile-firing by our allies? For the Soviets
to reason that any small retaliatory attack was probably *not* the advance

---

only one chance in ten of triggering SAC. After the European nation that is directly
involved in the particular potential provocation has been given IRBM's, suppose the
Soviets calculate an additional element of possible damage to them—say, by assigning
the same probability of one in ten to IRBM retaliation by the European power. The
destructive power of such retaliation is, however, estimated to be only one-tenth that
of SAC. Then deterrence of the Soviet provocation is measured by two elements of
possible damage to the Soviets. But, in the measurement, the chance of SAC retaliation
need fall only from its former value of 0.10 to 0.09 to leave expected damage to the
Soviet Union the same.

wave of an American attack, they must have both a sanguine view of our intentions and little fear that delay in any response on their part would compromise their ability to retaliate. Such a poised and confident appraisal in the face of actual thermonuclear attack hardly seems likely, to say the least.

The creation of little strategic retaliatory forces in Europe then appears to be unpromising as a means of increasing strategic independence among allies. As a means of collective defense, on the other hand, it may be inefficient. To create such forces may be to move them from places where they can be comparatively well protected to places where they cannot be, and to give an advantage to the Soviets' air offense because many of their short-range missiles and aircraft would find lucrative targets. And if the problem of coordinating our firings is not solved perfectly—which is a realistic expectation, given the necessity for government concurrence in such decisions—then these forces enhance the effectiveness of Soviet air defenses against staggered waves of attack. The attempt to resolve NATO's "strategic dilemma" by turning to the proliferation of little retaliatory forces seems to create more problems than it solves.

VI

Another prominent alternative proposed as a means of escape from the strategic dilemma is the bolstering of NATO's shield forces with nuclear weapons for tactical purposes. This proposal is sometimes offered as a supplement to proposals for the creation of retaliatory forces, and sometimes as an alternative. In either case, the political *mystique* of equality in weapon status is invoked. And there is a natural tendency on the part of finance ministers to regard the addition of nuclear weapons as a budgetary substitute for the supply of troops.

If we look only at the addition of nuclear weapons for tactical purposes, the reason for their great appeal in early NATO planning is evident. Military planners generated a requirement for shield forces to hold the line in Europe, and these requirements were not met. At the same time, the American stockpile of fissionable material was estimated to exceed that of the Soviets by a good deal. In the short run, we could obviously draw upon our superior supply of fissionable material to substitute for NATO's deficiency in troops.

But we must ask whether this obvious short-run possibility provides a tenable long-run basis for NATO planning. In the very short run, military planners in Europe understandably thought in terms of a

Soviet stockpile so small that the Russians could hardly divert any of it to tactical purposes in Europe. Presumably, in wars in which the Russians would use no or a very few nuclear weapons, not many of ours would be needed to redress our numerical inferiority in troops. Consequently, the damage inflicted by use of nuclear weapons in the theater might be so small that for the West it would compare favorably with the devastation that would otherwise be inflicted by Soviet invasion. But, as our war planning is projected for the future, one dominating aspect is clear. Both stockpiles of fissionable material and the ability to extract greater weapon effects from a given stockpile are steadily increasing. No longer can it be maintained that the Soviets would be so severely constrained in availability of fissionable material that they would not use many weapons in a tactical theater. After all, the United States has managed to create its awesome stockpile at the small annual cost of about one-twentieth of its national security budget, or about one two-hundredth of its gross national product. If stockpiles are strategically so all-important and yet, for a major power, so cheap, why should we not expect the Soviets to approach our stockpile levels in the long run? And even if we maintain a lead, will it matter much when absolute levels on both sides are very high?

So we face another dilemma in Western defense planning. If we seek to exploit our nuclear superiority tactically at a time when absolute levels of stockpiles are very high, we must be prepared for the explosion of a great deal more fissionable material in combat. If this occurs, and if the fissionable material is so packaged that both we and the Soviets get great weapon effects per unit of fissionable material—the crude direct way of maximizing military effects—then total damage in any tactical theater rises enormously. "Taking war back to the battlefield" is a fine slogan, but if it is used to rationalize unlimited theater employment of atomic weapons, it becomes a mockery to allies over whose territory they are being employed. The battlefield will be deep, because rear-located tactical air bases and missile launch sites are obviously prime targets, and logistic supply lines may well be. Hitting them hard and early is terribly important. And military commanders have compelling reasons to use big weapons rather than little ones to compensate for inaccuracy in their delivery. The battle line itself will probably be fluid. These are chilling prospects indeed for our allies, for the distinction between limited and total war becomes less and less discernible to them.

To cap their disillusionment, the economies promised by substituting tactical atomic weapons for troops turn out to be small and perhaps negative. True, a small force equipped with big-bang weapons can pack a large destructive power, thus permitting manpower economies for any given level of combat potential. But planning for full tactical use of atomic weapons in a context where the enemy's stock of such weapons grows steadily means that a higher and higher level of combat potential must be attained. Substituting bombs for troops reduces manpower requirements only as these requirements are inflated steadily by this associated factor. To put it another way, force requirements go up as estimated casualties soar in number, offsetting the substitution of atomic weapons for troops.

*Un*limited theater employment of atomic weapons clearly makes the contribution of shield forces in holding a frontier academic even if they can hold it. This way of performing the main function of the shield promises to devastate Europe, not to protect it. Given this prospect, we must expect that the incentive for Europeans to raise troops will be small. Moreover, if we expect use of nuclear weapons in Europe to be a substitute for the use of SAC, we raise the most troubling, because the most invidious, distinction among allies. In the event of war in Europe, our Continental allies would suffer damage that they would find indistinguishable from the damage of total war, while we might not—a prospect calculated to impair their morale even further. If, on the other hand, we think of such weapon employment as but a complement to SAC, Europeans must be expected to question its relevance. Because they are not really protected in the event of war, they must be interested almost exclusively in the deterrence of war. And, as argued earlier, the contribution that shield forces can make to deterrence is small and perhaps negative.

Perceiving this dilemma, advocates of tactical use of nuclear weapons have sought limitations upon the use of nuclear weapons in the theater that would clearly limit the amount of damage in the event of war. Beyond question, such limitations in many forms can be defined. Whether they can be relied upon is a different matter. The only sure way to limit damage from nuclear employment in the theater is to have our forces so concentrated and soft that the enemy need not devastate the countryside in order to eliminate them. This is obviously no military alternative. Or, if the primary impact of limitations is merely to limit the number of weapons that can be employed, we give away any stockpile advantage that we may have.

Consequently, those who argue for reliance upon limited employment of tactical nuclear weapons seek a type of limitation that still allows us nuclear superiority. Broadly speaking, the means of doing this is to use weapons that are inefficient in pure nuclear-engineering terms—that is, weapons with reduced military effects per unit of fissionable material. The obvious example is weapons whose yield is very small. But if we succeed in thus subordinating nuclear efficiency in a pattern of weapon usage that is advantageous to us, we face a tremendous problem in getting the Soviets to agree to the same limitations. If we accept the political onus attached to initiating widespread usage of nuclear weapons, with only sophisticated observers being aware of the great price we have paid in nuclear inefficiency in order to reduce damage, we are vulnerable to the counter of Soviet employment of weapons that are less compromised in their ability to inflict damage. In sum, if our nuclear advantage does not disappear anyway, it may not be translated into military advantage, not only because of limitations upon numbers of weapons, but also because we are forced to accept a greater penalty in weapon effectiveness than the Soviets.

The argument is often encountered that there are advantages to Western employment of tactical nuclear weapons quite apart from our stockpile advantage. Some assert that "nuclear weapons favor the defense," and our interests are supposed to be obviously on the side of the defense. But this proposition is doubly disturbing. If valid at all, the defensive advantage accrues only after nuclear hostilities are under way. When we must later counterattack in order to punish local aggression, as in Korea, this proposition offers us little comfort. And when we are on the defensive at the outset, as we expect to be, the one clear advantage that nuclear weapons would appear to confer is upon the side that initiates their employment, especially if it does so suddenly and in considerable numbers. And if we have made clear our intent to use nuclear weapons, an aggressor has an obvious interest in being the one to initiate their use in overwhelming power.

VII

Having considered the NATO strategic dilemma and the shortcomings of its popular resolutions, where do we stand? If nuclear weapons either for independent strategic forces or for widespread tactical employment are not very promising, what alternative do we have? In one sense, there is no satisfactory alternative. The decline in Western military power relative to that of the Soviets is, in its essentials, irremediable. We must reconcile ourselves to living in a state of far less security than we might have hoped. And in this, after all, we now have some training. Western peoples do find it hard, of course, to be realistically pessimistic, which explains why those proferring nuclear panaceas for the NATO strategic problem have found an eager and uncritical audience. But we must be realistic.

About NATO we need not become completely cynical. It is generally supposed that its early planners were nostalgically guided by World War II memories. But, even if they were, they may have planned better than they knew. What, after all, might a far-sighted planner have consistently advocated in 1949 if he had lost patience with old-fashioned concepts? An airpower extremist would have pointed out that it would take a long time to build conventional forces in Europe. Then, early planning was aimed, optimistically, at preparedness by 1954. An opponent of these plans might have argued for putting the resources instead into increased nuclear production and a better-prepared SAC that could have been ready as quickly.

There were glimmers of a public answer to this view even at the time, and probably there were other more effective answers behind the scenes. Secretary Acheson observed in 1951: "One reason why we cannot continue to rely on retaliatory air power as a sufficient deterrent is the effect of time. We have a substantial lead in air power and in atomic weapons. At the present moment, this may be the most powerful deterrent against aggression. But with the passage of time, even though we continue our advances in this field, the value of our lead diminishes."[8] It is true that in the same statement Secretary Acheson went on to say that "these defense forces would oblige the aggressor to use up his available resources, while his home sources of supply were being bombed," thus making his position consistent with the total-war philosophy that was officially controlling. However, questions of what we intended to have, while interesting, are not nearly as relevant as what in fact we do have. We have sizable integrated forces in Europe that we could not possibly possess had there been no major effort beginning in 1950. Without this build-up we should now be driven to rely upon massive retaliation, whether collectively or individually, as our sole defense in Europe.

What are our alternatives now? We can throw away the results of the NATO build-up, realizing some good-sized budgetary savings in the process. Or we can capitalize upon this considerable legacy from the past. There are some powerful arguments for the latter course. Beyond the compelling mutual interest of the Soviets and the West

---

[8] Hearings, Committee on Foreign Relations and Committee on Armed Services, U.S. Senate, 82nd Congress, 1st Session, on S. Con. Res. 8 (Feb. 1951): *Assignment of Ground Forces of the United States to Duty in the European Area*, p. 79.

in limiting damage in any hostilities, we need to remind ourselves of the extent to which old-fashioned conventional warfare is to Western advantage. We are not inferior to the Soviet Union and its European satellites in manpower or other resources. Given our great economic strength, we retain a comparative advantage in the conventional World War II-like warfare that is so expensive. And the lead times for increasing existing conventional tactical forces, while long, are much shorter than the lead times for creating new and intricate weapon systems for novel kinds of warfare.

These arguments are often countered by saying that, whatever their merits in the abstract, they are irrelevant because we have reached the point of no return in our military planning for nuclear warfare. This argument has considerable force, although it tends to be overstated. One's attention is caught by the novel trend rather than the familiar current situation. We are ill-prepared for nuclear war also. In our preparations we have compromised between conventional and nuclear warfare, and so are not as ready for either one as if we had concentrated upon it. That we should so compromise in order to have a flexible dual capability is sensible. That we should try to avoid compromise by being *thoroughly* prepared for both kinds of war is probably not sensible because it is too costly. The real issue is which capability—nuclear or conventional—should be subordinated to the other. Beyond the arguments already mentioned, there are two general considerations that support the unorthodox view that the tactical nuclear capability should be subordinated to the conventional. First, thorough preparedness for tactical nuclear war, as for strategic war, implies an ability to retain real capability after an enemy surprise attack with nuclear weapons. Buying such survival capability in a theater exposed to all kinds of Russian surprise-attack weapons is, if feasible, likely to be inordinately expensive. Second, technological developments in weapon systems promise to enhance markedly the effectiveness of non-nuclear defenses—so much so that the old label of "conventional" defense is perhaps no longer appropriate, although customarily used.

The problem of protecting American strategic forces based thousands of miles from Russian home bases promises to remain very demanding.[9] Protecting forces in Europe is much more difficult. Warning times are likely to be shorter; Russian missiles can be more accurate over shorter ranges; the yield of Russian warheads and bombs can be much greater because they need be carried or shot over much shorter distances; and so on. If a NATO military planner seeks to protect his

[9] See Wohlstetter, "The Delicate Balance of Terror," *loc.cit.*

capability against so formidable a threat of surprise nuclear attack, he naturally wants to eliminate all the "soft" spots in his system. He seeks some extreme combination of dispersed, alert, and hardened forces with sophisticated warning systems and protected supplies. And all cost considerations—the considerations that led to a build-up in Europe like that of World War II—are against him. Should we move from many airfields and missile sites to hundreds or thousands? Should we junk the expensive infrastructure and supply systems that were designed to provide continued operation and flows of supplies for a long conventional war, and provide new systems? Should forces be kept on hyper-alert status? Such questions can be multiplied. Some people will answer them affirmatively, and propose vast expenditures in Europe in order to be ready for the worst tactical contingency. Apart from political feasibility, such proposals are questionable—which of them can meet the fundamental test that the Russians cannot overcome their effects by changing their forces at lower cost to them?— but in any case, few would argue that they are likely to be adopted in anywhere near their entirety. It is the thoroughgoing proponent of the "new look" for nuclear preparedness in Europe who is unrealistic, not his critic who seeks to make NATO strategic pretensions consistent with the available assets—assets which were designed primarily for conventional war and whose costs have already been met in the main.

What dual capability, then, is it sensible to buy? Few would quarrel with providing alternative bomb racks for tactical airplanes so that they can carry nuclear or non-nuclear weapons. Certainly nothing so cheap should be neglected, however unlikely the contingency that we simultaneously desire and are able to strike in the theater with nuclear weapons. Other more expensive by-products for nuclear warfare are probably justified as well. Elaborate ground-to-ground guided missiles, on the other hand, are probably much too expensive and much too inaccurate to yield a profitable return in non-nuclear warfare, and therefore cannot be justified as an inexpensive by-product of conventional preparations. Ground-to-air missiles and other modern weapons, which are usually also described exclusively in terms of nuclear warfare, are a different matter. The argument that they have by-product value for conventional warfare is strong enough that it perhaps deserves to be inverted, with primary utility ascribed to their role in conventional warfare.

It is the great improvements in guidance that make missiles not only feasible in conventional warfare, but perhaps revolutionary. One main function of nuclear missile warheads is simply to compensate for inaccuracy. But to the extent that we make our weapons more accurate, the advantage of nuclear warheads declines. An anti-tank missile gains little advantage from a nuclear warhead if we have a high probability of hitting the tank, as recent developments may promise. In the case of ground-to-air missiles in particular, improved guidance looks especially attractive in conventional defense warfare. In conventional war, the life of an anti-aircraft battalion might coincide with the duration of hostilities. The battalion might get in many shots during repeated raids, and exact a level of attrition per raid that would be high enough to discourage conventional attacks. In the one-shot nuclear war, in contrast, a missile battalion may itself be the target of early and effective attack. Even if it survives, in delivering thermonuclear weapons the enemy can afford to let it exact a high price in terms of missile and aircraft losses. In short, the defensive guided missile may be especially useful in conventional war. Guidance developments may permit decisive hits at the wide-ranging tanks and airplanes that were main components of the old *Blitzkrieg*. In conventional war, the known advantage of prepared defense over the offense may become greatly enhanced. It would be a pity if our natural concern with nuclear weapon developments leads us to neglect the technological changes that can be incorporated to our advantage in preparing for conventional war.

If we accept the view that strengthened preparations in Europe for conventional, limited war rather than total war can contribute greatly to our defense, there remains the question of whether they are worth the cost. We cannot hope to provide a definitive answer, if only because the increment in security is incommensurable with sacrificed civilian alternatives. If we are persuaded, however, that such preparations reduce the probability of total war—because they reduce the danger of limited wars getting out of control much more than they increase the probability of limited provocations—we can note in passing some offsetting economies in military budgets that such preparations make possible. A lower probability of total war justifies spending less upon air defense. And the *great* merit of such clearly conventional preparations is that they promise to reduce devastation by weapon limitations that, whatever the incidence of mutual advantage for the two sides, are clearly defined. Because of this clarity, above all, they hold promise of reducing the danger of limited wars getting out of control.

It should go without saying that this alternative for our shield forces remains linked to the deterrent power of our main retaliatory forces. If we limit war, the limitations must be policed. Obviously there must be sanctions. Here, above all, is the place where strategic airpower must complement the tactical forces that will be operating under irksome restrictions, and here we must remain resolute despite the fearful stakes. SAC must continue to play the supremely important role of prime deterrent not only before war breaks out, but during war itself. The enemy must be made to think that violating the weapon limitations will probably bring against him a massive SAC strike. Then the terrible double penalty that he faces operates to dampen hostilities rather than aggravate them: (1) the local war serves to alert SAC and our air defenses, so that enemy chances of precluding retaliation by all-out assault diminish appreciably; (2) violating weapon limitations in the theater, his alternative way of raising the threshold of violence, runs a serious risk of giving SAC the enormous strategic advantage of the first strike.

The key to any policy of weapon limitations must be a reasonably clear-cut definition of the violations that would invoke massive retaliation. We cannot expect to find an unambiguous definition, but we can certainly hope for something less fuzzy than current notions about what will trigger massive retaliation. Hence we can reduce the chance of stumbling into total war. The definition of limits that possesses the greatest merit of clarity is simply non-use of atomic weapons.

Another possibility is to restrict the use of atomic weapons to the open seas or to those territories clearly recognized to be one's own. This is not by any means as clear a policy. Who defines one's territory? But this policy, if feasible, does permit the defender, but not the aggressor, to concentrate his troops, thus intensifying the normal numerical advantage of armies on the defensive and making a few troops go a long way. In these circumstances atomic weapons could be used against enemy aircraft and submarines certainly, and probably in a restrained way in tactical land operations. In land operations, each side would have powerful reasons to use fewer atomic weapons, and weapons that are cleaner and smaller, because the territory affected would be his own or that of his allies. These drastic limitations have obvious military disadvantages in terms of destroying enemy armies, but anything less limiting might well involve such levels of mutual destruction that fighting a war would be tantamount to losing it. In that case, why not pin everything upon strategic deterrence?

Given this general answer to what kind of a limited-war capability is sensible, we are left with the question, "How much?" In the immediate short run, not only are the shield forces unable to deter nuclear attack without SAC, but they probably could not hold against an assault that was all-out save for non-use of nuclear weapons. It is an open question whether we should aim for a limited-war capability in Europe so large that in the near and continuing future it could handle the latter kind of attack by itself. Such a force is clearly not beyond our means. And no other definition of the function of this force supplies much guidance to military planners in determining the size of required forces, although the convenience of making military requirements less intangible should hardly determine policy. But we must emphasize the great political gain that accrues if we are in such a position that only unambiguous nuclear assault need trigger massive retaliation.

I have avoided one of the questions raised at the outset, "Under what circumstances would a limited-war capability be used?" for the simple reason that I know no way to specify answers with any confidence. The very unpredictability of particular provocations, and the multiplicity of plausible ones, are what counsel ensuring ourselves by a capability that can handle the greatest in magnitude among limited provocations. The view that we are automatically prepared for any limited war if we are prepared for a big war has been criticized for the good reason that a different kind of capability may be at issue. But I am here advocating for NATO a conventional capability that is appropriate in kind as well as in amount for handling minor conflicts in and outside Europe. In contrast, the danger of the current trend toward nuclear emphasis is that our capability in Europe will be inadequate to handle the major threat and yet inappropriate in kind to handle lesser threats. Would this not be the worst of both worlds?

This entire argument has been cast in military terms, although certainly not because non-military considerations ought to be unimportant in choosing strategies. Rather the argument was designed this way because all too often good political arguments for non-nuclear limited-war preparations are dismissed as militarily unrealistic. The tragedy of much current discussion of these matters is that many cold-blooded considerations of military advantage for the West are taken as overruling humanitarian and political considerations, when they should be viewed as reinforcing them. There are enough genuine conflicts between these considerations without adding spurious ones.

It is not possible to maintain that a conventional limited-war capability in Europe is both militarily desirable and free. But I have tried to argue that it is militarily desirable. And additional political considerations whose treatment in any detail is beyond the scope of this chapter powerfully support this position. If a primarily non-nuclear posture even in Europe is militarily advantageous, then the moral arguments for it can be freely accepted and propagandized by the West. We need not be so anxious to put nuclear arms in hands that will especially alarm the Soviets and raise tensions needlessly. And, above all, we need not be so inhibited in proposing arms limitations and in responding to Soviet bloc proposals about them because of delusions that complete nuclear arming throughout the alliance is indispensable to our security.

CHAPTER 6

PROBLEMS OF COALITION AND DETERRENCE

BY MORTON A. KAPLAN

FROM the strictly rational point of view, NATO can persist as a going organization only if the member nations can protect their security better inside the organization than outside. Many of the factors that enter into a calculation concerning security depend upon technical considerations; and much of the information necessary to reach a correct conclusion is not in the public domain. Nonetheless, if estimates concerning these technical and military matters are considered hypothetically, it is possible to explore some of the problems that NATO faces in maintaining its cohesion.

These problems are very difficult to solve. Perhaps no good solutions are available. Much depends, of course, upon the risks that the Soviet Union is willing to run to exploit the potential divisiveness in NATO. If the Soviet Union is willing to run large risks, the most effective solution—confederation, or at least a genuinely supranational NATO military command—may prove politically infeasible (although perhaps this should not be assumed too readily). Other solutions that are more feasible, politically speaking, may not prove optimal if the Soviet Union exerts great pressure against NATO. There may be some merit, therefore, in attempting to test alternative solutions against the maximum pressure that the Soviet Union might generate.

I. PROBLEMS IN MAINTAINING THE COHESION OF NATO

In 1949, when NATO came into being, and for a number of years thereafter, the members of NATO had a greater rational interest in remaining within the organization than they did in leaving it. In the first place, the great cost to be avoided was Soviet domination. It was not considered that remaining outside NATO would reduce this threat, and to do so might have increased it. Nor, if war occurred, was it likely that having remained outside would remove a nation from the zone of hostilities. Moreover, the costs of non-nuclear war—the only kind the Soviet Union was then equipped to launch—were relatively low, as contrasted with the potential costs of nuclear war. The economic costs of contributing to NATO forces were not greatly different from the costs of independent national defense, unless a nation chose to demilitarize itself and entrust its defense entirely to others. Indeed, it could be maintained that NATO would improve the efficiency with which existing expenditures could be used for military purposes and, besides, that some of the financial burden could be shifted to the United States.

Note the difference between this situation and that of the interwar period. In the interwar period, collective defense would have required a decision to take action in the case of actual armed aggression by a dangerous nation, where the immediate threat to oneself was not clear. The situation was quite different in 1949. NATO was established in advance of the immediate act of armed attack and was designed to cover a situation that posed a diffuse threat to all its members. Only the United States was not in the immediate path of danger. Yet, since the United States was the only source of potential strength great enough to challenge the Soviet monolith, it could not attempt to shift responsibility to the European states, although it required their aid to build an effective counter-Soviet bloc.

Nuclear and, in particular, nuclear missile developments since 1949 seem to have changed the situation to such a degree that a reevaluation, even an agonizing reappraisal, of membership in NATO has become rationally appropriate for the member nations. The situation has been altered decisively by the emergence of the Soviet Union as a major nuclear power. This fact has added to the political, economic, and military difficulties that NATO faces. Entirely new classes of risks must now be run by the member nations, and their responses to Soviet challenges may depend, at least in part, upon their evaluation of these risks and their willingness to brave them.

In evaluating the alternatives available to NATO members in the nuclear age, a distinction must be made between two types of situations. One type is that in which missile and airplane bases are individually vulnerable to surprise attack. In this case, for the American deterrent to be effective, it is necessary to have more launching sites than the Soviet Union can knock out in a surprise attack—sufficiently more, in fact, to be able to inflict devastating retaliatory punishment upon the Soviet Union. If many of the facilities that can provide this margin of safety are of short or intermediate range, it will be necessary to have bases close to the Soviet Union, including bases in Europe. The second kind of situation may arise if hardness of basing or the mobility of nuclear weapons protects them against surprise attack. If, in addition, the weapons are ICBM's or long-range bombers, or are located in submarines that can cruise close to Russian shores, the need of the United States for nuclear bases in Europe will be reduced.

The first kind of situation is not unlike that which exists at present, and the second may possibly come into being sometime in the mid-1960's, depending upon technological developments. The second situation may never occur, however, if NATO cannot provide for the security of its members, including the United States, in the intermediate period. Therefore, the immediate problem for NATO is to ensure its viability in existing circumstances. This question will now be examined in its most general form.

II. The Immediate Problem for NATO

Let us assume that some fixed number of nuclear bases dispersed throughout the NATO area is required, at least for the present, to guarantee devastating retaliation even after a nuclear surprise attack by the Soviet Union. Below this fixed number, there is a declining probability of devastating retaliation. This number is also related by some direct function to the land mass of the Soviet bloc and the population and resources distributed over that land mass. Then any member nation of NATO that does not have a nuclear system of its own might infer that it could afford to refuse to permit use of its own territory for nuclear bases, provided only that dispersion of the required number of nuclear bases among the rest of the NATO nations was possible in the absence of its contribution. It would thus hope to keep itself from becoming a target in the event of all-out war between Soviet Russia and NATO, though at the risk that NATO would not protect it against nuclear blackmail or possibly even against non-nuclear attack.[1]

The argument for remaining outside the NATO nuclear system may be modified by moral and political considerations. In addition, NATO members cannot ignore a possible contagion effect—that is, the political effect upon other members' decisions of one nation's decision to remain outside the nuclear network. For instance, such a decision by England might lead to the collapse of the network, although a similar decision by Denmark probably would not. Moreover, the normal processes of political negotiation, which take place slowly and visibly, might induce most NATO members to cooperate—even

[1] For a discussion of this problem, see George W. Rathjens, Jr., "Notes on the Military Problems of Europe," *World Politics*, x, No. 2 (January 1958), pp. 182-201.

though NATO might be able to afford a particular nation's decision to remain outside the network—by holding forth collapse of the nuclear defense network as the alternative to general collaboration. And, although even this might not influence a truly irrational or stubborn nation, it might help to create a nuclear network in the face of the natural desire of individual members to shift nuclear risks to the United States and possibly some combination of other members. Yet nuclear risks do appear to be sufficiently frightening to call into question the establishment of an effective nuclear defense system, either under joint NATO control or under United States control.

III. The Relation Between the Present and the Future Problems of NATO

One inducement for the European members of NATO to cooperate with the United States in establishing nuclear bases in Europe lies in the fact that there may be a short period in which the American deterrent is not fully effective without such cooperation. This, however, involves the risk for these nations that they might become the site of nuclear war or that the Soviet Union might single them out for retaliation. If, as appears likely, the United States develops, sometime in the 1960's, an effective deterrent that is invulnerable to surprise attack and not dependent upon European bases, the European members of NATO might desire to thrust the entire burden of deterrence upon the United States. Yet, on the other hand, they might lack confidence that the United States would come to their aid at the potential cost of nuclear destruction in the United States.

The European members of NATO therefore might consider whether they are willing to run a present risk—that is, membership in either an American or a joint nuclear network—in order to reduce a possible future risk—abandonment by the United States. If, on the other hand, they can find a reasonably adequate solution for their future problems —perhaps the acquisition of independent nuclear systems—they might be willing to take the risk that the American nuclear system will deter the Soviet Union until the independent systems can be established. However, if independent nuclear systems do not really appear likely to solve the future defense problems of the other NATO members, there may be less resistance to running the present risks of membership in an American or a NATO nuclear network.

In order to explore the possibility that the United States can secure the cooperation of a sufficient number of NATO members to maintain an effective deterrent in the present period, it is necessary to examine in more detail the options open to the European members of NATO. So long as non-membership in an American or in a joint nuclear system appears to have important future advantages, the temptation to discount the present risks of non-membership will be high. Therefore, the options open to the European members of NATO must be examined for present and future advantages, with particular reference to the consideration that the present vulnerability of nuclear systems to surprise attack may not obtain in the future.

If the problem is considered systematically from the standpoint of a NATO member other than the United States, there are three general options available, within which there may be several variations. (1) It can choose to reject nuclear weapons entirely, (2) it can acquire an independent nuclear defense system, or (3) it can join some variation of a United States-NATO system.

IV. Denuclearization

The general argument for not permitting nuclear weapons on the soil of a nation has already been stated. A nation thereby reduces the danger that it will become the site of a nuclear war but increases the danger of nuclear blackmail and conventional attack. Not much more can be said about this alternative without a clear ranking of possible outcomes and a clear statement of attitudes toward risks. It could, however, be argued that this option does not genuinely reduce even the immediate risks, at least for the large European nations, if their refusal to accept nuclear weapons makes the American deterrent problematical at best. Uncertainty about the effectiveness of the American deterrent might trigger off a nuclear war, and even if a nation were not the direct object of an attack—Europe is small and the directional systems of missiles are subject to breakdown and large error—the general destructiveness of such a war might itself produce a situation nearly as dreadful. However, if all or virtually all of the European members made a joint decision to withdraw from NATO, Western Europe might be able to escape the worst consequences of missile warfare between the United States and the Soviet Union.

Some nations might choose this option on the thesis that the United States nonetheless would spring to their aid in the event of Soviet attack. However, if it were chosen by most NATO nations at a time when the independent American deterrent was not fully effective without European cooperation, the United States might not be willing to run the risk of protecting Europe against Soviet military attack. The political consequences of this state of affairs possibly might include the absorption of Western Europe into the Soviet sphere without the necessity of overt war. In this case, the danger of nuclear war would not have been eliminated completely, since, in the event of a future Soviet-American war, American nuclear weapons might fall on a Sovietized Western Europe. This, however, might seem a lesser risk; and, in any event, there would be some time discount. Moreover, the absorption of Western Europe in the Soviet sphere is not a foregone conclusion, even under the stated circumstances. Yet, it is difficult to believe that the option of denuclearization is a desirable one, except for the smallest members of NATO, which might be able to count upon American and NATO aid despite their choice of this option, if the cooperation of the large NATO members committed the United States to the defense of the general NATO area.

V. Independent Nuclear Systems

The alternative of independent nuclear systems during the intermediate period of the early 1960's has been proposed by some commentators, such as Rathjens and Kissinger, as providing the European members of NATO with the greatest protection at the least risk.[2] Such facilities—as distinguished from facilities controlled by the United States—could, of course, be used only on the decision of the nations in which they were stationed and for purposes which these nations approved.

It is questionable how effective independent European deterrents would be, either because most European members of NATO might not be able to afford maintenance costs even if the United States supplied the weapons free, or for geographic reasons. If, moreover, in the absence of supplementary bases in Europe, the American deterrent became ineffective for a critical period, it is not certain that such independent nuclear systems would provide an adequate solution during that period; in the last analysis, they would be close to the Soviet Union and vulnerable to Soviet IRBM's, and there would thus be a strong temptation not to use them. It may be argued, however, that such independent bases would be less apt to precipitate a Soviet nuclear attack than joint NATO bases, for it is unlikely that the European members of NATO would be willing to initiate nuclear war in

[2] Rathjens, op.cit.; Henry A. Kissinger, "Missiles and the Western Alliance," Foreign Affairs, xxxvi, No. 3 (April 1958), pp. 383-400.

Europe as a cheap form of defense. On the other hand, it may be argued, if a conventional war in Europe were being lost, the United States could not prevent the European members of NATO from using these weapons in self-defense. This would help to compensate for the fear that the United States might, at some future time, be willing to compromise a European war at the expense of the European members of NATO rather than risk Soviet nuclear attacks against the United States.

There are additional considerations. Thus, General Charles de Gaulle is reported to believe that French diplomacy would be considerably stronger if France possessed independent nuclear weapons. The question of the value of such weapons vis-à-vis the Soviet Union will be considered shortly. But the argument that such weapons would permit stronger diplomacy against minor states not directly connected with NATO or the Communist bloc is doubtful. One may note, for instance, that the British stockpile did little good at the time of Suez and it is doubtful that the French would risk the political costs of using tactical or strategic atomic weapons in the struggle in Algeria. Moreover, there is no inconsistency between joining a nuclear network and also having an independent stock of nuclear weapons for national policy purposes.

It has been claimed that, if individual European nations had sufficient nuclear capacity to inflict on the Soviet Union at least as much damage as they are worth to it (perhaps, more properly, at least as much damage as they are worth to some bloc other than the Soviet bloc, for these countries would after all be destroyed by nuclear war), they would have an effective deterrent against any rational Soviet nuclear attack.[3] However, the option of the independent nuclear system probably carries as much risk as either of the other alternatives in terms of the small nation's becoming the site of a nuclear war or of losing its independence.

Let us consider the option of independent nuclear systems during the period in which the nuclear weapons system would be vulnerable to surprise attack. It is quite true that the deterrent effect of the independent nuclear system might be considerable if the individual nation, even after a surprise attack by the Soviet Union, could do sufficient retaliatory damage to make the Soviet Union strategically vulnerable to an American surprise attack—in the sense that Russia would lose enough of its retaliatory capacity to inhibit its deterrent effect. That the independent capacity would be sufficiently great for this purpose, however, is quite doubtful. And, in the absence of the ability to do

[3] See Rathjens, *op.cit.*

sufficient damage after suffering a surprise attack, the problem takes on different dimensions.

Before a dispute between the Soviet Union and a small nation degenerated into warfare, bargaining would take place between two nations which face entirely different ranges of alternatives. If the threat of nuclear war is involved, one faces heavy damage and the other extinction. The one that faces extinction cannot rationally initiate a nuclear war unless it is virtually certain that such a war will ensue in any case. Moreover, the small nation, when standing alone, must face perhaps some possibility of surprise attack without ever being in a position to threaten to launch an attack of its own. And the existence of an independent nuclear system that is vulnerable to surprise attack is an open invitation to such attack or to nuclear blackmail. Indeed, possession of a vulnerable nuclear system is more likely to increase than to reduce danger. Successful blackmail might open Europe up to Soviet political penetration. To make sense, the independent nuclear system must be invulnerable to surprise; and the Soviet Union must believe the system to be invulnerable.

Suppose we project to a possible future when the independent nuclear system could be hard-based or hidden in the sea and largely invulnerable to surprise attack. Even if we then assume that the Soviet Union could not gain any advantage from a surprise attack, and that the attacked small nation could kill as many people in the Soviet Union or destroy as much in the way of resources as the small nation is worth, the deterrent effect of the independent nuclear capacity is not clear. Let us assume that the Soviet Union employs nuclear blackmail and, upon refusal of its demands, launches nuclear war. With this demonstration of its willingness to enforce its demands at the cost of nuclear retaliation, how many other small nations would be likely in the future to doubt the penalty of non-compliance? This means, of course, that by a deliberate initial sacrifice the Soviet Union could create a situation in which its future demands were quite unlikely to be opposed by small nations. In other words, the Soviet Union would take into calculation not simply the possible outcome of an individual exchange but the expected payoffs of a series of threats. On the other hand, the argument for independent nuclear systems would be stronger if these conditions were not given—that is, if the nation with its own nuclear weapons could cause sufficient damage to the Soviet Union to weaken it appreciably in relation to the United States, or if the USSR could not hope to improve its long-run position vis-à-vis the United States. This, however, is a doubtful possibility.

It may also be argued that the independent nuclear system permits the small nation to reduce the possibility of being forced into nuclear war, or that the independent nuclear capability can be used to limit the war objectives of the attacking major nation. Consider, however, the case when the Soviet Union engages in an initially non-nuclear war against the small nation. It is not clear that the independent nuclear system would reduce substantially the probability that nuclear war would take place, except under conditions that are not likely to prove comforting to the small nation.

The small nation may employ its independent nuclear system in either one of two ways in the event of war with the Soviet Union. It may use the system to launch a large-scale raid against the Soviet Union, or it may employ it in limited retaliatory raids. In either case, it is doubtful that the independent nuclear system would be very effective in limiting Soviet war aims or in limiting the means—for example, tactical nuclear weapons—employed by the Soviet Union to achieve those aims.

Large-scale use of the independent nuclear system against the Soviet Union has obvious disadvantages. Any use that approaches the maximum potential of the system presents the Soviet Union with a strong incentive to strike back in great force, since the Soviet Union already would have absorbed almost as much damage as the small nation was capable of inflicting. Thus such use would almost ensure destruction. For this reason, the threat to employ the independent nuclear system in this way is not likely to prove highly credible.

A more limited use by the small nation of its independent nuclear system, perhaps as part of a strategy of limited retaliation, would avoid the more obvious hazards of the large-scale use of such systems. But, even in this case, it may be doubted whether the advantages would outweigh the disadvantages. Limited use of the independent nuclear system would throw on the small nation the onus of initiating nuclear hostilities. The threat to break this taboo against the use of nuclear weapons might create countervailing pressures from both domestic and foreign opinion to which the small NATO member would be much more responsive than the Soviet Union. The threat would also serve to legitimize Soviet nuclear counter-retaliation.

Moreover, the Soviet Union has an advantage in the use of limited retaliation. Although it is conceivable that the threat to bomb Kharkov, for instance, might deter the Soviet Union from continued attack, the threat is not highly credible. If West Germany were at war with the USSR, would not a Soviet threat to bomb Bonn and Frankfurt in retaliation be likely to inhibit the carrying-out of the threat? It would not aid the cause of the small nation to step up the stakes by threatening to bomb Leningrad and Moscow, for the carrying-out of the threat would probably bring massive Soviet retaliation. For this reason, the threat would lack credibility. The reasonable use of limited retaliation depends, among other things, upon symmetries between the nuclear stockpiles and resource positions of the nations involved. Everything else being equal, it is not a good strategy for a relatively small nation with a limited stockpile.

The possession of an independent nuclear system cannot necessarily prevent the Soviet Union from initiating nuclear exchanges, for, if conventional warfare proves too difficult, the Soviet Union might initiate or threaten limited nuclear strikes to force surrender or at least a peace favorable to itself. The independent nuclear system is most likely to inhibit Soviet use of nuclear weapons when the Soviet Union is winning without their use. However, the small nation can achieve this fatal result even more cheaply by surrendering.

Without allies the small nation cannot win a non-nuclear war against the Soviet Union or even prevent Soviet victory. But it is also doubtful whether NATO could provide sufficient conventional support to halt a massive Soviet drive, although probing operations perhaps could be contained. Therefore, unless the United States is willing to use its deterrent to halt the Soviet Union in the case of a massive attack, the small nation gets no benefit from its independent nuclear system in this case. And if the United States is willing, the small nation does not need the independent nuclear system. Therefore, unless the additional small risk to the Soviet Union posed by the independent nuclear system deters it from attack in the first place, the system has little value.

Perhaps, however, the small nation fears a less than massive Soviet effort and desires only enough help from other nations to contain probing efforts or to deter the carrying-out of ambiguous Soviet threats. If we accept the basic premise underlying the independent nuclear system—that nations are not likely to risk nuclear warfare except in self-defense—the Soviet Union may be able to use a nuclear threat to isolate the object of its attack. Suppose, for instance, that in the event of a Soviet drive against West Germany, Russia threatened retaliatory raids against France if France sent troops to the aid of West Germany or permitted the use of its ports and transportation facilities to bring aid to West Germany. Again, if we accept the underlying premise, France is likely to depend upon its own nuclear system only in case of direct attack, to refuse to accept the risks involved in permitting the use of its ports and transportation facilities, and to advise West Germany to use its nuclear weapons to protect itself. Unless the United States could land sufficient support through German ports, effective conventional defense probably would be disrupted. This is but one instance of the kind of disruption that could occur. The more limited the Soviet aims and the more ambiguous the situation, the more easily could a conventional defense coalition be disrupted.

Perhaps, however, these events will never come to pass. The Soviet Union may be unwilling to run even low risks. Or, in the example given, France may come to see the probable end effect of an isolationist position and recognize a need to run a nuclear risk rather than to allow the Soviet Union to get away with its game of divide and conquer. But these are not substantial reasons for installing independent nuclear systems.

The independent system does not have great deterrent power and, if its adoption reduces even slightly the probability that the American deterrent will be used, the net deterrent effect of NATO defenses might be reduced. The adoption of an independent nuclear system does not increase the probability that other nations will supply conventional support in time of war, and, for political and psychological reasons, it may decrease the probability. Therefore, unless the independent nuclear system is the only alternative to complete lack of nuclear protection that the small nation has, this alternative is not very convincing.

Finally, one wonders how public opinion would bear up if smaller nations acquired independent nuclear weapons and withdrew from the alliance. Once the isolationist position of installing independent nuclear defense systems were adopted, the paralysis of governmental policy might increase at a rapid rate. Lonely, isolated, suspicious, and threatened with extinction, the Western European nations might thus well become subject to external blackmail and internal corruption and subversion.

VI. Combined Independent and Joint Nuclear Systems

The solution of combining the independent nuclear system with membership in a joint nuclear network is not greatly superior to the solution of independent nuclear systems. If the small nation can get sufficient American or other NATO support to hold off the attack, it does not need its independent nuclear system; if it cannot get such support, the system has doubtful utility for reasons made clear previously. The risk that Soviet use of tactical nuclear weapons or extensive Soviet war aims would set off retaliation from the joint system might deter the Soviet Union. But, again, it is doubtful that the independent system increases the Soviet risk substantially. However, the small nation may reason that the real deterrent effect of this solution stems from the fact that the use of its independent system may trigger the joint system, although, in the absence of this triggering, NATO would be willing to provide only conventional or tactical nuclear support.

Suppose a NATO member does attempt to pull the trigger in this fashion. If both independent and jointly controlled bases are in the territory of the nation from which a nuclear strike is fired, the Soviet Union cannot easily distinguish whether the attack came from the independent or from the joint system. Thus, it may be reasoned, in anticipation of a Soviet response that necessarily must be directed against the entire NATO system, the United States must permit the American or NATO system to be fired pre-emptively. If this assumption were accepted, an independent nuclear system in conjunction with a joint system would ensure the support of the general deterrent system and thus relieve the fear of appeasement by the United States. Moreover, since the Soviet response must be directed at the entire nuclear network and not just at the single independent system, the damage to the nation that unleashes general nuclear war might be limited, particularly if few bases were located in its territory. (Indeed, this would be an incentive to enter a joint system but to accept only a minimal number of bases, whether joint or independent, within national territory.)

If only one European member of NATO had such an independent nuclear system, it might have much to gain—although perhaps the United States would view the development with a jaundiced eye. If, however, all members of NATO had independent nuclear systems as well as bases belonging to a joint network in their national territory, there would be many fingers on many triggers—all capable of setting off general nuclear war under undefined circumstances. (If the circumstances under which the bases were to be used could be defined and agreed upon and the agreement policed, there would be no need for independent nuclear systems.) It is difficult to believe that the members of NATO would feel very secure in this kind of world or in a world where, even in the absence of a joint network, all the nations possessed submarine-launched missiles that might unleash general nuclear war. This solution protects against some risks but creates others that might be worse.

The Soviet Union might prove reluctant to initiate military hostilities in such a world, but it might also find that world so uncomfortable to live in that it would have an incentive to manufacture an incident that would justify a demand for the dismantling of the independent systems.[4] Indeed, it might even obtain support from European and American public opinion for such a move. The end effect might be the neutralization—and perhaps the Sovietization—of Europe.

Actually, however, the possibility of triggering general nuclear war is high only when both the American and the Soviet systems are highly vulnerable to surprise attack. If the Soviet system alone were vulnerable, it might not dare to attack in force; and if the American or joint system alone were vulnerable, the Soviet Union might carry out a counterforce strategy and then offer terms. If both systems were relatively invulnerable, the Soviet Union might simply launch a retaliatory or counterforce attack limited to the nation from which the first attack originated, rather than launch a massive attack that would lead to mutual suicide. If this last possibility turns out to be the case, the American or NATO system might not be triggered by the attack. Indeed, having resorted to nuclear war against the advice and desire of its allies, the small nation might harvest only ill will rather than nuclear support. Since, however, the assumptions on which these projections are made are not necessarily correct, it is conceivable that this display of valor or rashness (depending upon how one looks at it) might mobilize nuclear support, particularly if the impact of the use of nuclear weapons broke down the psychological barriers to their use, or created fears concerning possible Soviet responses, or changed American estimates of the scope of the stakes. Yet one can hardly consider these possibilities to be strong arguments for the adoption of the independent nuclear system, even when allied to a joint NATO system. Nor is it likely that the deterrent effect of this system upon the Soviet Union would be greater than that of an American or NATO system alone.

VII. DIFFICULTIES OF A JOINT NATO SYSTEM

If it is agreed that the options of no nuclear defense and of independent nuclear systems are very risky, the only remaining alternative to simple reliance upon the American deterrent is a joint NATO system.

[4] This point was discussed by Herman Kahn at the Princeton Conference on NATO strategy.

However, this solution also raises grave problems with respect both to its adoption and to its implementation. The difficulties of adoption have already been analyzed. Each member of NATO, except the United States, has an interest in shifting the potential costs of nuclear defense to the United States and perhaps some combination of the remaining NATO nations.

Even if the obstacles to instituting a joint system were overcome, it might prove difficult to implement that system. The fact that basically even the NATO system rests upon independent nations—especially the United States and, to a lesser extent, Great Britain—lies at the source of the difficulty. And the fact that, under NATO, the nation remains the locus of decision-making permits the concentration of a threat upon a particular member of NATO in a way not possible with respect to smaller political units within a nation. It would do little good to threaten New Jersey with extinction if it did not withdraw from the American nuclear defense network. United States military decisions are made by the national government and not by the states. Moreover, national decision-making is reinforced by ties of national solidarity which, at this juncture in world history, still constitute by far the strongest ties of any type of organized social grouping.

NATO, however, is not characterized by such strong solidarity or by fully integrated organizational ties. Therefore, by concentrating its threats on a single nation within NATO, the Soviet Union can create some of the same problems for a member that it can for a nation with an independent nuclear system. The exposed nation would still be threatened with extinction. However, this time the nuclear network would be alerted and might attack; therefore, the Soviet Union must also contemplate the possibility of its own extinction. Moreover, should war break out, the Soviet Union would have no strategic reason to concentrate its fire on the nation it threatened initially. Since the attack might come from any or all elements of the network, general strategic considerations would enter into Soviet calculations. This obviously diminishes the ability of the Soviet Union to concentrate its threat upon individual members of the nuclear network and—irrational considerations apart—diminishes greatly its ability to take advantage of the responsiveness within the nuclear network system to the demands of frightened public opinion or the desire to escape the common hazards of an effective alliance system.

If collective nuclear defense is the only alternative, and the United States controls the nuclear network system, Europeans might fear that that system would not be used in case of local war in order to spare the continental United States the danger of nuclear retaliation. If this concern were realistic, the possibility of successful blackmail would again be raised. On the other hand, if individual nations had control over the nuclear facilities within their borders, several difficulties would arise. In this case, the United States might fear that the nuclear system would be used for some local purpose for which it was unwilling to risk nuclear war. If a serial arrangement—such that facilities within one NATO nation are always under the control of another member of the alliance—were employed, this might raise the fear that the weapons would be misused for an insufficient purpose and that retaliation would take place against the unoffending nation within whose borders the weapons were based. If unanimous agreement were required before the network could be used, the possibilities of blackmail, irrational decisions, and paralysis would arise in an extremely serious form. If some modified and weighted majority voting system were used, these dangers would be reduced, but the chance of delay and ultimate paralysis would remain serious. Modern war situations may develop much too rapidly for such decisions to be subjected to a debate and voting process and, in any event, the wounds which divisiveness over such a decision might inflict would hardly be helpful in the conduct of war. Whatever disagreement there might be about any decision of this sort, to debate the matter at the time of conflict—even in secret— would surely be unfortunate.

A collective European system, only loosely related to a United States system, might eliminate some of these problems, but it would not do away with all of them. Moreover, if such a system did not have the ability to destroy the Soviet Union after a Soviet attack, the problem of blackmail would arise again in a very serious form. Europe is small in land mass and, at least at the present time, vulnerable to intermediate-range weapons. Group self-reliance under existing conditions might well increase fears that the United States would not spring to Europe's aid in time of conflict or might even lead Europe to increase its efforts to avoid involvement in a Soviet-American conflict. At best, a collective European deterrent, operating alone, is likely to be tenuous. Should successful blackmail of a single member of the network occur—a not unlikely possibility—the entire system might well collapse. Therefore, the problem of protecting Western Europe with an independent European deterrent remains very grave.

So long as the chief fear of the European members of NATO is the fear of involvement in nuclear war, they are unlikely to accept any joint

NATO system that might involve them in such a war against their will or for reasons they consider inadequate. It would seem that the formation of a joint NATO system depends upon a willingness to run nuclear risks and upon a reasonable guarantee that the system would run these risks only under circumstances that are agreed upon in advance. Thus a rationale must be provided for nuclear risks and the strategy based on this rationale must invoke these risks only under circumstances acceptable to the members of NATO.

VIII. The Limited Reprisal Strategy

The strategy of limited reprisal can provide a rationale for a joint NATO nuclear system. This, however, is not a sufficient rationale. A joint NATO system is not a good in itself. The limited retaliation strategy must also be adequate to the military problem of defending Europe against possible Soviet attack and it must do this at a reasonable level of risk.

The great attraction of a strategy of limited conventional war in Europe is that it does not seem to involve the huge risks of nuclear war. And, although a limited war strategy might not have the deterrent effect of massive retaliation, it can at least be employed at a cost that may seem acceptable. There are several reasons, however, why the strategy of limited war does not solve NATO's problem. NATO does not possess the conventional forces that can halt a massive Soviet attack, nor does it seem likely that the political conditions for raising such forces are likely to come into being in the next few years. Neither is there good reason to believe that NATO has a long-term advantage in the use of tactical nuclear weapons. NATO might be able to contain a Soviet probing effort. Indeed, it is valuable to have forces that can do this, for, in the absence of such forces, the Soviet Union might learn at little cost that the threat of massive retaliation is a bluff. (Of course, if the threat were not a bluff, the consequences also might be highly undesirable.) And the losing side in a European conflict might unleash nuclear war under uncontrollable conditions.

If the NATO forces do hold in the event of either massive or limited Soviet attack, the Soviet Union might employ nuclear blackmail to disrupt the NATO defense. One may not believe that the Soviet Union is likely to run this risk, but the possibility cannot be excluded. In this case, resort to massive retaliation remains to be considered. If one considers the probability that conventional NATO forces would not contain a conventional Soviet attack, that the Soviet Union might resort to nuclear threats if they did, and that limited war might give rise to unlimited nuclear war, the adequacy of the strategy of limited war becomes subject to serious doubt. One may ask whether there is not an alternative to limited war and massive retaliation. There is, provided that one is willing to accept the view that the potential costs of defense need not be related directly to the immediate value of the stakes of war, without consideration of future consequences. Indeed, it is precisely a failure to take this point of view that may permit the Soviet Union to exploit the organizational weakness of NATO.

Ordinary common sense might take the view that a particular stake of war is not worth defending if the costs of war would be obviously higher than the value of the immediate stake. This view had more plausibility in the nineteenth century—when there were many large nations with relatively equal military capabilities, and no group of nations had the cohesion of the Communist bloc—than it has at present, when, for practical purposes, only the United States and the Soviet Union have the capacity of major nuclear powers. In the nineteenth century, two nations at war with each other had to be cautious lest they so deplete their resources that a third nation could achieve a decisive advantage. If the NATO nations, however, were to accept the dictum that they could not pay more to defend a stake of war than the immediate, direct worth of the stake, the Soviet Union would have an incentive to make modest demands, the ultimate consequences of which would be ambiguous, and to back up these demands with large concentrations of military force and possibly also with nuclear threats. The acceptance of such demands would probably increase the Soviet incentive to make future demands. This clarifies the fallacy of any simple equation of the cost of defense and the value of the immediate stakes of war; it does not take into account future consequences, perhaps discounted because of future uncertainties. And one must also take into consideration the political and moral consequences of appeasement or surrender.

This does not imply that NATO must suffer eventual defeat if, on any particular occasion, it fails to resist a modest Soviet demand. But, unless there is some important reason for accepting the Soviet demand other than a fear of the military consequences, it is probably best to reject that demand. Indeed, a failure to respond strongly may only entrap the Soviet Union into taking future large risks that have unfortunate consequences for everyone.

If one is persuaded that an effective defense is necessary, regardless of the relation of potential costs to the immediate value of the stakes, one still must find some acceptable way to mount this effective defense. Massive retaliation does not commend itself, for obvious reasons. If adequate conventional forces are available, one may prefer to use these, provided the Soviet Union does not introduce nuclear weapons, rather than to take the risk that nuclear weapons, once used, may be used in an unlimited fashion. If, however, as appears likely, NATO will not have sufficient conventional forces to hold a massive Soviet attack, or to retake, for instance, a seized Scandinavian island like Bornholm, a different strategy may have to be employed. This may also prove to be the case if the Soviet Union attempts to use a nuclear threat to disrupt the conventional defense necessary to contain a probing operation.

A possible solution to this problem may lie in a strategy of limited nuclear reprisals, designed to communicate the unacceptable costs of continued war. A series of initially small or token raids against the Soviet Union or Soviet external resources might make credible the willingness of NATO to risk extensive costs to prevent defeat and might convince the Soviet Union that the costs of continued war would be unacceptably high.

Whether this strategy of limited retaliation can be employed reasonably depends upon the existence of certain strategic symmetries. If we assume that the retaliatory forces of both NATO and the Soviet bloc can survive a surprise attack, either because the deterrent forces are relatively invulnerable to attack or because there are too many bases to be knocked out in a single surprise attack, neither side can afford massive attack. Moreover, the ability of both sides to continue limited reprisals is symmetric, so that each side can reduce the resources of the other symmetrically. Carried to its conclusion, this process of retaliation would destroy both sides. There is at least some reason to believe that if war is forced to a level at which neither side can gain an advantage, and if neither side can force the war to a different level, a *status quo ante* solution would seem reasonable to both. This reasoning is reinforced by the fact that if either side were able successfully to insist on solutions more favorable than the *status quo ante*, it would gain eventual victory. And, if either side were to adopt the practice of agreeing to less favorable terms than the *status quo ante*, it would eventually lose. Therefore, if the intention to insist upon a *status quo* solution is communicated credibly, there are strong practical reasons for quick agreement upon the *status quo*. These considerations, however, make it clear that limited retaliation is not a good strategy for a small nation with a limited nuclear stockpile.

The great obstacle to agreement on a *status quo* solution when the strategy of limited retaliation is used lies in the difficulty of communicating credibly a willingness to continue to employ retaliatory attacks until war is called off. The threat of limited retaliatory attacks, however, is more credible than the threat of massive retaliation, because it does not involve the immediate danger of suicide. The threat of limited retaliation is also more credible if it is made before the enemy can establish his threat, for a failure to carry out one's threat when the stated conditions for employment apply involves the additional penalty of an exposed bluff. If the aggressor, in the absence of this threat, can shift this potential cost to himself by threatening nuclear retaliation if his demands are not met, he gives himself an additional reason not to back down. Therefore, the timing of the threat is important.

If the threat of limited retaliation must be carried out, a wide range of potential targets is available. The targets chosen in any actual case depend upon the nature of the situation. For instance, a minor Soviet probing operation might be met by a demand to withdraw and by a strike against a few Soviet ships at sea if the demand were not accepted. A more serious Soviet thrust might be met by a limited strike at Soviet oil fields. If the Soviet Union continued to be obdurate, eventually a small Soviet city might be hit, although warning should be sent to permit evacuation. Every effort should be made to avoid inflamed passions, but the Soviet Union cannot be permitted a sanctuary from which it can complete its aggression successfully. It must be admitted, however, that if the scale of attack begins to include cities, matters are nearly out of hand.

In the meantime, it cannot be assumed that the Soviet Union would merely continue its conventional offensive without responding to the limited retaliatory strikes. It might not really credit the willingness of NATO to continue its limited strikes or to increase their scope, believing instead that a counterstrike of limited proportions would soon call a halt to this activity. It might utterly misunderstand the rationale of the policy. Or it might decide to play on the organizational weakness of NATO and direct its counter-retaliatory strikes against specific members of the alliance rather than against NATO as a group. These difficulties are inherent in the nature of the situation; the last, in particular, is inherent in the nature of NATO. However, these considerations do not seem to outweigh the others that support the adoption of a strategy of limited retaliation.

IX. LIMITED RETALIATION AND A JOINT NATO SYSTEM

The advantages of a strategy of limited retaliation might be agreed upon; even so, this might not suffice to bring about a joint NATO system—in which case, the problem of creating an adequate deterrent would still be unsolved. It must be possible to combine the strategy with criteria for its application in such a way that it is plausible to ask the European members of NATO, as well as the United States, to trust its execution to NATO. Since NATO is unlikely in the near future to develop effective supranational political powers over the NATO governments, it would almost necessarily have to be the NATO military authorities to whom the execution of the strategy was entrusted.

To entrust NATO military, rather than political, authorities with the employment of nuclear weapons would not be as radical a departure from existing practice as it might at first appear, since the existing political controls over SAC's use of nuclear weapons may be less stringent than we have public reason to believe. Despite official statements to the contrary, it is difficult to believe that SAC commanders would not be permitted to unleash nuclear weapons without the prior consent of the United States government. The United States probably would be excessively vulnerable to surprise Soviet attack if SAC did not have the power of decision under certain circumstances.

Initial use by the Soviet Union of nuclear weapons probably would satisfy the criteria under which SAC is permitted to act. The criteria in the limited reprisal strategy could be satisfied either by Soviet nuclear attack or by failure on the part of the Soviet Union or a satellite to withdraw its military forces behind a defined border after a declaratory warning. Although this latter criterion could be made almost as clear as that under which SAC probably operates now, the provocation or urgency of the situation might not be considered as great. But even if this were true, the automaticity of the response is an essential factor in its workability. Moreover, the limited retaliation response, unlike the response to which SAC is probably at present committed, does not involve the same high immediate costs. The clarity of the suggested criteria for employment of the strategy of limited retaliation makes it possible to trust its execution to a supranational military command.

It is important to note that the NATO members gain an advantage from committing themselves to this strategy before the Soviet Union can particularize its counterthreats against any individual member. They ensure themselves of defense by both conventional and nuclear forces, if necessary. Yet the nuclear component would not be unleashed unless the Soviet Union, or one of its satellites, used nuclear weapons itself or refused to withdraw to a historically recognized boundary. Moreover, the Soviet Union could no longer gain an advantage from particularizing its threat, since a supranational military command controlling NATO weapons and bases would implement the strategy nonetheless, and in such a way that the Soviet Union must suffer costs without compensating gains. Thus, by joining the system, the NATO members protect themselves against their own susceptibility to blackmail.

There is a risk that the Soviet Union still might test the situation by a limited nuclear counter-reprisal before recognizing the credibility of the threat. This potential cost cannot be ruled out, but it must be weighed against the other advantages that stem from adoption of the limited reprisal strategy. Moreover, this potential cost is diffuse when the strategy is adopted; even if one thought that some Soviet counter-retaliatory act were likely in case the strategy of limited retaliation had to be carried out, the large number of potential targets and the ambiguity of an undefined future situation would make it easy to believe that counter-retaliation would be applied against someone else. In addition there is the possibility, even though we may not consider it rational, that the Soviet Union might respond by launching a massive nuclear attack. But this possibility seems to exist in the case of any strategy except that of surrender, and there is little information on which to quote relative odds for individual strategies.

It is an incidental advantage of a joint NATO limited retaliation strategy that nuclear bases in Europe would not be likely to invite Soviet attack even in the present period, when they are highly vulnerable to surprise attack. This is not true so long as their use is considered to be restricted to a massive retaliatory function; in that case, as a consequence of their vulnerability, they could be used only as part of a first-strike and not as part of a second-strike force—thus providing an incentive for a Soviet surprise attack. Even though their saturation in a surprise attack would invoke retaliation against the Soviet Union from that remainder of the American or NATO network which, by assumption, could not be eliminated in a surprise strike, nevertheless the reduction of the retaliatory striking force of NATO might be considered desirable by the Soviet Union in the event of war or serious crisis. However, given the adoption of a limited retaliatory strategy by NATO, this cost would probably be considered too high by the Soviet Union. This conclusion is reinforced by the fact that the European nations probably would be unwilling to trigger a Soviet massive counterattack by using European IRBM's in a massive attack when a quite acceptable alternative strategy like limited retaliation was available to them. For this reason, the installation of nuclear bases in Europe, as part of a joint NATO limited retaliatory strategy, does not increase substantially the probability of Europe's becoming the site of a large-scale nuclear attack in the present period, when these bases are highly vulnerable to surprise attack, and it would serve substantially to decrease the probability of war. Finally, if joint NATO bases in some future period were to become highly invulnerable to surprise attack and were possibly located outside Europe—perhaps in the sea—even this risk to Europe of becoming the site of nuclear war might be reduced substantially.

Note that there is greater reason to transfer effective supranational powers to NATO when adopting a strategy of limited retaliation than if either the strategy of massive retaliation or that of limited war were under consideration. The strategy of massive retaliation is fine if it actually deters the Soviet Union. The possibility, however, that it would have to be carried out might inhibit some NATO members from permitting NATO to involve them in the consequences of the strategy without their explicit consent at the time of decision. The members of NATO might be willing to allow the NATO command the authority to fight a limited war in their behalf. But many members would desire the right to veto a decision to resort to nuclear weapons if the war were going poorly, or they might desire the right to withdraw in case the Soviet Union used nuclear blackmail against them. Thus, so long as the prospect of nuclear involvement is so fearsome, the transfer of supranational powers to NATO is not likely to prove effective. If, however, the rationale of the strategy of limited retaliation were accepted—with its clear definition of the conditions under which and the purposes for which nuclear weapons would be employed—many of the barriers to the transfer of power of decision to the NATO military command would be removed. Thus, although the transfer of supranational powers to NATO would facilitate the employment of *any* strategy by NATO, the strategy of limited retaliation would provide the most effective rationale for such a transfer of power.

X. OTHER PROBLEMS OF THE JOINT NATO SYSTEM

One must recognize that even a strategy of limited retaliation implemented by a joint NATO system would not be adequate in situations like that of Berlin, where NATO might have to make the first overt military move, since the clearly defined criteria that permit operation of the strategy do not cover a case as ambiguous as this. But no strategy can solve this case easily. Consultation undoubtedly would be necessary before any response could be organized, and this again would permit the Soviet Union to exploit the potential divisiveness of NATO. Let us suppose, however, that the decision were made to abandon Berlin—bad in its consequences as this decision would probably be. In this case, one advantage stemming from the prior adoption by NATO of a limited retaliatory strategy is that the implications of this move for potential defenses, where the criteria for their employment apply, would not necessarily be highly dangerous to the morale of NATO; whereas, if a strategy of this kind is not adopted, surrender in the case of Berlin might seem to imply that NATO would surrender in the face of other Soviet threats made under less ambiguous circumstances.

Some problems will also remain in regard to extra-NATO considerations. Europe would hesitate to invoke an automatic strategy of this sort in other troubled areas of the world, and, in any event, the primary difficulties in most of these cases are political, so that military solutions would be inappropriate. Two expedients can be adopted for extra-NATO problems. The first and simplest—although not the most expeditious—is consultation. The second, which follows almost automatically from the detachment of NATO from other American commitments, is the separation of the NATO nuclear system from other parts of the American nuclear system. The major question that arises in this case is whether the United States would have an adequate deterrent apart from the NATO system. Eventually, with solid-fueled ICBM's and Polaris missiles launched from submarines, the United States may indeed have an adequate, independent system of deterrence, but there may very well be an intermediate period in which the American power of deterrence elsewhere in the world is in doubt.

The situation, however, is somewhat different than it first appears. This difference is both advantageous and disadvantageous. The American deterrent is stronger than it seems, because Soviet counter-reprisals against the United States would very likely bring the NATO system into play for defensive reasons, since the European NATO deterrent would probably not be effective if extensive damage were done to the independent American nuclear system. This very fact, however, constitutes a potential danger from the European point of view, and may somewhat inhibit European willingness to join a nuclear deterrence network with the United States. But the problem is not completely obdurate. National decision-makers are likely to realize that the very effectiveness of the deterrent system will make its use improbable. Indeed, European decision-makers might well be concerned lest the United States develop an effective deterrence system, independent of European bases, before the other member nations of NATO opt for a joint system. In this case, they might seriously fear the rise of American isolationism and the abandonment of Europe by the United States, which might wish to avoid the risks of intercontinental nuclear war.

Such fears may persist even though the question of whether NATO is desirable only as a temporary instrument for American strategy or whether the NATO system has a longer-range function in the American system deserves only one answer—namely, that the American interest in the security of Western Europe is an abiding interest. Even from a strictly military point of view, to fail to defend an area as defensible as Europe would cast serious doubt upon any defense short of the continental United States. And such a state of affairs would greatly increase the costs of employing the limited reprisal strategy, and also would greatly increase the probability of a misunderstanding that would lead to total nuclear war. The United States therefore cannot voluntarily omit Europe from its network in the future unless it is prepared to retreat into hemispheric or even continental isolation.

It is not necessary to belabor the reasons why such a decision would be undesirable from the American point of view. Even if one conceded the proposition that the American continent is large enough—together with submarines and other novel means of attack—to provide an effective deterrent to the Soviet Union, the fact is that international politics is not bounded merely by military considerations. Political and economic factors, and, above all, cultural values and moral obligations weigh heavily in the balance.

CHAPTER 7

NATO AND NUCLEAR SHARING

BY A. L. BURNS

WE shall seek to determine the feasibility and possible consequences of the following line of NATO policy: The Western
nuclear powers promise "big deterrents" to the individual NATO
allies (or, where appropriate, to groups of them), at the same time
guaranteeing them efficient nuclear support, both strategic and tactical,
against Soviet blackmail until nuclear weapon-systems adequate to
redeem the promise to share are available—all upon condition that the
allies begin allocating larger conventional forces (required for the preventing of limited Soviet aggression) to a joint NATO command. Possible effects of this policy will be considered at first generally, and
then as they might occur during three periods: (1) from the present
until the opening of the expected "gap" (that is, Soviet predominance
in long-range nuclear striking forces); (2) the time of the gap; and (3)
the post-gap period. Beyond this, further epochs of changing military
technology are doubtless to be expected, each tending to create a new
political situation. But we shall conclude our critique of nuclear sharing in NATO at the third stage when, as we shall suppose, at least
the USSR and the United States can readily produce retaliatory weapon-
systems, highly protected and likely to deter strategic attack.

Only one of the possible forms of nuclear sharing is here discussed.[1]
Others would include the gift by the United States of retaliatory strategic nuclear systems (or the nuclear warheads for the allies' own
solid-fueled IRBM's[2]) to the rest of NATO jointly, or to Continental

---

[1] For examinations of nuclear sharing in various forms, see George W. Rathjens,
Jr., "Notes on the Military Problems of Europe," *World Politics*, x, No. 2 (January
1958), pp. 182-201; M. W. Hoag, Memo. #144, in *Fourth Rand Political Exercise*, ed.
by E. W. Schnitzer, May 25, 1956, pp. 301-7; Roger Hilsman, "The Devolution of
Responsibility," in *East-West Negotiations*, ed. by Arnold Wolfers, Washington Center
of Foreign Policy Research, 1958, pp. 19-28; Paul H. Nitze, "An Alternative Nuclear
Policy as a Base for Negotiations," *ibid.*, pp. 28-38; *Report on the Present State of
European Security*, submitted to the Assembly of Western European Union, 4th
Ordinary Session, June 2, 1958, by the Committee on Defense Questions and Arma-
ments (hereinafter referred to as *Present State*); Richard S. Leghorn, "The Problem
of Accidental War," *Bulletin of the Atomic Scientists*, xiv, No. 6 (June 1958), pp.
205-10; Henry A. Kissinger, "Nuclear Testing and the Problem of Peace," *Foreign
Affairs*, xxxvii, No. 1 (October 1958), pp. 1-18; and Townsend Hoopes, "Overseas
Bases in American Strategy," *ibid.*, pp. 69-82.

[2] See the *New York Times*, January 13, 1959, p. 14, col. 5.

NATO without Britain; agreements by the United States to share strategic systems with NATO allies or other Western European nations severally and without condition; and distribution of tactical nuclear weapons by the United States. We should have to examine each of these alternatives separately if we were asked to choose between any of them and the sharing policy here under review. I am not of course committed to advocating the latter, either as the best form of sharing or as the best course in general open to NATO. Indeed, I would prefer a closer confederation of the NATO allies or, better still, some measure of arms control. It is partly as a lever in bargaining for these last alternatives that one might value the West's avowal of the policy we are to discuss.

The "big deterrent" systems to be promised the NATO allies are here thought of as designed to give any ally threatened with or subjected to a Soviet "first strike" the means of retaliating against the Soviet economy to an extent unacceptable to the Kremlin in any of the circumstances that might tempt Russia thus to strike first.[3] There-

[3] To determine this "extent" concretely for any particular ally's case, one would need both a great deal of military information, mostly classified, and also a willingness to trust one's intuitions as to what the Kremlin would consider unacceptable. Most writers on this subject have therefore chosen to represent the problem by means of calculi, sometimes in terms of game-theory, and always, one feels, more general and rationalistic than the situation justifies. Mr. Rathjens, for instance, ingeniously produces and then derides the "paradoxical conclusion that the weapon-requirements of a small state are greater if it has allies than if it does not" (*op.cit.*, p. 189). Game-theorists, similarly, have characterized the choice of arms that confront small NATO powers as a decision between options to play alternative series of games. Such approaches illuminate the facts as interpretative caricatures of the economic and strategic elements in all such choice today, and of the strongly determining influence exercised by apparently minor differences in the performance of weapon systems. Otherwise, the notion of "applying" game-theory or most of the other types of formal calculi to these situations of choice seems far-fetched.

Consider, for example, a NATO country such as Holland confronting the USSR, in a world where the United States and the United Kingdom dispose of nuclear weapons. Can the Netherlands and the Soviet Union then be said to have optimizable choices between alternative series of games? There seem to be three sorts of reasons why they cannot.

First, recommendations for an optimum strategy must be absolutely general—that is, irrespective of the idiosyncrasies of the contestants. But to ignore idiosyncrasies would be to deprive oneself of information, singular as to logical quantity, which might be highly relevant to the situation under study. We are contemplating Holland and Russia in the world as it is, not x and y in some finite schema.

Secondly, to designate a possible sequence of events as a series of games is to presuppose, among other things, (1) that the sequence comprises all the features in any way relevant to its own evaluation, and (2) that if more than one final outcome is possible, the complete array of probabilities of the alternative outcomes is known. These conditions are never met—not even when we consider playing an actual series of games! I consider an offer to gamble a dollar on each of three successive tosses of a coin which I believe to be unbiased. It would seem that I can discriminate, among offers of odds, between those that would be fair, and those that would favor or would disadvantage me. Yet I may recognize the possibility of other outcomes for which I could not even

fore the size and forms of weapons suitable to fulfill the promise must depend upon the whole complex of power-relationships obtaining, at the time of fulfillment, between the nations that by then belong to the nuclear club, as well as upon the adequacy of the stocks which the United States and the United Kingdom then dispose of. (Until further notice, we shall refer to the United States only, as the more powerful.) Should the United States have then regained power to deny the Soviet Union, by an American first strike, all hope of being able to retaliate effectively—that is, should the United States have regained a full "counterforce capability"—then each NATO member due to receive strategic nuclear weapons would require them only in the quantity and disposition and of the type that would rationally preclude Russia's initiating against the ally any strategic nuclear attack less heavy than would amply justify the United States' launching a first and conclusive strike against Russia's own strategic forces. We shall say that an ally possessing such strategic nuclear weapons would have a "triggering" deterrent. If, however, East and West are in a relationship of nuclear parity—if the United States could hardly expect to achieve more than stalemate by striking first at Russia, but could also be sure for its own part of easily forcing stalemate were Russia to strike first—then each NATO ally would need to be given, as its deterrent capability, retaliatory forces so thoroughly protected, of such penetrative and hitting power, and in such numbers, that even though Soviet forces were to strike the ally first and hard, the Kremlin would still have to reckon

---

guess the probabilities—for instance, that our games will be raided by the police, or that my opponent would abscond were he to win on the first or on the second toss. We *make* such gaming situations "rational" by discounting such real possibilities, which may be relevant to the evaluation of the series of games but are outside its formal properties; and thus game-theory is applicable to the playing of games, and even to some economic and strategic situations in which we are prepared similarly to discount. But it is "irrational" to ignore real possibilities in power politics.

Even if that were not so, the current possibility of nuclear annihilation introduces a third bar against game-theoretical analysis of the Netherlands-USSR type of situation. It is a requirement of such analysis that some finite though very small probability of the worst possible outcome shall be preferred to the near-certainty of some rather disliked alternative outcome. But when the worst possible outcome may be destruction of the planet, one cannot say that it would not be rational to reprobate that preference (cf. Pascal on the rationality of avoiding any chance, however small, of hell-fire!).

Because of all this, I cannot see the Dutch, in their deliberations whether to seek their own big deterrent, being helped at all by Mr. Rathjens' "particularly simple" definition of the offensive capability they would need: "The small state must have sufficient retaliatory capability to inflict a level of damage on the adversary equal to the residual value of the small nation to its large-nation adversary after the conflict" (*ibid.*, p. 184). The "residual value" would have meaning only if Russia might H-bomb Holland and everything else remain the same. Khrushchev himself would be hard put to it to set a number opposite that value.

with the prospect of losing, through the ally's retaliation, more of its economy than the destruction of the ally and any consequent increase of world-power could compensate for. This is what we shall mean by an ally's "(completely) independent deterrent." Though bare East-West parity would rule out the possibility of equipping NATO allies with triggering deterrents, America's recovery of a counterforce capability would, conversely, enable it to provide either the independent or the triggering variety, as should seem best.

Between the extremes of full United States counterforce capability and East-West parity, a gamut of power-ratios favorable to the West is possible. The nearer the counterforce extreme, the less independent of underwriting by the United States would the allies' deterrent forces need to be. But were the power-ratio to change greatly and come to favor Russia, the whole of NATO would find itself in a new and uncomfortable situation. This is now known as the "gap."

Such a position of Western inferiority would not imply that all types of nuclear sharing had become pointless, or even that nuclear forces developed without American aid by European nations would have no power to deter. High-confidence deterrents (for example, those discussed in the previous paragraph above) would indeed be precluded—even for the United States, and especially if there obtained, against an America-based SAC, some second-strike disparity produced by very superior Russian air defenses. In such a case, the Continental allies' limited resources and proximity to the Soviet homeland might give them, paradoxically, certain deterrent advantages. For instance, it has been suggested that British and Continental allies might acquire IRBM's, unalert and kept in protected stores, as insurance against nuclear blackmail of individual NATO members. Such forces would be usable only in a first strike of restricted effect. Therefore there would be no temptation for their controllers to employ them except as a very last resort; and since in any case such forces could not alone win a war against Russia, they probably would not much provoke her. But she could not be sure that to destroy them by nuclear bombing would not trigger the United States to a pre-emptive strike. One way of enhancing the credibility of the triggering effect would be to let the Kremlin know that those IRBM's, if used at all, would strike at Soviet air bases.

Against all such low-confidence measures, many of us would object that any increase in national security they might afford would be purchased with an increase in the number of human lives put at risk. But, as we suggest below, some NATO allies may try to develop their own low-confidence deterrents, partly to enable them to bargain with the United States for better weapon-systems.

The repercussions, the date and duration, the nature, causes, and existence of a gap are all matters of current debate. No one, however, appears to deny that in the fields of research and development the missile-weaponry of the USSR has progressed further than has the West's. We shall call this a "development gap." Should Eastern and Western technologies remain on more or less equal terms, the bridging of a development gap could take many years. It could, moreover, allow "production gaps" (that is, failures to produce enough of this available missile) to open up from time to time. Though the latter might be closed more readily—for example, through Western crash programs—they would tend immediately to shift the balance of world military power.

Eighteen months ago, it was possible to forecast a production gap for January 1959, on the grounds that by then the USSR would have an unmatched force of IRBM's, and also some ICBM's. Fears about the IRBM's were expressed in Congress long before the first Soviet claim to have launched an intercontinental rocket. But the possibility of so early a lag in production now seems to have been generally discounted. Concern is now focused on the period 1962-1964.[4] It is admitted on all sides[5] that the engines of Soviet missiles have greater thrust than those of the United States. The Russians' initial-guidance systems may also be the better—in putting satellites into orbit they seem to have succeeded more brilliantly, and from more taxing locations. Greater engine-thrust permits a larger thermonuclear payload (note, however, that Western achievements in "miniaturizing" the non-explosive parts of the warhead should contribute to the same effect). A better guidance-system increases accuracy. These Russian successes with accuracy and payload have a strategic significance beyond what may be suggested by a direct comparison with American performances in those directions. Megaton explosives accurately delivered could eliminate certain air bases and American ICBM sites with the use of fewer Russian missiles and therefore fewer Russian launching sites, which are likely during the first generation or so to be in shorter supply than ICBM's themselves.

Soviet anti-bomber defenses are supposed to be good, and improving. This factor, combined with Russia's missile potential just mentioned,

[4] New York Times, January 12, 1959, p. 16, passim.
[5] For example, by the Secretary of Defense, Neil M. McElroy, New York Times, January 25, 1959, p. 7, cols. 1-3.

might squeeze the retaliatory capacity of the United States to levels at which the Russians' confidence in their ability to win by a first strike would rise sharply. The United States nevertheless might retain, in SAC, a concurrent capacity of its own to strike first and win. Now, the more that each side came to credit both its own and the other's ability to win by striking first, the more explosive the situation would become. In such circumstances the NATO allies might well grow alarmed and demand the control of completely independent deterrent systems. On strictly logical grounds, however, they would have small reason to do so—for if Russia were then to launch a nuclear attack and confine it to Europe, she would be inviting the United States to pre-empt with an all-out strike against Russian forces. It would therefore be rather as triggers for SAC that separate retaliatory systems would contribute to the NATO allies' security. That contribution, furthermore, would be offset at least to some extent by an increased danger of the allies' systems' becoming targets in the course of a pre-emptive Soviet attack against the West. This in its turn would be forestalled only if the increment—comprised of allies' bases and sites —to the number of targets which the Russians would have to destroy by their pre-emptive strike would restore to the West as a whole an effective second-strike potential.

Fortunately, the most probable consequence of a production gap does not seem to be the creation of first-strike abilities for East and West—or, a fortiori, the establishment of Soviet predominance. Instead, it is to be expected that each side will entertain doubts (the Soviet Union rather less than the United States) about its own first-strike capacity; and also some inkling of the other's doubts, associated probably with a rather low confidence in its own ability to make a second strike.[6]

Political and moral considerations would still, presumably, weigh against the United States' striking first. We might also predict that NATO allies sharing the American picture of power distribution would seek to develop their own retaliatory nuclear forces, partly on the

[6] Objectively, one side's first-strike capability is the reciprocal of the other's second-strike capability. But a stable balance of power—or, as the case may be, of terror—depends upon the nature of and relations between the subjective convictions of the several nations' governments. Each government, that is, must make estimates about the ratios of national capabilities, about every other government's estimate of these, about the others' estimates of its own estimates . . . and so on indefinitely, though with diminishing significance. Thus stability might be ensured, at least for a short time, because of certain erroneous estimates of capability; and, equally, it could be upset by other combinations of error, even though the objective capabilities would have yielded a stable equilibrium.

questionable assumption that they might have some independent deterrent effect, but mainly as triggering deterrents or means of inducing the United States to provide more efficient weapons. Even the triggering hypothesis, however, would not bear examination if it were known that the power of the United States were declining so sharply that she would fear to intervene on behalf of an ally under Soviet attack, no matter how severe the provocation.

More explicitly, an ally's forces will have promise as a triggering deterrent only if the expenditure of Soviet strength required to eliminate them should be supposed to give the United States both cause and opportunity for a winning first strike against the unexpended Soviet forces. Whenever, on the other hand, such a pre-emptive strike by the United States would be likely to call forth unpreventable and devastating retaliation by the Russians, the possession of its own nuclear forces might *reduce* an ally's security, in the course of adding somewhat to that of the United States. For in the event of all-out war between the United States and the Soviet Union, the ally's weapon-system—near Soviet borders and consequently liable to be hit more heavily and more accurately than those across the Atlantic—would be a certain target for Russian attack and would thereby divert some punishment away from the American homeland. Vis-à-vis the United States as supplier of improved deterrents, the ally's bargaining power increases as the first-strike capability of the United States declines toward the level at which it could no longer afford to intervene on an ally's behalf; but when that point is reached, the ally's bargaining position collapses. Conversely, the triggering effect of the allies' deterrents should increase as the first-strike capability of the United States increases, and should continue to do so unless "Fortress America" becomes its preferred policy.

The allies' attainment of complete nuclear independence falls within quite a different purview. As we have defined it, independent retaliatory power is the ability, irrespective of whether any other nation is liable to intervene on one's behalf, to strike second against an enemy's economy. Clearly, an ally can be independent in this sense only if the Russians know that the weapons it has acquired could not be eliminated by their attack, and could subsequently penetrate their defenses with quantities of explosive intolerable to them. But weapons of this order seem beyond the power of the United Kingdom to produce within the next five years or so. A fortiori, other Western nations can hope to obtain them in the near future only from the United States.

The choice of weapons for a shared deterrent system would seem to be among (1) the submarine-and-Polaris combination (virtually safe from a first strike, but expensive, inaccurate, difficult to concert, and vulnerable to sabotage and other forms of unofficial war), (2) solid-fueled IRBM's in highly protected launching sites (easily controlled, cheaper, more accurate and powerful, but rather more vulnerable to a first strike and liable to concentrate fire on one's homeland), or—for a few of the allies—(3) ICBM's such as the Minuteman located outside Europe (again expensive, inaccurate, and perhaps requiring ground defense, but controllable, hardly vulnerable, and—best—far from home), or (4) some combination of these. Since the independent type of deterrent is likely to be preferred to the triggering type, at least as a means to national autonomy, the current trend of military technology—from vulnerable and slow-firing to protected and "press-button" missiles—would appear to favor the policy to be examined below, assuming that the West can close the gap. At least some of the NATO allies are able even now to provide themselves with a low-confidence triggering deterrent, which the United States would not much like, and which the allies themselves might be eager to exchange for the promise of an independent retaliatory system. The latter, on the other hand, might be built from the cheap and numerous solid-fueled weapons with which America, from 1965 on, is expected to close the gap.[7]

We should also consider the possibility of a different end to the missile race. What would follow if the USSR were to be first in the field with cheap and numerous solid-fueled ICBM's and with a highly effective anti-aircraft defense as well, so that it might strike first with diminishing fears of retaliation? It would be important that the West reply to such a Soviet predominance, not by a panicky attempt to enlarge its own capacity for striking first (since that would invite Soviet attack), but by adding quickly to the number of targets which the Soviet Union would need to strike first if it were to attenuate Western retaliatory power and force a surrender. As in the post-Sputnik crisis, the best way to add these new targets might be to emplace un-alerted nuclear missiles (but this time in hardened sites) as near as possible to vulnerable parts of the Soviet economy—that is, on the territories of Continental NATO allies. Unless the Russian air defenses were perfect, SAC might be usefully put in the air. But Continental allies could perhaps exact a stiff price from the United States for the

[7] *New York Times*, January 13, 1959, p. 14, col. 5.

privilege of adding to European targets.[8] In general such a remedy would make less feasible our policy of nuclear sharing, which thus is predicated upon the West's closing the missile gap, through developments such as the nuclear submarine and the Minuteman, before the Soviet Union achieves predominance, however briefly.

We have so far reviewed the broad context of military power in which it is proposed to follow our sharing policy. We must now show reason why anyone should want it.

II

H. G. Wells somewhere defined a nation as a group of persons afflicted or wishing to be afflicted with a foreign office. We might now say, ". . . with the power to start a nuclear war." Of course, this is not yet true without qualification, for some countries are aware of being still ensconced in locations that would not form worthwhile targets unless nuclear weapons were mounted there. But most European nations—fearing involvement willy-nilly in a Russo-American war, and desiring at least some voice in the critical decision—are apt to repeat Toynbee's sally: "No annihilation without representation."

Whether mere representation (for example, in a joint NATO command disposing retaliatory weapons) would satisfy is indeed a question. Any NATO ally could interpret the current situation to itself somewhat as follows: "We are committed to an alliance that may cause us to receive a nuclear attack upon the occasion of some American-Soviet quarrel whose origins we had nothing to do with. Yet we cannot be sure that the United States would see us through an experience of nuclear blackmail, let alone risk nuclear devastation in order to deter a conventional attack or nuisance raid against us—and even if it should, Russia may by then have gone so far ahead in the missile race that American help might be unsuccessful. Furthermore, there is insufficient evidence that the United States has sought to mend its pace: American

[8] For the contrary view, see Albert Wohlstetter, "The Delicate Balance of Terror," *Foreign Affairs*, xxxvii, No. 2 (January 1959), pp. 226-30, and especially p. 227: ". . . if the press reports are correct, the plans for I.R.B.M. installations do not call for bomb-resistant shelters. If this is so, it should be taken into account in measuring the actual contribution of these installations to the West's retaliatory power. Viewed as a contribution to deterring all-out attack on the United States, the Thor and Jupiter bases seem unlikely to compare favorably with other alternatives. If newspaper references to hard bargaining by some of our future hosts are to be believed, it would seem that such negotiations have been conducted under misapprehension on both sides as to the benefits to the United States." May not the "future hosts" have thought that they were being asked to turn their homelands into blotting-paper which would soak up attack by Russian manned bombers?

lead-times seem to be much longer than those of the USSR; critics of American strategic planning and military administration still complain of disorganization and waste; and many American leaders are more preoccupied with the soundness of their country's economy than with the preparedness of its defenses. Now if we had a deterrent of our own —large and invulnerable enough to provide, after suffering attack, a reasonable chance of doing some damage to the Soviets, though not sufficient to make them anticipate a first strike from us—we might reasonably assure ourselves that in the face of United States capabilities, surpassed though those be, Russia would not for any provocation or temptation that we might offer waste a part of her invaluable deterrent on us. We could thus resist Soviet nuclear blackmail; and as for pressure from conventional or tactical nuclear forces, we could meet that with tactical nuclear weapons of our own—supplemented by our few conventional forces, once we have those back from NATO command. And by posing greater prospective costs for a Soviet attack against us, we could avail ourselves of more and not less deterrent support from the existence of America's strategic forces."

Certainly, there are technical and strategic assumptions in that synopsis of the allies' temper which we shall have to question closely. But their motivating wish for nuclear autonomy—for at least some power to give or withhold consent to involvement in nuclear war— has, within the ultimate unreason of our world of sovereign states, its own reasonableness. When others possess such weapons, to acquire and retain ability to wield them oneself will usually be seen as a great national interest. Commentators on this side of the Atlantic sometimes speak as though there could be no other motive for withdrawal from NATO than surrenderist fears or pacifist scruples. Perhaps they should ask whether the European's expression of such doubts about the viability of the alliance may not be masking the very will to national independence that American critics desiderate.

Aspiration to the prestige that possession of a nuclear armory is thought to bestow should not be regarded as a *separate* cause of the lesser powers' search for private deterrents. Britain and France may have been motivated by such ambitions, as well as by more concrete expectations, but hardly Switzerland or Sweden. Greater prestige does attach to developing one's own weapons (though other kinds of "conspicuous production" might procure it just as well), yet Britain has to content itself with American vehicles for much of its bombload, and France is reported anxious to take up the offer of American nuclear submarines. Unaided development, especially of the delivery systems, is certainly more than most of the NATO allies could afford. On the other hand, marginal costs of the delivery systems and explosives which the United States would be mass-producing in any case, and which might be sold to allies, are said to be within the present defense budgets of a number of the NATO allies (though maintenance cost—a difficult figure to determine—seems to be high and increasing). One may doubt, therefore, whether France or even the United Kingdom would have paid for the "conspicuous production" of research and development if America had been willing to sell them nuclear weapon-systems in quantity.

The allies' reasons for wanting their own nuclear capabilities thus range from the superficial to those connected with the fundamentals of national existence. But to make a prima facie case for the sharing strategy which we are to examine, one need claim nothing more general than (1) that each NATO ally is or soon will be anxious to have its own big deterrent; (2) that the gap will not yawn so wide that even the United States may lose ability to retaliate; (3) that when the gap has been closed, each ally will be able to afford to obtain from the United States a system that actually would deter; and finally (4) that the United States itself is willing and able to share.

In the policy's first stage—which we assume to be initiated before or during the gap—the United States would need to make it clear that she would retaliate against the Soviet economy or forces if there were a direct nuclear attack or nuclear extension of conventional attack against any NATO ally. Unless the gap were imminent and only an increase in the number of bomber bases and missile sites close to Soviet borders could deal with it, she would also begin shifting the burden of her retaliation from slow-firing liquid-fueled IRBM's (and also from manned bombers?) based in Europe, to missiles based at sea, and to SAC on the North American continent and probably in the United Kingdom. From the allies' point of view, this nuclear redeployment would remove from their territories targets suggestive of a Western intention to strike first; from the American point of view, it would get rid of possible ambiguities—there would be no question of a host-ally's preventing retaliation on behalf of another ally. Meanwhile, the NATO allies, by increasing their contributions of conventional forces, would be raising to 30 divisions the present effective strength of little more than 15 effective combat-ready divisions[9] (including United States forces). American conventional and tactical nuclear forces need not be

[9] *Present State*, p. 11.

greatly increased,[10] but the nuclear-weapons battalions recently stationed in the United States would be maintained in Europe. Allied conventional forces could continue to receive training with tactical nuclear weapons but would have no cause, in terms of our policy, to be equipped with them. The resultant NATO force would be integrated, as at present, under a supreme command, but would then be given its own supplies and infrastructure. Above all, it would need complete power of movement and redeployment within the NATO zone. This last requirement would appear to entail a parallel diplomatic and political concerting of NATO, so that there might be a permanent political organ to which the Supreme Commander would be responsible. A joint force would thus have been provided by the Continental allies, the United Kingdom, and the United States, each of whose contributions would serve as sureties for the continued adherence of the nations that were supplying them.

From this first stage, the West could still pursue negotiations for effective arms control, if by then the prospects for it looked brighter than now. But otherwise, as the United States developed a protected deterrent and thereby closed the gap, NATO would be in a position to move to the second stage of nuclear sharing.

In that second stage, the United States (perhaps in conjunction with the United Kingdom) fulfills the promises made to each ally or group by providing a big deterrent for each. This weapon system will be manned and controlled from day to day by the recipients, but serviced and, when necessary, renovated by the donor. (Some arrangement such as that would ensure for the United States that the allies keep their side of the compact, and at the same time would allow the allies full strategic control of their deterrents. It would also answer to the technological resources of the two parties.) The purpose of the allies' deterrents is purely retaliatory, and they must continue to be maintained at levels thought sufficient to deter the USSR—no matter how its capabilities should improve—from attacking the recipient nation.[11]

Meanwhile, the Continental allies, possibly with British help, would take over from Continent-based American forces the task of filling out NATO's joint capabilities at the conventional and tactical-nuclear levels. The United States presumably would want this done, and the allies' doing it might go toward their payment for big-deterrent capacities they had received.[12] NATO would have been preserved in its

[10] Indeed, a polite threat to decrease them might well bring the allies around.
[11] The problem of "sufficiency" is further discussed below.
[12] In most cases, side-payment will also be necessary, and bargaining will therefore

essentials (the ensuring of measures for joint defense against the likelier forms of attack), while the interests that might have broken it up—the inclination of the United States to keep the bulk of its forces in Fortress America, and the wish of each ally to have no finger but its own on the trigger of its strategic weapons—would have been fulfilled. It now remains to be seen whether, stage by stage, the policy is practicable.

III

The very first condition to be satisfied before entering upon the first stage would be that nearly all NATO countries should find the later stages practicable and desirable. Logically, then, we should begin with the last. But perhaps it will suffice if we remember that each step in implementing the policy must survive criticism.

In particular, all allies must face at the beginning of Stage I some prospect of the missile gap. Its first effects have been construed by some European opinion as making NATO more important for the United States and perhaps rather more costly and dangerous for the allies than it was in the mid-1950's. These opinions, however, reflect the relative weapon-holdings of 1957-1958. We must try to guess whether things would look different if the Soviet Union should be on the brink of possessing a qualitatively comparable but quantitatively superior air force and air defenses, several hundred solid-fuel ICBM's with nuclear warheads, and four hundred or more conventional submarines, as against the United States' geographical advantage in disposition of bases, its variety of first-generation missiles (mostly in small quantities),[13] and its few nuclear submarines. Would that distribution tempt the allies to doubt whether the United States would intervene if they suffered nuclear attack, or induce America to consider giving NATO a rather lower priority than in the past?

Far from remaining the advantage that, under the aegis of earlier weapon systems, they used to be, a large number of weaker allies may now overstrain a leading power such as the United States; and their neutralization or changing of sides might be part of the price that a predominant Soviet Union would try to exact. Not our strategy alone, indeed, but the existence of NATO itself would appear to depend upon the signs that America can produce of being able (1) to prevent

---

take place from time to time. The important thing is that donors and recipients would each have something they might withhold from the others.

[13] C. J. V. Murphy, "Defense: The Converging Decisions," *Fortune*, October 1958, p. 119 *et seq.*

the gap from widening overmuch, and (2) to bridge it quite quickly.

Conversely, NATO powers that intend to stand by the alliance and the United States connection would be well advised to help now in lightening the load upon America's capacity for weapons research and development. Since alarm over Sputnik has not after all produced a grand coalescence of Western military effort, the lesser powers might help by providing adequate conventional and other forces within their capacity. America for its part should understand that development of an armory capable of surviving Russian attack is a diplomatic as well as a military necessity.

Contemplation of a possible gap may induce the wealthier allies to forestall our policy by a different method. Just as Switzerland and Sweden—non-NATO powers lacking formal alliance with the United States—have begun to consider acquisition of nuclear arms, though at first for tactical use only, so France, for example—already developing nuclear weapons, and unwilling to divert larger forces from Algeria to a joint NATO command—may decide to go her own way, relying on a low-confidence deterrent, her own conventional forces, and the intervening barrier of Middle Europe to protect her from Soviet attack. This may seem, to a nation ambitious to regain Great Power status, much more attractive than would be the policy we are examining, since "going it alone" promises immediate independence, instead of our policy's chancy and qualified promises. United States advisers, however, may be able to demonstrate that the obvious objections against reliance on a vulnerable deterrent and a low-confidence strategy apply to France's current essay in complete independence, just as they apply against any proposals for supplying smaller NATO countries with unprotected retaliatory forces in the pre-gap period.

Adjectives like "vulnerable" and "low-confidence" are not absolute, and they tend to oversimplify our picture. The mere existence of the United States as a nuclear power can be thought of as endowing France with a certain degree of triggering deterrence. Similarly, the French can safely discount any possibility that the whole of Russia's missile force would ever be used against France. Furthermore, a low probability that French retaliation would succeed in destroying many Soviet cities might yet deter Soviet attack, even though there were a high probability of Russia's coming off scot-free.[14] A recognition of

[14] It may be that certain finite but low probabilities of very heavy damage are simply ignored by adventurous nations, while conservative ones continue to take them into consideration. There could be close coincidence of preferences over all higher ranges of probability, and yet the adventurous nation may just stop weighing the unpleasant possibilities when, say, maximum possible damage to itself becomes less than 4 per

low probability of maximum military success is not equivalent to a low confidence in one's general ability to stand the Russians off. France (so her rulers might argue), though unsupported in most military and political situations, would not be entirely alone in the very worst extremity: her would-be attacker would have to consider the possibility that he was setting off a *general* nuclear war. This consideration might tilt the scales against France's accepting our policy. After all, the promise of a protected deterrent, if and when that is available, and meanwhile the obligation to buy a never-quite-certain support by the United States at the cost of allocating more French troops to NATO, might seem to France the worse alternative, at once risky and poor-spirited. In assessing our suggested scheme, then, we must recognize the possibility that France or Britain or even Western Germany could effectively prevent its being started by quietly declining, and instead proceeding to develop their own nuclear weapons.

During this first stage, however, the United States might guard against such defections and might strengthen the weaker powers' trust by increasing its commitments of conventional and tactical nuclear force to the more vulnerable parts of the European zone. Of course, this is a medicine that must be used with care, for too great a total build-up of NATO "shield" forces might mislead Russia about the West's intentions, and too great a proportion from the United States might defeat a chief American concern in the exercise—that the NATO allies should increase their contributions to the joint force, and eventually take over the whole burden. (This would be a net saving for the United States, reduce reliance on the triggering aspect of allied deterrence, and provide a useful talking point with the Soviet bloc.) Yet some such American allocation of tactical forces will be required in any case to offset the effect on NATO morale of withdrawing strategic and retaliatory forces to less vulnerable regions. The reallocation might appear in United States accounts as the immediate cost of keeping NATO intact, the condition of the whole operation being that the allies should also increase tactical allocations. American nuclear battalions at present stationed in the United States would seem to be the contribution costing least; but we must also remember their possible alternative uses to America on other fronts of the cold war.

The most tempting form of attack on NATO in the pre-gap period seems to be some mixture of *coup d'état* and swift occupation by Soviet

---

cent probable. Individuals sometimes differ that way in their envisioning and weighing of risks, and so may nations.

conventional forces, probably against a background of readied but unused tactical nuclear units. Nuclear blackmail of a selected NATO ally should not begin to be promising unless and until the gap actually opens. It would therefore seem to be in the interest of the Continental allies that they and the United States should act to strengthen the NATO shield. Against this, we must recognize the dissuasive prospect of their having to pay for more conventional forces.

Could Britain and the European allies find between them the 15 extra divisions required to bring joint NATO forces up to the strength that most authorities say will be necessary? Very likely they could; but it is at least doubtful on present showing whether anyone would be willing to do so. Provision of conventional forces confers little prestige, and withdraws labor from the productive part of the economy in somewhat the same proportion as do nuclear forces. It is not easy for smaller allies, who make the lesser but nevertheless significant contributions, to hand over their armies to a joint command exercised by Americans, Germans, and Frenchmen (cf. the unwillingness of the United States, on past occasions, to submit its own troops to foreign command). For such nations, the example of Duncan Sandys' 1957 White Paper on defense, and perhaps also the policies of General de Gaulle, may prove highly infectious.

Current United Kingdom policy affords a precedent which could gravely mislead small Continental powers. For Britain the new weapons restore in some measure the advantages of the English Channel. But nations like Denmark, or the Benelux complex, may one day face ground attack despite possession of tactical nuclear weapons. It would be one thing to use retaliatory forces for vengeance after a devastating nuclear attack, but quite another to initiate their use against a powerful but selective drive by Soviet conventional forces—with the much more powerful Soviet armory of nuclear weapons available to prevent nuclear reprisal by the West. If a small country is prepared to go down fighting rather than surrender before conventional attack, conventional resistance offers a less forlorn hope than does suicide through the dispatch of a nuclear strike against strong Soviet defenses. As I have assumed in this chapter, the only thing directly and unconditionally deterred by a big deterrent is another big deterrent. If this is true, then the Continental allies of NATO, unlike Great Britain or the United States, require frontier-guarding forces.

Our policy seems to involve grouping the smaller NATO powers into units that might in the long run manage jointly to control a protected deterrent system. Foundations for that state of affairs, where they do not exist already, need to be laid in the period before the gap opens. Excluding for the moment Britain and perhaps France—as already in the nuclear club—the more obvious "potentially nuclear" units, in order of increasing unlikelihood, seem to be Western Germany, Italy, Benelux, Norway and Denmark, and Greece and Turkey. Benelux, with an advanced industrial population of twenty million or so, could probably agree and look forward to operating a joint deterrent. Norway and Denmark together are less than ten million. They possess coastlines and traditions that might be helpful in operating a seagoing strategic force; but whether they could underwrite and eventually manage a joint deterrent is a question of more tactical detail than we can here command. It may be that instead of grouping them together, we should think of Denmark as West Germany's and Norway as Britain's special ally in the nuclear field.

If other NATO powers are promised deterrent packages, Greece and Turkey are likely to expect them also. Some authorities might consider this alone as sufficient warrant for ruling out our scheme. The two countries, it is thought, might use the weapons against each other; or Turkey at least, militant as it is, might rashly turn them on the USSR. Even together, they would have much less chance of financing and managing the weapons than would smaller but more advanced nations. This seems to me a weightier objection than the other. The best of a bad set of alternatives may be for a virtually separate arrangement to be made between the United States (the United Kingdom being at present too unpopular) and these two old enemies, with a view to maintaining an independent retaliatory force in the Eastern Mediterranean, in the command of which Greece and Turkey would both have a role. This is not a satisfactory solution, and the area forms the western marches of that world-region perhaps most open to Russian aggression. I would therefore regard the positions and reactions of these two NATO allies as a certain objection to our whole policy.

Indeed, the grouping problem would be among the most difficult faced by proponents of our policy. For the larger European nations, the decision whether to develop one's own nuclear weapons or to buy a deterrent from the United States at the price of staying in NATO has a major economic component which helps to make it more calculable. Many of the smaller nations, on the other hand, would be retrieving little more of the substance of national sovereignty by sharing group control of a deterrent than they would by continuing to rely directly on a powerful protector such as the United States. Yet if America is eventually forced to make separate agreements with each national partner, not much of the reality of military power (apart from a conventional capability that might or might not be retained) will be left to NATO. Many of those countries, moreover, have strategic importance beyond their size, because they occupy flank positions which the West does not wish to have fall into Soviet hands. Only one element in this part of the situation does not tell against the feasibility of our policy: the smaller countries, especially those with Iron Curtain frontiers, are the ones that stand most in need of conventional and other territorial defense.

We must now ask what steps the Soviet Union could or would take against our policy in the pre-gap period. Of course, if it believes that its predominance in weapons will increase indefinitely, a scheme destined to bear fruit only upon a contrary condition should not disturb it very much. If, on the other hand, it envisages the gap either not opening or closing quickly again, then defeat of the policy should be among its objectives. Soviet countermeasures might include threats and blackmail, the use of military force, and proposals for arms control to freeze the nuclear situation.

Some Western opinion (including the writer's) would for various reasons prefer arms control to the policy under discussion. As an aid in precluding accidental nuclear war, our policy has only the following features to commend it above a *laissez-faire* attitude to the spread of nuclear weapons: (1) since the packaged big deterrents would be presumably of one type and supplied from centers under Great Power authority, the policing of an arms control scheme in the post-gap period might be rather more practicable than in a nuclear anarchy; (2) if the policy were adopted, work on nuclear weapon development would presumably cease in NATO countries other than the United States and probably the United Kingdom; and (3) the proposing or initiating of the scheme might induce the Soviet to look more favorably on arms control than it does at present. But the Continental allies might not favor arms control under such conditions, especially as they would need to find very large conventional forces if Russia could not be bargained into reducing hers.

If the Soviet Union should use threats and nuclear blackmail to prevent NATO countries from agreeing to the scheme, the political foundations of the scheme itself—in particular, of the degree of trust which the allies would be prepared to put in the United States during the earlier periods—would be severely tested. An American presence on the Continent is part of the scheme, and would be for the allies perhaps the strongest inducement to disregard Soviet threats. The

NATO powers should not adopt any sharing policy unless they can be confident that the alliance is proof against blackmail. Civil defense capabilities for the allies could be another prophylactic: if a country knew that, given time to evacuate, it could save a large part of its population from anything but an all-out strike, it might call bluffs less equivocally than otherwise. Finally, the Kremlin would need to recognize that NATO would be strengthened whenever the USSR was caught bluffing.

We should admit that conventional Soviet attack against NATO countries intending to adopt our policy would be feasible in some cases—but little more so than it is already. Soviet invasions of Norway and Denmark, for instance, would not be worthwhile merely in order to rule out the possibility of a Scandinavian-controlled deterrent (United States bases in Norway are a different matter, because they would be more readily usable in an American surprise attack). Something else would have to be procurable from such a venture; and even if it were successful, there would be no way of telling in advance whether the maneuver would not turn out to have strengthened the remainder of NATO.

Soviet nuclear attack upon an ally which had contracted for but not yet received its deterrent is a different matter—one that would transpose the situation at once into a Russo-American conflict of wills. A failure to respond on the part of the United States would of course destroy its influence throughout the world, which might persuade Russia to risk the consequences, were it not that they would include the possibility of all-out nuclear war or of an aborted conflict that would certainly produce complete mobilization of American and other resources against the aggressor. On the whole, we may conclude that Soviet Russia would run grave risks if it were to oppose our policy by threats or by force; but that a diplomatic offensive condemning it and proposing arms control might have a real chance of defeating the scheme and of neutralizing many of the Western allies.

How does our scheme in its first stage, before the gap has grown wide, stand up to examination? As a military conception, it seems to survive review at least as well as the present arrangement. Most of its difficulties are political. In some aspects, though not in all, it would cost the United States rather more than what appears to be present policy. During this first stage, it would cost the NATO allies much more. Further, they would have to abandon at the outset some insignia of sovereignty (especially France, of course) in order to regain later, perhaps, a nuclear independence that some of them might consider all too hypothetical. Small NATO powers would have to stomach the additional disadvantages of strategic grouping. Finally, the upshot of the first stage might not be the beginning of nuclear sharing, but the beginning of arms control.

IV

How would our policy survive the gap? This is virtually to ask about the general prospects of NATO during that period, for the inauguration of our scheme would merely have strengthened conventional defenses in the NATO area and transferred some American retaliatory forces to extra-Continental sites. At this stage of the analysis, then, the only rivals to our scheme which we need here consider would be others designed to deal more appropriately with the shortage of missiles and its consequences, which will be by far the greatest of the threats to NATO cohesion. What would the Continental allies be left to choose but capitulation, or unarmed or at best armed neutrality, if the United States should lose all ability to redeem its promises?

Most commentators rule out such a possibility, thinking it more likely that the Russians will gain some substantial advantage in missiles as well as conventional weapons, but that they and everyone else will expect the disparity to be short-lived and of doubtful military effect. With previous weapon systems, such a declining predominance would have afforded them the most conclusive of motives for launching world war. Now, we may expect that they will use their temporary advantage to make bloodless gains, probably by exerting pressure in a number of different areas at once. So long as the United States was maintaining an edge or at least parity in nuclear forces, the grand Soviet strategy of making trouble had to be implemented in one part of the world after another, because of some Soviet scarcity of resources. With the position likely to be reversed, we must face the possibility of simultaneous challenges, perhaps backed directly by conventional force, in many of the areas of the cold war. The West being unable to deal with all of them, Russia should be bound to make killings somewhere. This would present old worries to the NATO allies with new force: granted the United States were bound to give way in some region, would that region be Europe? If this predicament arises, and if the West European answer on the whole is "Yes," our policy in particular and the Atlantic Alliance in general fall to pieces. What might persuade the allies to answer, "No"?

As in the previous period, trust would be induced less by any declaration of policy, or promise, than by American commitments on the Continent, and large contributions to a joint NATO force. A salutary gesture, if the United States could afford the risk, might be to reinforce its contribution and to place all American NATO forces under Continental command, insisting meanwhile that that command have complete freedom to move, under a single control, anywhere in the NATO area. If it were known that danger to the United Kingdom had also increased, by virtue of United States nuclear bases there and by Britain's honoring of commitments in other parts of the world, Continental suspicions of an Anglo-American hedging operation might be stilled. Lastly, the allies would expect to see a mobilization of resources in the United States, demonstrative of the conviction that holding the line around the world and particularly in Europe was worth a degree of strain within the American economy.

If measures such as these were taken against a decline of confidence, Europeans themselves could be expected to make their contributions to morale. On the other hand—if our assumption about simultaneous and ubiquitous Soviet pressure is correct—allies who were safeguarding colonial possessions and overseas interests would be in danger of thus appearing to neglect Europe for selfish ends. In this respect, the Soviet Union would have such countries on the horns of a dilemma, since Communist-encouraged victories against the French in Africa or the British in the Near East might lose only less prestige for the West than would American reversals against Soviet machinations in Iran, Pakistan, and elsewhere.

Allowing for all the imponderables in this inadequately defined situation, I suppose that our policy would be a little more likely than not to survive the missile gap. The Soviet Union could be more certain of effective gains in the Middle East, Africa, and the Far East than in Europe. If Europe collapsed, to be sure, much of these other regions would go also (unless the United States could salvage what colonial powers had been unable to defend). But the risks to the Soviets of a European adventure would be far greater than those of operations in the grey areas.

Perhaps I should emphasize once again that our policy could not cope with a large and prolonged Russian predominance in weapons. If the gap is believed to be a gulf, then one finds it difficult to imagine NATO staying intact under any guise. We must now consider, however, the contrary assumption: that at some stage—for example, as American crash programs designed to obtain invulnerable quick-fire missiles begin to pay off—a new era of parity will be foreseen.

Our policy will reach a crux at that point. Allies belonging to the scheme will at once enquire about delivery dates for their promised big deterrents—all the more urgently if there has been erosion of the Western position. Russia might very well take this opportunity to "offer" the United States an arms-control scheme, more or less as an ultimatum—that is, she could threaten to seize "preventively" some area in Europe or the Middle East, unless it were agreed that only existing nuclear powers should have the right to nuclear weapons.

Some such stratagem might very well succeed. Divergent interests might then come to the fore within NATO. While march-lands in peril of Soviet conventional attack might be willing to forego their nuclear share if everyone else would, the wealthier and less endangered powers might try to insist that the United States fulfill its promises. In that event, American opinion might be torn between the prospect of a more or less permanent *détente* with the Soviet bloc, and that of a large array of Western nuclear powers.

It is impossible to say how such alternatives might seem to compare under such conditions. Much would depend upon political affairs elsewhere, and upon non-military factors. World-settlement, even on a basis of division between East and West, has considerable attractions, as well as ominous undertones, at any time. But if the Soviet Union, for instance, could not guarantee that China would never acquire nuclear weapons unless others also acquired them, the West as a whole might decide to reject the offer.

We shall now conclude this study with a brief survey of our policy's prospects in the post-gap era. The writer has been at no stage convinced that better policies could not be thought of. This one, however, has seemed worth considering as an alternative to *laissez-faire*—for it does appear likely that if NATO countries and others are left to their own devices they will certainly try to get nuclear weapons for themselves, if necessary at the inordinate expense of developing them from scratch, and at the grave risk of finishing up with a vulnerable big deterrent and insufficient means of dealing with pressures and attacks short of nuclear assault. The temptation is to think that the alternatives are: conventional weapons for Europe—or nuclear weapons for each of the several powers. But many more permutations are logically conceivable, and some of these are practical possibilities. The advantage of our policy over that favoring a joint nuclear force as well as a joint conventional capability for NATO[15] is that nations patently do not

[15] See *Present State, loc.cit.*

trust a supranational collective with power over the initiation of nuclear war. Its advantage over a policy of individual nuclear and conventional forces (the *laissez-faire* policy which we put into the mouth
of the discontented ally—see above, pp. 159-60) is that, though the
several European countries are not separately capable of withstanding
Soviet conventional attack—the likeliest sort—they would be capable
of doing so jointly. And, from the West's point of view, its advantage
over the various disengagement policies involving total or nuclear demilitarization of the Germanies would be the retention of West Germany's ground forces by NATO command, and the continuance of
pressure of example that might detach Eastern Germany from the
Soviet bloc. Against the latter advantage of our policy must be set the
possibility that a militarily strengthened Western Germany which remained in the Western camp might well frighten back into conformity
with Moscow such promising liberalizers as Poland.

We have already considered likely Soviet reactions to our scheme,
and have argued that from time to time it could form a useful lever
for the reopening of arms-control negotiations. We saw, however, that
the Soviet Union might be able to pose dilemmas for both the would-be
receivers and the would-be giver of protected deterrents just before
these were handed over. Supposing that such crises could be weathered,
we must now ask whether in the post-gap situation, with Continental
nations and groupings in possession of their private deterrents, the
Soviet Union could then effectively interfere with the system established
in accordance with our policy.

What do we suppose that Russia would then be facing? In Europe,
she would confront about 30 divisions. Assuming that these could,
but need not, use tactical nuclear weapons, we may argue that the
Soviet Union could not launch a probably successful conventional
attack unless it were prepared to use ground forces in such concentration that they would provide easy targets for tactical nuclear weapons.

The writer is also assuming that a large-scale ground attack by
the Soviet Union, employing tactical nuclear as well as conventional
forces, would be recognized as opening up the serious possibility of
strategic nuclear retaliation, or at least of a great Western strike against
Soviet bases and locations. At this level, Soviet strategists would have
to take account of far more Western retaliatory forces after the gap
than before it. Would this imply for the Kremlin that a unified
counterforce strike by United States, United Kingdom, and Conti-

nental ICBM's and other weapons could put the Soviet bloc in a war-losing position?

That is another highly technical question which this chapter cannot resolve. But if the answer were "Yes," we could infer that the Soviet Union would be forced into a low-confidence strategy—for example, into threatening to select one or a few of its attackers at random and concentrate all possible retaliation there. Against an alliance such as NATO, some of the low-confidence strategies would probably suffice to deter—supposing deterrence were at all required. If, on the other hand, even a first strike by *all* of NATO would not yield it a certainly winning position, the situation would seem to be the "stand-off" of accepted deterrent theory. But in that case, might not the Soviet Union be able to blackmail *each* NATO power separately?

Again, we become involved in military technicalities. Our policy is feasible only if highly protected retaliatory weapons are *now* known to be procurable within a few years (otherwise the allies may lack confidence that the United States will be able to provide big deterrents). We have been assuming, perhaps rashly, that packages of these might be handed over once the United States is mass-producing them, each of which could inflict second-strike damage unacceptable to the USSR. We have also suggested that a second-string deterrent effect might operate insofar as the Soviet Union might fear that a strike against a Continental NATO power, through the combined effects of attrition of the Soviet attack and retaliatory damage to the Russian homeland, might invite American and possibly other strikes against a weakened and yet patently aggressive Soviet Union. But the alternative we are now exploring (of Soviet forces also more or less invulnerable to a unified first strike) seems to eliminate the possibility of such a second-string deterrent factor.[16]

The tendency of the last few paragraphs is to suggest that, whatever the degree of vulnerability of the Soviet forces, there would be little prospect for them of direct military success against the NATO system as we imagine it after the gap. But many NATO countries have over-

---

[16] It might be restored for a time if, along with the big deterrent package, NATO allies were to be offered a highly effective defense against manned bombers and air-breathing missiles. Such a move could be countered by the Soviet Union only if its forces were so particularized that those devoted to carrying out threatened strikes against Continental NATO powers were completely independent of those committed against the United States and the other NATO allies, and if it could be guaranteed that the confusion resulting from a victim's retaliation against Russian resources would not disturb the Soviet Union's deterrent posture toward America and the others. The costs of that kind of particularization are very high, and would not be worth the Soviet Union's undertaking unless (contrary to our fundamental assumption) there were also serious weaknesses in the first-stage deterrents which we are supposing to have been received by the NATO countries.

seas territories which might be threatened in ways that could influence their mother-countries—for example, France and Britain. Those, however, are the countries most likely to dispose at an early stage of retaliatory forces of their own, some of which might be transferable to the defense of their threatened interests.[17]

So far then, our strategy—if it could be developed to the final stage—would appear to pass the tests of a post-gap world. One difficulty remains for our policy, and it might prove insuperable. What assurance could be given that the new big deterrents would not swiftly become obsolete—say, through increasing accuracy of Soviet IRBM's, and development of Soviet contra-missiles?

Becoming a nuclear power may be thought of as marking, for the typical NATO ally, a point of no return. Could it very readily creep back into the shelter of United States protection should its deterrent prove ineffective? The problem of possible obsolescence is serious enough for the superpowers, which have great industrial and technological reserves giving them a prospect of countering their rivals' military innovations. For the lesser powers, possible obsolescence of the deterrent means possible susceptibility to blackmail at the least.

If the latter is a serious consideration, there can be little doubt that as a long-term security measure our policy would be inferior, from both America's and the allies' points of view, to a strategy leading to federation of all the Western powers, and a consequent sharing of research potential and instruments of defense—something not at present contemplated. But if enough allies come to expect a rate of obsolescence of deterrent weapons that they could not hope to keep up with, our policy will not attract them. This last difficulty must therefore remain as a question-mark at the end of our discussion.

Our policy can be objected to at a number of points. Perhaps no single objection is quite conclusive, nor do many of them seem cumulative. Other and diverse strategies may be preferred for various reasons—strategies as different as Western federation and thorough arms control. It may be an advantage of ours that it leaves both of those open as alternatives until its own final stage.

Our last word must be to insist again that the whole policy depends on technicalities. Unless protected deterrents are already known to be procurable early enough and in sufficient quantity, the case for nuclear sharing probably falls.

[17] It has been suggested that NATO powers armed with retaliatory forces might be inveigled by Soviet diplomacy into using them as levers against each other. This does not seem plausible. Such conflicts of interests as there are among the nations of the alliance are not likely to become so intense.

CHAPTER 8

SURPRISE ATTACK AND DISARMAMENT

BY THOMAS C. SCHELLING*

I

THE term "disarmament" has covered a variety of schemes, some ingenious and some sentimental, for cooperation among potential enemies to reduce the likelihood of war or to reduce its scope and violence. Most proposals have taken as a premise that a reduction in the quantity and potency of weapons, particularly of "offensive" weapons and of weapons that either deliberately or incidentally cause great civilian agony and destruction, promotes this purpose. Some schemes have been comprehensive; others have sought to identify particular areas where the common interest is conspicuous, where the need for trust is minimal, and where a significant start might be made which, if successful, would be a first step toward more comprehensive disarmament. Among these less comprehensive schemes, measures to safeguard against surprise attack have come, since the President's first "open skies" proposal in 1955, increasingly into prominence.

The focus on surprise attack has not been advertised as an abandonment of interest in a more ambitious dismantlement of arms; rather it represents the philosophy of picking an area where success is most likely, in order to establish some tradition of successful cooperation. The search for safeguards against surprise attack has generally been considered, in our government and elsewhere, not as an *alternative* to disarmament, but as a *type* of disarmament and a possible step toward more.

Nevertheless, though surprise-attack schemes may be in the tradition of disarmament, they represent something of an innovation. The original open-skies proposal was unorthodox in its basic idea that arms themselves are not provocative so long as they are clearly being held in reserve—so long as their stance is deterrent rather than aggressive. The proposal was also unorthodox in its dramatic reminder that, important as it may be to keep secrets from an enemy and in some matters to keep him guessing about what our plans are, it can be even more important to see that the enemy is *not* guessing about our in-

* The influence of the author's RAND colleagues on this chapter, too great to cite in detail, is greatly appreciated.

tentions toward surprise attack *if in fact we are not planning any such attack*. In the philosophy of the open-skies idea, we are interested not only in assuring ourselves with our own eyes that he is not preparing an attack against us; we are interested as well in assuring *him* through *his* own eyes that *we* are preparing no deliberate attack against *him*.

The importance of not keeping that particular secret has an analogue in our alleged political inability to attack first. As General Leslie R. Grove remarked a year ago, "If Russia knows we won't attack first, the Kremlin will be very much less apt to attack us. . . . Our reluctance to strike first is a military disadvantage to us; but it is also, paradoxically, a factor in preventing a world conflict today."[1] We live in an era in which a potent incentive on either side—perhaps the main incentive—to initiate total war with a surprise attack is the fear of being a poor second for not going first. "Self-defense" becomes peculiarly compounded if we have to worry about his striking us to keep us from striking him to keep him from striking us. . . .

A novel aspect of surprise-attack schemes is therefore that they not only involve the *exchange* of vital information—information about each side's readiness to attack the other—but recognize that each side may have a *unilateral* interest in revealing the truth about his own intention, if in fact his intentions are only to strike back, not to strike first. Their implications go even further: it could be an advantage, in the deterrence of surprise attack, to have no *capability*, not just no intention, of exploiting a first strike. While our political capability or incapability of striking first may be determined by inflexible institutions or past history, our military capability to strike first—not just to survive a first strike and strike back—can be our own decision; it depends on the kinds of forces we create and the manner in which we deploy them. The surprise-attack problem, if viewed as a problem of reciprocal suspicion and aggravated "self-defense," might suggest that there are not only secrets we prefer not to keep, but military capabilities we prefer not to have.

Of course, it is even better if the other side does not have them either. So there may be advantages in considering the surprise-attack problem one for negotiation rather than unilateral action. Still, it is a significant feature of surprise-attack schemes that some of the restraints that might be negotiated in a bilateral agreement are reinforced by a nation's own unilateral security motives, and not necessarily at odds with them.

[1] *New York Times*, December 29, 1957, p. 20.

II

The innovation involved in the shift of attention to surprise-attack schemes goes even deeper than that. It has to do with what is being protected by the scheme, and what armament situation the scheme takes for granted. An anti-surprise-attack scheme has as its purpose not making *attack* more difficult but making *surprise* attack more difficult. It seeks, that is, to reduce or eliminate the advantage of striking *first*. It must assume that if the advantage of striking first can be eliminated or severely reduced, the incentive to strike *at all* will be reduced and war made less likely. But what is the advantage of striking first?

It is widely accepted that the United States of America has the military *power* virtually to obliterate the USSR, and vice versa. And it is widely accepted that if either side struck the other's homeland a major nuclear blow, the nation so hit would have a powerful *incentive* to strike back with equal or greater force. But if either side can obliterate the other, what does it matter who strikes first? If we and the Russians are going to be nearly obliterated, do we seriously prefer to live a day longer than the Russians, rather than let the Russians outlive us for a day? The answer, of course, is that we are not particularly concerned with outliving the Russians by a day; we are worried about whether a surprise attack might have sufficient prospects of *destroying our power to retaliate* to be undeterred by the threat of retaliation. It is not our *existing* capacity to obliterate Russia that deters a Russian attack against us, but our capacity to retaliate as it would be *after* being attacked ourselves. And in the calculation we must assume that a Russian first strike, if it came, would in the first instance concentrate on knocking out precisely the power that we rely on for retaliation.

There is a difference between a balance of terror in which *either* side has the capacity to obliterate the other, and one in which *both* sides have the capacity, no matter who strikes first. It is not the "balance" —the sheer equality or symmetry in the situation—that constitutes "mutual deterrence"; it is the *stability* of the balance. The situation is symmetrical but not stable when either side, by striking first, can destroy the other's power to strike back; the situation is stable when either side can destroy the other whether it strikes first or second— that is, when *neither* in striking first can destroy the other's ability to strike back.

The difference between a stable and an unstable balance of terror is illustrated by another offensive weapon against which no good defense was ever devised—the pistol.[2] The "equalizer" of the Old West made it possible for *either* member of the hostile pair to kill the other; it did not assure that *both* could kill each other. The tense consequences of this weapon system can be seen on TV almost any night. If one is face to face with a potential enemy and both are armed with pistols, the advantage of first shot aggravates any incentive to shoot. The survivor can argue, "He was about to kill me in self-defense, so I had to kill him in self-defense." Or, "He, thinking I was about to kill him in self-defense, was about to kill me in self-defense, so I had to kill him in self-defense." But if everyone who was shot were assured of living long enough to shoot back with unimpaired aim, there would be no advantage in jumping the gun and no reason to expect the other to try it.

The special significance of surprise attack thus lies in the possible vulnerability of retaliatory forces. If these forces were themselves invulnerable—if each side were confident that its own forces could survive an attack, but also that it could not destroy the other's power to strike back—there would be no powerful temptation to strike first. And there would be less need to react quickly to what might prove to be a false alarm.

Thus surprise-attack schemes have as their most *immediate* objective the safety of *weapons* rather than the safety of *people*.

Again, to state the point differently, surprise-attack schemes—in contrast to other types of disarmament proposals—are based on *deterrence* as the fundamental protection against attack. They seek to perfect and to stabilize a situation of mutual deterrence. This means that they seek to enhance the integrity of particular weapons systems, not to dismantle or to degrade those systems. Paradoxically, it is precisely the weapons with the most inhumane capabilities that a surprise-attack scheme seeks to preserve—namely, the weapons of retaliation, the weapons whose mission would be to punish rather than to fight. Deterrence of a major enemy assault depends mainly on weapons that threaten to *hurt* the enemy afterward, not to disarm him beforehand. A "good" weapon—to push this philosophy all the way—is a weapon that can only hurt *people* and cannot possibly damage the other side's strategic striking force; such a weapon is profoundly defensive in that it provides its possessor no incentive at all to strike first and initiate

[2] A military historian, commenting on the alleged "historical truth" that there has never yet been a weapon against which man has been unable to devise a counter-weapon or a defense, reminds us that "after five centuries of the use of hand arms with fire-propelled missiles . . . no adequate answer has yet been found for the bullet." Bernard Brodie in *The Absolute Weapon*, New York, 1946, pp. 30-31.

a major war. But clean weapons with the capability of seeking out enemy missiles and bombers—that is, with the capability of destroying "military" targets—are "bad." They are the weapons that *can* exploit the advantage of striking first and consequently provide a temptation to do so; they lose their special advantages if withheld until after the enemy strikes (and in some cases may even find no targets if they strike second); they consequently provide a temptation to strike first.

When we have identified the surprise-attack problem as one that concentrates on the possible vulnerability of each side's retaliatory forces to surprise attack, we have identified the point at which surprise-attack schemes differ drastically from more conventional notions of disarmament. We have also identified the source of a number of anomalies and paradoxes that have to be faced if we are to recognize the virtues and defects of particular schemes and to comprehend the motives behind them. It is at this point, also, that we begin to question whether surprise-attack schemes can be viewed as "first steps" toward more comprehensive disarmament in the traditional sense, or instead are incompatible with other forms of "disarmament." Can measures to protect SAC be viewed as first steps toward its dismantlement? Can we initially take cooperative measures to perfect and safeguard each side's capacity to retaliate massively, in the interest of mutual deterrence, and do it as a step toward eliminating the threat of massive retaliation from a tense and troubled world?

Or should we instead recognize surprise-attack schemes to be a practical compromise—an implicit acceptance of "mutual deterrence" as the best source of military stability that we are likely to find—and a recognition that though we may not be able to replace the balance of terror with anything better, there is nevertheless much that we can do to make that balance stable rather than unstable?[3]

III

Once we have identified the surprise-attack problem as one that resides in the possible vulnerability of either side's retaliatory force

[3] In case the reader feels that the argument presented here is correct in principle but uninteresting in fact because the continuous invulnerability of our retaliatory forces is assured beyond any worry, I should like to refer him to Albert Wohlstetter's cogent discussion in "The Delicate Balance of Terror," *Foreign Affairs*, xxxvii, No. 2 (January 1959), pp. 221-34. If he feels that the argument is too exclusively preoccupied with the problem of major surprise attack by one central power on the other, to the exclusion of considerations like limited war, retaliatory threats against third-area aggression, the role of NATO, the significance of the Sino-Soviet alliance, and so forth, the point is acknowledged. One of these interrelations is touched on briefly in the final pages of this chapter.

to a first strike by the other, it becomes necessary to evaluate military strength, defensive measures, and proposals for the inspection or limitation of armament, with precisely this type of strategic vulnerability in mind. We do not, for example, assess American and Soviet strategic forces by counting up the bombers, missiles, submarines, and aircraft carriers on both sides, as though we wanted to see who could put on the most impressive peacetime parade; we have to consider instead what it is that the Russians have that they could effectively use in a surprise attack aimed at the destruction of our retaliatory forces, what we could expect to have left over if they did execute a skillful first strike, and what these residual forces could do to the Soviet Union on a punitive mission. For this kind of estimate, it is of no great help to know that we have as many bombers or missiles as the Russians, or twice as many, or half as many, on the day before the attack. More pertinent is the question of how many separate targets we present to the Russians and what forces the Russians would require to carry high-yield weapons in coordinated fashion to those targets. If we have a thousand combat-ready bombers but they are concentrated at a hundred enemy-aiming points, and if the enemy can, in some cases, hit two or more of our bases with the same bomber, enemy long-range aircraft measured in scores rather than in thousands may be enough to cause us concern. This reduced figure is significant not only in assessing the adequacy of his long-range force, but in assessing the likelihood of his sneaking past our warning system. Of course, if we have planes that are sheltered against his weapons, or hidden from them, or safe in the air when he arrives, or able to get quickly off the ground before he can reach them, his problem is much harder. Similarly, to make an impressive promise of Russian devastation we do not need anywhere near all of our home-based and overseas-based bombers, since a fraction of them might do enormous damage in Russia. But all of these considerations remind us that in judging the adequacy of our strategic forces a parade-ground count of who has the most planes or the most bombs or the most missiles hardly begins to approach the problem. By the same token, the question of "who is ahead" in the arms race is not particularly relevant; the answer will usually be: *whoever strikes first*. And if we have to plan on the conservative assumption that the other side may strike first, this does not mean just that we need more of everything than he has; it more likely means having a different configuration of things. Not more of a striking force of the kind that is best for a first strike, but a more invulnerable retaliatory force of a sufficient size to guarantee a punitive mission adequate to deter anyone who contemplates it. Two hundred bombers safe against attack are worth as much as 2,000 that have only a 10 per cent chance of survival if the other side sneaks in first.[4]

It is not just our striking force that has to be evaluated in the light of a possible surprise attack; an assessment of defensive measures also comes out quite differently if we put primary reliance on deterrence and concentrate on the preservation of our deterrent force. Chicago cannot be hidden, buried in a blast-proof cavern, or kept ten miles off the ground; but concealment, dispersal, hard shelter, and airborne alert are meaningful defenses where defense really matters—in preserving the deterrent force. Similarly, an active air defense of Chicago that has only a 50-50 chance of saving the city from a multi-megaton bomb would be a discouraging prospect, and we have little promise that we could even do that well; but an active defense that could guarantee the survival of half our strategic striking force would be evaluated quite differently. It may be more than enough to guarantee the Russians a prohibitive cost or risk in retaliation. Again, a defense of Chicago that requires the enemy to triple the size of his attack may be a poor prospect for us, since this may only mean a few extra tens of millions of dollars' worth of Russian aircraft to kill some millions of Americans. But a defense of our retaliatory force that requires the enemy to triple the size of his attack may substantially increase the enemy's difficulty in sneaking past our warning system, and therefore appreciably change his estimate of the likelihood of successfully precluding retaliation.

IV

The same kind of calculation is pertinent to an evaluation of proposed arms limitations. If we look just at the problem of a Russian attack on the United States, it appears that ICBM's will make it immaterial to the enemy whether he shoots us from close up or afar; accuracy may not make much difference with a multi-megaton bomb fired at metropolitan areas. If the Russians, to take a numerical illustration, could expect to land half their missiles within, say, a five-mile radius when they shoot them from 5,000 miles, and if the lethal radius of the bomb itself is five miles or so, a metropolitan target poses so little problem from 5,000 miles away that it might not even be worth the expense of moving up close for a better aim. They could shoot us from deep in south-central Russia and have an even chance of landing

[4] An eloquent discussion of this point is in Wohlstetter, *op.cit.*

within a five-mile radius with a single shot, 3-to-1 odds of getting at least one weapon in if they shot two, and 7-to-1 odds of getting at least one in if they shot three. At that rate, 300 weapons would knock out seven-eighths of any hundred American cities they selected; and the most they would gain by moving up close would be to cut the required number down toward 100.

But suppose instead they are trying to hit an American missile or bomber that has been sheltered with reinforced concrete. If the sheltered weapon can stand 50 pounds per square inch or more of blast over-pressure, an enemy missile with a megaton warhead would have to strike within about a mile of the target. If, now, that hypothetical ICBM that could hit within a five-mile radius at 5,000 miles could be moved up to within 1,000 miles, and if we assume that its accuracy is proportionately improved (as might very roughly be suggested for a ballistic missile without a terminal target-seeking capacity), it would still be a correct calculation that with three times as many missiles as aiming points it could knock out seven-eighths of the aiming points. If we had 400 missiles and they wanted to be sure we were left with no more than 50, they would need 1,200 by this calculation. What happens when we put them back to 2,500 or 5,000 miles?

They do not need just two and one-half or five times as many missiles to accomplish the same destruction of our missile force. With a median error of one mile per thousand of range—as in our illustrative example —they get half their missiles in a two and one-half-mile radius at 2,500 miles; only about one in 9 or 10 will land within a mile of target. At 5,000 miles, with half falling inside a 5-mile radius, only about one in 30 will land within a mile of the aiming point. Thus the requirements to knock out 350 of the 400 missiles of our hypothetical example are of the order of 3,000-4,000 and 10,000-12,000, respectively. Moving them back from 2,500 to 5,000 miles could thus raise their requirements by several thousand missiles! This is only a hypothetical example, but the principle is evidently pertinent. There is an order of magnitude of difference between the comparative cost to them of shooting cities at 2,500 or 5,000 miles, and of shooting *hard-sheltered* retaliatory missiles or planes (small target points) at those two alternative ranges. (For unsheltered missiles or planes, of course, the city-target computation is more nearly pertinent.[5])

On some questions, emphasis on the surprise-attack problem may

[5] The example assumes a point target, circular-normal error distribution, weapon effects as given in *The Effects of Nuclear Weapons*, ed. by Samuel Glasstone, Washington, D.C., 1957.

lead to a downright reversal of the answer that one would get from more traditional "disarmament" considerations. Consider the case of a limitation on the number of missiles that might be allowed to both sides (if we ever reached the point in negotiations with Russia where an agreement limiting the number of missiles was pertinent and in-spection seemed feasible). Suppose that we have decided, from a con-sideration of population targets and enemy incentives, what number of missiles we should have to have left over to be able to carry out an adequately punitive retaliatory strike—that is, the number of missiles that we should have to be capable, in the enemy's eyes, of having left over in order to deter him from striking. Suppose, again just for illus-tration, that we estimate that we would need 250 missiles left over after his first strike in order to strike back in a sufficiently terrifying way so that, if he anticipated it, he would be deterred. Consider how many missiles he needs in order to leave us with no more than 250 for various initial numbers which we might have. And suppose—again to simplify calculation—that his accuracies and reliabilities are such that each of his missiles has a 50-50 chance of killing one of our mis-siles, and that ours are sufficiently dispersed so that no one of his mis-siles can knock out two or more of ours at the same time.

If we have 500 missiles, he needs 500 to wipe out *half* of ours, leaving us but 250. If we have 1,000 he needs 2,000 to reduce our residual supply to *one-quarter* of its starting level. If we have 2,000 he needs 6,000, and so on. As we double our own number—using the illustra-tive .5 figure for his reliability and accuracy—we force him not just to double his own, which is already a multiple of ours, but to increase even the multiple of ours that his starting supply has to be.

From this point of view, a limitation on the number of missiles would appear to be more stabilizing, *the larger the number permitted*. This would be so for two reasons. First, the larger the number on both sides, the greater is the absolute number of missiles expected to be left over for retaliation in the event that either side should strike first, and therefore the greater is the deterrence to an attempted first strike. Second, the larger the number of missiles on both sides, the greater must be the absolute and proportionate increase in missiles that either side would have to achieve in order to be capable of assuring, with any specified probability, that the other's left-over missiles would be less than some specified number after being attacked. Thus if one side were to cheat and to disguise and conceal extra missiles, or to break the engagement and race to achieve a dominant number, the difficulty of doing so would be more than proportionately enhanced by any increase in the starting figures on both sides. In fact, if the numbers to begin with are high enough to strain the budgetary capacities of the two enemies, and within these budgetary capacities the number of missiles is high, stability might be imposed by the economic limitation on what either side could do relative to what it would have to do to achieve mastery.

Here is a case, then, in which an "arms race" does not necessarily lead to a more and more unstable situation. For anything like equal numbers on both sides, the likelihood of successfully wiping out the other side's missiles becomes less and less as the missiles on both sides increase. And the *tolerance* of the system increases, too. For small numbers on both sides, a ratio of 2 or 3 to 1 may provide dominance to the larger side, a chance of striking first and leaving the other side a small absolute number for striking back. But if the initial numbers on both sides are higher, it may take a ratio of 10 to 1 rather than 2 or 3 to 1 to have a good chance of striking with impunity; neither side needs to panic if it falls behind a little bit, and neither has any great hope that it could draw far enough ahead to have the kind of dominance it would need.

This greatly simplified view of a "missile duel" is much too specialized to be a strong argument for arms races rather than disarmament. But it does demonstrate that within the logic of stable deterrence, and of schemes for the prevention of surprise attack, the question of more versus fewer weapons has to be analyzed on its merits in individual cases. It is *not* a foregone conclusion that disarmament in the literal sense is the direction that leads to stability.

There is another arms-limitation issue that may lead to different conclusions, whether we are worried about the general problem of attack or the peculiar problem of surprise attack. It has to do with the implications of continued improvement in missiles, and the value of inhibiting missile research and development if we thought a system of inhibitions might be feasible. It is widely argued that with improving accuracy and yield of missiles the balance of mutual deterrence becomes less and less stable, and that consequently it would be useful to freeze missile technology as much as possible. The argument essentially rests on the question of how many missiles it takes to knock out a missile; with sufficient accuracy and reliability it may take little more than a 1-to-1 ratio, on the assumption that one knows where his targets are located. As indicated above in connection with zonal limitations, the number of missiles required may rise disproportionately with increases in aiming errors. As missiles get more accurate, and can carry higher-yield warheads, they become more and more capable of destroying other missiles; and the tolerable inequality in the number of missiles on both sides becomes less and less. So if there were any way to prevent improvement in the accuracy of missiles, we might enjoy an era in which each side could easily have more weapons than the other side could possibly knock out, even with very disproportionate numbers on the two sides. Missile research, by making the missiles more accurate, is thus a force for instability.

But the important thing to inquire is whether further improvement in missile technology will have a *net* effect that raises or lowers the vulnerability of missiles to each other. (To sharpen the point, I am ignoring the relation of missiles to other weapons, or of one kind of missile to another.) It is true that the reduction of aiming error lowers the number of missiles required to kill a missile, and hence makes for instability. But improvements in the design of missiles may also make them easier to shelter—smaller, less elaborate logistically, requiring shorter exposure before firing, and so forth. Considering the replacement of liquid-fueled by solid-fueled missiles, or the replacement of visible and immovable ICBM's and IRBM's by concealed and mobile Polaris submarines, there is much to suggest that technological innovation may do at least as much for the invulnerability of missiles as it does for the counter-tendency, the potency of a missile against another missile. In general, if we think of the possibilities of developing less vulnerable missiles by putting them under water, by hiding them, by moving them frequently, and so on, there is no strong presumption that the situation will get worse as missiles become more potent and more flexible. This is another dimension of the "arms race" in which the balance of terror may possibly become more stable, not less so; at least, there is no necessary presumption that we should wish to freeze missile technology even if we could.

Incidentally, if the argument above on numbers is a valid one, it reinforces the argument favoring improvements in missile technology. An important result of advancing technology may be reduction in the cost of a missile with given performance. Thus, for a given budget, improvement in missile technology may increase the number of missiles of given capability that one can have. If stability comes with larger numbers, cheaper missiles may be stabilizing.[6]

[6] It is not being implied that the line of reasoning presented here is the only pertinent one. The possibility of error, accident, or mischief might (or might not) be greater with the larger number of missiles. The purpose of this chapter is not to settle the question of whether we should feel more at ease with larger or smaller numbers of

Our attitude toward missile submarines, and toward the problem of devising submarine-detection techniques, should be much affected by whether we are worried about enemy attack or enemy *surprise* attack. If the submarine proves to be for many years a fairly invulnerable site for anti-population missiles, we should perhaps view it not as an especially terrifying development but as a reassuring one. If in fact the best we can hope for is mutual deterrence and we only want the balance to be stable, then the Polaris-type missile carried by a submarine of great mobility and endurance may be the kind of weapon system that we should like to see in adequate numbers on both sides. If it should prove to be both undetectable and highly reliable, it would have the advantage of not needing to strike first in order to strike at all, of not fearing that an aggressor might hope to knock out the very forces that were supposed to deter him. True, it might seem more reassuring if we had the power to destroy the enemy's missile subs but he did not have the power to destroy ours; but if the power already exists on both sides, and we cannot wish it away, then the most we can hope for is that this capacity to destroy each other will itself be sufficiently indestructible so that each side is in fact deterred. From that point of view, we perhaps should not even wish that we alone could have the "invulnerable" nuclear-weapon submarine; if in fact we have either no intention or no political capacity for a first strike, it would always be helpful if the enemy were confidently assured of this. His own manifest invulnerability to our first strike could be to our advantage if it relieved him of a principal concern that might motivate him to try striking first. If *he* has to worry about the exposure of *his* strategic force to a surprise attack by *us, we* have to worry about it, too.

These thoughts also give us a peculiar feeling about the scientific search for submarine-detection devices. We have all read that the Navy is urgently seeking a better system of defense against submarines. There is no question but that we have to devote ourselves intently to the problem. Yet we ought simultaneously to *hope* that the problem is insoluble. If it is insoluble (in the relative sense in which a technical problem can ever be insoluble) and submarines are destined to be comparatively safe vehicles for a decade or so, stable mutual deterrence may be technologically possible. If submarines prove to be vulnerable themselves, for reasons yet to be discovered, arms technology is lamentably less stable than we hope. We have to *try* to detect submarines,

---

missiles on both sides but to indicate that the answer is not automatically implied by our attitude toward "disarmament."

because we cannot afford to let the Russians find a technique that we do not know, and because we have to learn all we can about detection to make our submarines less detectable; but like a person who has entered into an agreement with a partner whom he cannot trust, we may search like the very devil for a loophole, knowing that our partner is searching just as hard, while hoping that no loophole is to be found. (Like two antagonists with pistols and no bullets, searching desperately for bullets, we hope that if there are any we find them first; but we can also hope that there aren't any.)[7]

Once we have pressed the argument this far, we may as well carry it all the way. If our problem is to guarantee to an enemy that we have the capacity to strike a punitive blow after being struck ourselves—and to assure him that we know that he knows it so that we are under no temptation to doubt the potency of our own deterrence and strike first—we should find virtue in technological discoveries that enhance the anti-population potency of our retaliatory weapons. If it is logical to take measures to guarantee that a larger proportion of our retaliatory forces could survive a first strike on them, the same logic should make us welcome an increase in the potency of those that do survive. As Bernard Brodie has said, "When we consider the special requirements of deterrence in the minimal or basic sense of deterring a direct attack upon oneself, it is possible that one can see some utility in the super-dirty bomb. Since the emphasis has to be on making certain that the enemy fears even the smallest number of bombs that might be sent in retaliation, one wants these bombs to be—and thus to appear before the event—as horrendous as possible. This objective is advanced by making the bomb super-dirty, which incidentally also makes accuracy of delivery relatively unimportant."[8]

The novelty of this reasoning disappears as soon as we recognize that the "balance of terror," if it is stable, is simply a massive and modern version of an ancient institution: the exchange of hostages. In older times, one committed oneself to a promise by delivering hostages physically into the hands of one's distrustful "partner"; today's military technology makes it possible to have the lives of a potential enemy's women and children within one's grasp while he keeps those women and children thousands of miles away. So long as each side has the manifest power to destroy a nation and its population in response to

---

[7] Because this chapter is about principles, not about submarines, I can perhaps be excused for pretending that undetectability on short notice in the open sea is equivalent to invulnerability in my example.

[8] Bernard Brodie, "The Anatomy of Deterrence," *World Politics*, xi, No. 2 (January 1959), p. 187.

an attack by the other, the "balance of terror" amounts to a tacit understanding backed by a total exchange of all conceivable hostages. We
may not, of course, want to exchange quite *that* many hostages in
support of this particular understanding with this particular enemy.
But in a lawless world that provides no recourse to damage suits for
breach of this unwritten contract, hostages may be the only device by
which mutually distrustful and antagonistic partners can strike a bargain.[9]

V

This line of reasoning is not simply an enormous rationalization for
an arms race. It does indeed suggest that "disarmament" in the literal
sense, aimed indiscriminately at weapons of all kinds—or even selec-
tively aimed at the most horrifying weapons of mass destruction—
could produce instability rather than stability, and might have to be
completely successful in order not to be disastrous. Nevertheless, there
is an important area of arms limitations that is not only compatible
with the foregoing analysis but is suggested by it.

It suggests making a distinction between the kinds of weapons that
are peculiarly suitable to the exploitation of a first strike and weapons
that are peculiarly suitable to the retaliatory role. At one extreme is
the "pure" strike-back type of weapon: the relatively inaccurate vehicle
with a super-dirty bomb that can kill just about everything in the
enemy's country *except* a well-protected or well-hidden retaliatory
force, and that itself is so well-protected or well-hidden as to be invulnerable to any weapons that the other side might possess. Ideally,
this weapon would suffer no disadvantage in waiting to strike second
and gain no advantage in striking first. At the opposite extreme is a
weapon that is itself so vulnerable that it could not survive to strike
second, or a weapon specially designed to find and destroy the enemy's
retaliatory forces before they are launched, that would lose most of its
usefulness if it were held until the other side has already started something. These "strike-first" weapons not only give their possessor a
powerful incentive to strike first, and an incentive to jump the gun
in the event of ambiguous warning rather than to wait and make
absolutely sure; they are a tacit declaration to the enemy that one

[9] It should be emphasized that I am discussing only the problem of major surprise
attack here. The implications of the "hostage" concept for, say, civil defense policy
depends on its relation to other contingencies as well—limited war, mischief by a third
party, less-than-massive retaliation, and so forth. Some of these interrelations between
surprise attack and other military contingencies are touched on in the final pages of
this chapter.

expects to strike first, and they consequently invite the enemy to strike a little before *that* and to act with haste in the event he thinks that we think it is time to act quickly.

Between the extremes of the "pure" strike-first weapon and the "pure" strike-back weapon, there are the weapons that can strike first but do not need to, that can survive and serve the retaliatory purpose but that also might have an important effect on the other side's retaliatory forces if used first. Perhaps most weapons fall in this category if reasonable precautions are taken for their protection. So we cannot make a nice distinction between first-strike and second-strike weapons, extolling the one and disparaging the other in our approach to the surprise-attack problem. If we were to consider eliminating all weapons that had any possible effect against the other side's retaliatory forces, or that enjoyed any advantage in being used first, there might not be enough left with which to promise retaliation.[10] But surprise-attack negotiations might usefully concentrate on the opposite extreme.

The most obvious candidates would be exposed weapons, vulnerable weapons. It might seem anomalous to insist to the Russians that they cover any nakedness of their strategic forces, or for them to suggest that we protect better some of our own. More likely would be suggestions to abandon weapons that were provocatively exposed to the other side. Note how different in spirit this would be from the "ban the bomb" orientation. Whatever the propaganda implications of such a topic, it at least has the merit of viewing deterrence as something to be enhanced, not dismantled.

Second, restrictions on the deployment of forces that affect their counterforce potency rather than their counterpopulation potency might be sought. They will not be, until there is candid recognition that surprise-attack schemes are to be deliberately aimed at protecting, not degrading, each side's strike-back capability. The discussion above of the effect of range on missile requirements, whatever its specific merits, suggests that this category of limitations may not be empty.

Third, there may be some useful exploration of cooperative measures, or mutually accommodated modes of behavior, that reduce the danger of war by misapprehension. Even voluntary exchange of information might help, if we and the Russians can unilaterally pick modes of behavior that, when the truth is known, are reassuring. This is presumably the idea behind proposals for inspection of air traffic in the north polar area; and there may be some other types of activity in

---

[10] Furthermore, we are taking nothing but the surprise-attack problem into account here.

which there could be mutual benefit from some traffic rules. What is attractive about this category of measures—as about a candid discussion of the evils of strike-first weapon systems—is that they may make possible some understandings that do not have to be embodied in formal agreements, and facilitate unilateral accommodations on both sides.

Fourth, there may be arrangements to cope with crises and emergencies that threaten to explode into an unintended war. A later section of the chapter discusses this point at some length.

Fifth, there may be measures that, by making surprise less likely, make a first strike less attractive. This point brings us back to the open-skies type of proposal.

VI

Most of the public discussion of surprise-attack schemes during the last few years has related to measures that might reduce the likelihood of surprise, rather than measures to limit what weapons could do if surprise were achieved. The open-skies proposal was based on the idea that, with sufficient observation of each other's military forces, neither side could achieve surprise in an attack and, lacking the advantage of surprise, would be deterred.

The technical problem of devising a practical inspection scheme that could yield each side adequate warning of an attack by the other has probably become not only much more difficult to discuss, but much more difficult to solve, since the first open-skies proposal was made. With hydrogen weapons reducing the number of aircraft that might be needed in a surprise attack, with missiles promising to reduce the total time available between the initial actions in readying a strike and the explosion of weapons on target, and with mobile systems like missile submarines to keep under surveillance, it looks as though pure inspection unaccompanied by any limits on the behavior of the things to be inspected would be enormously difficult or enormously ineffectual. The idea of examining photographs for strategic indications of force movements and concentrations is simply obsolete. The problem now would seem to be one of intensive surveillance of strategic forces by a vast organization that could transmit authentic messages reporting suspicious activity within at most a few hours, and eventually within a few minutes, in a way that is not intolerably susceptible of false alarms. There is no practical assurance that this could be done; and it must be kept in mind that a system of this sort cannot get a real test until the day that "This is not a drill" puts it to its only trial.

This does not mean that inspection schemes against surprise attack have no prospect of success. What it means is that a scheme providing for *nothing but inspection* may have very poor prospects. But if one cannot send observers out to follow all the aircraft, missiles, and submarines wherever they go, one can still consider calling the aircraft, missiles, and submarines to assemble where they are more easily watched. If restrictions on the deployment of forces are used to make the task of inspection more manageable, something may be accomplished. But though there may be promise in the idea of a combination of inspection and weapon limitations, there are also some serious problems.

One is a possible incompatibility between the need for inspection and the need for concealment. When missiles become sufficiently accurate, it may become almost impossible physically to protect one's own retaliatory forces by the sheer provision of cement, or, if not impossible, exceedingly costly. Mobility and concealment may then have to be the source of security for the retaliatory forces; if the enemy can hit anything he can locate, and kill anything he can hit, he has to be made unable to locate it. To the extent that he can have our own retaliatory weapons under continuous surveillance he has continuous information on their location.

In other ways, an inspection scheme on the scale required for protection against surprise attack might yield excessive information about the disposition of the other's forces and make them more vulnerable. It is widely known, for example, that there was a time when hurricane winds immobilized an extremely large portion of the B-36's that then comprised our principal retaliatory threat. The implications for surprise attack of such an event differ widely, depending on whether the enemy just knows in a general way that this kind of thing can happen to us, or instead has definite information when it occurs and knows exactly whether or not he has clear sailing for a few days. Imagine the state of tension that could occur if *either* side's strategic-force personnel began to suffer a severe epidemic that threatened to immobilize them temporarily before the eyes of the other side's inspection. Much better —if we and they are occasionally to land in a very unalert position for reasons that are impossible to prevent, at least once in a while—that neither of us should be in a position to know too much about the other's occasional disabilities.

Finally, while there may be arrangements that have a high probability of providing warning of the other's preparation for an attack, the value of the system depends on what one can do if he does get warning. One can prepare to send off his own anticipatory strike, hoping to get in first; but this is an unattractive course if the warning is ambiguous. A false alarm then leads to war. And while the enemy's knowledge that we would strike quickly if we had warning may be an important deterrent to his initiating any preparations for an attack, his fear of our acting suddenly on the basis of a false alarm may raise his estimate of the likelihood that war will eventually take place anyway, and increase his incentive to mount a preventive attack that evades detection. So it would be helpful to be able to use a warning for something other than a signal for mounting our own attack.

At the other extreme we could ignore the warning, just letting it come. But there are probably things we should do to "get ready." And if the things we can do to get ready appreciably reduce the likelihood that his attack will succeed—that is, if they raise the likelihood that we can retaliate severely—we may want to make a quick announcement to the enemy that we are ready, in the hope that our improved posture will deter his final decision.

The important question now is what we do that constitutes getting ready. If the answer is simply, "Be more alert," there is another question, "Why weren't we more alert in the first place?" Most of the obvious things that one would do if he had warning of an attack are things that one probably would like to do perpetually in view of the ever-present possibility of an attack. And if our Strategic Air Command is continually doing its best to reduce the time it takes to get aircraft ready and off the ground in the face of warning, or to keep the doors tightly shut on sheltered aircraft, or to keep aircraft safe in the air in combat-ready condition, there may not be much more that it can do on short notice.

There is an answer to this last objection, but it is not altogether satisfying. It is that there are things that a nation can do in the face of imminent attack that it could not do continuously and indefinitely. One can evacuate or go underground, but not forever. One can get his retaliatory forces safely off the ground, where they are no longer targets for enemy bombs; but they cannot stay in the air forever. One can put men on 24-hour duty, but not for many days in a row. One can ground all commercial aircraft to raise the reliability of the warning system, but the economic loss might be exorbitant if commercial and private flying were forsworn for all time in the interest of making enemy aircraft more recognizable. One can provide more air crews per plane, to get around the fact that people have to sleep, but this is expensive. There are, in other words, things that one can do to "get ready" in the face of expected attack that one cannot be expected to have been doing all along. But assuming that the things that should have been done all along actually were being done, and that the enemy was tempted to try a sneak attack in spite of our preparations, the important question is how much we can improve our posture within the time available once we get warning.

There is another question: How long can we keep it up? Suppose we cannot physically keep all aircraft in the air at all times, as is true, and that it may be too costly in all respects (accidents as well as jet fuel) to keep as many as half of them in the sky on the average, but that a substantial increase in the number aloft can be effected on short notice if a serious warning is received. This might well mean that the enemy would not be deterred by our ordinary posture, but would be deterred by the posture we can adopt when we get warning. Does this mean that he quits as soon as he sees that we have gotten ready? Or might he just wait until the gas is gone, the pilots are tired, and the planes have to come down again?

This is the problem of "system fatigue" that is likely to plague any super-alert stance that one could take. And if for the first few hours or days one has done literally everything that can be done to maximize safety in the very short run, the resulting fatigue may make the system even more vulnerable, during the recuperation period, than it originally was under "normal" procedures. If the enemy knows this and can predict it, may he not just wait until fatigue sets in, perhaps hoping that the job will be even easier once our response has been exhausted? And must we not, anticipating this, strike in anticipation? Does this not make "super-alert" a self-defeating activity, hence an irrelevant one?

The answer to this has two parts. First, one must try to design a super-alert response that has good endurance and little fatigue, recognizing that this means compromising its peak effectiveness. Second, one may have to engage in some kind of crash disarmament negotiations with the enemy during the period that one has in fact taken measures to ensure his own invulnerability of retaliation. If we can keep up a super-alert for twenty-four hours, we have twenty-four hours during which to attempt to demand or negotiate some degree of Russian "disarmament" that is both tolerable to the Russians and sufficiently reassuring to us to permit us to return to "normal" rather than to proceed with total war. This might mean devising and instituting a much more ambitious scheme of anti-surprise-attack measures than had been politically feasible during the earlier period. It would mean negotiating not just under the ordinary pressure of knowing that sneak attack is a long-term danger, but doing it with clear notice that if measures to make successful first strikes impossible have not been devised, agreed upon, and taken by a quick deadline, war by mutual consent has become inevitable.

It would probably not be enough, in these circumstances, for the Russians to return to the *status quo* of the day before. In one sense we might feel safer than before; we would have more confidence in the warning system, because it had actually worked, and the Russians would have less confidence in their ability to escape detection. But there would be two very unstable factors. One is that the Russians would have learned how not to launch a surprise attack, and might in the process have learned a good deal about how to do it in some other way, having seen the way our response worked. The second is that the record would show unmistakably what conclusions the Russians had been led to by their calculus of the advantage of attack, and we would be under no illusion about their willingness to attack if they thought they could get away with it. Furthermore, the Russians, knowing that we know their motives, would know that we will be even quicker to respond to ambiguous warning in the future, and that any temptation we may have had toward preventive attack would have undergone a legitimate increase. Thus our *intentions* toward each other would have been badly destabilized. We are no longer *suspicious* of each other's intentions; we are *certain* of them!

These reflections do not prove that extra warning would be either useless or embarrassing. What they indicate is that warning by itself may not be enough. Extra warning does provide an *opportunity*, but the opportunity has to be exploited with skill. And preparations for what one would do in the contingency may have to be made well ahead of time. There is barely time to deliver an ultimatum to the Russians when we catch them preparing to attack. Deciding what ultimatum would both meet our needs and be tolerable to the Russians not only is intellectually difficult; it is technically difficult, depending on such things as procedures to verify compliance. We could probably only deliver an effective ultimatum if we had thought ahead of time about what it should contain.

VII

There are two quite distinct criteria for judging the efficacy of an inspection system, or for designing the system itself. One is how well the system gets at the truth in spite of the subject's best efforts to conceal it; the other is how well it helps the subject to display the truth when it is in his interest to do so. The distinction is pertinent to the contingencies in which one's enemy and oneself may (at least momentarily) have a strong interest in conveying the actual truth rather than in disguising it.

Inspection schemes are ordinarily judged by how they perform against evasion—against clandestine activities that are hidden or disguised, against efforts to drown the inspection system with interference, or to degrade it by spoofing, or to impose administrative obstructions. They are designed on the premise that the enemy (or "partner") will try to convey false information, that being what the scheme is designed to guard against. Since the schemes are designed to detect "illegal" activity, they have to presume that such activity will naturally be accompanied by skillful efforts to avoid detection. Reliability is measured by how much the other party can get away with if he cheats as shrewdly as he can.

But a very different notion of the reliability of a system, and perhaps a quite different system, is involved if we reverse the premise. How good is the system if the other party in fact wishes to convey true information? What is the best system for observing, verifying, and transmitting credible and authentic evidence of the truth on the assumption that the other party wishes to convey the truth and will try to submit the kind of evidence that does indeed convey it? The difference is like that between a scheme for discovering the guilty and a scheme for permitting the innocent to establish alibis. A policeman may be unable to tell whether I am participating in a gang fight around the block, if in fact I *am* participating in it; but if I am *not,* and I want to establish the truth, I can go sit beside him until the crisis is over. The *kind of evidence* that I would use to establish falsely that I am innocent may be different in character from the evidence that I would use to establish it if it were true. And a scheme that has little reliability for finding the truth if I wish to conceal it may have high reliability for verifying the truth if in fact my interest is in providing incontestable evidence. Roughly speaking, one system arrives at a presumption of innocence in a negative way, by an absence of positive evidence to the contrary; the other scheme relies on positive evidence, and is pertinent to the particular situations in which the subject's own interest is in letting the truth be known.

The difference between these two situations is pertinent to the distinction between a scheme to minimize the fear of *deliberate* surprise attack and a scheme to minimize the fear of inadvertent, or "accidental," or unintended war—the war that results from a false alarm, or from a mistaken evaluation of the other's response to a false alarm, or to a wrong interpretation of a mechanical accident, or to the catalytic mischief of a third party interested in promoting war, or to a situation in which the apprehension by each side that the other may be about to pre-empt explodes by feedback into a war by mutual panic. In the one case, that of a planned, deliberate, surprise attack, the aggressor has every reason to disguise the truth. But in the case of "inadvertent war," both sides have a strong interest in conveying the truth if the truth can in fact be conveyed in a believable way in time to prevent the other side's mistaken decision.

Misapprehension of Attack

Consider this question: how would we prove to the Russians that we were not engaged in a surprise attack, when in fact we were not but they thought we might be? How might they prove to us that they were not initiating a surprise attack, if in fact they were not but they knew that we were afraid they might be? Here is a case in which each side has an interest in the truth; it is the other's bad intelligence that is the culprit. If they think we are striking when in fact we are not, and we cannot prove that we are not, we may end up by being struck pre-emptively by them or by deciding that we have to strike quickly after all, simply because, being expected to, we can no longer afford not to, their misguided effort at pre-emption having become inevitable.

Evidently it is not, as a general rule, going to be enough just to tell the truth in order to convey the truth convincingly. There may indeed be some situations in which sheer verbal contact is enough to allay each side's suspicions; just to take a wild example, if the Russians suffered an accidental nuclear explosion on one of their own bases, it might be helpful to both sides if they could simply reassure us quickly that they knew it was an explosion, that they were not interpreting it as a harbinger of an attack by us, and so on. But in most of the cases that one can imagine, it is insufficient simply to assert that one is not engaging in a strategic strike or that one is not in a menacing posture. There has to be some way of authenticating certain facts, the facts presumably involving the disposition of forces. We would have to prove not only that we were not *intending* to exploit our position, but that our actual position was one that *could not* be exploited to doublecross the enemy if he should take us at our word and restrain his own forces.

Misapprehension During Limited War

Consider another instance. Suppose in the course of a limited war one side or the other takes an action that, though actually within the scope of limited war, might be misinterpreted as a strategic strike. Suppose we, for example, used the kinds of aircraft that would alternatively be used in a strike against Russian bases, and flew them in directions that might be interpreted as aimed at the Soviet Union itself—as might be the case if they were flying from North African bases or the Mediterranean fleet to countries near the southern border of the Soviet Union. Alternatively, suppose that Soviet aircraft flew a limited war mission that could be interpreted, on the basis of the momentary evidence we might get, as a strike at all of our overseas bases and carriers, but that was actually a limited strike and not part of a general effort to destroy United States retaliatory power.

The question arises whether there are any means by which to reduce the likelihood of misinterpretation in this case, where misinterpretation might lead one side either to take off in anticipated retaliation, to pre-empt as quickly as it could, or to get into a super-alert status that had a high proclivity toward false alarm. The side making such use of potentially strategic weapons might well wish to convey some "truth" about the limit to its intentions. Assertions alone might in this case be of some help, since they would provide voluntary advance warning to the other side of a kind that would seem to be pretty genuine evidence that one did not have in mind a major strike. One might, that is, literally ask the enemy to get into an alert status, thereby doing something that would hardly be reasonable if one were really about to enlarge the war at one blow to an all-out counterforce strike. But in addition to just stating what one was doing, and giving warning in the process, one might wish to give additional factual evidence about the number and location of weapons involved, or other characteristics of the sortie, so that the enemy could check the truth of the assertion. This is not an easy thing to do, since the side engaging in the sortie would not wish to give away too much truth or the sortie itself would be spoiled; but quite possibly one would wish to provide both an indication of limited intentions and some reliable means for the other side to check them. And even if one did not wish to give any true information about the sortie actually planned, one might wish to bend over backward to demonstrate that complementary actions—actions involving other forces in other parts of the world that would almost certainly take place if this were an all-out counterforce strike—were in fact not being taken.

Reciprocal Misapprehension

Consider another case that was described by Gromyko at a press conference in April 1958: "After all, meteors and electronic interference are reflected on Soviet radar screens, too. If in such cases Soviet aircraft, loaded with atomic and hydrogen bombs, were to proceed in the direction of the United States and its bases in other states, the air fleets of both sides, having noticed each other somewhere over the Arctic region, under such circumstances would draw the natural conclusion that a real attack by the enemy was taking place, and mankind would find itself involved in the whirlpool of atomic war."

Assuming for the moment that the situation described might conceivably arise, how might the interacting misapprehensions of both sides be slowed down and reversed? If there were some way of reversing motion on both sides, in a properly phased and authenticated way, a kind of balanced withdrawal by mutual consent might be possible.

The bargaining environment is not a propitious one. At best there would be a very few hours in which to conduct the negotiations, and at worst no time at all. The requirements for a successful outcome can analytically be divided into two parts. First, there has to be discovered some "solution"—some pattern of action that reverses the trend toward mutual attack, and that constitutes a dynamically stable withdrawal to a less menacing alert status, one that yields neither side a dangerous advantage in the process, and that is within the physical capabilities of the forces concerned. The second requirement is that compliance somehow be observable, verifiable, and provable. We cannot carry out our part of the bargain unless we have trustworthy means for monitoring the other side's compliance, and the same is true for them. Conceivably we would have an interest in cheating, if we should think it a splendid moment to go ahead with a surprise attack that we had never had the initiative to get started in the first place; but it is overwhelmingly more probable that we should wish in these circumstances for a cheat-proof monitoring system that we could submit to, so that if we did comply with our part of the bargain, the other side would have no doubt about it. The problem is essentially one of contract enforcement. And the motivation in this case, for each side, is to convey the truth as best he can if in fact he complies with the plan.

This example not only makes clear the need for some *prior arrangement* for observation and verification, in view of the very short time available for bringing inspectors to the scene; it also demonstrates how important it is to have thought ahead of time about what kind of proposal to make, and to have designed one's own flight plan in a way that could take maximum advantage of any means we might have for deliberately giving the enemy true information in the event it becomes desperately necessary to do so.

This case also may illustrate the difference between the two criteria for reliability of an inspection system. It might be very difficult to design radar that would *always* catch the enemy—and by which he could always catch us—in an attempt at sneak attack; it is quite another question how to design radar so that if we both wished to invite voluntary surveillance, we could submit in a convincing way. In one case we are, in effect, evading his radar surveillance as best we can. In the other we may deliberately "parade" in front of his radar, or submit to other means of long-distance recognition, so long as he does the same for us. A system that is designed to minimize evasion may not be one that is best designed to take advantage of the motives that are brought to bear when two parties who admittedly distrust each other find it profitable to strike an agreement.

Warning of Actual Attack

Even in the case of an enemy effort at a deliberate sneak attack, arrangements for the revelation of true information might prove to be useful. If we imagine a situation in which we actually received tactical warning of a planned surprise attack—especially one involving, say, submarines or surface vessels so that the evidence might exist as much as a day or so in advance of the planned strike—the question always arises of what we should do with the warning. As indicated earlier, there are three main categories of behavior for us, aside from just waiting for the attack and getting ready for it. One is to announce to the Russians that we know it is coming, hoping that the loss of surprise will deter them from carrying out the plan. A second is to pre-empt quickly ourselves, enjoying the moral satisfaction of being in the right but suffering the certainty of war. The third is to make demands on the Russians, insisting on the withdrawal or surrender of their advance forces, insisting that they account for the disposition of their strategic forces, at least until they have been forced out of their advanced positions, and the like. We might go further and insist that a crash disarmament program must be agreed upon now or never. But however far our demands went, they would require some rather extensive means of observing compliance of a kind that probably could not adequately be improvised within the short time available—certainly not unless we had made some plans of our own about what to ask for and how to observe it, and possibly not unless there were previous arrangements on the part of the Russians that made them capable of revealing their own behavior in order to demonstrate compliance.

In other words, in a case of this sort—presumably the most "favorable" case of planned surprise attack, namely, the case in which we do get advance warning—any strategy on our part between the extremes of instant pre-emption and a passive declaration of readiness would require some kind of ambitious inspection arrangement. Having in existence a scheme that could, with last-minute modifications, locate and identify Russian forces and monitor their withdrawal into a less menacing posture would probably be essential. It might also be essential to the Russian incentive for compliance that we be able to demonstrate enough about the disposition of our own forces to assure the Russians that we are not doublecrossing them in the event that they do comply.

Longer-term Surveillance

The difference between these crises and emergency situations and the longer-term problem of policing arms limitations or inspecting against the danger of surprise attack is in the kind of evidence that is required and in the strength of the motivation to provide it. The more "leisurely" process of inspecting an arms agreement, or even of observing against the danger of surprise attack, is generally viewed as depending mainly on *negative evidence*—that is, the *absence of evidence*. One reduces the probability of missing such evidence by enlarging and intensifying the system; and one supposes that the problem of evasion is made somewhat difficult by the fact that successful evasion may require keeping particular activities hidden from view over a long period of time. But in a crisis one requires more certain evidence; one does not have time to get leads and follow them up; there is no time to try the system out and enlarge it or intensify it if it does not work. Consequently, a crisis agreement would have to rely on *positive evidence*—not the absence of evidence that the other side is cheating, but positive evidence that one is not cheating. Instead of looking for evidence about what the other party is *not* doing, one demands evidence that shows what he *is* doing. And the reason why such evidence might be forthcoming in a crisis is that the motive to provide it—the greater urgency of reaching an understanding or an agreement that depends on it—may be enhanced in such an emergency.

Why not design a system that requires positive evidence for the longer-term problem, too? The answer seems to be that it may make unacceptable demands on the participants. Actually, a limitation on the deployment of forces—say, a limit on the number or percentage of aircraft that could be out of sight in the air at any given time—would be essentially a means of giving positive evidence of where a sizable fraction of the aircraft is, relying on negative evidence only with respect to the remainder permitted to be out of sight. But to require "positive evidence" of the identity and location of every airplane at all times might give too much information to the potential enemy, and, of course, might destabilize the situation with respect to surprise attack by making each side's retaliatory forces more vulnerable to counterforce attack. Furthermore, the provision of positive evidence may require drastic actions that could not be tolerated as a continuous state of affairs but might readily be acceptable in particular emergencies. Grounding all commercial aircraft to improve surveillance and warning might be an example. So there does seem to be a special correlation between positive-evidence systems and *crisis* arrangements for inspection or limitation. But the correlation should not be exaggerated; certainly if the United States is *not* cheating on an agreement and is *not* preparing an attack, we have an interest in submitting to a sufficiently rigorous examination to prove it and to get full credit, and to minimize the Soviet incentive to cheat or pre-empt in "self-defense."

Intensity of Use of Surveillance System

In some cases the difference between a positive-evidence system and a negative-evidence system is a matter of scale or intensity. If we had technical means of identifying individual aircraft and establishing their position, a "normal" anti-surprise-attack inspection scheme might provide for only limited use of the technique, perhaps on a sample basis, perhaps covering only aircraft outside the borders of the country concerned. But if it ever became essential to the striking of a quick bargain that each side be able to reassure itself as to the exact identity and location of every enemy aircraft, each side might in such an exceptional circumstance agree to a complete census of aircraft, either immediately or in some phased fashion that would keep each side about equally knowledgeable of the other's forces during the course of the census. Similarly, part of a regular inspection scheme might involve a limitation on the areas where aircraft could patrol, for the purpose of keeping down noise levels and permitting readier identification of unknown aircraft. In time of acute emergency, however, both sides might be strongly motivated to agree to ground all commercial aircraft and to channel military flights in a way that would drastically eliminate interference and permit identification.

Overbuilding the System

For the purpose of being prepared for crises and unforeseen situations, there is consequently a good argument for overbuilding an inspection system relative to the use that has been agreed on. Having stand-by capacity to enlarge or intensify the system, or to augment it with additional facilities and inspectors, may have a good deal to do with the usefulness of the system in time of crisis. To put the point differently, we should not judge the reliability and usefulness of a system solely in terms of the motivations of the participants during "normal" operations; we should recognize that occasions may arise when there is a powerful motive for crash negotiations on arms limitations, at least momentary limitations, with no time available for setting up observation and communication systems *ad hoc*.

To be specific: in the event that there should be established an inspection system to monitor an agreement to suspend nuclear tests, we should consider carefully how both sides might take advantage of the inspectors and their facilities in case an acute military crisis occurred. The mobility of the inspectors, their location, their communication facilities, their technical training and surveillance equipment, their trustworthiness, and their numbers should be evaluated and designed not just with nuclear-test detection in mind, but with some view to their serving a desperately critical need for a means of inspection, verification, and communication in a crisis that threatens both us and the Russians with inadvertent war.

VIII

Any scheme involving inspection or limitation of weapons or their use should be subjected to the test of considering what happens to it in the event of limited war.

As discussed above, an inspection scheme could possibly be helpful during such an occasion by minimizing certain explosive misapprehensions of both sides about each other, and might help to prevent mistaking limited actions involving each side's SAC for an all-out action or a pre-emptive effort. At the same time, an inspection scheme could be a great hindrance to the conduct of the limited war itself: it might be in a position to see too much, particularly with respect to strategic forces, once the activity level was geared inside the United States or the USSR to some third-country war. In this event, there would be powerful incentive for one side or the other to break the agreement, to propose its suspension, perhaps to accuse the other side of abusing the system, to drown it with interference, or otherwise to renounce, destroy, or degrade the system with every effort to put the blame on the other side. If this happened, it might mean that the long-term possibility of an effective surprise-attack or arms-limitation scheme would have suffered a permanent setback, the whole idea having become discredited.

It seems necessary to try to design the system with the limited-war contingency in view. An example of how the design of a system might be affected by making allowance for the possibility of limited war is the question of who should operate the system. There would probably be great advantages to having any surprise-attack inspection system operated by the nationals of the principal participants in the scheme, Russians inspecting the United States and Americans (or Americans, British, French, etc.) inspecting the Soviet Union. The problem of trust—of seeing with one's own eyes—may be critical in an inspection scheme that requires a response so quick that there is no time for confirmation procedures. And there may be practical reasons for supposing that, at least at the initiation of a scheme, the technical and organizational problems of using a United Nations or neutral-personnel system would be too great.

But perhaps the possibility of the system's having to survive a limited war might suggest additional reasons for considering the introduction of neutral or United Nations personnel—if not at the beginning of the scheme, at least later when they can be trained and organized. There might be appreciably more tolerance to, say, Swiss observers at American installations than to Russian or Chinese, if we were engaged in a war in which American soldiers were being killed by Russian weapons, Russian-supported forces, or Russian forces themselves. Imagine the furor that an unsympathetic newspaper could raise if patriotic American newspapermen could not get into Cape Canaveral, while a bunch of "Bolshevik spies" were made welcome in the place at a time when American soldiers were dying overseas through the efforts of the compatriots of these very guests at America's most secret bases. Or consider Russian (or Chinese) observers at our Far East strategic air and naval bases during an attempted invasion of Quemoy or of Taiwan itself. Our ability to tolerate Swiss, Swedes, Indians, or even Finns might be much higher. (In case it proved hard to agree with the Russians on just who is "neutral," it might not be necessary to have the same "neutral" nationalities policing both sides.)

This personnel question may be important in itself; but it is raised here only as an illustration of how one's judgment of the effectiveness, reliability, and durability of an inspection scheme may depend a good deal on how severe the tests are that we think the scheme may have to meet. The possibility of limited war is one of these tests.

IX

From the foregoing considerations, it is not at all clear that the stability of the balance of terror—the lack of temptation to deliberate surprise attack, and the immunity of the situation to false alarm—will be greatly affected by the military arrangements that we try to work out with the Russians. As nature reveals her scientific and technological secrets over the coming years, we may find that each side can (if it does what it ought to do and does it rapidly enough) substantially assure the invulnerability of its own retaliatory forces irrespective of what the other side does, and assure it in a way that is manifest to the other side, so that a powerfully stable mutual deterrence results. Alternatively, nature may have planted mischievous secrets ahead of us, so that we and the Russians continually find new ways to destroy retaliatory forces at a faster rate than we find new ways to protect them. There is only a hope—no presumption—that, even with great ingenuity and the best of diplomacy, we and the Russians could find cooperative measures to arrest that trend toward instability. So we may get stability without cooperation, or we may not find it even with cooperation. Still, some kind of cooperation with the Russians, or mutual restraint, formal or informal, tacit or explicit, may prove to make a significant difference in the stability of the balance of terror; and the stakes of course are very high. Although we cannot be sure that a deliberate policy of collaborating in order to render each side's retaliatory forces invulnerable would make any difference, we have to consider that it might, and ask ourselves whether in fact we should want a perfectly stable balance of deterrence if we had the option before us. Would we really be interested in a far-reaching and effective anti-surprise-attack scheme if we knew of one, and if we thought the Russians would accept it?

Although it would be nice to know that the Russians could not be tempted into a deliberate planned sneak attack, and nice to know that they were so sure we wouldn't try it that they would never jump the gun in panic, it can nevertheless be argued that our ability to deter anything but a major assault on ourselves depends at least somewhat on the Russian belief that we might be goaded into deliberate attack. The Russians might not believe this if their retaliatory forces were substantially invulnerable to a first strike by ours. It can be argued that we would shrink except under the most extreme provocation from any retaliatory strike that had no significant chance of eliminating or softening the Russian return strike. According to this argument, a pair of *invulnerable* SAC's is a pair of *neutralized* SAC's; and while that might be the best kind in a completely bi-polar world, it is a luxury that we could not afford in the existing world—a world in which there is a large "third area" in which we wish to deter Russian aggression by a threat more credible than that of mutual suicide.

Can we threaten to retaliate, not just to resist locally, if the Russians unquestionably possess the military capacity to return us a blow of any size they please? Have the strategic forces any role when each is invulnerable to the other, except to neutralize each other and to guarantee, by their joint existence, their joint disuse?

There is a role available to them. SAC would still be capable of carrying out "retaliation" in the original sense of the term—namely, in the punitive sense. If the threat of knocking out Russian or Chinese cities was originally thought to be potent because of the sheer pain, economic loss, disorganization, and humiliation that would be involved, and not mainly because the military posture of the enemy in the immediate area of his aggression would be greatly affected, the main ingredient of the threat would still be present even if the other side's SAC were invulnerable.

The threat of *massive* retaliation, if "massive" is interpreted to mean unlimited retaliation, does indeed lose some credibility with the loss of our hope that a skillfully conducted all-out strike might succeed in precluding counter-retaliation. There probably are circumstances under which we might try to launch an all-out preventive or pre-emptive strike if there were appreciable hope that the Russians would be physically incapable of destroying us in return, and especially if the damage they could do in return could be held to really modest proportions. And to eliminate this possibility (besides eliminating an important motive for a Russian first strike on us!) does indeed seem to reduce somewhat the potency of our deterrent threats.

But if we were ever to consider *limited* or *graduated retaliation* as a means of putting pressure on the Russians to desist from actions intolerable to us, or to consider extending a limited local war inside Russian borders in a way that maintained the pretense of local military action but was really intended to work through the sanction of civilian pain and the threat of more, this kind of retaliatory action, and the threat of it, seems to enjoy *increased* credibility with a reduction in the vulnerability of both sides' strategic forces. It does, paradoxically, for the same reason that *all kinds of limited war might become less inhibited as the possibility of all-out surprise attack became unavailable.* The risk involved in a bit of less-than-massive retaliation would be a good deal less than it is now because the fear of an *all-out* strike in return should be a good deal less. The fear that our limited retaliation would be mistaken for the first step in the initiation of all-out war should be less; to mistake our limited retaliation for the initial step in mutual obliteration, the Russians would have to believe that we were literally prepared for suicide.

There might be a greater moral antipathy toward retaliation when its purely punitive nature—its anti-civilian nature—became more clearly recognized. But if as much skill is used in devising the rationale, the formula, the limits, and the ostensible connection between the punishment and the crime as is used in limiting a local war, this moral inhibition might not seem so great as to make the threat appear innocuous to the Russians. The civilian casualties that resulted from the limited local war in Korea might not seem less repugnant than the Russian civilian casualties in a war of limited retaliation—say, a nuclear weapon on Vladivostok.

On balance, it looks as though the threat of wholesale retaliation would indeed become less credible, while the threat of limited retaliation (even on a scale that deserves the word "massive") would become a great deal more credible. This is not to argue that limited retaliation, entailing the risk, if not the certainty, of limited counter-retaliation, and so forth, is in no danger of producing total destruction, either slowly or by explosion into greater and greater retaliatory strikes, or would not be horrendous to contemplate even if kept limited. The problem of limiting a war of retaliation may be no easier than that of limiting local war, and it may be harder. Furthermore, the precepts that ought to govern our strategy and behavior in a limited war of retaliation may require some new thinking, and not be obtainable by simple translation of the precepts that we believe in for the conduct of limited local war. But the kind of mutual restraint required in a Korean war is not wholly different from the self-discipline that would be required in a limited retaliatory war. Limited retaliation may appear implausible only because we have not become accustomed to the idea as we have to limited local war during the last several years. We have researched, conversed, and argued about limited local war, particularly since the Korean experience demonstrated that the species existed. Had our atomic monopoly lasted longer, we might have thought about limited retaliation long enough to get used to it. Our widespread confidence in the possibility of limited local war, as compared with the rather widespread skepticism about the limited use of direct retaliation, may partly reflect our greater intellectual familiarity with the one than with the other.

The argument here does not, however, depend on making an exchange of limited punitive blows appear safe and attractive *compared with limited local war*, but safe enough and attractive enough compared with all-out war to be a credible threat (and not a called bluff) *in any case where we may have to rely on the threat of retaliation.* In any event, it is not true that there is *no* retaliatory role for SAC in a world in which both sides' SAC's have become stabilized through their impotency to destroy each other. The SAC's would be "neutralized" only in respect of potential attacks on each other; they would still possess their punitive role, which was the original role envisaged for our SAC when only our side had a long-range nuclear-weapon capability. And this punitive role provides a basis for a deterrent threat. And while the threat of *all-out* punishment may lose credibility with the achievement of invulnerability by both sides' retaliatory forces, the threat of limited retaliation may well gain it. Whatever our immediate judgment about the net effect of this on deterrence in third areas, it should be clear that there is a possibility here that cannot be dismissed out of hand, a possibility that may substantially offset the loss of the all-out retaliation threat and may conceivably outweigh it. We cannot therefore deprecate a world of invulnerable SAC's simply by reference to the need for third-area deterrence; it must be demonstrated that one particular deterrent threat is more potent than the other one.

Only an extreme optimist can think that we may ever have a clear choice of accepting or rejecting a scheme that would guarantee to make both sides' retaliatory forces totally and continuously invulnerable. But this question of what would happen to third-area deterrence, and the limited-retaliation possibility that it calls to mind, are at least pertinent to the question of what we might let ourselves hope for.

CHAPTER 9

BRITAIN AND NATO

BY DENIS HEALEY

FOR the first ten years after the war, Britain's thinking about military problems was completely overshadowed by the prior need to construct a political framework of alliances within which her defense efforts might have a meaning. The year 1945 found Britain, relatively much weaker than before the war, facing much greater demands on her limited resources. What remained of the system by which she used to protect her world interests was scattered throughout the power vacuum between America and Russia, under heavy pressure not only from Soviet imperialism but also from local nationalism. During the whole period that the Labour government was in office, its foreign policy was dominated by the need to find new sources of power and to liquidate any inherited responsibilities which were not essential to national survival. In practice this meant transferring authority in the Empire wherever possible to the local inhabitants and implicating the United States in the protection of Europe and the Middle East. The United States was the only potential ally with which association would not mean a net drain on Britain's power.

In 1946 American support for the ultimatum which led to Russia's evacuation of Northern Persia gave at least a temporary security to the Middle East. In 1947 Britain's withdrawal from Greece jostled the United States into accepting responsibility for the security of the Eastern Mediterranean. It was a longer and more difficult process to commit America to the defense of Western Europe. In 1948 the Marshall Plan gave America a stake in the economic survival of the area; her military undertaking required not only the demonstration of Soviet hostility at Prague and Berlin but also some evidence of Britain's readiness to lead the defense of Europe, as provided in the Treaties of Dunkirk and Brussels.

The Dunkirk and Brussels Treaties had little military significance. Their essential function was to attract an American commitment with real meaning. Lord Montgomery tells in his memoirs how he found it impossible as CIGS to persuade the British government to make the treaties a military reality by stationing more forces on the Continent. The fact is that there was at this time no prospect of organizing any effective defense for Western Europe without American support; and after her experience in 1940 Britain was determined never again to risk losing the bulk of her army at the outset of war by making unsound military dispositions for purely political reasons.

Even when America finally did make her own commitment in April 1949, most Englishmen in authority felt that NATO's main value was as a political instrument which put Western Europe under America's atomic umbrella. The caution shown by both sides during the Berlin blockade made it seem fairly certain that neither Russia nor America would risk a world war. And military planning went forward inside NATO for the first twelve months without any real sense of urgency.

In Britain itself the military were working on the official assumption that no major war was likely for ten years, and were concerned mainly to digest the lessons of World War II for their own particular service. No clear strategic concept had yet emerged for the defense of Europe in global war. In any case, each of the services already had immediate practical tasks to perform in the overseas territories for which Britain was still responsible.

With the outbreak of the Korean War, the whole picture changed completely. It was almost universally assumed that Korea exemplified a new Soviet technique of war by proxy which might be applied at any moment somewhere in Europe. Thus the purely political guarantee of American involvement contained in the North Atlantic Treaty was no longer considered sufficient to deter aggression.

Scarcely anyone noticed that in Korea America had withdrawn her political commitment together with her troops, and that it might have been the formal disavowals of strategic interest made by Secretary Acheson and General MacArthur rather than the evacuation of American forces which invited the aggression. On the other hand, it was quite reasonable to believe that the Korean War itself, even if no other local aggression were committed, might spread into global war irrespective of the wishes of either side. In any case, the British Chiefs of Staff now adopted the assumption that major war was possible within three years, and for the first time began to plan seriously for that contingency.

Again, the essential precondition of effective military action was full-scale American cooperation from the outset. The Labour government, now clinging precariously to office with a majority of only six, introduced a rearmament program which involved spending £4,700 million in three years. The economic and social sacrifices it entailed led to a major split in the Labour Party itself and contributed to Labour's defeat in the General Election of October 1951. There is no doubt that the main reason why the Labour Cabinet consciously assumed the political handicap of so daunting an arms program was not so much the belief in its military necessity as such, but the feeling that unless Britain gave a dramatic and unequivocal pledge of her readiness to lead Europe in building a serious military force on the Continent, the United States might not be prepared to make her indispensable contribution. The first aim of British military policy was still to strengthen the deterrent by increasing the probability of America's atomic response to aggression in Europe. The essential conditions to achieving this aim were to obtain General Eisenhower as Supreme Commander of the Allied forces and to station American troops in force along the threatened frontier.

Nonetheless, with the prospect of general war now seriously envisaged for the first time, Britain was also concerned to develop a practical strategy for NATO in case the deterrent failed.

Military thinking in Britain at this time was in many ways similar to Soviet military thinking today, if the picture presented by Raymond L. Garthoff[1] is to be trusted. Though it was agreed that nuclear weapons had great value as a deterrent, they were not considered as necessarily decisive in actual warfare against the Soviet Union. But British planners were obsessed by two implications of Russia's nuclear armament—she had exploded her first atomic bomb in 1949. In a future war, if Russia was able to drop atomic bombs on the Channel ports and beaches, it would be impossible for Britain either to evacuate large forces from the Continent as at Dunkirk or to carry out another "Overlord" for their return. On the other hand, Britain would be unable to survive Soviet atomic bombardment if the Russians possessed airfields and launching sites on the Continental coast of the Channel. London's ordeal during the days of the V 1 and V 2 was still fresh in Britain's memory.

Thus, if war came, Britain must keep the Red Army as far east as possible, even if this meant tying up the bulk of her armed forces permanently on the Continent in peacetime. This was a complete reversal of the thinking which had dominated Whitehall a year or two before. But there were good grounds for it. Russia's acquisition of atomic weapons had made it necessary, and America's commitments under NATO had made it feasible.

There was at this time little prospect of a serious conflict between Britain and the United States on the need for a forward strategy in NATO. Though America had her advocates of a peripheral strategy, particularly in SAC, she still depended on medium-range aircraft to

[1] In *Soviet Strategy in the Nuclear Age*, New York, 1958.

deliver her atomic weapons, and therefore needed foreign bases even for a peripheral strategy. No European country was prepared to accept American bomber bases without obtaining an American commitment to help in its defense. Under the conditions of 1950, America had no alternative to the forward strategy which Europe itself desired.

On the other hand, once NATO had accepted the concept of a forward strategy, America was in a strong position to impose her own terms for making the contribution without which such a strategy would be impossible. She did so by obtaining Europe's reluctant agreement in principle to a defense contribution from Germany as well. The British government considered the demand for a German contribution as premature in both the political and the military sense. It foresaw the political difficulties in both Germany and France which did delay agreement in practice for almost another five years. And while it was possible to plan for the defense of France and the Low Countries even without German troops, the addition of German troops would involve extending the defense commitment up to the Iron Curtain itself, thus increasing NATO's responsibilities together with its capacity. But though Britain argued strongly that the German contribution should be limited for the time being to an increase in size and armament of the Federal police forces, she had to bow, like the other European powers, to the American ultimatum.

France achieved more to delay German rearmament by refusing to permit it except in the framework of a federal European Defense Community. But when after four years' negotiations France herself rejected the EDC Treaty, Britain's alarm at the possible consequences led her to make a pledge to the Continental powers which apparently involved a break with her basic principle of avoiding military commitments in Europe unless they were shared by the United States. In fact, Eden's promise to keep the equivalent of four British divisions in Western Germany until the end of the century was so hedged about with qualifications that Britain has already been able to reduce her land contribution to NATO by almost half without violating the words of her pledge. But by violating its spirit, she has cast a doubt on the sincerity of her concern with European defense which has infected all recent discussions of NATO strategy.

All this, however, was far from the mind of the British government when NATO began seriously to discuss a European strategy in 1950. The general trend of informed opinion in Britain in the months following the outbreak of the Korean War is well represented by the

contemporary report of a Chatham House Study Group.[2] This put
the target for an Atlantic force to hold a front in Europe at 50-55
divisions (at least one-third of them armored), a tactical air force of
5,000 jet fighters, and 1,000 tactical bombers. It went on: "Generally
speaking, the American and British task for a period of three to five
years appears to be this: to furnish the hard core of elite divisions and
air squadrons under one command and stationed in and close to Germany, for the defence of western Europe, while France and other members of the Atlantic Council build up around it an integrated European
force. . . . In time it should be possible—if the German contribution
is made available—for the United States and Britain to hope for a
lightening of the burden. But until that prospect is far clearer than
it is now, it is they who must take the strain. And even that can only
be done if the American readiness to send arms and war supplies is
matched by an equal readiness to station more ground forces in
Europe."[3]

This was the sort of thinking which led the Labour government to
condemn itself to electoral defeat in 1951 by undertaking to spend on
defense an average of 10 per cent of the national income over the next
three years, and to seek a German military contribution.

The Conservative government which succeeded it held views which
were different in some important respects, although at the Lisbon Conference in February 1952 it accepted military targets for NATO which
corresponded closely to those quoted above from the unofficial Chatham
House Report. However, from the moment it took power, the Conservative government held that its predecessor's program could not
be carried out in as little as three years, and that to attempt such a
task would inflict irreparable damage on the British economy. In its
second White Paper on Defense, in 1953, it decided not only to spread
the program over a longer period, but also to hold it to a lower peak.
Electoral considerations probably played some part in this decision.
In more than one country, those parties which are pledged primarily
to cut government expenditures nowadays find little scope for this
activity except in the field of defense, which commands less organized
support among the voters than other fields. But there were also more
relevant grounds for this shift in British defense policy.

It soon became apparent that the Lisbon targets were practically unattainable, and that only Britain and America were making a serious
effort to achieve them. Yet the danger of war did not appear to be

[2] Royal Institute of International Affairs, *Defence in the Cold War*, London, 1950.
[3] *Ibid.*, p. 73.

growing. The course of the Korean fighting in 1951 showed what care both sides could take to prevent the dangerous extension of a local war. Moreover, Russia made no attempt elsewhere to repeat the Korean experiment of aggression by proxy. One of the chronic difficulties in obtaining support for NATO's military demands is that NATO'S supporters claim that it has achieved its political aim of preventing Soviet aggression in Europe while simultaneously admitting that it has failed to achieve its military targets. After ten years of reiteration, this is bound to weaken public confidence in the will and the ability of the military to limit their demands to what is necessary.

Even during the first critical months of the Korean campaign the Conservatives had been less disposed than the Labour government to fear general war, although they shared its desire to see America committed as fully as possible to the defense of Western Europe. Once the American commitment had become a fact, with the appointment of General Eisenhower and the dispatch of more American formations to Germany, the new British government was satisfied so long as it could ensure the continuation of this commitment, framing its policy inside NATO to achieve this political end rather than to implement a purely military strategy. Churchill himself had always believed that Western Europe's immunity depended on the American atomic umbrella. More than the Labour leaders, he saw NATO as a political instrument for tying SAC to automatic retaliation if Europe were attacked, rather than as a military instrument for the defense of Europe if the deterrent failed.

On the other hand, he recognized that America would not keep troops in Europe unless some attempt was made to find a strategic role for them in war, and unless America's European allies showed themselves ready to cooperate in fulfilling this role. Thus when the RAF argued that NATO should formally admit that Western Europe's security depended upon the deterrent of air-atomic retaliation, and should trim its ground forces accordingly, Churchill rejected its advice for political reasons, and continued to support the concept of forward defense. Moreover, the Continental governments knew that their peoples would not support NATO unless they could be persuaded that its aim was to defend them from occupation by the Red Army. One experience of "liberation," even in the pre-atomic age, had been enough. On the other hand, the Continental countries showed no readiness to make the sacrifices required to implement a forward strategy. The proportion of their defense expenditure to national income, like their period of military service, remained constantly below that of the peripheral powers, Britain and the USA.

This failure of the Continental allies to make sacrifices equal to Britain caused more and more irritation in London as the postwar seller's market began to disappear, and Britain faced more serious commercial competition from European countries which carried a lighter military burden. Britain has always depended heavily on the exports of her engineering industry, which was particularly hard hit by rearmament. This problem assumed increasing prominence in each successive White Paper on Defense after 1952. Britain particularly resented competition from Western Germany, which, though it made some financial contribution to Western defense even before its own rearmament got under way in 1955, was able to devote its engineering industry wholly to investment and foreign trade.

Meanwhile Britain was waking up to the strategic revolution wrought by the staggering advances in military technology. The problem first presented itself in the appallingly rapid rate of obsolescence which stultified much of Britain's defense expenditure. Despite a level of military spending which imposed crippling burdens on the British economy, the British services never seemed to have enough up-to-date equipment in operational use. The history of military aircraft production, particularly fighters, became a major political scandal. It was the need to rationalize defense production which first compelled the British government to re-examine its strategic assumptions and to seek a unified defense policy to cover all three services. This was a slow and spasmodic process, made no easier by continued changes in the political control of the services—there were seven different Ministers of Defense between October 1951 and January 1957.

The first public product of the strategic reappraisal came in the Defense White Paper of 1954,[4] for which Churchill himself was believed to have a large personal responsibility. Naturally enough, at this stage in the discussion, the 1954 White Paper was an uneasy compromise between the traditions and vested interests of the individual services and the demands of new weapons which were only just coming into operational use in Britain. It was revealed that "atomic weapons are in production in this country and delivery to the forces has begun. . . . An air-to-air [guided missile] weapon will be the first to come into service and surface-to-air weapons will follow. . . . Clearly, within a limited defence budget we may not be able to afford both new weapons and conventional forces of the present size. But the balance between the

[4] Cmd. 9075.

two can only be decided in the light of the situation as it develops
over the years ahead. The new weapons can in any event only be introduced gradually as they become available."[5]

The division of opinion about NATO strategy was reflected in the
passage: "The Government will continue to regard it as a defence
measure of the first importance to maintain the strength and efficiency
of the British forces on the Continent assigned to the Supreme Allied
Commander Europe. The primary deterrent, however, remains the
atomic bomb and the ability of the highly organized and trained United
States strategic air power to use it."[6]

However, Britain herself intended to build her own atomic striking
force to ensure the destruction of Soviet targets which directly threatened her and might not have a high priority for SAC. This must, for
economic reasons, be accompanied by a reduction in Britain's land
forces. The reduction would fall not in the NATO area, but overseas,
entailing the replacement of foreign garrisons by a central strategic
reserve. Such a shift would be possible because, "as the [atomic] deterrent continues to grow, it should have an increasing effect upon the
cold war by making less likely such adventures on the part of the Communist world as their aggression in Korea. This should be of benefit
to us by enabling us to reduce the great dispersal of effort which the
existing international tension has hitherto imposed on us."[7]

The practical implications for British defense policy of these general
propositions might have been considerable. However, they were almost
nullified by another passage which gave the individual services an opportunity for maintaining all their traditional demands. If the deterrent
failed and global war were forced upon us, it was likely that "such a
war would begin with a period of intense atomic attacks lasting a relatively short time but inflicting great destruction and damage. . . ."[8]
But this phase might be followed by a period of "broken-backed warfare during which the opposing sides would seek to recover their
strength, carrying on the struggle in the meantime as best they might."[9]
Therefore, besides active forces able to withstand the initial shock,
Britain must have reserve forces capable of rapid mobilization behind
the shield.

It was still assumed without argument at this period that the West
could "keep the lead we now hold in technical development on which
we must rely to offset the preponderance of the Communist states in
manpower."[10] The few voices, like that of Professor P. M. S. Blackett,

[5] *Ibid.*, pp. 5-6.   [6] *Ibid.*, p. 4.   [7] *Ibid.*, p. 5.
[8] *Ibid.*   [9] *Ibid.*   [10] *Ibid.*

which warned that the West could not rely on maintaining such a lead were treated as defeatist, if not fellow-traveling. But a little later America's belated publication of the effects of the explosion of the thermonuclear bomb had a tremendous impact on the British government, which was then still led by Winston Churchill. It removed most of the remaining doubts about the atomic revolution in warfare, and started in Britain the debate about the diplomatic and strategic consequences of nuclear weapons which is now shaking NATO to its core.

The British White Paper on Defense in 1955[11] was devoted almost entirely to examining the impact of the thermonuclear bomb. It recognized at the outset that a much smaller number of H-bombs less accurately delivered would provide a much more efficient deterrent than the very large number of accurate fission bombs till then believed essential for deterrence. For this reason it would be worth Britain's while to provide herself with an independent thermonuclear striking force. But the Russians, too, were "clearly following the same policy; though we cannot tell when they will have thermonuclear weapons available for operational use."[12] In other words, the availability of the thermonuclear weapon would allow a larger number of powers to contemplate the independent development of their own deterrent, and also reduce the time required to produce it.

So far as Europe was concerned, Britain was more certain than ever that the threat of nuclear retaliation would be an effective deterrent. "The knowledge that aggression will be met by overwhelming nuclear retaliation is the surest guarantee that it will not take place."[13] For understandable reasons, government spokesmen refused even to discuss the possibility that Russia's growing power to respond in kind to nuclear retaliation by America might make America more reluctant to commit herself to such retaliation on behalf of her allies. But in fact most of the strategic debate in Britain since 1955 has taken this possibility as its starting point. The real argument between the government and its critics has been about the best way of coping with America's reluctance to remain tied to a NATO strategy of massive thermonuclear retaliation.

The government has on the whole taken the view that America's reluctance to initiate strategic nuclear warfare could be overcome if NATO adapted its local strategy so as to commit the United States automatically to some form of nuclear warfare in the European theater itself. NATO did in fact take a decision in this sense as far back as December 1954. But the decision had only limited political meaning

[11] Cmd. 9391.   [12] *Ibid.*, p. 3.   [13] *Ibid.*, p. 6.

so long as there were hardly any nuclear weapons available to the NATO commander himself and their use was subject to a veto from Washington. The NATO Council decision in December 1957 that strategic as well as tactical nuclear weapons should be widely distributed among the European allies which desired them was partly designed to make an all-out nuclear response to Soviet aggression more probable, though the fact that the warheads remain under American control still limits its effectiveness in this respect. However, under this theory, the essential function of NATO's nuclear weapons remains deterrence, not defense. Now that Russia is as well prepared for tactical nuclear warfare as the West, the role of atomic weapons in Europe is primarily to "raise the stakes" and so increase the NATO deterrent, as explained by Mr. Dulles,[14] rather than to provide the possibility of effective local defense. The early hope that battlefield nuclear weapons might give special advantages to the defending side seems to be weakened by recent exercises. Certainly the British government's main aim in NATO has been to counter America's reluctance to make a total response to aggression in Europe by making her physical commitment in the danger area more complete and inextricable.

The government's critics, including not only the official Labour Opposition but also some prominent Conservatives—notably former Defense Minister Antony Head—have argued, however, that America's reluctance to be committed to total war on behalf of her allies must be met by providing an effective response to aggression in Europe which is short of total war. They argue, on the one hand, that if a local aggression takes place and the only alternative to appeasement is total war, the Americans, and the British too, for that matter, might choose appeasement. And, on the other hand, they have been impressed, particularly since the Hungarian rising, by the possibility that fighting might break out on the frontier even though the Russians did not intend it; in such a case, a deterrent strategy is irrelevant and it is vital to have military forces which are capable of smothering the outbreak without risk of total war.

The debate on this issue, however, which is now raging in all the NATO countries, has been distorted in Britain by considerations not directly relevant to the technical problems of European strategy.

The first factor is the long-standing determination of the British Army, now supported by the government, to end compulsory national service as soon as possible. While the Navy scarcely takes any conscripts

[14] John Foster Dulles, "Challenge and Response in United States Policy," *Foreign Affairs*, xxxvi, No. 1 (October 1957), pp. 25-43.

at all, and the Air Force relies on them for a little over a third of its strength, and that entirely in non-combatant roles, nearly half of the Army's manpower has been conscripted for the last ten years. Moreover, the Army has had to use conscripts on a large scale as fighting troops and junior officers. Conscription is a particularly wasteful way of providing the British Army with operational manpower, since nearly three-quarters of the conscripts are always undergoing training, making great demands on the regular army for instructors. Moreover, much of the six to twelve months of a conscript's operational life is spent traveling to and from stations like Hong Kong or Malaya which may be many weeks away by sea.

Even when the conscript is actually available for operations, he tends to be inferior in both training and morale to the regular soldier. As warfare becomes more complicated, the inferiority of the conscript becomes ever more marked. And so long as a large part of every army unit consists of conscripts who have just arrived or are just about to leave, enthusiasm for joining the regular army is lower than it could be. The disadvantages of conscription have been aggravated in Britain by the refusal of both the political parties to consider selective service. As a result, the government has always called up more conscripts than are actually needed, and a proportion of these have inevitably wasted their time.

The first move toward abolishing conscription came in 1955 when knowledge of the effects of thermonuclear bombing persuaded the government that conscription was no longer required as a means of producing large numbers of trained reserves for total war. A White Paper on National Service then stated: "In a nuclear age the conception of reserve forces waiting to take part in large-scale conventional war is out of date. In the initial stages of such a war the reserve manpower of the Services will, in the main, be required to help to maintain the life of the nation and to deal with raids and sabotage."[15] Now that conscription was required primarily to provide troops for immediate military commitments, the government decided to reduce the annual intake by calling men up more slowly. Two years later a new Defense Minister decided to cut the Gordian knot outright.

In his famous Defense White Paper of 1957,[16] Duncan Sandys decided to go all out for the total abolition of conscription by 1962, the last conscript being called up in 1960. This assumed that by 1962 Britain could make do with an army of only 165,000 men—a figure which some informed persons claim was reached, not by making an honest

[15] Cmd. 9608, p. 5.   [16] Cmd. 124.

estimate of Britain's military commitments in 1962, but by making the most optimistic possible guess at the potential increase in regular recruiting during the intervening years. So far as regular recruiting is concerned, there has been so great an increase in the last twelve months that the government claims to be confident of reaching its target. On the other hand, the Report of the Advisory Committee on Recruiting in October 1958,[17] which was endorsed by the government, argued that the target could not be achieved unless during 1958-1962 one in three of all available young men volunteered for regular service on reaching the age of eighteen. No one believes that so high a recruiting rate is possible; but many argue that the Committee was far too pessimistic in assuming that 64 per cent of Britain's young men would not be available for recruiting either because of their profession or because they were medically or otherwise unfit.

Though the government has undertaken to introduce some form of compulsory service if voluntary recruiting fails to meet the target, there is a widespread belief that, if the shortfall is a small one, it will lower its target instead. And since Britain's overseas commitments are exclusively national and cannot be transferred to others, the reduction is most likely to come in her contribution to NATO in Europe. Indeed, Britain's desire to end conscription has already led to a greater reduction in her NATO forces than her allies believe justified. And it may also have influenced her views on the strategic concept which NATO should follow.

The other external factor which has exerted a major influence on British views about NATO has been the development of Britain's military commitments overseas and the failure of her allies to support them. The major part of Britain's land forces have been serving outside Europe ever since the end of the Second World War, either as garrisons in the long chain of imperial bases from Gibraltar to Hong Kong or in active operations against large-scale terrorism in Malaya and Cyprus. For many years there were also substantial British forces carrying out occupation duties in Austria and Trieste or supporting the United Nations campaign in Korea. Apart from adopting the appropriate political measures—which ultimately succeeded in Malaya—there are obvious limits on Britain's ability to reduce her military commitments in the Colonies. She therefore sought and obtained formal permission to reduce her NATO contribution in case of emergency in her overseas territories.

[17] Cmd. 545.

A much more serious problem arose over Britain's interests in the Middle East. Besides sharing with the rest of Western Europe a vital economic interest in access to Middle Eastern oil on reasonable terms, Britain also has a unique financial interest in the existing system by which Middle Eastern oil is produced and marketed. This special national interest is most dramatically illustrated by the stupendous contribution made by Kuwait to the dollar reserves of the Sterling Area and to the investment funds of the London capital market. For many Englishmen, particularly if they are Conservatives, even more important than Britain's material interests in the Middle East is the symbolic value of Britain's semi-imperial position in the area.

Most Conservatives felt that ever since the war Britain had been unnecessarily abdicating from her imperial heritage through weakness of character, a misplaced sense of guilt, Socialist heresy, and pressure from American vested interests masquerading as anti-colonialism. After the Persian oil dispute, this feeling acquired pathological violence. When Colonel Nasser nationalized the Suez Canal Company, many people in Britain positively welcomed his act as providing an opportunity for that display of military force in the area which they considered an indispensable precondition for restoring British influence. America's refusal to countenance such a display without better legal grounds led to the Anglo-French conspiracy on the ill-conceived and worse-executed Suez campaign. The isolation of Britain and France inside NATO over Suez led to a frightening explosion of anger in Britain against the alliance as a whole and the United States in particular. Besides the Conservative politicians, at least one senior civil servant in a key position began talking as if America's "betrayal" must mean the end of NATO.

In this atmosphere the acquisition of an independent thermonuclear striking force became an absolute priority for the British government, while for a large section of the British people the H-bomb became the indispensable symbol of national greatness. Randolph Churchill spoke for this section when he told the American Chamber of Commerce in London: "Britain can knock down twelve cities in the region of Stalingrad and Moscow from bases in Britain and another dozen in the Crimea from bases in Cyprus. We did not have that power at the time of Suez. We are a major power again."[18]

The impact on NATO of Sandys' 1957 White Paper was to some extent distorted because he and other government spokesmen deliberately presented it so as to excite this element in British opinion. In fact

[18] *The Times* (London), November 14, 1958.

it represented no dramatic shift in the current of British defense policy as it had been developing since 1952. Indeed, its novelty consisted in the fact that for the first time the British government was drawing the practical conclusions for defense organization from the strategic assumptions which it had stated quite unequivocally in 1955. Because it was impossible to defend the British people against thermonuclear attack, British policy on global war must consist entirely in deterrence. The considerations which had led the Labour government in 1950 to aim at holding the Russians in Europe as far as possible to the east were no longer relevant, given the present capabilities of Russian air power—with the IRBM just around the corner.

Thus Britain was no longer prepared to make major economic sacrifices for a NATO strategy of forward defense whose only purpose was to encourage the Continental countries in clinging to illusions which had been out-of-date for years. In the discussions which followed inside NATO about the projected British troop reductions in Germany, however, Britain does not seem to have pressed this strategic argument, for fear of raising unnecessary opposition. Instead she concentrated on the economic argument that she was making a disproportionate sacrifice and overstraining her balance of payments. But statements made by leading British figures—notably Lord Montgomery, even before he retired as Deputy Supreme Allied Commander—show clearly enough that the troop reductions were felt to be justified in any case because Western atomic striking power has ruled out any possibility of a major Soviet attack on Western Europe for at least ten years.

In fact, NATO itself has dropped the idea of forward defense as it was conceived by the Lisbon Conference. Apart from their function in triggering off massive retaliation, the task of the ground forces is now seen not as to hold the whole front against a major Soviet attack, which would in any case involve full-scale thermonuclear retaliation, but as to smother frontier incidents and to block any limited and local aggression whose success might prove fatal to the morale of Europe as a whole. The British government would argue that the task of smothering frontier incidents does not require the thirty divisions SHAPE demands, while the second task assumes a Soviet readiness to risk global war which does not now exist, but which might be encouraged if NATO too obviously prepares to limit its liabilities. In any case, experience has shown that the use or threat of armed force by the Soviet Union on local issues is more likely to drive the West together on a massive arms program than to demoralize and disintegrate the alliance.

The Labour Opposition, and an important section of Conservative backbenchers, are less sanguine about Soviet intentions, and less ready to be tied to a suicidal strategy if any fighting develops in Central Europe which it is beyond the very limited capacity of the present NATO forces to contain with conventional weapons alone. They doubt whether it would be possible to prevent limited atomic war in Central Europe from spreading rapidly to all-out thermonuclear world war. So while recognizing that the distribution of "tactical" atomic weapons to the NATO forces will strengthen the deterrent against a major Soviet attack, they fear that it might also weaken the Western will to offer effective resistance to a military challenge which is presented ambiguously—for example, one which arises out of frontier fighting for which the initial responsibility is unclear. Thus they have tended to support NATO criticism of recent British troop reductions in Western Germany.

Up to this point, both sides to the argument about NATO strategy assume that the alliance remains united in its reaction to attack on any one of its members. But, in the long run, a much more serious challenge to NATO is presented by the line of reasoning which lay behind Britain's decision to build a thermonuclear striking force, which, like the American SAC, lies wholly outside NATO. The main argument publicly used by the government to justify this decision has been that the British H-bomb would "strengthen" the Allied deterrent, though how and to what extent it would do so have never been explained in detail. The secondary argument implicit in much of the government propaganda for the H-bomb is that it would enable Britain to use military force for pursuing her special interests outside the NATO area, without having to rely on United States support if she were again threatened, as at Suez, with thermonuclear attack by Russia—*v.* the quotation above from Randolph Churchill.

But a much more important reason for Britain's decision than either of these is the belief, once incautiously expressed in Parliament by Duncan Sandys himself, that as America comes to rely less on overseas bases for her own atomic striking force, her strategic interest in defending Western Europe may decline so dramatically as to threaten her support for NATO. Indeed, even before America acquires a fully intercontinental striking force, Russia's ability to inflict intolerable damage on the United States itself may make automatic nuclear retaliation by SAC a far less credible deterrent than it was a few years ago.

British strategic thinking nowadays is much concerned with the distinction between "active" and "passive" deterrence. Active deterrence

is defined as the threat to initiate global thermonuclear war in response
to an aggression which is limited, in the sense that it does not put the
survival of the deterrent's possessor directly at stake. The doctrine of
"massive retaliation" was an example of such active deterrence. Passive
deterrence is defined as the use of thermonuclear striking power to
deter a direct all-out attack on one's national existence by displaying the
capacity to inflict intolerable damage on the aggressor's homeland even
after he has struck the first thermonuclear blow at one's own. A country
which aims at active deterrence against, say, the Soviet Union must
have a thermonuclear striking force hundreds of times larger than one
which aims only at passive deterrence. For, since it plans to strike the
first thermonuclear blow, it must aim primarily at ensuring its own
survival by destroying the enemy's power to retaliate in kind. In fact,
most experts believe that in a few years' time such an aim will become
unattainable even for the richest and most advanced country in the
world. Apart from the difficulty of locating the tiny targets presented
by underground and undersea missile bases, the weight of nuclear explosive required to destroy them might threaten the survival of the
human race itself.

Passive deterrence, on the other hand, requires only sufficient thermonuclear striking power to inflict damage on the aggressor which is out
of proportion to what he would gain by defeating the country concerned.
Since it assumes that the enemy has already struck the first thermonuclear blow, it can ignore his military bases and concentrate on major
population centers and agglomerations of economic power. Even a
small country could contrive sufficient dispersal of its striking force
to have a good chance of keeping some retaliatory power intact. And
if it were close to the Soviet Union, it might find a relatively un-
sophisticated delivery system sufficient for its purpose. Sweden, for
example, might well feel itself immune from Soviet attack if it was
thought to have the capacity for dropping one H-bomb on Leningrad. However, if Soviet interception techniques improve, the number
of weapons required to saturate Russia's defenses could rise beyond
the capacity of a small country.

On the other hand, the value of a small but independent thermonuclear striking force in passive deterrence is reinforced by the possibility that a single H-bomb exploded in Russia, whatever its country
of origin, might trigger off a general thermonuclear exchange between
Russia and the West. So far as the potential aggressor is concerned,
this possibility adds a small and variable risk of massive retaliation to
the more calculable probability of losing a few cities. And so far as

the United States is concerned, an independent H-bomb may give any of her allies a degree of influence over her use of SAC more certain than could be secured by any purely institutional arrangement.

There is little doubt that the main aim of the British thermonuclear striking force is to provide passive deterrence for Britain in case America drops her present policy of active deterrence for NATO as a whole. Though some Englishmen believe that the political likelihood of Russia presenting Britain with the sort of threat to which passive deterrence would be relevant is too small to be worth preparing against, the majority, including the leaders of both the political parties, feel that the additional expenditure required to mount a passive deterrent on the basis of Britain's existing atomic resources and delivery system is small enough to be worth making. This majority might dwindle dramatically if its assumptions about the low cost of a passive deterrent prove to be mistaken.

What is more controversial is the British government's attempt to carry out a policy of active deterrence with a capacity which is adequate only for passive deterrence. The 1958 White Paper on Defense, for example, included the passage: "But it must be well understood that, if Russia were to launch a major attack on them [the Western powers], even with conventional forces only, they would have to hit back with strategic nuclear weapons."[19] And there has been much talk in government circles about the possibility that when America loses her strategic interest in Europe, Britain will be able to step into her shoes by providing the necessary atomic umbrella for the Continent. Moreover, there is some evidence that the government may be spending more on its thermonuclear striking force than would be required for strictly passive deterrence, though nothing like enough to make a strategy of active deterrence credible. This line of criticism, which is broadly supported by the Labour Party, was well summarized in two articles by the *Times* Defense Correspondent on October 15 and 16, 1958, which concluded:

"If we believe that America will not defend us because of her vulnerability, we cannot credibly pretend that we, with our much greater vulnerability, will risk our extinction for NATO. The possession of an independent deterrent cannot therefore be used as a substitute for limited war forces.

"We must also recognize that the threat of Russian nuclear blackmail which gives us a military justification for having our own deterrent is the least likely of the various Communist threats that face us. We

[19] Cmd. 363, p. 2.

should give first priority in our defence preparations to the cold war, which is with us all the time; second priority to limited war, which the deterrent can no longer be relied on to deter, because of the nuclear stalemate; and last priority to global war preparations."

Of course the government has not been so single-minded in the pursuit of the Sandys policy as both its friends and opponents sometimes suggest. Ever since the publication of the 1957 White Paper, the individual services have been fighting a rearguard action—and not without success—against its implications for them. As in the United States, a conflict of vested interests between the services is apt to produce a mixture of incompatible strategies. On the other hand, some of the inconsistencies in the government's words and deeds are due to its legitimate desire not to hasten the reduction of America's strategic interest in Europe, to which it is trying to adapt its defense policy in time. One of the major problems facing the democracies in framing their defense policies arises from the difficulty of maintaining public support for existing strategies while simultaneously explaining the need to adapt strategy and weapons to the changes which may be expected over the next ten years—a difficulty which has troubled Secretary McElroy in the United States just as much as Duncan Sandys in the United Kingdom.

Thus, as the implications of the thermonuclear stand-off sink in on both sides of the Atlantic, military staffs and political leaders are more and more exercised by the problems of limited war as the only sort of war which the West can afford in the future. But official discussion of limited war, in Britain as elsewhere, is inevitably confused by a natural wish not to weaken the deterrent by casting doubt on the certainty of retaliation by SAC to any attack on Western Europe. In discussing the Central European problem in particular, the confusion has been confounded by the fact that some parties to the argument see limited warfare in the area—particularly limited atomic warfare —as a means of strengthening the trip wire which leads to massive thermonuclear retaliation; while others see it as a means of replacing massive retaliation by a less suicidal and more credible strategy. Still others believe that it can fill both roles at once.

Thus, when Britain first agreed to the use of nuclear weapons by SHAPE in 1954, she did so wholly as a means of reinforcing the American deterrent. It was not until 1956 that the government half-heartedly hinted at the possibility of limited atomic war as something which might happen in reality without leading to global war. The 1956 White Paper included the passage: ". . . we have to be prepared for the outbreak of localised conflicts on a scale short of global war. In such limited wars the possible use of nuclear weapons cannot be excluded."[20] On the other hand, one of the government spokesmen in the debate on this White Paper defined a limited war as one in which nuclear weapons were not used.

The debate on the 1958 White Paper was only a little less confused on this issue, though the Minister for War, Christopher Soames, made a statement which was at once precise and discreet: "The real danger," he said, "lies in the fact that an unscrupulous nation playing upon the natural abhorrence and reluctance of the Western world to launch into a mutually devastating nuclear exchange might indulge in military adventures, or encourage other countries to do so whilst giving them thinly-veiled support. This is a field in which no government can say in advance to what weapons they would need to have recourse in any of the possible different sets of circumstances. . . . [We] would use the doctrine of minimum force. We would not deploy more forces, nor would we have recourse to bigger explosive power, than what was absolutely necessary to protect our interests. What is important here is that the Western world, and we in particular, should devote a sufficiently high expenditure to conventional weapons, so that we will not be in a position of having to resort to undue force."[21] Unfortunately this admirable statement was a *cri du coeur* from the Minister responsible for an army which is being starved of the weapons it would require to implement such a policy, for the sake of providing the air force with weapons it could not afford to use except in the most unlikely contingency of all—a direct nuclear attack on Britain herself.

Not surprisingly, most of the public discussion of limited war has been confined to politicians in opposition and to experts of no party at all. The Labour leaders have recently committed themselves to a fairly comprehensive doctrine on the subject which may be summarized as follows: if ever Britain finds herself engaged in fighting, she should use the minimum force required to bring the fighting to a halt—but not to "win the war." They recognize that the essential condition for limited war is limited war aims and that the old slogan, "There is no substitute for victory," must be replaced by the slogan, "There is no substitute for survival." Most interested opinion in Britain would agree that so far as the limitation of warfare itself is concerned, limiting the theater of war has been proved possible in Korea and elsewhere, while limiting targets within the theater is perfectly feasible. There is still,

[20] Cmd. 9691, p. 4.
[21] Hansard, February 27, 1958.

however, a widespread feeling that, though a clear distinction between conventional and nuclear weapons is easy to maintain, it would be well-nigh impossible in actual warfare to maintain a distinction between the various types of nuclear weapons, and that the employment even of small-yield nuclear weapons would make the limitation of targets and even of theater much more difficult to maintain.

However, most of this discussion must remain largely theoretical. For the fact remains that Britain by herself cannot afford to produce a wide enough spectrum of options to permit her to apply the doctrine of limited force, particularly while she is diverting so much effort to the maintenance of her thermonuclear capacity on a scale which is probably larger than required for passive deterrence. The obvious answer is to seek within NATO that specialization of function and production which was envisaged when the concept of balanced collective forces was first launched. The slogan of "interdependence" has indeed been heard increasingly over the last twelve months on the Prime Minister's lips. But so far it has been applied in practice only to relations between Britain and the United States, from which Britain can hope to be the net gainer, and hardly at all to relations between Britain and the Continent, which is still seen as a net drain on Britain's scarce resources.

Moreover, it is difficult to see how Europe and the United States could ever afford to commit themselves in the long run to genuine interdependence in the military field unless each member of the system thus created felt confident of its ability to commit the rest to its defense in an emergency, and was itself prepared to be so committed when another was under attack. This was possible—indeed, was a reality— in the days when America had a direct strategic interest in the defense of Western Europe and ran only a marginal risk in committing herself to retaliation on its behalf. The situation is so different today that it is difficult to see how the mutual confidence required for strategic interdependence could be created by anything less than full political federation. There was a time during the Anglo-American honeymoon from 1946 to 1950 when there seemed to be the possibility of a slow development in this direction. But apart from Norway and Holland, the rest of Europe has always been indifferent or hostile to the concept of an Atlantic Community, and enthusiasm in Britain and the United States seemed to dwindle rapidly, particularly after 1952.

The existing divergence between the strategic situation and interests of America and her European allies is well illustrated by the course of the current argument about NATO strategy. America seeks a strategy of limited war on the Continent which would relieve her of the commitment to automatic thermonuclear retaliation. But any strategy for limited war in Europe not only weakens what is left of the great deterrent, but may imply suffering for the Continental countries which is for practical purposes indistinguishable from that involved in global atomic war. This is particularly true of a strategy which involves the use of nuclear weapons on the battlefield. A strategy for purely conventional defense, on the other hand, besides being politically unacceptable to the Continent in practice, however attractive it might be in theory, could always be outflanked if the Russians themselves chose to introduce the tactical use of atomic weapons, facing America once more with the choice between suicide and abandoning her allies.

It seems probable that in this situation most of the Continental countries in NATO will follow the British lead in trying to build a passive deterrent for themselves as soon as they are physically capable of doing so. It is true that a passive deterrent is a sure protection only against direct all-out attack on the nation possessing it. But most of the Continental countries have no immediate strategic interests outside their national frontiers in any case. There remains the theoretical possibility of nuclear blackmail or limited aggression, but a country which had the power to destroy a few Soviet cities would feel fairly secure against this risk. The declared interest of Sweden and Switzerland in acquiring nuclear weapons is an obvious pointer for countries at present in NATO.

The cost of producing nuclear weapons, and even more of constructing the delivery system required to make them effective, is likely to compel countries which begin building their own deterrent to reduce their contribution to whatever collective forces NATO then maintains. Moreover, as the power to initiate thermonuclear war spreads to more and more governments in NATO, membership in the alliance may seem to confer more risks than security. If every country with atomic weapons could be relied on to use them rationally—that is, exclusively as a passive deterrent—there would be little to fear. But experience suggests that a country which has just acquired atomic weapons may suffer from a rush of blood to the head and be tempted to use them for diplomatic purposes which involve great risks, even if not for actual warfare. German Defense Minister Strauss, for example, has said that when his country has atomic weapons, she will be able to compel both East and West to take the problem of German reunification more seriously. Statements in Paris about the French H-bomb have been much more extravagant. There can be no guarantee that this type of thinking will not prevail when the problem is faced in practice.

Once a country comes to feel that it can guarantee its own security against Soviet attack, it may well begin to consider using its nuclear forces to pursue exclusively national interests outside the alliance itself. Yet the risks it runs in such adventures are bound to threaten other members of the alliance. European anxiety about Chiang Kai-shek's behavior during the Quemoy crisis imposed real strains on NATO, even though Taiwan is not directly allied with America's Atlantic partners. Such anxieties would have been enormously multiplied if Chiang had had nuclear weapons under his own control. Or, to take another example, if nuclear weapons had been given to Turkey or Greece, they would have been just as likely to have increased the division between these countries over the Cyprus issue as to have strengthened their unity against possible Soviet attack.

The spread of thermonuclear weapons does not threaten only the internal stability of the Western alliance. It also threatens the precarious stability created in the world as a whole by the fact that at present major atomic striking power is confined to two countries which, though hostile, are widely separated from one another in space and— by comparison with some other countries—are fundamentally satisfied with the *status quo*. The interest shared by Russia and America in preventing any extension in the possession of atomic weapons, except under their control, is suggested by the extent of their agreement on the need to end nuclear tests. For the greatest importance of a nuclear test ban would be in impeding the spread of nuclear weapons. No new country can build its own nuclear weapons system unless it is allowed to test its products. And since the main value of nuclear weapons is in deterrence, it is essential that a new country should be able to prove that it actually does possess these weapons by successfully exploding them.

Some of the dangers attendant on the spread of atomic weapons could be reduced if it were possible to devise an acceptable system for the supranational control of atomic weapons within the Western alliance. A recent American study[22] discounts the possibility of America herself joining such a system, but argues that she should persuade or compel her European allies to create one for their own weapons. But in practice this means pooling the decision to make peace or war, when war means total destruction. America has so far confined herself to establishing common control of atomic weapons in NATO only in

[22] Ben T. Moore, *NATO and the Future of Europe*, New York, 1958.

the negative sense, by keeping the warhead in her own hands while entrusting the means of delivery to those of another, thus giving each the power of veto. But this is no precedent for a purely European system of control, since it has been possible only because America retains the major part of her atomic striking power outside the system. In fact, she has lost nothing by accepting such a control system, because her allies would not allow her to station the weapons in their territory at all unless they had the power of veto over their use. And her allies lose nothing by accepting it, since they cannot now have atomic weapons at all unless they give America the same power of veto. The situation would be entirely different if a system were required to provide total control over the use of atomic weapons produced by individual countries inside Europe. It is difficult to conceive of France, particularly under its present leader, agreeing to give each of her allies the right of vetoing the use of the weapons she plans to start producing next year, and through which she hopes to recover status as a great power. The problem is even more difficult if it is desired to produce a system which allows positive control—that is, which would ensure that the weapons were used by the community as a whole whenever one of its members so desired.

Yet only a system of positive control would meet Europe's strategic need if America's atomic umbrella were withdrawn. As in the case of military interdependence in general, interdependence in atomic weapons is difficult to conceive under any circumstances short of the complete fusion of national sovereignties in a political federation. And though six of the Continental countries have committed themselves to move over seventeen years toward political federation through economic union, the difficulties of establishing collective control of their atomic weapons are more likely to prove an obstacle than an incentive to this end. In practice, collective influence over the use of nuclear weapons is most likely to be achieved by distributing some of the weapons themselves so as to give individual members of the alliance a chance—which will vary according to the politico-military circumstances of a given crisis—of triggering off the whole of the alliance's atomic power.

At the moment it looks as if technological and economic difficulties may ensure that France is the only new Western country to produce its own atomic weapons within the next five years, though it would be unwise to rule out the possibility of a scientific breakthrough which could make atomic weapons much cheaper and easier to produce. But this is a field in which coming events cast their shadow long before.

Even though the United States and Britain may wish to discourage their partners from following their example, it is quite impossible for those members of NATO which are farthest from the danger zone to deny a more exposed ally weapons which their enemies already possess and which they themselves consider vital for their own defense. There is obvious scope for bargaining in which an ally will demand access to America's nuclear armory against making a more effective contribution to the collective forces. General de Gaulle's *demarche* about the missile bases in France suggests a general trend. Experience with the Tripartite Agreement on rationing the supply of arms in the Middle East shows that it may be impossible for one side in the cold war to operate a system of arms control in its own camp without the cooperation of the other side in the cold war.

For this reason, a problem steadily assuming greater prominence in Britain is whether it is possible to reverse the whole trend of the last thirteen years and to base the security of Western Europe on some form of cooperation with the Soviet bloc in the regional limitation and control of weapons and forces. It is recognized by both sides in this debate that such cooperation with the Soviet Union would be possible only on the basis of unity and strength inside the Western alliance. And the main disagreement is not so much about the desirability of such a security system in principle, as about whether the West is yet sufficiently strong and united to undertake negotiations to this end. The Labour Party, which has now officially committed itself to aim at a form of disengagement in Central Europe, believes that NATO's bargaining position is likely to get weaker rather than stronger as time passes and that the Russian leaders may become less willing to negotiate a settlement than they appear at present. The Conservative government, on the other hand, is disinclined to weaken still further its declining popularity inside NATO by pressing issues which neither the American nor the German government is yet ready to discuss.

However, neither side believes that there is any immediate prospect of disengagement in Central Europe in its full sense, meaning the physical evacuation of the area by both the Soviet and NATO forces and the political neutralization of the countries thus exposed. The most the Labour Party hopes for as a first step in this direction is an agreement on the limitation and control of armaments on both sides of the Iron Curtain in Central Europe, leaving the existing alliances untouched and the American and Russian troops confronting one another along the Iron Curtain as at present—though in smaller numbers. It believes that the latest revision of the Rapacki Plan provides a good basis for negotiations to this end. The Conservative government in fact put forward similar proposals with American agreement in 1955—indeed, it was only the accident of convenience in conference tactics which led to these proposals being called the Eden Plan rather than the Dulles Plan.

Hugh Gaitskell, the Labour Party leader, has repeatedly stressed that his proposals for disengagement in Central Europe should be seen not as a diplomatic alternative to NATO but as a strategic alternative for NATO. For whatever agreement were reached with Russia on the precise military and diplomatic status of Central Europe, a strong Western alliance would be required to provide sanctions against its violation. That is why the Labour Party has always refused to consider any form of disengagement which would mean the total evacuation of the Anglo-Saxon forces from the Continent. Its own proposals envisage merely the relocation of the American and British troops in the Low Countries and northern France. Perhaps it is worth pointing out that as of January 1959 the Western governments' official proposals for a German settlement concede the military feasibility of disengagement in principle by offering to keep NATO forces out of the present Soviet Zone when German reunification has taken place and the Red Army has withdrawn to Poland or points east.

I believe myself that as the implications of the thermonuclear stand-off come to be recognized more fully, it will be seen that the problems of protecting the *status quo* under the Labour Party plan for disengagement would resemble in principle but be simpler in practice than those of protecting the present *status quo*. For fighting would begin, if it began at all, on the eastern frontier of Poland rather than in the center of Germany. And the existence of a strong buffer of conventional troops between the atomic forces of both sides would reduce the risk that a frontier incident or local explosion might lead to an unnecessary thermonuclear holocaust.

This of course assumes that Russia would not attempt a massive military invasion of the whole of Europe after disengagement had taken place. But Russia could hardly hope to gain more by such an invasion than she holds at present by the peaceful occupation of Eastern Europe, while the risks of thermonuclear destruction she would run would be out of all proportion to the gain. If Russia were really prepared to run such risks, she would not agree to disengage in the first place, since she is in a stronger position to exert military pressure on

Western Europe from where she stands today than she would be if she withdrew to her own territory.

Here again, there is less disagreement than appears between the two sides to the debate on disengagement in Britain. Both of them believe that, with all its obvious imperfections and dwindling credibility, the thermonuclear deterrent is likely to retain its efficiency for some time in preventing Russia from deliberately initiating global war. And they both feel that the difficulty of keeping a war limited in Central Europe will deter Russia from pursuing her aims there by piecemeal local aggression. But while the supporters of disengagement fear that the continued division of Germany may produce an explosion in the Soviet Zone which could drag the great powers into nuclear war against their will, its opponents believe that the danger of such an explosion would be greater if the Red Army were known to be on its way out of Eastern Europe. The other disagreements expressed by the two sides are probably due more to the difference between the inhibitions of office and the license of opposition than to genuine conflicts of judgment on the issues themselves. An opposition party can afford to look further ahead and to speculate more freely about the future than any government.

It is perhaps worth making a final point about the difference of political climate in Britain and the United States concerning strategic problems in general. It seems to an outsider that the American people, who came face to face with their vulnerability in total war only a year ago with the launching of the Soviet Sputnik, still believe it is possible to find a military policy which would restore their nation's historic immunity by guaranteeing absolute security against all possible threats. The British, on the other hand, have come to accept the fact that armaments can offer only a precarious and relative security. Having already suffered much destruction in the Second World War, they have now grown accustomed to the idea that they cannot survive in total war, and they believe that the Soviet leaders are realistic enough to know that Russia too is indefensible against thermonuclear attack. And they feel that knowledge of her vulnerability in total war will discourage Russia from using her superiority in conventional forces to attempt limited local advances against Western Europe—although this danger is not wholly insignificant.

Thus the fundamental argument in Britain is shifting from purely military issues to the political assumptions on which defense is based. It is between those who believe that the stability now offered by a bipolar balance of terror may be shattered so soon that it is urgently necessary to probe Soviet readiness to cooperate in measures of arms control, and those who feel that there is plenty of time before this problem need take first place in British and Western thinking. The division emerges most clearly in the debate about Britain's H-bomb. Some of the former group, who are by no means confined to one party, would like Britain to declare now that she would stop producing her own nuclear weapons in return for a sure guarantee that no countries other than the United States and the USSR would produce them in the future. Some of the latter group would like to increase the number and variety of Britain's nuclear weapons considerably before negotiation on the major problems begins in earnest.

No one doubts that there is bound to be an increase in the number of countries with their own atomic weapons unless there is agreement either inside NATO on the positive centralized control of these weapons or between NATO and the Soviet Union on measures of disarmament which would reduce the desire and ability of other nations to acquire them. Both of these alternatives to thermonuclear anarchy require a degree of international confidence and cooperation which seems unlikely at present. Even among those in Britain who regard the spread of atomic weapons as the most urgent problem facing mankind, there are some who are reconciled to the possibility that it may be some years before either solution emerges clearly as a practical choice. In the meantime, British thinking about NATO strategy is likely to remain, like that of other powers, an uneasy compromise between the inheritance of the past, the realities of the present, and fears or hopes which can only be confirmed in the future.

CHAPTER 10

GERMANY AND NATO:
THE REARMAMENT DEBATE, 1950-1958

BY GORDON A. CRAIG

ONE of the most encouraging signs of progress within the NATO military alliance in 1958 was the growth in strength and proficiency of the German *Bundeswehr*. At a time when other countries were finding it difficult to raise their quotas and when France's colonial troubles were constituting a continual drain upon her European forces, the West German army became the largest national contingent in the NATO shield. By the middle of the year the Federal Republic had raised seven divisions for the Western alliance—three motorized infantry divisions, two armored divisions, a parachute division, and a mountain division. As of that time, those divisions were not, it is true, at full strength; but it was expected that this deficiency would be corrected by the end of the year; and German military officials predicted confidently that by 1961 five more full divisions would be in the NATO order of battle.

This progress was reassuring to those who had begun to doubt that they would ever see German troops. The creation of a German contingent as part of the Western alliance had, after all, been discussed in Europe and the United States as early as 1948, and it had been agreed to, in principle at least, by the majority of the NATO Council in September 1950. But, although planning got under way almost immediately, with the creation of *Dienststelle Blank* at the end of that year, it was not until March 1954 that the constitutional law of the Federal Republic was amended to give the government rights over German citizens in matters of defense; and actual provisions for raising troops had to wait until the EDC debate was over and the London and Paris agreements were ratified. The first tangible sign of progress came when the *Bundestag*, in July 1955, passed a bill authorizing the raising of 6,000 volunteer troops; but, even after that, it took a full year before the German legislature had completed its work on a Soldiers Law, which defined the rights and responsibilities of members of the armed forces, and a Service Law, which provided for the creation of a conscript army. This series of delays had been long and exasperating and had led even the patient *New York Times* to complain about "quarrels over technicalities" and to hint that further procrastination would raise doubts about Western Germany's reliability as an ally.[1]

In retrospect, it is clear that technicalities and details of military legislation were less important in slowing the progress of German rearmament than other factors. Since 1950 the German people and their leaders have been seriously divided on basic questions concerning the political and economic aspects of the task of rebuilding a German military establishment, the strategic usefulness of such a force in the light of the conditions under which it might be called upon to fight, and the way in which German membership in a Western defense community would affect the chances of future reunification of the nation. Despite the delivery of German formations to the NATO command, these differences of opinion still remain.

I

The first phase of the long debate over the merits of German rearmament began in 1950 and continued, with varying degrees of intensity, until the Paris treaties were signed in October 1954. The prevailing characteristic of the discussion in this early stage was its academic tone and its tendency to avoid any thoroughgoing analysis of concrete military problems. Indeed, when military issues were touched on at all, they were treated in terms of the past, as if any new conflict that might break out would differ in no significant respect from the Second World War. And even this kind of discussion, which did not get very far beyond comparisons of the number of divisions on each side of the Iron Curtain, was mainly restricted to military circles.

In parliamentary discussion, it was the political rather than the military aspects of the question that received most attention. In general, government spokesmen argued that the rearmament of Germany within a Western defense community was necessary for two reasons. It would, in the first place, be the most expeditious method of freeing Western Germany from the restrictions of the Occupation Statute, of laying the ghost of the ancient Franco-German hostility, and of effecting a union betwen Germany and the Western Powers. In Konrad Adenauer's eyes, in particular, rearmament was primarily a diplomatic gambit, although this should not be construed in such a way as to cast doubt on the sincerity of his desire for Western European integration, for which he had, indeed, worked since the mid-1920's.[2] In the second

[1] *New York Times*, editorial, June 29, 1955.
[2] See Gordon A. Craig, *From Bismarck to Adenauer: Aspects of German Statecraft*, Baltimore, 1958, p. 138.

place, it was argued that the Korean War proved that, whatever the deterrent value of the U.S. Strategic Air Command, it was expedient to have ground forces as an additional discouragement to local aggression. The projected German divisions would comprise such a defensive force and would, the argument ran, give the Federal Republic security in the east while it was regaining its freedom in the west.

The opponents of German rearmament—if we leave aside those who argued from pacifist conviction, or from fear that a new army would undermine Germany's still fragile democratic institutions, or from mere disinclination to perform military service—also made their case, for the most part, by political reasoning. Any move to raise troops in alliance with the West, they insisted, would precipitate a Soviet attack on Germany or—at the very least—harden Soviet resistance to the idea of a future reunification of the divided nation. The Social Democratic Party, which led the opposition, made much of these arguments and, in addition, suggested that the Western Powers could be expected neither to raise enough troops to deter Soviet aggression nor to stand by Germany if aggression came. In the debate over the EDC treaties in 1952, a Socialist speaker argued further that, since Western Germany was not a member of NATO, she would have no control over any troops that she raised and no effective means, therefore, of forcing the British and French to give priority to the defense of German soil in the event of war.

Later on, when the Federal Republic did in fact become a member of NATO, the Socialists—as Hans Speier has pointed out[3]—conveniently abandoned this early argument and came out in opposition to the NATO tie; and this demonstrates how much the debates on German rearmament were dominated by the dictates of political expediency rather than by any true desire to grapple with the realities of the security question. With the bulk of their party still holding to their traditional doctrinaire opposition to militarism, the Socialists used any argument against rearmament that seemed useful at a given moment, while the government answered all criticisms with bland assurances that all would be well once the troops were raised. That the level of sophistication in this debate on strategy was not high is illustrated by a speech of Franz-Josef Strauss in March 1952 in which (addressing himself to the argument that a new army would cause a new war in a country still recovering from the ravages of the last one) he stated that he was confident that the government and its

---

[3] Hans Speier, *German Rearmament and Atomic War: The Views of German Military and Political Leaders*, Evanston, Ill., 1957, p. 162.

Western friends would be able to find "a strategic conception according to which Germany cannot become the theater of a conflict."[4] Nor did the Chancellor hesitate to lend his authority to the view that membership in the Western defense community would somehow, for reasons which he did not reveal, make it wholly impossible for Germany to become a battlefield again.[5]

Thus, until the very end of 1954, the cloudiest possible conceptions of defense possibilities circulated in public; and no one seemed to have the slightest curiosity about actual strategic plans which were, presumably, being drafted in *Dienststelle Blank* and at SHAPE.

II

This situation was radically changed by military developments that followed the signing of the Paris treaties in October 1954. The treaties themselves, by admitting the Federal Republic to membership in NATO and authorizing her to raise and maintain a military establishment of 500,000 officers and men, including twelve combat divisions assigned to the NATO command, transformed what had appeared to be an academic debate into a discussion of concrete and immediate problems and stimulated speculation concerning the actual use to which the German NATO units would be put. For the first time, German periodicals with national circulation began to publish circumstantial articles on strategy, and some of these were soon pointing out that, in the event of aggression from the east, NATO forces would apparently conduct themselves according to the classical principles of land warfare, with the forward units making a dogged withdrawal from the Elbe to the Rhine, holding on as long as possible to each successive line of resistance in order to gain time for the Allied build-up behind the Rhine and the massive counterthrust that would be delivered by it.[6]

The thought of what this kind of war would mean in a country as thickly settled and as highly organized as Western Germany shocked many Germans and weakened their enthusiasm for the newly achieved tie with NATO. The most dramatic expression of this reaction was the attempt made by Colonel Bogislaw von Bonin, in defiance of his superiors in the Defense Ministry, to win support for a strategic plan which rejected the NATO concept of retreat and counterattack in favor

---

[4] *Ibid.*, p. 161.

[5] See, for instance, his clear statement on this point in *Frankfurter Allgemeine Zeitung*, March 17, 1955, p. 4.

[6] See, for instance, *Der Spiegel* (Hamburg), November 3, 1954, p. 18; and Adelbert Weinstein, in *Frankfurter Allgemeine Zeitung*, November 2, 1954.

of a mobile defense along the zonal border, conducted by an independent German army of 150,000 volunteers, armed with the most powerful anti-tank weapons. Bonin's dismissal and his subsequent campaign in the press aroused wide public attention.[7]

Meanwhile, however, a new source of anxiety had been revealed. In December 1954, the NATO Council decided that all of the alliance's future strategic plans would be based on the assumption that NATO forces would use atomic weapons to defend themselves against an attack from the east; and, six months later, as if to show that they meant this, NATO forces carried out an elaborate air exercise called *Carte Blanche*, which was designed to demonstrate the capabilities of tactical atomic weapons against enemy bases and lines of communication. At the end of the simulated bombing, in which 3,000 planes were flown and 335 bombs "dropped," observers calculated that—apart from the damage to military objectives—1,700,000 Germans had been "killed," 3,500,000 "wounded," and an unknown number affected by radiation.[8]

This was sobering in the extreme. *Carte Blanche* seemed to some critics to prove the utter pointlessness of rearmament, while by others it was cited as proof of the emptiness of the government's assurances and the inconsistency of their views on strategy. While the Socialists scornfully recalled the Chancellor's promise of German immunity from battle damage,[9] independent journals questioned the ability of a force, which—if Field Marshal Montgomery was to be believed— would automatically resort to atomic weapons regardless of the nature of the attack to which it was subjected, to meet the kind of aggression most likely to be experienced (small-scale local incursions and guerrilla warfare combined with political subversion) without touching off an all-out nuclear war. In a widely read book called *No One Can Win the War*, the military expert of the *Frankfurter Allgemeine Zeitung,* Adelbert Weinstein, wrote that a war that involved the use of atomic weapons would cause "dreadful damage in certain areas in Germany and terrible losses of life among the populace" and that "any German must on that account reject such a strategy." If it was true that the only defense lay in the use of atomic weapons, then there was no military means of attaining national security, which must therefore be sought by political means. Weinstein actually suggested that one way

---

[7] See Gordon A. Craig, "NATO and the New German Army," in *Military Policy and National Security,* edited by W. W. Kaufmann, Princeton, N.J., 1956, pp. 221ff.

[8] *Ibid.,* pp. 225ff.

[9] See the speech of Erich Ollenhauer reported in *Das Parlament* (Bonn), July 6, 1955, p. 5; and remarks of Fritz Erler reported in *Der Spiegel,* July 13, 1955, p. 8.

of promoting such a political solution would be for the Federal Republic to adopt something like the Bonin strategy of strong zonal defense by conventional arms, while requesting her NATO allies to withdraw their troops beyond the Rhine. The Soviets, he suggested, might be more amenable to negotiations for a security pact and other desiderata if Western Germany were not so obviously a Western strategic glacis.[10]

All of these criticisms—and an additional one stressed by Weinstein and by the Czech military specialist Miksche,[11] to the effect that the coming of nuclear weapons necessitated a radical revision of the traditional organization of land armies and particularly of the divisional structure, and that those planning the new German army were still in this respect operating on the basis of outmoded ideas[12]—were used by opposition speakers in the heated military debates that were held over the next two years. In the *Bundestag* discussions of the Volunteers Bill in July 1955 and in the debate on the Service Bill a year later, the Social Democrats insisted that the government had no reason to call for conscription; if it was not tied to obsolete ideas and was not intent on building up the kind of army that had fought the last war, it would see that a small army of volunteers would serve its needs perfectly well. Then as later, however, the chief Socialist argument was that no army, large or small, that fought with NATO could protect Germany from the horrors of nuclear war. "The strategy of NATO," Fritz Erler cried in the debate of July 1956, "leaves no room for doubting that an armed conflict in Europe—even with [the participation of] 500,000 German soldiers—will not remain a conventional conflict. The NATO plans are based upon immediate and direct employment of atomic weapons in the event of a conflict in Europe."[13]

There can be no doubt that these attacks embarrassed the government, for the rejoinders of its spokesmen were often lame and some-

[10] Adelbert Weinstein, *Keiner kann den Krieg gewinnen*, Bonn, 1955, pp. 53, 62.
[11] Lieut. Colonel F. O. Miksche, *Atomic Weapons and Armies*, New York, 1955, especially Chapter 6.
[12] "Modern armies will adjust themselves to atom war by keeping their tactical units smaller than in former times and allowing armed bands to be created which will have to dispense with any kind of train. They will therefore be highly mobile and armored, provided with a considerable amount of communication equipment, and will carry their own supply staffs with them. In a few years, therefore, there will be no divisions of the present type; what will remain will be only a tactical unit which we will have to give another name, since the designation 'Division' would be antiquated and would give rise to false impressions. This development, which is not to be halted, is a further argument against the overhasty organization of twelve German divisions of the old type." Weinstein, *Keiner kann den Krieg gewinnen*, p. 60.
[13] Quoted in Speier, *German Rearmament*, p. 207.

times inconsistent. They tried so far as possible to avoid any detailed discussion of NATO strategy, and to dispose of the awkward decision of December 1954 by denying its existence or intimating that it would soon be changed. In the debate of July 1955, Franz-Josef Strauss, already rapidly emerging as the chief government spokesman on military matters, used a combination of promises and evasions to defend the government's demand for authorization to raise troops. For Germany to fail to meet her commitments under the Paris treaties would, he said, be faithless and politically disastrous. Failure to raise conventional forces would mean that atomic weapons would surely have to be used immediately on the outbreak of a war, whereas an increase in NATO's conventional forces, by the addition of German contingents, might actually advance the coming of atomic disarmament. In any case, Germany's contribution to NATO would make it a more effective organization and, because of this, the Federal Republic would have "the right of influencing NATO plans in the light of German interests."[14] In the debate of July 1956, Kurt-Georg Kiesinger followed the same line in seeking to meet the Socialists' continued references to the NATO decision of December 1954. It was wholly possible that the NATO Powers might decide *not* to use atomic weapons, he said, but they could do so only if they had enough conventional troops to be able to escape the alternative of mere capitulation to aggression. In asking for a conscription bill and an army of half a million men, the government was, therefore, doing its bit "to the end of avoiding the use of the most horrible of all means of destruction, if the worse comes to the worst."[15]

The government bills weathered the parliamentary storms of 1955 and 1956 because of the numbers and the discipline of the coalition deputies rather than because of the persuasiveness of their arguments. It may be that Theodor Blank (who was dropped as Defense Minister in October 1956) really believed that German rearmament of the kind advocated since 1950 would both deter Soviet aggression and make the use of atomic weapons unnecessary if it nevertheless came. It is doubtful whether either Franz-Josef Strauss (who succeeded him) or the Chancellor ever put much faith in these prophecies. If they did so, they now changed their minds in a radical and dramatic manner, for in the fall of 1956 they began to urge the necessity of providing the new German army with tactical atomic weapons.

[14] *Das Parlament*, July 20, 1955, p. 12.
[15] Quoted in Speier, *German Rearmament*, p. 210.

III

Konrad Adenauer's reversal of position in this matter could hardly have been more abrupt. As late as August 1956, he had reacted violently to stories that had appeared in the *New York Times* concerning projected force reductions that would seriously cut the number of American troops in Europe and to explanations that these reductions were to be balanced by the introduction of more atomic weapons.[16] In a statement printed in the official *Bulletin* of the West German government, the Chancellor said bluntly: "I would like to stress that I regard shifting the principal emphasis to atomic weapons at the present time as a mistake." To meet an attack from the east with tactical atomic weapons would almost certainly "trigger an intercontinental rocket war.... I am of the opinion that it is of special importance to localize small conflicts that may occur, and for this we need divisions with conventional weapons."[17] Yet, only a month later, Adenauer was talking with his allies about the possibility of equipping the *Bundeswehr* with tactical atomic weapons.

It has been suggested that the Chancellor was talked around by the new Defense Minister Strauss or by the U.S. Assistant Secretary of Defense, Donald Quarles; but it seems more likely that domestic resistance to military conscription, now increased by the stories of the imminent American cutbacks, had the strongest influence in determining his position. At the end of September 1956 the Chancellor had felt it necessary to make concessions to this feeling, and had announced that the term of service for conscripts in the new defense force would be reduced from eighteen to twelve months. The inevitable effect of this upon the projected force levels of the *Bundeswehr* made the introduction of nuclear weapons a logical substitute for reduced manpower.[18]

The Chancellor's request for tactical atomic weapons could not, of course, be immediately satisfied. As the December 1956 meeting of NATO demonstrated, the Federal Republic was not alone in desiring to acquire such weapons, and the United States government possessed neither the stockpile nor the necessary authority to satisfy them. Discussions of possible arrangements went on among the allies throughout the course of 1957, but no real progress had been reached by the end of the year. It was impossible, however, to prevent rumors of what was

[16] *New York Times*, July 13, 14, 15, 1956.
[17] *The Bulletin* (Press and Information Service of the German Federal Government), August 21, 1956, p. 1.
[18] The most satisfactory account of all this is to be found in Speier, *German Rearmament*, Chapter 12. See also *Der Spiegel*, October 3, 1956, p. 11.

in the wind from reaching the German public, which became increasingly concerned over the prospects opening before them. Press reports of the NATO Council meeting of December 1957, which indicated that the sharing of atomic weapons had again been discussed, brought public feeling to a head and touched off the public debate on atomic weapons that raged during the first six months of 1958 and exceeded in violence any previous public discussions of strategy questions.

In the foreign affairs debate in the *Bundestag* in January, the Socialists—especially Ollenhauer, Carlo Schmid, and Erler—tried to elicit information from the government bench about plans to accept atomic weapons for the army or to allow the construction of rocket ramps on German soil.[19] The ministers did not seem prepared to answer their questions and took refuge in technicalities or generalizations, which did nothing to reassure public opinion.[20] The matter was raised again in another full-scale debate in March, and this time it was apparent that the Chancellor had decided to indulge in some plain speaking.[21] Spokesmen for the government reaffirmed their faith in the political and military strategy of the Western alliance and argued that, until such time as a comprehensive disarmament agreement was concluded among the Great Powers (and the Soviet Union had apparently no interest in such an agreement), the Federal Republic's security was necessarily bound up with NATO. This would probably mean that, sooner or later, the *Bundeswehr* would receive tactical atomic weapons for, in view of Soviet advances in weapons technique, it was only natural that NATO must bend all its efforts to acquire and equip its forces with the most modern armament, including rockets and nuclear weapons.

The Chancellor himself was brutally frank. "I want as many Germans as possible to hear this," he said. "If an important part of NATO doesn't possess weapons as strong as those of its potential opponent . . . then it has neither significance nor importance. If the strategical planning of NATO—and we must naturally and will naturally test this— desires that we too, the Federal Republic, make use of this development of weapons technique, and if we hesitate to do so, then we automatically leave NATO" and are left at the mercy of the Soviet Union. Unless controlled disarmament were attained within the near future, the gov-

[19] See *Das Parlament*, January 29, 1958, pp. 4f., 13f., 15f.
[20] See the speeches of Adenauer and Strauss, *ibid.*, 14f., 17f.
[21] On Adenauer's motives, see *Die Gegenwart* (Frankfurt a.M.), April 5, 1958, p. 199.

ernment must be authorized to accept the strategy and the weapons prescribed by NATO planners.[22]

The Defense Minister pushed this argument home. Even the opposition must admit, he argued, that until controlled disarmament came into effect, there was a threat of war. In view of this, what was the opposition's military policy? It surely did not believe in passive resistance; and, if it believed in an army at all, it could hardly believe in equipping it with arms inferior to those of its potential antagonist. How could troop morale be maintained in such circumstances? "We do not wish to equip the German army with tactical atomic weapons, . . . we are prepared to accept any prohibition of atomic weapons on the basis of control and balance of strength in the sphere of conventional weapons. Our allies are completely free to make such declarations on behalf of Germany. We are not, however, prepared so to weaken the defense potential by our 'No' that it might be a source of hope to the aggressor that he could take over Europe without the risk of a third World War."[23]

This revelation of the government's intentions released passions in the *Bundestag* which awakened unhappy memories of debates in the last years of the Weimar Republic and led one writer to say that "the *Bundestag* had discredited itself, the parliamentary system of government and democracy."[24] During the debate, no real attempt was made to discuss the issues systematically, and neither side sought to win the other by reason and persuasion. The speakers for the SPD obscured the fact that the government's intention of accepting arms would be conditional upon the state of general disarmament talks and described the government's policy variously as an indulgence of Strauss's desire to play at soldiers, an indication of the Chancellor's subservience to John Foster Dulles, and a sign that the military caste was reasserting its dominance in German life. Speakers for the government tended to deny that there was room for honest doubt on the atomic issue and to regard oppositionists as pro-Communists and neutralists. Throughout the debate there was a deplorable amount of what Theodor Eschenburg called "mouth anarchy,"[25] as deputies exchanged such epithets as "liar," "scoundrel," "shameless lout," "out-and-out tramp," "headhunter," "poisoner of wells," "mass murderer," and the like. The trauma that Hitler had left behind, one journal noted, was revealed repeatedly: an

[22] Adenauer's speech is in *Das Parlament*, March 26, 1958, pp. 4-5.

[23] *Ibid.*, pp. 8-11.

[24] F. R. Allemann in *Die Zeit* (Hamburg), March 27, 1958. See also Michael Freund in *Die Gegenwart*, April 5, 1958, pp. 200ff.

[25] *Die Zeit*, April 10, 1958, p. 1.

SPD deputy compared Adenauer to Goebbels, and the CDU deputies ostentatiously left the chamber; the Chancellor complimented an opponent, who happened to be an ex-Communist, on his "dialectical training and skill"; an FDP deputy accused the government deputies of having learned about communism from Alfred Rosenberg; a Socialist compared the government request for authority to accept atomic arms to Hitler's enabling law of March 1933; the whole opposition, during some words in praise of the Chancellor by CDU deputy Kiesinger, chanted "Heil! Heil! Heil!"; and so on.[26]

The posing of the atomic issue had, in short, revealed how deep the division was between the government and the opposition and how passionately the different points of view were held. The debate ended, as was expected, with a majority in favor of a resolution empowering the government to continue to build up its military strength within the NATO alliance, and in accordance with its strategy, until such time as general and controlled disarmament was agreed upon.[27] But the SPD was unreconciled and determined now to carry the issue to the country, by encouraging provincial governments to hold popular referenda on the atomic arming of the Bundeswehr.

In adopting this tactic the SPD showed an utter disregard for the lessons of history and for the facts of constitutional law. Certainly the history of the Weimar Republic, which on more than one occasion was involved in grave civil disorders as a result of popular referenda promoted by the extreme left and right, should have been enough to discourage resort to this method. Moreover, from the legal point of view, there was no provision in the Basic Law for such referenda; for, during the drafting of that law, Theodor Heuss had argued persuasively that the popular referendum was of advantage only to demagogues. Decisions in the Federal Republic must, it had been decided, be made by its representative assemblies. The SPD sought now to get around this by asking the provincial governments to pass special laws authorizing the referenda on the atomic issue, ignoring the fact that the Basic Law reserves foreign affairs and national defense to the Bundestag; and it succeeded in persuading the Senates of Hamburg and Bremen to act as it desired.[28]

It cannot be said that the referendum campaign, which went on

---

[26] Das Parlament, March 26, 1958, pp. 12, 30; Der Spiegel, March 26, 1958, p. 15; P. W. Wenger in Rheinischer Merkur (Bonn), March 28, 1958, pp. 1, 3; ibid., Easter 1958, p. 2.

[27] Das Parlament, April 2, 1958, p. 27.

[28] See Der Spiegel, April 30, 1958, pp. 15f.; Theodor Eschenburg in Die Zeit, April 3, 1958, p. 4; M. Gräfin Dönhoff, ibid., May 15, 1958, p. 1.

until late May, when the government secured injunctions from the Supreme Court at Karlsruhe forbidding all referenda on the subject, or the accompanying "Fight Against Atom Death," which was pushed in all parts of Germany, threw much light on the complicated strategic issues at stake. The crowds which assembled to hear SPD speakers were regaled with oversimplified formulas like "The question is posed whether we prefer suicide or the salvation of peace and of our wives and children," while their eyes were fed with signs reading "Strauss wants atom bombs; we want to live" or "*So etwas wie Hiroshima findet Adenauer prima.*"[29] Sometimes the meetings seemed to have little spontaneity, but to have been elaborately arranged by trade union or local government pressure.[30] But it would not be wise to overestimate the importance of these factors or to deny the sincerity of most of those who felt that some popular action was called for to stop the government's course. The intensity of their feeling was heightened by the intelligence that atomic arming might come sooner than had been expected at the time of the March debate, for in April the defense ministers of the NATO countries met in Paris and, at the conclusion of their meetings, Strauss gave an interview in which he indicated that decisions had been reached that would affect the armament of German forces and increase the risks the Soviets must run if they tried aggression.[31]

Nor should this movement be regarded only, or even primarily, as a movement of Socialists and trade unionists, for it affected many people who could not be labeled as either. Private societies like the *Aktionsgemeinschaft gegen die atomare Aufrüstung der Bundeswehr* carried on propaganda and sent protests and resolutions to NATO meetings.[32] University students, following the example of some of their professors, arranged demonstrations—groups from ten universities, for instance, marching in May in protest against armament plans.[33] And both the Evangelical and the Catholic Church were profoundly stirred by an issue that seemed to raise moral and ethical problems that were quite as serious as the political and military ones.

The Protestant Church was affected more seriously than the Catholic by the atomic question. It included a radical wing whose position was illustrated by Dr. Heinemann's cry during the March debate: "Better dead than mass murderers!" Churchmen like Niemöller and Gollwitzer argued seriously that a soldier with atomic arms could not be considered

[29] Josef Müller-Marein in *Die Zeit*, April 24, 1958, p. 1.
[30] Müller-Marein, *ibid.*, May 8, 1958, p. 1. Cf. *Frankfurter Rundschau*, May 2, 1958, p. 2.
[31] *Wehrkunde*, vii, No. 5 (April 1958), p. 277.
[32] *Frankfurter Rundschau*, May 7, 9, 1958.
[33] *Ibid.*, May 20, 1958, p. 1.

as being in a state of grace, and Niemöller was said to believe that it would be the duty of a Christian to betray the position of rocket ramps to the enemy rather than condone their use. At the synod meeting of the Evangelical Church in Berlin in April and May, there were so many resolutions against the atomic arming of the *Bundeswehr* that a special working group had to be set up to deal with them; and, although the radicals were not strong enough to push through a resolution condemning the Federal Republic's policy, they came close to breaking up the meeting by the violence of their tactics.[34]

Extremists of the Niemöller stripe were not, of course, unopposed. Within the Protestant Church eloquent voices were raised against their using the Gospel as an argument against measures that were designed, after all, to protect the West against a declared enemy of Christianity. "Worse than atomic weapons is the life of slavery in the East," wrote one pastor who knew from experience the truth of what he was saying;[35] and Emil Brunner pointed out that "since no pacifist voices can be raised in Russia, [where] short shrift is made of pacifism . . . one ought to realize that, in propagating unconditional pacifism here, he is making himself a pacemaker for [a power with] an unscrupulous will to war."[36] In a widely discussed statement issued in May, seven Roman Catholic moral theologians quoted the Pope as saying: "There are values of such importance for the common life of human beings that defense of them against lawless attack is fully justified. . . . A people that is threatened . . . cannot, if it wishes to act in a Christian manner, remain in passive indifference." The means of defense, they added, must be proportioned to the nature of the threat. The use of atomic weapons was not necessarily immoral; but to cry, "Better red than dead!" was certainly a denial of Christian responsibility.[37]

The whole period from April to July was filled with these and similar debates, waged with earnestness and passion in all parts of Germany. Yet, in the latter month, the Federal Republic's allies were given one encouraging indication that, despite the misgivings of many Germans, the great majority was still in favor of the Chancellor's foreign and military policies. The Social Democrats had elected to make atomic arming of the *Bundeswehr* the principal issue in the provincial elections

[34] *Rheinischer Merkur*, Easter 1958, p. 3; *Die Zeit*, May 1, 1958, p. 1; *The Bulletin*, May 6, 1958, p. 3; Gerhard Baumann, "Atomrüstung im Widerstreit der Meinungen," *Wehrkunde*, vii, No. 8 (August 1958), pp. 420ff.; *Der Spiegel*, May 14, 1958, p. 50.

[35] Baumann in *Wehrkunde*, vii, pp. 420ff.

[36] *Neue Zürcher Zeitung*, May 13, 1958.

[37] *Frankfurter Rundschau*, May 7, 1958, p. 2; Baumann in *Wehrkunde*, vii, pp. 420ff.; Alois Schardt in *Rheinischer Merkur*, October 17, 1958, pp. 4f.

in North Rhineland-Westphalia, and the CDU had responded by calling upon voters to rally to the defense of NATO.[38] The elections were
held on July 6 and gave the Chancellor's party an absolute majority of
the vote. One respected observer said that "the majority of the voters
of North Rhineland-Westphalia (and that is one third of all voters
in the Federal Republic) has announced that their confidence in Adenauer is greater than their fear of misuse of atomic weapons";[39] and
Die Welt of Hamburg agreed that "a representative segment of the
population has indicated that it will no longer oppose atomic armament."[40]

IV

This was doubtless reassuring to Franz-Josef Strauss, whose strenuous
efforts to build up the *Bundeswehr* as quickly as possible had been
based, ever since he became Defense Minister in October 1956, on the
assumption that atomic weapons would be in its armory. Two months
after the elections in North Rhineland-Westphalia, the Defense Minister was able to demonstrate some of the results of his work. In the
first part of September 1958, *Bundesheer* and Allied units conducted a
four-day series of exercises in the Oberpfalz, in which 10,000 troops
participated and which included the combined operation of armor
and infantry and a bridge-building exercise and night river-crossing.[41]
In the exercises of the 5th *Panzerdivision*, the movement, concealment,
and control of troops were good, and both command and troops responded flexibly to an attack by Italian paratroopers. During the crossing of the Rhine at Neuwied, the work of the engineers was precise
and fast, and the march discipline of the infantry division employed
was excellent. In general, the technical planning and execution of the
different phases of the simulated fighting showed that the training of
the troops was more than adequate. The fears of those who had felt,
on the basis of strong anti-military tendencies manifest among German
youth in 1954 and 1955,[42] that conscripts would not be good soldiers
were not borne out in these maneuvers, nor were the gloomy prophecies
of those military writers who felt that the emphasis placed in the
Soldiers Law upon the rights of the individual soldier would make
for slackness and lack of discipline.[43] On the contrary, Adelbert Wein-

[38] F. R. Allemann in *Die Zeit*, July 4, 1958, p. 1.
[39] Robert Strobel, *ibid.*, July 11, 1958, p. 1.
[40] Cited in *The Bulletin*, July 8, 1958, p. 2.
[41] *Frankfurter Allgemeine Zeitung*, September 11, 12, 16, 1958.
[42] On this, see Craig in *Military Policy and National Security*, pp. 198f.
[43] For examples of this kind of criticism, see Werner Picht, *Wiederbewaffnung*,

stein wrote that the new soldiers "seem to be *fixe Burschen* [smart fellows] who go about their task with a swing and are supplied with an adequate share of sound common sense." Thanks to the devotion and the hard work of the officers and the ability of the conscripts to be inspired by them, the German units looked very good.[44]

Foreign observers seemed to agree. Both American and English journals had little but praise for the conduct of the troops in the final phase of the *Bundesheer*'s autumn maneuvers, which was held at Bergen-Hohne in the last week of September. These exercises, in which 12,000 troops, 3,000 wheeled vehicles, and 680 tracked vehicles participated, included the firing of anti-tank rockets, a massive tank attack preceded by two atomic detonations, and a drop by a company of paratroops.[45] The last of these, which was executed in a wind strong enough to have justified postponement, and in which four men were hurt, showed that there was no lack of determination in the new army; and the exercises as a whole—*The Times* of London felt—showed that the troops had "a high grade of personal responsibility and spirit."[46]

The maneuvers at Bergen-Hohne had a special interest for professional observers, since they provided a glimpse of the new divisional organization of the *Bundesheer* which was expected to be in effect by 1959. According to current plans, the new "unitary division" (*Einheitsdivision*) was to be composed of two Grenadier Brigades and one Armored Brigade—and these formations would differ significantly from existing fighting units. They would be self-sufficient formations of mixed arms, each of which—in addition to its armored and grenadier battalions—would have its own anti-aircraft, communications, and supply units and an artillery battalion comprising two companies of 10.5 cm. guns and one mortar company. Two of the new brigades were tested at Bergen-Hohne—a Grenadier Brigade under the command of Brig. General de Maizière and an Armored Brigade under Colonel Lüder—and, although minor deficiencies became evident, the mobility of the formations and their responsiveness to command were so impressive that Defense Minister Strauss announced, on the last day of maneuvers, that the *Bundesheer* had found its profile and that priority would now be given to the creation of more of the new-style brigades.[47]

Pfüllingen, 1954; and Friedrich von Stulpnagel, "Vom künftigen deutschen Soldaten: eine Antithese," *Wehrkunde*, III, No. 10 (October 1954).

[44] *Frankfurter Allgemeine Zeitung*, September 16, 1958.

[45] *Ibid.*, September 26, 27, 1958; *Frankfurter Rundschau*, September 27, 1958.

[46] *The Times* (London), September 28, 1958.

[47] *Frankfurter Allgemeine Zeitung*, September 27, 1958, p. 3; and, especially, Ernst-Otto Maetzke, *ibid.*, September 29, 1958, p. 2.

The strategical concept underlying the projected divisional reorganization seems to have been designed to meet professional objections to previous plans for the defense of Western Europe, by increasing the possibility of effective defense along the zonal border. If Colonel von Bonin's one-man revolt against the mobile defense concept had led to his dismissal from office, his ideas had survived and had been taken up by other writers—by Kissel, Zitzewitz, and others in military journals like *Wehrkunde*,[48] by Adelbert Weinstein of the *Frankfurter Allgemeine Zeitung*, and by the widely read strategical thinker, F. O. Miksche. In a book published in 1958,[49] this Czech critic had, in a sense, summarized the views of this whole school by arguing that, even though the nuclear revolution had come to stay, one could not win a street fight or prevent infiltration with atomic bombs. The military advantage in future war would lie with the side that, in addition to its nuclear weapons, possessed a strong, armored, and mobile infantry armed with conventional weapons; and NATO in particular needed a zonal defense strong enough to make impossible a Soviet penetration that had not been preceded by the kind of concentration that was vulnerable to atomic attack.[50]

That these ideas have not been entirely disregarded in West German defensive planning seems reasonably clear. In an interview during the September maneuvers, Defense Minister Strauss said that the *Bundesheer*'s new strategy might be called a "modernized Bonin plan," with the new highly mobile brigades taking the place of Bonin's anti-tank and armored units. In his plan, he made clear, they would operate behind a strong border defense composed of militia units and army infantry—"Stone Age soldiers," as he called them—who would probably be deeply entrenched and would be supported by territorial militia who were responsible for local defense in rear areas.[51] As in the case of Bonin's plan and the preferred plans of Miksche, the objective here would be to create a border defense strong enough to discourage aggression by indicating that deep penetration could be achieved only with a massive effort and very heavy casualties.

The major difference between Bonin's views and those of Strauss is that Bonin, in his anxiousness to make it clear to the potential enemy

[48] See, for instance, Horst von Zitzewitz, "Grenzschutz gestern und morgen," *Wehrkunde*, VII, No. 3 (March 1958); and Hans Kissel, "Zur Verteidigung Westeuropas," *ibid.*, No. 6 (June 1958).

[49] Oberstleutnant Ferdinand Otto Miksche, *Der Atomkrieg findet nicht statt*, Stuttgart, 1958.

[50] See Otto von Habsburg's comments on Miksche's views in *Rheinischer Merkur*, September 5, 1958, p. 3.

[51] Adelbert Weinstein in *Frankfurter Allgemeine Zeitung*, September 12, 1958, p. 2.

that the *Bundesheer* was a strictly defensive force, thought solely in terms of conventional weapons when he planned the arrangement of his blocking units,[52] while the present Defense Minister seems to believe that this is no longer possible. Thus, although the armament of the new Grenadier and Armored Brigades does not include atomic artillery, the support weapons of division and corps will include tactical atomic weapons; and the brigade commanders will be able to recommend to division headquarters the kind of atomic blow they want and the time and place of delivery, in cases where they can no longer control the situation with conventional weapons alone.[53] There seems to be little doubt in Strauss's mind that, in the event of aggression from the east, the use of tactical atomic weapons would be inevitable and that atomic rocket artillery would be the best security against regional breakthroughs. Although he has described his strategy as one of graduated deterrence, he does not seem to believe that the strictly conventional phase of any future war would be of long duration.[54]

At the end of 1958, the Defense Minister was devoting much of his energy to perfecting the new divisional organization and procuring modern armaments for the *Bundeswehr*, but he was also expressing the view that an effective defense system would demand certain other things as well. It was clear, for one thing, that provision had to be made for a much larger territorial army than the Republic possessed. It was the Minister's view also that the existing conscription law would have to be amended in order to give trainees more field service than the existing twelve-month law permits; and, if lengthening the period of active service proved to be politically inexpedient, he was inclined to believe that three months of field training might be added immediately after the completion of the recruit's year of service and then deducted from his later reserve requirements.[55] Finally, it was his firm belief that no defense plans would be realistic until the *Bundestag* passed a Law for Emergency, placing all the resources of the nation in the service of defense in the event of war and giving legal authority to the military to guide necessary evacuations, to restore order in bombed civilian centers, and to perform other emergency tasks.[56] Here Strauss seemed to be thinking along the same lines as Major Wilhelm Kohler

---

[52] In one version of his plan, Bonin admitted the possibility that the zonal defense forces might have to call on NATO forces for support by tactical atomic weapons. See *Der Spiegel*, March 30, 1955.

[53] Maetzke in *Frankfurter Allgemeine Zeitung*, September 29, 1958, p. 2.

[54] *Frankfurter Allgemeine Zeitung*, September 12, 1958, p. 2. Cf. Adelbert Weinstein, "Was ist stufenweise Abschreckung?" *ibid.*, June 30, 1958, p. 1.

[55] *Ibid.*, September 16, 1958, p. 3; *Der Spiegel*, October 1, 1958, pp. 15f.

[56] Weinstein in *Frankfurter Allgemeine Zeitung*, September 12, 1958, p. 2.

who, in a perhaps not entirely spontaneous article in the April issue of *Wehrkunde*, argued that, if possible, 80 per cent of the population of all districts lying within 150 kilometers of the zonal borders should be evacuated before the actual outbreak of a war and that detailed plans should be drawn up so that every citizen would know in advance by what means of travel, in what group, at what time, with what special duties, and with what required supplies he would be expected to move west.[57]

The likelihood that Strauss's plans for extending the field service of recruits would be approved in the near future was not great; and the mere mention of Kohler's evacuation plan in the popular press was enough to cause public dismay and business indignation in towns close to the border.[58] Even so, as the year 1958 came to an end, the Federal Republic's NATO partners had good reason to be pleased with the demonstrated strength and effectiveness of the *Bundesheer*.

V

Since 1950 the Adenauer government had doggedly followed a policy of rearmament within the framework of the Western defense community and, in doing so, it had defeated its domestic opponents in every crucial trial of strength. Yet it is safe to say that, at the end of 1958, the number of informed and responsible critics of Adenauer's policy and the NATO strategy to which he clung was increasing. The principal reason for this was that, despite the undoubted diplomatic successes that the Chancellor had won by his adherence to the West, he had not gained the prize that he had promised the German people in 1954; the "policy of strength" had not impressed the Soviets sufficiently to make them grant German reunification on Western terms. Increasingly now, men were beginning to ask whether a policy of undeviating loyalty to NATO could be expected to bring reunification on any terms.

The crux of the problem lay in Western insistence that a reunited Germany must have no restrictions upon its sovereignty and must be free to join the NATO alliance if it saw fit to do so. A Soviet Union in the throes of domestic disaffection and involved in revolutionary disturbances in the satellite countries might possibly be willing to countenance this solution to the German question; the Soviet Union that had won such impressive diplomatic, economic, and scientific

[57] Major Wilhelm Kohler, "Das Flüchtlingsproblem in der Bundesrepublik Deutschland," *Wehrkunde*, vii, No. 4 (April 1958).
[58] See *Der Spiegel*, April 30, 1958, pp. 22f.

triumphs since the end of 1956 would hardly be inclined to do so. The Federal Republic and its allies were left, therefore, with the choice of holding stubbornly to their present position or seeking a road to unification on a different basis. Even if they were permitted to do the former—and, after Khrushchev's note of November 1958 on Berlin, this seemed doubtful—to do so would be to admit that military expediency was the only determinant of Western policy; and many Germans agreed with the Socialist Fritz Erler, who wrote in April 1958, "I deplore the argument that for strategic reasons West German military participation in NATO is a higher necessity than the establishment of a free united Germany which is protected and limited by other instruments than the actual NATO solution."[59]

To such persons, the idea of some kind of disengagement by the military forces of the major powers seemed to offer at least a possibility of escape from the impasse to which Western policy had come at the end of 1958. This idea had, of course, been advocated by individual politicians and publicists ever since the signing of the Paris treaties;[60] but it had not had much impact upon the popular consciousness until the end of 1957, when the Polish Foreign Minister Rapacki made his proposal at the meeting of the United Nations Assembly for the creation of an atom-free zone in Central Europe, when George Kennan urged the consideration of mutual withdrawal of Soviet and NATO troops from Germany, and when the Soviet government combined both ideas in letters addressed to Konrad Adenauer and other heads of state. The Soviet letter of December 8, 1957, offered a standstill agreement on armaments pending preparations for general disarmament, a ban on the use of nuclear weapons in all Germany as well as in Poland and Czechoslovakia, and the withdrawal of Soviet troops from Eastern Germany if the allies would match it by pulling their forces out of their European bases.[61]

Konrad Adenauer's first response to this proposal was given at the NATO Council meeting in December 1957 and was surprisingly cordial. The Chancellor stated that he had read the letter from Bulganin "with great attention" and "would see no objection to attempting to inquire through diplomatic channels from the Soviet Government what precise conceptions form the bases of these proposals."[62] This statement was greeted with something akin to enthusiasm in Western Germany,

[59] Fritz Erler, "The Reunification of Germany and Security for Europe," *World Politics*, x, No. 3 (April 1958), p. 368.
[60] See, for instance, Weinstein, *Keiner kann den Krieg gewinnen*, pp. 57f.
[61] *New York Times*, December 11, 1957, p. 1.
[62] *Ibid.*, December 17, 1957, p. 1.

and Adenauer was credited with transforming NATO policy and laying the basis for fruitful negotiations with the Soviets.[63] It came, therefore, as a shock to many when, in a radio address on January 15, Adenauer attacked the proposals for an atom-free zone as a Soviet maneuver to destroy NATO and prepare the way for the Communist domination of Europe,[64] and when, a week later, he repeated this in an answer to Bulganin's letter of December 8.[65] The cartoonist Flora must have summed up the feelings of many when he drew a picture captioned *"Der sehr gestrenge Herr Papa,"* showing a stern-faced Adenauer dragging a small and wistful Michel away, while a balloon labeled "Rapacki Plan" floated off into the air.[66]

The parliamentary opposition took up the question of disengagement in the debate on foreign affairs in the *Bundestag* on January 23-24, 1958. After Foreign Minister Heinrich Brentano had opened this discussion with a report of the steps taken at Paris to improve the coherence of the NATO alliance, Dr. Mende of the Free Democratic Party submitted a series of questions to him. Was the government, in talks with its allies, prepared to insist that the question of German reunification must be discussed in any summit negotiations entered into by them? Did they intend to promote unification itself by following up Rapacki's proposals, or were the Chancellor's radio address and his answer to Bulganin—both of which the speaker resented as high-handed, since Adenauer had not seen fit to consult party leaders or the *Bundestag* Foreign Affairs Committee before making them—to be taken as the government's final word? Did the government intend—as the speaker clearly hoped it did—to use Kennan's proposal for a solution of the German question as the basis of discussions with the four powers?[67]

The first of these questions Brentano answered with a simple affirmative, and the third by stating that he did not regard the Kennan proposals as worth serious discussion.[68] With respect to the Rapacki pro-

[63] *Ibid.*, December 20, 1957, p. 1; January 5, 1958, p. 12. See also *Frankfurter Allgemeine Zeitung*, December 19, 1957, p. 1; M. Gräfin Dönhoff in *Die Zeit*, December 26, 1957, p. 1.

[64] *New York Herald Tribune*, January 16, 1958, p. 1; *The Bulletin*, January 21, 1958, p. 2.

[65] *New York Times*, January 22, 1958, p. 1.

[66] *Die Zeit*, January 23, 1958, p. 1.

[67] *Das Parlament*, January 29, 1958, pp. 3-4.

[68] "We have busied ourselves with this question longer, more intensively, and more earnestly than the former ambassador Kennan. . . . The Federal Government has no intention of proposing to the four powers, as a sensible solution of the German question, that the Federal Republic and the German people should be armed for partisan war and for the werewolf ideology that goes with it" (*ibid.*, p. 4). This last is a reference to Kennan's suggestion that Germany would be better defended by paramilitary forces and a civil resistance movement making its defense "at every village

posal, the Foreign Minister took the line that, far from promoting
the cause of reunification, it would merely confirm the present division
of Germany, for it could be implemented only if the Pankow government were a contracting party. He had already said that the government had no intention of asking its allies to agree to limitations upon
their armaments, for—even if the Federal Republic had the right to do
so—this would lead only to their withdrawal from Germany. This
would weaken Western defenses "without our getting a single step
closer to a relaxation of tensions, to controlled disarmament, or to the
solution of the German problem." In answer to Mende, he repeated
those arguments, making clear that the government did not intend to
make concessions until it had tangible assurances that they would not
be dangerous.[69]

These answers did not satisfy the Free Democrats, one of whose
speakers lamented that Adenauer had disappointed all those who believed that his attitude in Paris was the beginning of a "de-Dulles-
ization" (*Entdullexsionierung*) of German policy;[70] they did not satisfy
the Socialists, who had long criticized the NATO tie as a barrier to
negotiation with the Soviet Union[71] and who saw in Brentano's answer
another manifestation of this; and they did not convince independent
commentators, who felt that the government's attitude toward the
Bulganin note was unnecessarily cavalier. Writing in April 1958, the
Socialist deputy Fritz Erler said, "We should discuss the proposal
seriously, instead of calling it 'unrealistic,' as many of our leaders call
every proposal that might lead out of the deadlock in which we now
find ourselves." By showing willingness to negotiate, the government
would not be tying its hands. There were many variants of the disengagement idea, none of which pretended to be a definitive solution.
"The readiness is the decisive point," Erler wrote. "If the West is not
adaptable, it will be immobilized on the German problem and leave
all initiative to the USSR."[72] Erler was supported on this point by an
editor of the important journal *Aussenpolitik*, who wrote later in the
year: "Things become either better or worse. They don't stay the same.

---

crossroads" than by regular military formations. See George F. Kennan, *Russia, the Atom and the West*, New York, 1957, pp. 63-64. This suggestion awakened unhappy memories of the last days of Nazi resistance, and whenever Kennan's plan was mentioned in debate, the cry "Werewolves!" was apt to follow. See the exchange between Carlo Schmid (SPD) and Kiesinger (CDU) later in the debate (*Das Parlament*, January 29, 1958, pp. 7f., 14), and Erler's defense of Kennan's proposals (*ibid.*, p. 15).
[69] *Ibid.*, pp. 1, 4.
[70] *Ibid.*, p. 10.
[71] See the SPD Press Officer's statement in *The Bulletin*, March 18, 1958, p. 5.
[72] Erler in *World Politics*, x, pp. 371f.

Germany will be united one way or another. The inactive partner yields the field to his opponent."[73]

Such writers as these have been particularly critical of the government's assumption that *any* step in the direction of disengagement would necessarily be disastrous from a security point of view. A denial of atomic weapons to the *Bundeswehr* or rocket bases to Western Germany would, they feel, cause no real military disadvantage and might, if offered in negotiation, be productive of unexpected political gain. Further steps of disengagement need be taken only in return for security arrangements that promised to be effective. Since Germany could neither afford, nor safely be allowed to possess, a military establishment of the size necessary to protect her against all future attack, it would be reasonable to place her within the kind of security system proposed in the Gaitskell plan and to give her the further protection of a mutual guarantee by the United States and the USSR. Only after such arrangements had been made would it be reasonable to think of a phased withdrawal of NATO and Soviet troops, from both Germanies, from Poland and Czechoslovakia, and perhaps from the countries of the Danubian basin as well. If such disengagement got under way, it was to be hoped that the reunification of Germany would proceed in stages corresponding to the troop withdrawals; but even if this were not possible, reunification must follow inevitably upon the end of occupation. And if, in the course of all this, Germany's tie with NATO was broken, did that really matter? The West could hardly doubt that a united Germany would remain a cultural, political, social, and economic part of the Western family of nations, and Germany could hardly doubt that the West would fight to protect its being overrun by the Soviet Union at some future date. The alliance would remain in fact, if not in law.[74]

The advocates of disengagement are not so naïve as to forget that there are many technical problems that would have to be solved before anything like the process described above could be realized (problems of inspection, phasing, security during withdrawal, equalization of advantage after withdrawal, and the like); and they are under no illusions concerning the political difficulties involved in all this. They are willing to admit that the Soviet Union may not have the slightest desire to grant reunification and that Western offers of disengagement may—as Secretary Brentano prophesied—be referred, one way or an-

[73] Wilhelm Wolfgang Schütz, *Das Gesetz des Handelns: Zerrissenheit und Einheit unserer Welt*, Frankfurt a.M., 1958, p. 41.
[74] *Ibid.*, pp. 84-108; Erler in *World Politics*, x, pp. 372-77.

other, to the East German government, which can hardly be expected to be enthusiastic about reunification. But until this is known for sure, every effort should be made to promote negotiation; and, while this is being done, care should be taken to avoid jeopardizing future negotiation by present tendencies in military policy.

For this reason the SPD, at its party congress at Stuttgart in 1958, supplemented its stand in favor of negotiations to investigate the possibility of creating "militarily thinned-out areas," with a statement on military policy which was somewhat more coherent than earlier statements of this traditionally anti-militarist party.[75] This admitted that the dangers of Germany's present situation required her to possess an effective fighting force, but that this should not be too big and should not be armed in a provocative manner. "In its defense effort the Federal Republic must observe a proper relation to that of its immediate neighbors, in particular the German military force on the other side of the demarcation line.[76] For this purpose it is far more suitable to maintain volunteer troops which are fewer in number but very well trained than a mass army based on general conscription. . . . For their task of protection, such troops should not be equipped with instruments that are not designed to protect but only to destroy: atomic weapons and rockets. Such troops . . . would, in case of a military emergency, require supplementation, for which purpose it is necessary to have local volunteer units previously trained in short periods of military service."[77]

Government spokesmen have jeered at the vagueness and lack of imagination shown by this statement of military policy, and have charged that the blanket repudiation of atomic weapons is unrealistic in view of recent weapons developments.[78] But the Socialists have not been alone in arguing that the actual acceptance of atomic weapons by the *Bundeswehr* and the erection of rocket ramps in the Federal Republic will seal the division of Germany, if it does not precipitate a Soviet attack, and in urging that military policy must, after all, be guided by state policy which, in West Germany's case, must have reunification as its objective.

[75] It was not coherent enough to satisfy a number of German journalists. See F. R. Allemann in *Die Zeit*, May 29, 1958, who said that the SPD was clinging to "the withered tufts of a quasi-revolutionary utopianism"; *Der Spiegel*, May 21, 1958, pp. 18f.; *Frankfurter Allgemeine Zeitung*, May 21, 23, 24, 1958.

[76] It is known that some Socialists, including Erler, believe that the West German army should be as large as the combined forces of East Germany, Poland, and Czechoslovakia. *Frankfurter Allgemeine Zeitung*, May 24, 1958.

[77] *The Bulletin*, June 3, 1958, pp. 4-5.

[78] See the speech by Strauss in *Das Parlament*, July 30, 1958, pp. 4ff.

Thus, at the end of 1958, interest in proposals of disengagement—which Konrad Adenauer had tried to kill in January and John Foster Dulles thought he had buried in May at Copenhagen—had revived sharply[79] and was exerting increasing influence on the debate on defense and rearmament which had continued in Western Germany since 1950.

[79] See Drew Middleton in *New York Times*, December 7, 1958, section 4, p. 5.

CHAPTER 11

ALTERNATIVES TO NATO

BY PAUL H. NITZE

IN discussing alternatives to NATO, there are several possible approaches to our subject.

One approach is to focus on prediction. We can look at the present status of NATO in comparison with its status at various times in the past. We can analyze the forces which appear to be behind the trends of change that have taken place. We can then attempt to extrapolate those forces and trends forward in time and arrive at an estimate of the new situation we will probably face at some time in the future. This should give us an insight into the various alternatives to, or major modifications of, NATO which would seem possible in that new situation.

A second approach is to concentrate on a functional analysis. What today are the major elements of NATO and what are their functions? How could those elements and functions be modified or changed over the spectrum of conceivable alternatives?

A third approach is to examine, not what is likely to happen, nor what conceivably could happen, but what we should be trying to make happen in the interest of over-all policy.

These three approaches are not mutually exclusive. In fact, they are complementary. An extrapolation forward of current trends gives one a sense of the real problems which must be faced and of the limits of the solutions that are within the realm of the practically possible. A survey of the major elements of NATO, of their functions, and of the full spectrum of conceivable alternatives helps to point up possibilities which might otherwise be overlooked. Finally, a discussion of probable trends and conceivable alternatives would be meaningless unless we eventually came to grips with the policy question: in what direction should the will and effort of the United States be directed to mold the future rather than merely to adapt to it?

Before getting into the substance of these three approaches, it may be useful to define a little more precisely what we mean by an alternative to NATO. In addition to new systems which would involve the elimination of NATO or its supersession by a new organization, changes in NATO so substantial as to exceed a mere modification or development of the alliance are considered to be alternatives to it. These could include such radical changes as the elimination from the membership of NATO of one or more of its principal members—the United States, the United Kingdom, France, or Germany—or the addition of sufficient non-Atlantic members to destroy its present regional character. They could include changes in its organizational structure that would strengthen its cohesion so radically as to make NATO a confederation, or that would weaken it so radically as to reduce it to a mere political commitment. Furthermore, it is possible to conceive of changes in the philosophy underlying NATO so radical as to constitute an alternative, even though no change were made in its membership or in the form of its organization. Today it is assumed that a collective defense of the NATO countries is possible and that, in the long run, the USSR can be made to accept and live with that fact. If the reverse assumption were to be accepted, the purpose of NATO would logically become that of finding the best accommodation possible with the USSR. Such a change in the basic assumption underlying the purpose of NATO would constitute as radical an alternative as any of the others suggested.

I

Let us now turn to the trends of the past, the principal forces that seem to have been behind those trends, and their extrapolation into the future. These trends can only be suggested in a most tentative way. The period of history with which we are dealing is too close to us for a more precise judgment.

The following trends come to mind: The first is a trend from political commitment to collective defense and then back toward re-emphasis upon political commitment rather than collective defense. NATO began as a treaty registering mutual commitments of its members. The relevant commitment was that of the United States to come to the support of Western Europe should it be attacked. Very quickly this basically political commitment was transformed into the beginning of a collective defense posture. With the commitment of American, British, and Canadian divisions to Europe under an American supreme commander, this trend took a major forward stride. It continued until the force goals set by the Lisbon Conference failed of implementation. Since that time, there has been a steady weakening of the collective defense posture of NATO relative to that of the Soviet Union. The corollary has been greater reliance upon the political commitment, backed by the deterrence provided by SAC.

A second trend has been that affecting the role of the United States within NATO. Originally the pressure was from the European members, who sought greater United States initiative and leadership. For a period that leadership was willingly provided by the United States and was cooperatively accepted by the European members. There followed a period of more hesitant leadership by the United States and even that leadership was accepted with increasing reluctance. The culmination of this trend found its expression in the Suez crisis. There has been some recovery since, but American leadership, either in its provision or in its acceptance, is today not to be taken for granted.

A third trend was, at first, increasing NATO pressure against the Central European satellites of Russia, followed, since the suppression of the Hungarian uprising, by increasing Soviet bloc pressure against Europe.

Now, what have been the forces which have underlain these trends?

One force has been a decrease in the incremental advantages which Europe could expect to receive from the United States connection. As European economic recovery has progressed, economic assistance has come to be of marginal rather than of fundamental importance to the principal European countries. With the full commitment of such United States military forces to the Continent as it appears reasonable to anticipate, additions to NATO non-nuclear military strength must of necessity come largely from the European countries themselves. Another factor in Europe's decreased expectations has been the greater emphasis in United States policy on United States interests rather than on the collective interests of the NATO members considered as a group. This has caused them to expect less United States support for European interests in non-NATO areas such as the Middle East and South Asia.

A second force has been the fundamental change in nuclear power relationships. The most important components of this force have been the growth in Soviet nuclear stockpiles, the lead the Soviets seem to have established in long-range missile technology, and the impressive indications of relative Soviet progress in basic research and rate of economic expansion. Another component has been the progressive nuclearization of war planning and preparation on the Western side, and increasing public knowledge in the West as to the probable effects of such a war on civilians. This second force has tended to offset the strength of the deterrence which the United States connection could be expected to provide and to increase the risks to the European countries implied by that connection.

A third force is to be found in the shifting power relations and political strains within NATO. One component in this force has been the growing power and political stature, first, of Germany, and now possibly of France, vis-à-vis England. In the early days of NATO, the combined influence of the United States and England could usually bring unity into NATO policy decisions. Today that is no longer true. Another component has been the divisive effect of such issues as Cyprus, Algiers, the China policy of the United States, the free-trade area, and Icelandic fishing. On the other side of this equation, one should, however, mention the diminishing distrust and growing rapport between France and Germany. The growth in stature of the Community of Six, adding the Common Market and Euratom to the Coal and Steel Community, provides the prospect both of increased strength and cohesion on the Continent and of difficult problems to be worked out between the Community of Six and the other NATO and OEEC members.

A NATO structure which has shown these trends and which has been affected by these forces is now to be tested by a concerted Soviet pressure drive. At present this drive is centered on the exposed position of Berlin and the desire of the German people for reunification, a reunification which can take place only with Russian consent. The context of this drive is a weakened NATO relationship. The Soviet objective is the elimination of United States forces and influence from Berlin, from Germany, and from Europe.

It is in the light of this impending test of NATO that we must examine conceivable alternatives.

II

Now, what are the principal elements of NATO and their functions, and are there alternative methods of satisfying these functions?

We can list five elements. The first is the drawing of a line which will give the Soviet bloc clear notice of the American commitment to intervene should the line be violated. The second is the presence of sufficient American forces in Europe to make it clear that we intend to honor the commitment. The third is the provision of sufficient collective forces to restrain a substantial probing attack—a military attack short of a major invasion of Western Europe. The fourth is the provision of ready and secure forces properly positioned to deter a major Soviet attack. The fifth is an organizational framework and political symbol around which the principal Western powers can coordinate their political, economic, and general power so as to create a power center adequate to balance the coordinated general power of the Communist bloc.

Now, the drawing of a line which will define a United States commitment to intervene, should it be violated, can be done in several ways. It can be done by unilateral declaration by the President. It can be done by joint resolution of the Congress. It can be conveyed to Moscow through diplomatic channels as a specific and concrete warning. The question is whether the Soviet leaders will believe that we really mean it; that in the face of the overwhelming military and very great political power which they can mobilize against a particular position, we and our allies will, in fact, take serious and effective action if the line we draw is breached.

One of the factors which tends to make a commitment credible is the formality and authority of the procedure by which it was originally registered. The most formal and authoritative commitment the United States can make is obviously a treaty commitment. The requirement of approval by two-thirds of the Senate ensures that the decision to enter into the commitment is not one of individuals, or of a single party, but is a solid expression of national will and intent. A loss of national honor would be involved if the United States were to back down on a treaty commitment under pressure. Bilateral treaty commitments covering Western Europe would not be as logical a solution to the problem of drawing a line as the present NATO multilateral treaty. It is doubtful whether the Senate would be likely to accept them as an alternative unless the most compelling considerations were advanced. In summary, there are other ways of drawing a line, but these other ways are less credible and serious than the present NATO commitment.

Regarding the second element we have listed—the presence of sufficient United States forces in Europe to make it clear that our commitment is backed by a serious intention—we are again concerned with convincing the USSR that we really will act if the NATO line is breached. Today Russian forces could not overrun the Continent without overrunning the five and one-half United States divisions stationed there. It is hardly conceivable that we could permit those divisions to be overwhelmed without bringing to bear against the USSR the full force of every weapon we possess. The presence of these forces in effect transfers the weight of Russian pressure from Western Europe to the SAC bases in the United States. Is there any alternate means by which a similar deterrent to Soviet military pressure against Europe can be provided? Perhaps a smaller number of American divisions, reinforced from time to time in periods of crisis, might have substantially the same effect. It is difficult, however, to conceive either how these forces can be kept indefinitely in Europe except under the legitimization of their presence provided by NATO, or how any deterrent of equal persuasiveness could be substituted if they were to be removed.

The third element which we have listed is the provision of sufficient collective forces to make it possible to restrain a substantial probing attack—a military attack short of all-out war. American forces permanently stationed on the Continent should not, in the long run, be essential to the performance of this function. An adequate number of German, French, and Italian divisions properly equipped should be able to do so. The presence of United States and British forces does, however, tend to stiffen the line. In any case, some form of collective defense understanding would seem to be required if any of the Western European countries is to stand up to and throw back a probing attack of any considerable strength. To stand up alone against even a two- or three-division attack which includes Soviet forces is more than can be expected of any of the Western European powers.

The fourth element is the provision of ready and secure forces properly positioned to deter a major Soviet attack. This element has three components. The first is the provision of shield forces on the Continent. As pointed out earlier, these forces have been permitted since Lisbon to decline in relative strength. The second is the provision of tactical nuclear forces to back up the shield. Against larger Soviet forces similarly equipped, they contribute largely by knitting together the deterrence of the shield with that of the sword. The credibility of the sword itself, however, is now subject to question, except as against the most extreme provocation. It is not always recognized that there is an inverse relationship between the strength of the sword and the degree of provocation which it can be expected to deter. With the advent of Soviet ICBM's, a successful counterforce strike by SAC (even in riposte to an attack on Europe and thus with benefit of the first nuclear strike) becomes hardy credible. It therefore becomes of the utmost importance to all members of the alliance that the contribution of the shield to deterrence be increased and that the power of the sword, relative to Soviet forces, not be permitted to decline further.

The relevance of NATO to the shield forces is obvious. A question, however, can be raised as to the longer-term importance of the contribution which the NATO countries, other than the United States, can make to the sword. The importance of NATO in this regard is less clear than it once was. Today, a number of alternative solutions are conceivable for the future. The most obvious is reliance upon the

Polaris-submarine system at the periphery and the Minuteman system at the center. However, in a world in which nuclear weapons are each capable of destruction over a large area, sheer geographic extent and diversity of defense and retaliatory means become important factors. It is by no means clear that reliance upon any one or two weapon systems can give such certainty of retaliation as to provide a sufficiently credible deterrent. Furthermore, the Polaris and Minuteman systems have not yet been fully developed and tested. Until these phases have been completed and the actual systems are in place, geographic diversity of retaliatory means is of the utmost importance. Western Europe alone, or the United States alone, does not provide an adequate base for a credible deterrent against a provocation short of an all-out nuclear attack. Each is therefore dependent upon the other. Without NATO the means of satisfying this interdependence for defense are difficult to imagine.

The fifth element we have listed is the organizational framework and political symbol provided by NATO as a center around which the Western powers can coordinate their political, economic, and general power so as to create a power center adequate to balance the coordinated general power of the Communist bloc.

It can be argued that NATO provides only a weak organizational framework; that as a political symbol it is somewhat tarnished by its necessary concentration on military defense; that as a power center it is too exclusive and alienates rather than attracts those nations in the Middle East, Asia, and Africa where the general power of the Communist bloc presents its greatest challenge; and that more important than a regional organization and a regional political symbol are the strength, wise policy, and unity of the individual nations. There is some substance to these arguments. The fact remains, however, that strength, wisdom of policy, and unity among nations do not come about easily or automatically. NATO has played an important role in bringing the North Atlantic powers closer together than they would have been without it. If NATO were to be done away with today and nothing substituted in its place, it is quite possible that the centrifugal forces always present even between nations whose basic interests are close together might well become dominant. It is quite conceivable that the major continental Western European nations, in the absence of NATO, would put their primary reliance on the Community of Six and hope that a third-force position—a position of neutralism— would carry them through the international storms to be anticipated.

Before discussing further the full range of possible political alternatives to NATO, let us turn to the third of our methodological approaches, the approach from the standpoint of policy.

III

The principal policy issue affecting NATO today concerns two potentially conflicting objectives. One objective is to increase the power and firmness of the West in standing up to the adverse power of the Communist bloc. The other objective is to surmount the adversary relationship between East and West and work out some system of relationships between them which is more satisfactory and less hazardous than the present bleak confrontation.

These two objectives are not necessarily in conflict with each other. It can be argued that the greater the relative strength of the West to that of the East, the less have been the tensions between the two sides. After the rapid build-up of strength in the West occasioned by the Korean War, and during the uncertain political relationships and readjustments in the East following Stalin's death, we saw the first Geneva Conference and the "spirit of Geneva." This is undoubtedly an oversimplified analysis. Many other developments were concurrently taking place. These included the shift in Soviet doctrine from the concept of capitalist encirclement to that of two camps, coexistence, and the prospect of socialist encirclement of capitalism. Nevertheless, with the decline in relative Western strength and cohesiveness since the first Geneva Conference, we have seen an increase in tension which culminated, in 1958, in the virtual ultimatum concerning Berlin.

There are, however, legitimate grounds for deep anxiety concerning the long-range continuation of the present bleak confrontation, and therefore grounds for the consequent effort to find some alternate road. There is growing public realization of the hazards involved in a potentially unstable nuclear "stalemate" in which great advantages may accrue to the side striking the initial blow. There are risks that, even with an extensive and protracted effort by the West to balance the power of the East, positions of importance to the West will be eroded and lost. Under the circumstances, much of Western public opinion demands that some more direct solution to these growing hazards be found through a negotiated settlement or partial settlement. A wide variety of proposals have been put forward. Some of them imply the elimination of NATO, or at least some alternative to it.

The proposal most seriously debated is that an area in Central Europe be made into a buffer zone between East and West—that there be a disengagement between the military forces of the United States and the USSR from their direct confrontation in the heart of Europe.

The degree of disengagement proposed has covered a wide spectrum. The more modest proposals call merely for a ban on nuclear weapons within some defined area or a general thinning of military forces on both sides within such an area. The intent, however, is that these modest steps be but the initial steps in a process which will then proceed to a more complete disengagement. The more radical proposals call for the prompt reunification of Germany, the withdrawal of Germany from NATO, the withdrawal of all United States forces from Europe, and the withdrawal of Russian forces behind the Bug River, back behind the boundaries of the USSR.

A series of issues immediately arise in considering these proposals. One issue is the degree to which the proposed concessions and withdrawals on both sides are reasonably symmetrical and equitable in their effect. In 1948, some of us in the State Department were of the view that an agreement which achieved the substantial withdrawal of Russian forces behind the Bug River would be so highly beneficial in its effects, even if United States forces were symmetrically withdrawn from Europe, that the West should strongly press for such an agreement. The most compelling reason against making such a proposal was that there seemed to be no possibility whatever that the Russians would agree to it. That they would not was fully confirmed during the meeting of the Council of Foreign Ministers at the Palais Rose in Paris in 1949. This experience emphasizes the second issue—the question of whether any given proposal will in fact be negotiable.

But let us go back, for a moment, and go a little more fully into the situation as it existed in 1948 and 1949. Those in the Policy Planning Staff who favored disengagement at that time were of the view that if Russian forces were withdrawn behind the Bug, a very substantial political reorientation was certain to take place in all of Central Europe. It was our hope that this reorientation would take place gradually and with discretion. We did not see how the reunification of Germany in a form acceptable to the Bonn government could be prevented if Russian military forces were not directly present in support of the East German regime. Far from wishing Germany or any other part of Central Europe to become part of NATO, it was our thought that the influence of the NATO powers would be directed to keeping Central Europe a buffer area incapable of disturbing the security of the West or of challenging the East. The United States monopoly of atomic weapons was considered a sufficient strategic guarantee to ensure that the USSR did not violate the agreement.

Today the correlation of forces is quite different from what it was in 1948 and 1949. There is no longer an American atomic monopoly to guarantee any such agreement as might be made. But, more importantly, it is now the Russians who can hope that the effects of even a superficially symmetrical agreement will lead to the eventual withdrawal of American influence from Europe as a whole rather than to a withdrawal of Russian influence from Central Europe. Respect for the brute power of the USSR, and for its will to use superior strength to prevent forces antagonistic to the Soviet Union from coming to power, has certainly grown in Central Europe since the suppression of the Hungarian uprising. It is, however, to be doubted that there is any genuine loyalty or enthusiasm for the satellite Communist regimes or any radical decrease in the underlying hatred of them on the part of the mass of the people and the intellectuals. It is, therefore, highly doubtful that the USSR would, even today, accept any form of agreement which would, in fact, result in the withdrawal of Soviet forces behind the boundaries of the USSR.

Even if it could be demonstrated that the USSR would not possibly accept any agreement which entailed the complete withdrawal of its military forces from Central Europe, it can be argued that the West should put forward such a proposal merely for the political and propaganda effects of advocating it. I believe the argument on the other side—that the effect of putting forward such proposals would be more unsettling to the West than to the East—deserves consideration. In any case, it is the purpose of this chapter to discuss the real alternatives of possible agreements rather than the political and psychological tactics of the process of negotiation.

A further issue arises as to whether a buffer zone created by the withdrawal of the military forces of the major powers really would contribute to a continuing reduction of tensions and of the danger of war. It has frequently been pointed out that the withdrawal of United States military forces from South Korea did not prevent war breaking out there. An area of unsettled political control, a so-called power vacuum, is more apt to result in conflict and in war than is the direct confrontation across an established boundary of the military forces of opposed major powers. More basic political issues than mere distance between opposed forces should be settled if a program of disengagement is to have any lasting effect. If the intervening area is recognized by both sides to fall within the power sphere of one or the other, the disengagement is apt to result in decreased rather than increased possibilities of friction and of war. In 1948 it was our purpose that the intervening area would come to be governed by regimes responsive to the will of the peoples of Eastern Europe—in other words, that it would be in the power zone of the free world—even if it were militarily neutral. If the Soviets had indicated a willingness to withdraw their troops at that time, we would have interpreted it to mean that they accepted such a political solution to the problem of Eastern Europe. Today an evacuation of United States troops from Germany or from Europe would probably be interpreted by the Soviet Union, and by many Europeans, as acceptance by the West that all of continental Europe was thereafter to lie basically in the power sphere of the USSR. The USSR for many years might well make no very direct demands upon the individual European nations, but the essential question of who is to decide the most basic issues—those potentially involving war or peace in the area—would, in their view, have been decided. The situation of Europe would then be comparable to the present position of Finland.

It can be argued, as George Kennan has argued, that Europe is in no condition to face another major war—be it a nuclear war or a war fought merely with conventional weapons—and that those things which are generally considered by students of defense matters to be necessary if there is to be an effective and credible deterrent to Soviet attack are either too costly and ignominious to be seriously considered, or more apt to invite an attack than to deter one. If one accepts this analysis, the USSR is already in a position in which it can decide the basic issues of Europe—those involving a decision on peace or war in the area. In logic, it would then clearly follow that nothing essential would be risked by disengagement. An agreement to disengage would merely reflect the true power situation which had already been created by other factors. It would decrease the risk of war arising from a misunderstanding of those more basic power relationships.

Concerning this basic issue, NATO and its functions are of secondary importance. In 1948, we were not concerned with German membership in NATO or with the presence of substantial American ground forces on the Continent. The United States atomic monopoly seemed to satisfy the basic military strategic requirement. The withdrawal of Soviet military forces behind the Bug would give an opportunity for the inherent political forces within the area to find a more normal and hopeful mode of expression. Formal organizational instrumentalities such as NATO seemed to be of secondary importance. Looking at today's very different situation, it can still be argued that the formal organizational instrumentalities should not be a bar to whatever may be wise from the standpoint of policy. If it were to be assumed that the USSR would today accept an agreement under which the military forces of the USSR would withdraw behind the Bug, that German reunification would then follow in some manner not wholly artificial and Communist-bound, and that the USSR could reasonably be expected to live with such developments for an extended period of time because of purely political restraints upon her doing otherwise, then it would be intelligent to work out alternative organizational arrangements which would not impede such an agreement. This is merely to say that organizational arrangements such as NATO should not stand in the way of an agreement which would have the effect of permanently rolling back the USSR from its unnatural position in the heart of Europe.

Thus two lines of approach have been advanced to justify disengagement. One is that the NATO countries are militarily so weak and so incapable of remedying their weakness that any attempt to persist in the present confrontation is apt to lead to a hopeless war, a war brought on by a miscalculation on our part as to the realities of the power situation. The other argument is that disengagement will result in great political victories for the West. These are assumed to include withdrawal of the Soviet Union from the heart of Europe, the reunification of Germany, and the growth within Central Europe of governments and economic institutions which, though they might differ substantially in form from American institutions, would be responsive to the will of the people in the area. These two approaches would appear at first view to be inconsistent. In George Kennan's analysis they become consistent because of the very great importance which he gives to political factors relative to military factors. In his opinion, twelve German divisions, backed by the general political restraints upon the USSR against its bringing its superior military capabilities to bear, are adequate to give Germany a high degree of security; and the attempt to achieve a greater degree of security involves an excessive United States presence in Europe, an excessive reliance upon nuclear defenses, and a dangerous freezing of the present line across Europe.

The relative importance of political and military factors is not easy to define. Few students of the matter would deny the priority of political considerations over military. That relative military capabilities are an important component of the over-all political situation, however, is hardly to be denied. In 1939, and again in 1950, the West rightly regretted that it had not paid more attention to this component in the preceding years of relative peace. Today it may well be true that we are putting excessive reliance upon nuclear armaments. But to agree to this is not to say that a favorable political future for Europe and for the West is to be foreseen if we concede to the USSR a commanding and unchallengeable military position with respect to Europe.

Let us now attempt to relate our discussion of disengagement to our preceding discussion of alternatives to NATO. The point which seems to come out most clearly is that NATO is not an end in itself but an instrumentality in support of a particular line of policy. If one is persuaded that a radical change in policy is advisable, then radical alternatives to NATO may be in order. If one believes that political restraints against the USSR using a preponderant military position can be relied upon, then there is little point in drawing lines and guaranteeing them by multilateral treaty arrangements. The presence of United States forces in Europe is then unnecessary. European forces can be adequate to deter any minor probing attacks. A general restraint against the Soviet Union initiating nuclear war can be provided by Polaris and Minuteman systems. A new political symbol and organization that is less oriented toward military matters and perhaps less exclusive in its membership would then be desirable.

The question of whether such a radical change in policy is advisable rests, at least in part, on an assessment of fact. The crucial judgment concerns the reliance that one can put upon the leaders of the Soviet Union being restrained by non-military, non-NATO, political considerations. No one would deny that such considerations exist. The Soviet leaders would obviously prefer not to engage in military operations beyond the borders of the USSR and would recognize the adverse reaction within Russia and beyond their borders of initiating such operations. Are these considerations strong enough, however, to supervene against other considerations which might tempt the Soviet leaders to exploit a position of unchallengeable military superiority? The evidence that they are is hardly sufficient to warrant placing upon it the principal reliance of Western policy.

IV

The varieties of disengagement may constitute the currently most interesting class of proposals implying an alternative to NATO. There are, however, other important classes. One such class includes the proposals which would lead to union, federation, or at least confederation within a given area and which would thereby supersede NATO or make it irrelevant.

Two separate strands of thought can be identified as lying behind these proposals. One strand is the thought that an excessive dedication to national interests leads to chauvinism, national rivalries, and international tensions; and that there is, therefore, virtue in any arrangement which will subordinate dedication to national sovereignty and national interests to loyalties to some much larger political entity. The other strand is the thought that very large and highly integrated political units are necessary to survival in today's world.

The most radical of the proposals advanced advocate world government or a United Nations so strengthened as to constitute a close approximation to world government.[1] These proposals raise two basic issues. The first is the question of how the power of decision and the power of enforcement of decisions are to be organized and who is conceived of as ending up with effective control of these powers. The second is the question of feasibility.

Most of the proposals for world government assume that the power of decision and of enforcement will be organized through democratic institutions roughly comparable to those which have evolved in the Western world, and that the effective control of these powers will be exercised by the peoples of the world in their own interest. The role of leadership and of political parties and the difficulty of conceiving of political parties operating effectively across regional and continental lines seem to be ignored. That the Communists would accede to any system which did not assure them of the prospect of exercising effective control over the processes of decision-making and of enforcement seems inconceivable. If this judgment is accepted, the proposals for world government become merely one expression of the policy that flows from the belief that international tensions and the risk of war are, in the world of the future, the supreme evils, and that even a world controlled by the Communists is preferable to a divided world.

The more modest proposals for union, federation, or confederation accept the prospect of a politically divided world and of the dangers of tension and of war which are inherent in this prospect. The object of these proposals is to improve the unity and strength of the peoples in the area concerned rather than to eliminate tension with other areas. Again we have the question of how the power of decision and of enforcement are to be organized and the question of feasibility. We also

[1] There are other proposals for increasing our support of the United Nations which do not imply world government. These are discussed in Section V below.

have the further question as to whether closer union among a select group of free-world countries will strengthen or divide the free-world system as a whole.

The project which is furthest advanced and which most nearly meets the test of feasibility is the Community of Six. With respect to certain specific functions the institutions which have been created by the Community of Six go beyond the mere coordination of national policies. The agreements contemplate progress toward full political unity. It is yet to be seen, however, how the power over vital decisions such as those affecting Algeria or the reunification of Germany is to be organized and enforced and where the locus of effective power is to be. The French appear to believe that the locus of effective power will be in French leadership. The Germans and the Dutch hardly share that view.

At the present stage of development of the Community of Six, no question of an alternative to NATO arises. NATO continues to be necessary as an over-all political and defense umbrella under which the evolution of the Community of Six can proceed.

In this context, the question of an alternative to NATO could in the future arise in one of two ways. The Six might come to believe that the risks and disadvantages of the United States connection outweigh its advantages, and that such cohesion and strength as they can develop among themselves must be their reliance for survival. The Six might be able to make it not worth the candle for the Soviet Union to attack them directly with military force. It is hardly conceivable, however, that by themselves they could carry much weight in major political issues in other parts of the world. The task of providing a balance to the Soviet system in world politics would then fall squarely on the shoulders of the United States, either alone or with the British Commonwealth.

The other way in which an alternative to NATO could arise in this context would be if the United States decided to withdraw its effective support from the Continent or from NATO as a whole. In that event, problems similar to those mentioned in the preceding paragraph would arise, though from the opposite cause.

It has been suggested that an independent strategic nuclear deterrent in the hands either of the individual continental European powers, or of the Community of Six, would significantly change the otherwise gloomy prospects of the above contingencies. It is doubtful, however, that the USSR is going to be much deterred by nuclear systems which it could at any time eliminate by an initial strike of its own. To provide nuclear systems which could survive an initial Soviet strike is no easy or cheap task, particularly with limited geographic resources. Perhaps Polaris, Minuteman, or some yet undiscovered system will provide such a capability in the future. But, even then, the credibility may be low that such systems will in fact be used other than in reply to the utmost provocation—a provocation tantamount to the threat of national destruction. There is thus little prospect of escape from the necessity for a broad coalition including both Europe and the United States if the general power of the Soviet system is to remain balanced.

Projects for political union or confederation in areas greater than NATO or smaller than NATO, therefore, do not appear to offer much hope as feasible or effective alternatives to NATO.

V

One further class of possible alternatives to NATO deserves to be mentioned. This class of alternatives addresses itself to the question of the exclusiveness of the NATO club.

It can be argued that the principal threat to the free world is not that of military attack or military pressure against Europe. The more immediate threat is continuing economic and political pressure against the so-called "grey areas," backed by the growing general economic power and productivity of the USSR. From this point of view, continued emphasis upon NATO and its military problems is detrimental rather than helpful. To many in Asia, Africa, and even Latin America, NATO is an exclusive club of those who are predominantly of the white race, native to the Western culture, and highly industrialized. It is a club from which they are excluded and the existence of which impinges upon their prestige and their aspiration for an equal place in the sun. What is generally called anti-colonialism, now that colonialism is on the way to being liquidated in most areas of the world, can be more directly equated with resentment against this exclusiveness than with resentment against colonialism as such. It is directed as much against the United States as against those European countries that still maintain colonial possessions.

If one starts from this set of considerations, one is led to a search for institutional arrangements which are non-exclusive and in which the new and emerging nations of the grey areas can participate as equals, not necessarily in power and prestige, but in qualification for membership. The obvious institution is the United Nations. Many of the proponents of greater emphasis upon that organization do not have in mind transforming it into a world government. They have in mind a shift of United States emphasis from NATO, the exclusive institution, to the United Nations, the inclusive institution. They recognize the limitation which the Soviet veto in the Security Council places upon the effectiveness of the United Nations as a decision-making organ. However, they believe that that limitation is overbalanced by the fact that the United Nations can have a positive influence in the areas that are most directly threatened, while the influence of the NATO powers, insofar as they act through NATO, will in these areas be negative. The NATO powers acting as NATO powers in the Middle East, for instance, can only succeed in generating antagonisms.

Only in its most extreme form does this line of thought suggest an alternative to—or rather the liquidation of—NATO. Under this proposal the essential functions of NATO could be dealt with in the following manner. The Charter of the United Nations gives guarantees against the use of military forces across national borders. The individual NATO nations could re-emphasize their determination to live up to their commitment to the Charter if the boundaries of the NATO nations, or the boundaries of other members of the United Nations, were breached by military force. They could deploy such military forces as might be necessary to demonstrate their will and ability to live up to these commitments pursuant to bilateral arrangements with the countries concerned. The coordination of policy could take place through normal diplomatic channels. The principal overt force of Western policy would be directed to building political and economic strength where it was really needed, in the threatened grey areas of the world.

Another proposal along the same general line is that there be negotiated a general Article 51 pact in which all the nations considering themselves threatened by military aggression might participate. This again would be non-exclusive as between North Atlantic and grey-area countries. The emphasis, however, would be on defense against military aggression, while the former proposal places the emphasis upon defense against economic and political pressure.

Both of these proposals meet with a cool reception among European countries. It is even doubtful whether in the current climate of opinion the more radical alternatives which flow from this line of thought would find wide acceptance in Asia or in Africa. The issue of relative emphasis to be placed upon meeting the threat of military aggression in Europe or of dealing with political and economic pressure in the grey areas is, however, a very real issue indeed.

VI

If we think back over the various alternatives to NATO which we have discussed and consider the grounds which are advanced in support of and in opposition to them, a number of points seem to emerge.

The way in which the threat to the free world's security is evaluated and the line of policy advocated obviously bear a relationship to each other. The interesting question is the nature of the causal connection between the two. Sometimes one has the impression that those advocating a line of policy evaluate the nature of the threat, not on the basis of such objective evidence as exists, but in terms that support the line of policy which they find most congenial. Those interested in the economic development of the underdeveloped areas tend to see the threat largely in economic terms, while those interested in military policy tend to see it largely in military terms. Evaluation of the threat, in logic, should be an operation independent of the policy preferences of the evaluator. On the other hand, policy is not merely a reaction to a threat. It is in part a constructive process independent of the nature of the threat. The difficulty is in keeping the various considerations that bear on policy sufficiently distinct from each other so that policy can be analyzed with some degree of rationality.

Judgment as to whether an alternative to NATO should be pursued depends in part, then, on as objective as possible an evaluation of the threat. If the facts justify a judgment that the threat is almost solely economic and political, some radical alternative to NATO would be in order. If the facts justify a further judgment that the threat is primarily directed against the Asian-African countries and not against Europe, the range of alternatives is further narrowed. If the facts justify the reverse of these judgments, only those alternatives which would increase the military strength and cohesion of the Atlantic countries would seem to be in order. If, however, the facts support the more usual evaluation that the threat is complex, covering all fronts and all modes of attack, including the possibility of a military threat to Europe, then the question becomes one not of an alternative to NATO, but of the proper place of NATO within a much broader structure of policy which includes as one of its parts the military defense of Europe.

More difficult to analyze is the proper weight to be given to efforts to strengthen the West in its adversary relationship with the Soviet-Chinese-Communist world and the weight to be given to surmounting or mitigating that relationship. Here we not only need a judgment of the threat and a sense of the thrust of our own purpose, but we must also judge the feasibility of meeting the threat, on the one hand, and of mitigating the adversary relationship, on the other. The question of feasibility continually recurs in choosing between longer-range policies. In the short run, most policies which differ substantially from current policy appear to be infeasible and generally are. But where policy modifications have as their object effects to be achieved over a number of years, the evidence of experience is that much more can generally be done than at first seems possible.

In conclusion, it may be appropriate to re-emphasize the obvious point that consideration of alternatives to NATO is merely another way of considering the alternatives to over-all Western policy.

CHAPTER 12

NATO DEFENSE IN AN UNCERTAIN FUTURE

BY KLAUS KNORR

IN an excellent article on the strategic situation, published in January 1959, Alastair Buchan censored the "absolutists" who, at one extreme of possible positions, plump for disarmament at any price or, at the other extreme, suffer from "nuclear obsession" and remain addicted to the outdated strategy of massive reprisal. He praised the writers who, occupying the middle ground, think total war improbable, believe limited conflicts more likely, and stress conventional forces as a means of deterrence. The assumption uniting this constructive group, he says, is that "the Soviet-American strategic deadlock is now fundamentally unbreakable. . . ."[1]

Despite some ominous inferences which had been drawn more than a year before from Soviet successes in launching earth satellites and ICBM's, many, if not most, experts until recently held a position similar to that of Mr. Buchan, although the unpublished report of the "Gaither Committee" was rumored to have reached some upsetting conclusions. It was not until Mr. Wohlstetter's article in *Foreign Affairs* appeared in January 1959,[2] and subsequent reappraisals came to a head during the Congressional hearings early in 1959, that the alarming view spread rapidly that the thermonuclear striking power of the United States might soon become decidedly inferior to Russia's, and that the "unbreakability" of the Soviet-American strategic deadlock was seriously in doubt.

This nasty shock has been a reminder of the obvious, but frequently ignored, fact that in matters of present and especially future defense strategy uncertainty is appallingly prevalent. On this subject—error in regard to which may prove fatal to entire societies—it is almost literally

[1] "Their Bomb and Ours," *Encounter*, XII (January 1959), p. 12. Mr. Buchan shares this assumption, though he believes that during the next three to eight years, the "balance of terror" will pass through a dangerous phase because of the hair-trigger sensitivity of the American and Russian strategic forces (p. 13).

[2] Among other writings carrying similar implications, see Bernard Brodie, "The Anatomy of Deterrence," *World Politics*, XI, No. 2 (January 1959), pp. 173-91, and Herman Kahn, "How Many Can Be Saved?" *Bulletin of the Atomic Scientists*, XV, No. 1 (January 1959), pp. 30-34.

true that nobody knows and everyone guesses, and that even the best guesses may prove radically wrong. This difficulty is compounded if ignorance, misinformation, and wishful thinking are added to the factor of uncertainty.

If American air power were headed for a period of substantial weakness, the implications for NATO strategy would be exceedingly severe. Although, as Hoag points out earlier in this book, SHAPE began in 1957 to discard the view that massive retaliation is the exclusive deterrent to Russian aggression in Europe, the security of the NATO allies has continued to rest primarily on the retaliatory threat of SAC. As late as November 1958, General Sir Richard Gale, Deputy Supreme Allied Commander Europe, stated: "The stationing of Allied forces in countries where aggression is likely to take place is a certain way of defeating this well-known Soviet method [of infiltration]. It is the realization . . . [of] the head-on clash of military forces with the consequent threat of massive retaliation that is the deterrent. This in a nutshell is the whole concept of the shield and the sword."[3]

Therefore, what happens to the sword is crucial to the security of the alliance. Similarly, any consideration of changes in NATO capabilities—such as the diffusion of nuclear weapons in Western Europe, or resort to conventional forces for deterring limited attacks—must be governed by the prospective state of SAC.

I. THE NUCLEAR BALANCE OF POWER

What has shocked a large proportion of the informed public, though evidently not the American Administration, is the appearance of the "missile gap." A missile gap can be one of missile *development* and/or missile *production*. A development gap undoubtedly had existed for some time before 1959, for the Russians had first-generation ICBM's with admittedly larger thrust and possibly more reliable guidance than did the United States. These advantages mean greater accuracy and larger nuclear warheads, and hence more destructive power per missile. At the beginning of 1959, it seemed likely that the missile gap had also become, or shortly would become, a production gap in the sense that, over the next few years, Russia would produce more operational missiles than the United States. The important controversial questions were: How many more? And how heavily does a missile superiority of various hypothetical sizes weigh in the strategic balance of power?

[3] *NATO Letter*, VI (December 1958), p. 17.

The Russians announced before the end of 1958 that they had started to produce ICBM's "serially"—which is their term for mass production. According to the American defense budget proposed for the fiscal year 1959-1960, about 200 Atlas and Titan missiles are planned to become operational by 1961. During the hearings in January 1959, Secretary of Defense McElroy admitted that, in 1961, the Soviets might have an ICBM superiority of 3:1. This would seem to permit prediction of 500 or 600 Soviet ICBM's by 1961. According to some non-official guesses, the USSR might have as many as 300 or 400 ICBM's by the end of 1959, and rapidly increasing superiority through the early 1960's.[4] Of course, nobody in the West *knows* what Soviet production rates are now or will be in the future. It *is* known, however, that the Russians have a significant developmental lead, that they are industrially and economically capable of producing and emplacing hundreds of ICBM's during a two-year period, and that they have repeatedly surprised the West by the speed with which they have improved their military capabilities. One need not be an alarmist, therefore, to assume that it is well *possible* for the Soviets to acquire several hundred ICBM's by the end of 1960; and that, depending on future American production plans, the "gap" could go on increasing for several years.

The Administration denies that a missile gap of the size admitted by Mr. McElroy will make the United States strategically inferior to Soviet Russia. It points to our present 3:1 superiority in intercontinental bombers, to the large bombs which these bombers can deliver, and to the superior accuracy of the plane-delivered over the missile-delivered bomb. Based on these considerations, it is evidently the Administration's plan to economize on the production of first-generation missiles and await the development of more sophisticated models—for example, the hard-based, solid-fueled Minuteman and Polaris—before going into substantial mass-production, which is generally foreseen for the middle 1960's. In the interest of economy, then, the Administration has decided—so far as missiles go—to travel light for a number of years.

Nobody *knows* with assurance whether or not the calculated risk which the Administration is willing to run is realistic or foolhardy. However, again known possibilities are such that the risk of a Soviet surprise attack on the United States may well be substantial and, indeed, dangerously high. And more important than any missile gap of development or production may be a lack of prompt adjustment in

[4] For example, Thomas R. Phillips, "The Growing Missile Gap," *The Reporter*, xx (January 8, 1959), p. 11.

American strategy to the problem which the gap poses. The Russians might well be able to mount a crippling surprise attack on SAC if they arrive at a position permitting them to fire 300 ICBM's in a first blow and to reserve enough striking power for a second attack on the United States.[5] The Soviets might calculate that, of any small number of SAC planes that would escape destruction, only a still smaller number would penetrate their active air defenses (on which the USSR has spent a larger proportion of its defense budget than the United States), and that the damage which any remaining bombers might inflict could be further cut to an acceptable level by evacuation and improvised protection against fallout.[6] Indeed, the Russian leaders would have some grounds for expecting that the United States might not use the remnants of SAC for automatic retaliation.[7] In this hypothetical example, after all, the fact that SAC did not deter a Soviet first strike is the end of the first round. Retaliatory action by the United States would start a second round in which Russia's unexpended forces would threaten to lay waste American cities *if* the United States reacted to the Soviet surprise attack by bombing Soviet cities. And the Russians would be sure to let the United States know the series of events to be expected.

This hypothetical example is not a prediction that the USSR will be in a position to undertake such a surprise attack, or would do so if

[5] Suppose that the USSR can destroy SAC bases overseas with its superior forces of IRBM's and that there are about 50 SAC targets in the United States, both air bases and planned ICBM sites being "soft." We may have to credit Russian ICBM's with a possible combination of size of nuclear warhead, accuracy of delivery, and performance reliability that would enable as few as 100 missiles to wipe out all targets of SAC power in the United States. Such a combination of Soviet missile properties is *possible*, even if not probable over the next few years. But if we had to concede to Russia 300 or 400 ICBM's, available for a first strike, these properties could, of course, be considerably relaxed. Moreover, should Russia decide on a surprise attack, she would probably launch a mixed force. She might additionally commit submarine-based missiles of a 200- or 300-mile range (which, it is generally conceded, she may well have). Although to do so would diminish the chances of effecting complete surprise, the Russians might also use their bombers—all of which, according to Air Force testimony, the United States could not hope to intercept. If only 10 or 20 got through—not necessarily through the Dew Line—they alone could destroy a substantial number of SAC bases. This threat would be especially great if, in order to minimize the chance of giving warning to SAC, Soviet bombers were committed in a sneak attack rather than in a massive saturation attack. (The estimate of 50 SAC home bases, as well as Mr. Mc-Elroy's estimate of a 3:1 missile ratio between the USSR and the United States, are to be found in as unofficial a publication as *Time*, February 23, 1959, p. 22.)

[6] Kahn, "How Many Can Be Saved?" *loc.cit.*

[7] Deterrence of a Russian attack, however, requires the United States to make in advance a credible threat of answering a Soviet counterforce strike by a strike against Soviet cities with whatever force is left to it. It may be difficult to make this contingent threat effective without organizing now for such a counterstrike, which would be close to automatic after a Soviet attack had occurred. And if such an attack actually took place, the question of the best American response would depend on the size and composition of the forces which survived the attack.

it were. Even if it were, its decision might be affected by a host of considerations, such as uncertainty over exactly how much of SAC might be wiped out, should Soviet operations not go according to plan; or by Soviet expectations about the level of the chances of being subjected to American surprise attack, by deliberate plan or accident; or, not impossibly, by non-military reluctance, including moral costs, to inaugurate all-out war. The only point is that the assumed conditions might plausibly prevail, and that such an attack must be regarded as a possible—and more than an improbable—contingency. And such an attack would, under the assumed conditions, bring disastrous results— heavy damage to the United States population and economy if this country automatically initiated the second round of thermonuclear blows; or, if it did not, at least for some time the United States would have only a capability so weak that it might be destroyed by a second Soviet attack. Even if Russia did not undertake a second strike, she would most certainly exploit our rather helpless position, not only by putting demands on the United States, but also by blackmailing our allies, who would be equally helpless.

On the other hand, if the missile gap should widen enough to give the USSR a substantial lead in emplaced ICBM's as well as IRBM's, without bringing about Soviet surprise attack, the American capability for crippling the Russian air force would be likely to decrease because of the increase of military targets in the USSR. This would be especially true if Russia were to disperse or hide the missiles in each squadron to a greater extent than is, for the time being, the case in the United States, or if it hardened the launching sites. Furthermore, the airplane is likely to become increasingly vulnerable to active defenses; and if stand-off bombs are fired from aircraft a few hundred miles from the target, the plane as a delivery instrument might lose some of its vaunted advantage, for the bombloads would be smaller (since the launching facility must be carried) and the accuracy of their delivery less than is true in the case of dropped bombs. It must also be remembered that this factor of diminishing Soviet vulnerability comes on top of two disadvantages in the American capacity for launching a first strike. American intelligence on the location of Russian targets is not as good as Soviet intelligence on American targets; and political and moral restraints narrowly circumscribe United States opportunities for launching a first strike, and render an American surprise attack on an unalerted Russia virtually impossible. As a result, a counterforce strategy on the part of the United States—that is, a strategy aimed at hitting the sources of Soviet offensive air power—might become increasingly difficult, if not impracticable. Indeed, it may be doubtful that even now the United States, depending on planes, has a substantial counter-force capability against an *alerted* Russia, just as Soviet aircraft hardly have a substantial counterforce capability if SAC is on alert.

The conclusion suggests itself that, from now on until sometime in the mid-1960's, the Western military posture will probably become weaker on the all-out war level than it has been. How much it will decline must remain uncertain and controversial. On the worst assumptions, it might crumble dangerously; on more favorable assumptions, the decline will be moderate. What will be the consequences of these possible developments on the security of our NATO allies? The following inferences seem plausible.

First, NATO security is obviously affected by the high probability, if not certainty, that the United States will become more vulnerable to a Soviet surprise attack than before. If the worst possible contingency materialized—namely, that the USSR could and did launch a surprise knockout blow, leaving the crippled SAC unable to inflict more than moderate damage on Russia—Western Europe would obviously be defenseless.

Second, the security of Western Europe would also be jeopardized if all-out war were not precipitated deliberately, but broke out by accident, and the situation led to a Soviet first strike or simultaneous first strikes by the two big powers. During the next few years, the strategic situation will be highly unstable—especially if war is considered likely—because a first strike would, as Rathjens points out, confer great advantage on the country striking first. In fact, the technical premium on a first strike would be especially great for the United States because of its increasing vulnerability to Soviet missile attack and because, for some time, the bomber will probably remain an excellent though deteriorating first-strike instrument.[8] Under these circumstances, a high degree of sensitivity and automatic reaction will be built into the retaliatory systems, and the chances of a reaction to mistaken signals will be substantial.

Third, the United States, it would seem, has—as Brodie put it—lost

[8] Because of the vulnerability of airfields to ICBM's, the bomber would be a poor instrument for a second strike, although the bomber can of course be upgraded by improved warning systems, harder bases, and maintaining an appreciable proportion in the air at all times (which is tantamount to "air basing"). Vulnerability is also great in the case of the first ICBM squadrons, which are being emplaced above ground. On the other hand, aircraft would be good for a first strike, because they can deliver large bombs with accuracy—an advantage that is, however, affected by the state of active air defense in Russia and the degree of warning received by Soviet defenses.

the "absolute deterrence" which permits the threat of massive reprisal to be widely used.[9] Russian fears of massive retaliation will decline and somewhat diminish the expectation that the United States would threaten all-out war in response to lesser Soviet attacks in Europe. The credibility of an all-out SAC response would suffer especially if, by multiplying missile targets, the Soviets sharply reduced their vulnerability to a counterforce attack and, at the same time, enhanced their own power of retaliation. As was brought out at the Princeton Conference on NATO strategy, the utility of a limited-war strategy to deter all but massive ground attack on Western Europe depends markedly on whether or not SAC has a counterforce capability (with a countercity capacity in reserve) and hence the ability to reduce the damage which Soviet retaliation could visit on the United States. Only in that case can SAC threaten reprisal to deter the Soviets from violating the limits on limited war. For the reasons indicated, the American counterforce capability may decrease during the next few years.

Fourth, despite the declining credibility of SAC's threat of massive reprisal to Russian threats to, or attacks in, Europe, at least an ambiguous SAC threat remains, and the Soviet leaders could *not* be sure of the American reaction so long as the United States retained, as it probably will, a considerable first-strike capacity. More than the smallest doubt would make them hesitate to expose themselves to an American first strike or to put SAC on an alert which would reduce its vulnerability to a Soviet attack. (If the USSR acquired offensive power of absolute superiority—the capacity for "absolute deterrence" mentioned by Brodie—it might be tempted to launch a surprise attack on SAC before attacking Western Europe.) Soviet doubt would also permit an alerted SAC to police the limits of a limited war in Europe. Thus, the prospect appears that, compared with past conditions, the United States will be in a better position to protect Western Europe against direct assault than to protect itself.

Fifth, during the next few years a substantial first-strike capability will be the great remaining, though probably diminishing, military asset of the United States—an asset especially valuable for the protection of Western Europe. Even vulnerable IRBM's stationed in Europe would help to maintain this asset. As Rathjens and Schelling point out, superior accuracy at the shorter distance from targets makes IRBM's particularly effective as a counterforce weapon. However, such missiles of high offensive power and great vulnerability (so long as they are not hard-based, and are in fixed locations) are also extremely "provoc-

---

[9] Brodie, "The Anatomy of Deterrence," *loc.cit.*, p. 175.

ative" to the USSR; and, should the Soviet Union decide on a surprise all-out attack, damage in Western Europe would be the greater, the more such missiles were emplaced there. Yet, viewing the security posture of Western Europe as a whole during the next few years, this conditional drawback would seem more than balanced by the increase in America's deterrent power and hence in her ability to protect NATO. It is not clear that Western Europeans have given this chain of relationships sufficient thought.

Sixth, while a substantial missile gap, should it develop, would probably not lead to a Soviet surprise attack so long as the Russians had to reckon with the possibility of large-scale counterdamage, Moscow would certainly find it advantageous to exploit its missile superiority in diplomacy, in more or less veiled threats, and in military aggression so limited that an American threat of massive retaliation might not take place or could be safely suspected as bluff.

The above considerations would, of course, be affected if, during the next few years, the United States were to take more protective measures than were being planned early in 1959. Marginal remedies—such as keeping more SAC bombers, equipped with bombs, in the air at any one time—would help. But an increase in Atlas and Titan production, and their bunched emplacement above ground, would probably not be the best and quickest countermeasures. A rapid multiplication of hard targets, which the USSR would have to locate and hit, would seem to be the most efficient step. IRBM emplacements abroad and possibly placement of guided missiles on available Navy ships would be promising. Accelerated development of Polaris and Minuteman would help. But most of these countermeasures would require expensive crash programs.

Thus far, this analysis has been confined to the unstable period until the mid-1960's. The general expectation is that, thereafter, the thermonuclear stalemate will become dependably "unbreakable," because more sophisticated missiles will be protected by hard bases, widely dispersed, or movable. Therefore, they would be protected against surprise attack and a counterforce strategy would no longer be attractive. At that time, indeed, the nuclear arms race would presumably be suspended, for—at best—the number of missiles required for a successful surprise attack on the enemy's retaliatory force would be enormous and immensely costly to produce and emplace.

However, in view of past occasions when seemingly safe expectations have been rudely upset by events, we should be more cautious and less sure of the promised advent of a stable "balance of terror." As between the United States and the Soviet Union, it is not the availability of

bombs but bomb delivery that is the key problem. Technological innovations and their military exploitation may surprise us; the missiles we
are awaiting may deliver less than they now promise; we may overestimate the hardness of bases and underestimate future difficulties
impeding exact bomb delivery and the surveillance of submarines; the
Polaris-submarine system may turn out to be very costly; and we cannot
be sure that a counterforce strategy will necessarily be shunned. As
Schelling asks, what if both sides always find new ways of destroying
retaliatory forces at a faster rate than they find new ways to protect
them? It may well happen that the protection of deterrent power, far
from automatic, can be achieved only by dint of continuous hard effort
and at great expense.

Assuming, however, that the mid- or late 1960's will leave both sides
only with the power of *passive*—not *active*—deterrence, how would
this development impinge on the security of Western Europe? On
the one hand, our NATO allies would share in the benefit of a more
stable system which is less likely than its predecessor to result in the
accidental outbreak of all-out war. On the other hand, however, stable
deterrence on the level of all-out war does not mean *over-all* military stability. On the contrary, as was observed at the Princeton Conference, such a situation would increase the chances of lesser aggression,
because both sides would have a supreme interest in avoiding mutual
devastation. This would greatly increase the danger of Soviet nuclear
blackmail directed against individual NATO countries, unless they
possessed a credible passive deterrent of their own or shared effectively
in a joint deterrent based in Europe. Similarly, the risk of Soviet limited
attack would rise unless such attack were deterred by an effective
limited-war capability at the disposal of SHAPE. But, even in this case,
a European-based passive deterrent would be indispensable in order
to deter Russia from associating strategic nuclear threats with a ground
attack. Whether or not the threat of limited reprisal would be superior
to that of massive reprisal for these purposes will be taken up below.
The important point to recognize is that, with the United States possessing only a *passive* deterrence (no counterforce capability), the threat
of massive reprisal by the United States can rationally no longer be
expected to protect Western Europe against Soviet aggression.

II. Nuclear Dispersal in NATO

As one participant in the Princeton Conference on NATO remarked,
the purpose of nuclear dispersal in NATO is for our allies "to obtain
the means of deterrence by possession rather than association." The

pros and cons on such dissemination of independent national deterrents present a picture of baffling complexity. To help illuminate the problem, it seems best to distinguish, as above, between two ensuing periods—first, from the present until the mid-1960's, by which time ballistic missile capabilities will presumably be more or less protected against attack; and, second, the period thereafter, when such missiles will have become fully developed and tested and will be at least technologically available, and probably produced in considerable numbers in the USSR and the United States.

Among the NATO countries, the chief motivation for acquiring independent deterrent forces rests on two factors—the diminishing credibility of strategic nuclear protection by the United States, and the fact that the reluctance of the European allies to supply a sufficient limited-war capability makes them more dependent on deterrence by strategic nuclear weapons. It is now possible for nearly all NATO countries to secure American IRBM's under the double-veto system, which requires a concurrent decision by the United States *and* the ally before the weapons can be fired. These are not therefore *independent* weapons. However, during the period until the mid-1960's, few European countries can hope to develop—as distinct from acquiring outright from the United States (which so far is prohibited by Congressional law)—appropriate weapon systems of much consequence without at least technological assistance from the United States. The United Kingdom *might* have been able to do so, but it is now getting this assistance. It is doubtful, however, that even France could achieve much if left entirely to her own resources. She might produce a fair number of bombs, at least of the Hiroshima type, and she will have some planes. Yet the production of a substantial and sophisticated weapon system would be beyond her means. Even now the French are experiencing greater difficulties with the development of a bomb than had been expected. What is difficult for the United States should be more difficult for its allies.[10] If these countries were determined to develop and produce missiles of their own (plane-delivered bombs becoming of lesser value), they would do best to concentrate on the solid-fueled weapons of the future, skipping the stage of the first-generation missiles. It is doubtful that even the British Blue Streak, a liquid-fueled IRBM, will be developed and made operational before it is technologically obsolete.

Whatever the European allies would achieve on their own during

[10] In 1959 alone, the United States plans to spend nearly $7 billion on missile programs alone (President Eisenhower's annual Message to Congress on the State of the Union, January 1959). Almost all of this is for research and development.

the period, then, should not as such cause much worry to Soviet Russia. Their deterrent power would be grossly vulnerable to a surprise attack.[11] Indeed, it would probably be a rather sickly deterrent. As Healey observes, its utility would lie primarily in involving SAC and, as he believes, would offer the Europeans a better trigger for this purpose than a joint NATO system could. It is not, however, clear that an independent nuclear capability would give our European allies a free finger on the SAC trigger. In any crisis raising the question of a strategic counterthreat, an ally would take risks if it proceeded to use nuclear bombs, without consulting the United States in a manner that might come close to leaving the final decision to the United States. To be sure, the deterrent value of the triggering device depends ultimately on Soviet expectations. Could the Russians be sure that hostile action against a European NATO country would not bring SAC into action? They probably could not unless the United States dissociated itself from its ally's military course of action—a contingency which is difficult to imagine, unless the ally acted irresponsibly. But is not all this tantamount to saying that Soviet fears of American intervention are doubtfully, *if at all*, affected by what a NATO ally could do with its own independent retaliatory ability? In other words, does this ability add anything to deterrence? With or without an independent deterrent, a threat against or an attack on a European NATO nation would alert SAC and give it the opportunity for a first strike. The Russians would be reluctant to do this so long as the United States commands a substantial counterforce capability. It can indeed be argued—as do Rathjens and Kaplan—that the net deterrent effort of the trend toward independent retaliatory systems will be negative. The Soviets might ask themselves: would there be any need for independent systems if the threat of SAC on behalf of the American allies had not become less credible? And, so long as an independent nuclear capability is to serve primarily as a mechanism for triggering American intervention, would American IRBM's, under the bilateral control system now in force with Britain, not prove more effective in this respect, as well as a great deal cheaper? To call a small triggering capability "independent" comes, after all, close to self-deception.

During the period under discussion, an independent retaliatory capacity would be more valuable than allowed above under the more pessimistic expectations about the missile gap. But under the worst as-

---

[11] By placing missile sites in or under major cities, a very small country could deny Russia the choice between a counterforce and a countercity attack, and thereby make reprisal against an aggressor somewhat more credible than it would otherwise be.

sumption—a devastating surprise attack by the Soviets—independent deterrents would do no good. They could not save Western Europe if the United States went down in defeat. However, should the missile gap grow to be broad and prolonged, the USSR would be more likely to exploit its temporary but substantial superiority by threatening the West and pressing it into diplomatic defeats. Under these circumstances —still leaving the United States, however, with some first-strike counterforce ability—American threats of strategic reprisal would become decreasingly credible to Moscow, and an independent retaliatory capability would, as Burns points out, stiffen European NATO allies against nuclear blackmail.

In these matters, self-deception is not entirely worthless, and its destruction by sober analysis not entirely beneficial. Up to a point—but only up to a point—the very belief in having deterrent power will create deterrent power; and when it comes to bargaining in a situation of nuclear blackmail, ignorance—that is, overestimation of one's assets—tends to improve one's bargaining power. But the outside world will not make it easy to sustain illusions for long. The Soviets would have every incentive to press enlightenment. More important, since we are now considering a situation dominated by very pessimistic assumptions about American thermonuclear power, American behavior, if at all adjusted in the direction of realism, would make it harder for Western Europe to maintain illusions about its own capability for deterrence.

Regarding the period after the mid-1960's, the above considerations would require no basic revision if the second period were essentially like the first—that is, if the now firm expectation of ballistic missiles that are highly invulnerable to strategic attack proved unfounded, and one or both of the big nuclear powers could manage an effective counterforce capability. Over the longer run, of course, more Western European countries would have the capacity for building an independent retaliatory force—albeit, in the absence of American assistance, only at great cost. But *they* could scarcely manage independent counterforce capabilities which, in the age of solid-fueled and fairly hard-based or mobile missiles, would obviously be much more expensive to achieve than they are now. Even the United Kingdom would find it hard and almost certainly prohibitive to maintain a continuous retaliatory system—that is, a system which would be up-to-date in all its parts as the technological arms race went on. Under this assumption, therefore, the European NATO allies would, as before, remain highly dependent on the deterrent power of the United States; and the possession of an independent capability would not make much sense unless the United States retained or regained a counterforce capability.

Assuming, after the mid-1960's, a world of retaliatory systems which are highly invulnerable to direct attack, and hence would be counter-city rather than counterforce capabilities, the picture changes radically. At present, it seems to be the official British view that, under these conditions, an independent capability would be useful to a country in order to deter nuclear blackmail and limited aggression *against itself*, the expectation being that no country would use its capability—which if used would bring sure and massive destruction to itself—in order to protect an ally against either nuclear blackmail or limited attack.

It must be granted that a threat to use a pure countercity force on behalf of an ally ranks low in credibility, for it is a threat involving the acceptance of massive destruction. Without a counterforce capability, the United States could not be expected to attack Russia unless it were attacked itself. It must also be granted that an independent retaliatory force might have substantial deterrent power against the threat of all-out war. However, the amount of damage which the blackmailer will expect from the blackmailed country is a matter of critical importance. The Soviets, for example, might not be deterred by an independent re-taliatory system if they calculated its penetrative power to be small, if they could reduce casualties by civil defense measures, if they were willing to pay a stiff price for being able to threaten other countries afterward more effectively, and if they had serious doubts that the black-mailed country would actually follow through with its counterthreat and prefer mutilation to surrender. A "small" country—that is, a country of decidedly lesser military capability than the USSR—would therefore be safer as a member of a *joint* system which could better meet some or all of the critical conditions—provided an effective joint system were feasible. A joint system could threaten the USSR with more damage. But an effective joint system would have to leave little or no doubt that it would react to a threat to one of its members.

The same question arises when an independent retaliatory force is considered as a deterrent to limited attack. Again, the destructive power of the system, as registered by the USSR, might be a critical factor; and again the doubt might arise whether a small country, at-tacked alone, would actually prefer suicide to surrender. And it is probable that Russia would accompany a limited attack with the declaration that she would use part of her retaliatory force if the limited attack were resisted.

If all retaliatory systems were fairly invulnerable, it might be easier for a small country to react to nuclear blackmail or limited war by threatening—and, if necessary, by carrying out—limited rather than "massive" strategic reprisal. However, Kaplan points out that the success of this alternative strategy also depends upon symmetry between the retaliatory forces, and is therefore not good for a nation with a rather limited stockpile of bombs and a small delivery capacity. For this strategy, he believes, a joint system would be superior. But asymmetry of military capabilities is probably not very important under this strategy. The threat to destroy one big Russian city may give Moscow pause if the gains from its aggressive behavior are comparatively small. The important asymmetries concern comparative capacity and willingness to absorb damage involved in the strategy.

Even under the circumstances now assumed, the independent retaliatory systems of small countries could not guarantee prodigies of deterrence. Nor would the systems be cheap, for the technological arms race would not necessarily come to a halt. To be sure, should only pure countercity capabilities prevail (as yet a doubtful assumption!), the NATO allies could not rely on the United States for protection against nuclear blackmail, and a good independent force would afford considerable—indeed, indispensable—protection against threats of all-out attack. It also seems clear, however, that a joint NATO system would, if practicable, be far superior to the independent solution.

III. Limited Reprisal

I can add only little to what has been said by Kaplan, Rathjens, and Schelling about the merits and demerits of limited rather than massive strategic retaliation. This is a possible strategy demanding more study than it has so far received.

The immediate rationale of such a strategy is clear. Facing nuclear blackmail or limited war, a country—especially one without counterforce capability—should find it easier to make a counterthreat of limited than of all-out retaliation, and to follow through with the threat should it fail to deter. As Kaplan argues, an exchange of limited punitive blows appears *relatively* attractive, particularly when the *immediate* value of the stake involved in Soviet aggression is modest, so that concession seems preferable to accepting the risk of suicidal devastation, even though a series of such Russian moves would eventually risk the complete defeat of the country or group of countries.

The strategy consists of convincing the opponent—if necessary, by repeated limited nuclear attacks—that the *status quo* is preferable to the damage involved, and especially to letting the process continue until both sides are destroyed. The strategy is a bargaining strategy, permitting negotiation while the process of mutual reprisal goes on, and would work most satisfactorily if a return to the *status quo* could be achieved after only one exchange of token raids on military targets or, still better, if the mere threat would suffice. Thereafter the strategy would seem to lead to an increasingly unstable position. Everything else being equal, the value of the strategy would also rise if the country subject to aggression had no capability for stopping limited ground attacks—that is, it can be regarded as a partial substitute for a limited ground-war strategy.[12] And, as Schelling remarks, limited retaliation could become an important strategy if both sides possessed exclusively a highly protected countercity force (no counterforce capability!)—a situation in which limited attack would be less inhibited.

Three critical points, however, are in order. First, the capacities of the USSR and a "small" country to pursue this strategy may be highly unequal. As mentioned above, there may be appreciable and relevant gaps in ground forces, in strategic nuclear capabilities, and in public determination. Indeed, one important question of asymmetry might arise from differences in political organization. Adoption of the strategy of limited reprisal requires going through a series of decisions involving acceptance of increasing damage to oneself and hence a degree of *sang-froid* that governments of democratic countries may find it hard to muster.

Second, Schelling points out that it may be harder to keep the limits on an exchange of limited reprisals than on a limited war with surface forces. Indeed, since the challenge involved in the first and each following limited blow is exceedingly public, it would be difficult for the other side to stop retaliating; and, once cities were hit, it is hard to see how one could count on the continuation of restraint. To this must be added the risk of an accidental lifting of the limits because the first or any particular limited attack is misinterpreted as part of an all-out blow.

Finally, the deterrence value of a strategy of limited retaliation remains unclear. The threat of limited reprisal may be more credible than the threat of all-out retaliation, though this seems doubtful to me; but

[12] However, superior ground forces would increase the bargaining power of the USSR. It can be argued that, if everything else is symmetrical between the two parties in a strategy of limited reprisal, some ground-force holding capability is essential to the success of the strategy. See Glenn H. Snyder, *Deterrence by Denial and Punishment*, Research Monograph No. 1, Center of International Studies, Princeton University, January 2, 1959, p. 10.

the deterrent power of the threat is surely inferior to the threat of massive reprisal. Even if a country pursuing this strategy, and challenged to
follow through, initiated a blow or a series of reciprocal token strikes,
it would not necessarily be credible to the opponent—if only for the
political reason mentioned above—that the sixth strike was certain to
follow the fifth round. And what if mutual blows on strictly military
targets proved inconclusive? Would it be easy to step up the level and
begin hitting individual cities?

IV. NUCLEAR SHARING

Two major forms of sharing strategic nuclear weapons are possible
in the NATO alliance. One would be for the United States to sell
strategic weapons to *individual* allies; the other, to establish a joint
nuclear capability controlled by NATO, including the United States.
Other possible forms of sharing are a purely European pooling arrangement, without American membership; a combination of joint
and independent capabilities; and arrangements for sharing American
weapons know-how—but not American weapons.

On the basis of the foregoing analysis, there is little to be said for a
United States policy of giving American nuclear weapons outright to
our NATO allies during the next few years. To do so would be of
very doubtful value to the security of our allies and of still more doubtful
value to the United States. Under these circumstances, sharing American IRBM's under the double-veto system would be the best arrangement. As was also indicated, however, the case for sharing during this
period would be strengthened appreciably if American strategic power
were to deteriorate to a very dangerous extent.

European-controlled capabilities will make a great deal more sense
—though not as much as is sometimes claimed—if the mid-1960's
usher in a prolonged period of missiles which are hard to knock out
by a first strike. Indeed, it would be difficult, in that event, to deny
our allies weapons which we already have.

Nevertheless, even under such conditions, there is a great deal to
be said against a sharing policy. First, independent retaliatory systems
in the hands of smaller countries afford no reliable protection against
the threats of nuclear blackmail or limited war. Especially, they do
not guarantee the determination to make defensive use of these weapons
automatic or near-automatic—a condition which is an essential ingredient of credible deterrence. Second, the over-all security of our
NATO allies would suffer if possession of a retaliatory capability were

to induce them to neglect other military preparations for limited war, for it is not easy to stop limited aggression by threatening a reprisal which involves unacceptable damage to oneself. Third, the emergence of additional nuclear capabilities tends to increase the danger of all-out war being precipitated accidentally. Fourth, the diffusion of such capabilities tends to increase the chances of irresponsible employment. Fifth, the last two risks would be compounded—to a level that is regarded as unacceptable by many observers—as the emergence of new retaliatory systems encouraged their emergence outside NATO as well. Sixth, any increase in the number of strategic nuclear systems will present additional obstacles to the conclusion of agreements on arms control or disarmament.

This is a formidable list of objections which will weigh more heavily in the United States than in Europe, but ought not to be shrugged off by our European allies. Whether we attach more weight to the pros or the cons depends largely on how a complex, dynamic, and uncertain situation is assessed, and on the relative importance conceded to each argument. It would be miraculous if everyone came to the same conclusion, based, as it must be, on intuition and personal value schemes as well as rigorous reasoning. It is my personal conclusion that, in all likelihood, the motivation for acquiring independent retaliatory systems is strong enough to make their spreading inevitable; and that, on this view, sharing would give the United States the opportunity to exert some control over this development and thus to maximize its possible benefits and, above all, minimize some of its grave disadvantages.

If widely accepted, this conclusion should not, in my opinion, induce the United States to *press* strategic nuclear weapons on individual allies or a collective allied arrangement. On the other hand, we should not delay the inevitable by dilatory action. Since the problem is grave and the choice of solution unsettled for nearly all NATO countries, the United States should enlighten its allies about the dissatisfactory aspects of *all* possible solutions, and especially about the dubious utility of independent deterrents. And it should then say in effect: If you are still determined to go ahead, let us see how we can together minimize the risks and the other disadvantages to be expected.

The establishment of a group capability, supposing that most allies volunteered for membership, would have great advantages over any other approach. A merged and hence larger capability would tend to command greater deterrent power than several small independent systems. Pooling would also be much cheaper and, indeed, give very small countries access to a capability which, on their own, they could not afford for economic reasons. The danger of accidental war and irresponsible use would be reduced if one capability took the place of several. Finally, a collective scheme would present lesser impediments to the negotiation of arms controls.

The great trouble with the joint approach—as Healey and Kaplan point out—is, of course, the great difficulties standing in the way of its adoption and implementation. Even if a joint scheme proved negotiable, it might not be a mechanism for making effective decisions. The crucial problem—as stated at the Princeton Conference—is that each member would want his fingers on both trigger and safety catch. Healey is correct in saying that each country would claim the right to use the collective system in its own defense; and this means that other countries would run the risk of involvement in nuclear war when they themselves were not under pressure or outright attack. This central difficulty leads to the major objection that a joint system is impossible without federation and that federation among the NATO members is politically unfeasible.

For the time being, the unfeasibility of federation must be granted. It is less clear that federation would be indispensable. Sovereign nations are able to bind their freedom of decision in very important matters. They do so when they conclude an alliance. To be sure, the issues at stake in an efficient—that is, tightly centralized—joint capability are of formidable consequence—though somewhat less so for the United States than for its allies, since this country would not, and could not be expected to, contribute more than a portion of its strategic forces to the pool. And yet, the arrangement would not seem as much of a departure from the present situation as is often assumed. The Russians may see in NATO, as it now is, a great deal of "jointness" on the strategic nuclear level. This is, in fact, what many of our allies hope.

The impediments to organizing a joint NATO capability are admittedly great. But they should not be regarded as insuperable before different methods have been examined and their acceptability tested on the political level. Such proposals as that made by Kaplan deserve careful exploration. To define ahead of military crises the precise conditions under which the joint capability would be used, and how it would be used, would have the double advantage of prompt, though not hasty, response—it would have a significant "automating" effect—and of ensuring members against their own susceptibility to being victimized by threats. On the views expressed above, there is time—until the mid-1960's—to study the problem, test solutions politically and, if possible, set up the pool. And it would become the United States to take the leadership in this matter, and take it boldly and imaginatively. By doing so, the United States could most effectively advocate the conditions of sharing which should be insisted upon. They would include conditions to minimize the risks of accidental war and the irresponsible use of weapons. Another condition would be to make sharing revocable in the event that satisfactory agreements on arms control proved possible in the future. And there would be good reason for demanding, as Burns suggests, that—in exchange for receiving a share in American nuclear weapons—our allies provide a substantial capability for deterring or meeting limited Soviet attacks on the ground.

Provided these conditions were met, the United States should even consider supplying strategic nuclear weapons to a joint establishment of which it was not a member. A joint West European pool would go some way toward resolving the awkward problem which is raised if the United States is part of a joint system while also maintaining an independent capability. Since the United States is probably the only NATO country over the long run willing to run risks in opposing substantial Communist aggression in other parts of the world, this country could not throw all its strategic nuclear capability into a common NATO pool. Our European allies, however, would understandably fear that, under such an arrangement, the USSR could make no practical distinction between American forces in and outside the pool; and that they would therefore run grave risks of being involved in American policies over which they had insufficient or no control. I do not claim that separating the American capability entirely from a West European capability would fully solve this dilemma. But such separation would seem to mitigate it appreciably.

Should a joint system prove unfeasible, the United States must decide on whether or not to help in the development of *independent* national capabilities. As stated above, this is a possible solution far less desirable than a pool; and pointing out the drawbacks may, in fact, make a joint system less objectionable. But the less desirable solution may be the only feasible one; and if the emergence of independent capabilities is regarded as inevitable, the United States would do better to assist it in exchange for conditions designed to lessen the drawbacks of independent capabilities. Not all these drawbacks are susceptible to minimization. In addition to the disadvantages identified above, one more calls for consideration. Healey may be right in predicting that the independent solution is likely to dissolve the alliance. The prediction, however, calls for qualification. In the less likely event that independent nuclear deterrents would fully protect each ally, there would be no loss in the dissolution of NATO as a military alliance. As a defense mechanism, NATO is a means to an end, and dispensable if the end is served by other means. Yet in the more likely event that independent capabilities provide *in fact* only a partial and precarious solution to the security problem of each member, a weakening of NATO ties could only reduce each ally's security more than it would be increased by the acquisition of "independent" deterrents. The real danger in this particular matter is that the owners of an independent retaliatory force will overestimate its effectiveness and underestimate its costs—in short, fall prey to self-deception.

Kaplan points out that little is to be gained by combining a joint system with an independent nuclear deterrent. This is, however, what may happen if a half-abortive attempt is made to establish a joint system. It would be difficult psychologically for the United Kingdom to assign all its forces to the pool, if only because the United States did not. And should France produce some bombs, she would find it difficult to make this assignment either because Britain did not, or for specifically French reasons. Imponderables aside, there is, however, as Kaplan concedes, one rational reason for retaining at least a token force; this is to possess the ability to trigger off the joint system without depending on joint decisions—an advantage of great importance if the joint system has not been given a good built-in capacity for making, in the face of crisis, decisions that will effectively protect each member. This objective, of course, would be invalid if the joint system were designed to give each ally full protection against Soviet military aggression.

V. LIMITED WAR FORCES

As Healey observes, Western European governments are by and large reluctant to tolerate the possibility of limited surface war and—aside from the threat of massive retaliation—to provide forces for deterring or suppressing limited attack.[13] Yet if both sides are unprepared to accept the destruction they would suffer in total conflict, the threat of all-out response to limited attack on all but the most massive scale may be incredible and hence fail to deter. To make the threat as a bluff would be exceedingly dangerous; for we would be without defense if the bluff were called. And should limited war break out, by accident

---

[13] See also the excellent analysis of Arnold Wolfers, "Europe and the NATO Shield," *International Organization*, xii (Autumn 1958), pp. 428-34.

or design, to face the all-or-nothing decision of either surrender or self-destruction is a horrible position to contemplate, and this especially so if the challenge is minor or ambiguous. To face this potential dilemma of the all-or-nothing condition year after year, and perhaps decade after decade, may prove to be beyond the morale resources of some Western nations. The all-out threat, to be sure, remains indispensable for making the enemy stick to limited objectives and to limits on the use of force. What is dispensable is making the strategic threat operative *immediately* upon the outbreak of aggression, and the *postponed* threat may well deter, provided both sides labor under the heavy constraint of wanting to avoid nuclear devastation. Because the postponed threat is indispensable, as well as for the reasons stated earlier, a limited-war capability has more than minor and highly subsidiary uses only if the United States retains a counterforce capability or, as a minimum, if the European countries possess—for policing the limits on limited war—the threat of a countercity capability. As Rathjens observes, the NATO alliance may be good for a limited-war strategy even if it should lose value as an all-out alliance.

To many people in Western Europe, reliance on massive retaliation for deterring limited aggression seems attractive, because such a defense strategy makes smaller demands on military manpower and economic resources than a mixed strategy. Ultimately this position turns on a question of basic values, but only ultimately. If a society has full knowledge of its choices and decides to accept the risk of national surrender rather than military conscription and a somewhat lowered standard of living, its decision is rational in the sense that it knows what it is doing. But it is incumbent on each nation's leadership to see to it that prevailing value priorities are applied with a reasonably full knowledge of the consequences of choice. Regarding the economic burden of a dual capability, it is worth remembering that the establishment of a joint strategic capability, with weapons coming from the United States, would cause substantial savings.[14]

It is often asserted that a limited-war strategy cheapens the deterrent value of the all-out threat. But this cannot be demonstrated. It is true that this strategy tends to increase the probability of limited aggression. This tendency, however, may have little more than a gratuitous effect of this kind if, in the absence of counterforce capabilities, the threat

[14] Buchan, for example, suggests that, were Britain to give up the building of an independent nuclear force, she could furnish six divisions to SHAPE's forces ("Their Bomb and Ours," *loc.cit.*, p. 17). However, Buchan mentions the further condition that Britain would have to forego the maintenance of large garrisons outside Europe.

of massive retaliation becomes increasingly hollow. And it can be argued, furthermore, and most forcefully, that the maintenance of a dual capability tells the opponent that we know our business and are going about it in a soberly calculated way, that we intend to employ the final threat with circumspection but do intend, if necessary, to employ it. And regarding the damage to be reckoned with under the two alternative strategies, Hoag points out correctly that we face a question with an indeterminate answer. Under a limited-war policy, we increase the probability of wars which are likely to be less devastating; under the alternative policy, we reduce the likelihood of any war, but make it a war of probably tremendous devastation. Which product of the two pairs of probabilities will be the more serious?[15]

The question of which kind of limited-war capability the NATO alliance should provide is by now more interesting than whether a limited-war strategy should be adopted at all. As Hilsman indicates, SHAPE has begun to revise its policy of downgrading the limited-war strategy adopted after the Lisbon phase. This does not necessarily mean that the revision will be completed at SHAPE. Military planners in the Pentagon are by no means united on the subject; official British policy seems to favor tactical nuclear arrangements for the shield forces; so does French opinion and a considerable body of German opinion, including Defense Minister Strauss (see Chapter 10).

To my mind, Hoag presents a most convincing case for a *primarily* conventional capacity—always provided, of course, that the West commands the strategic nuclear backing for *any* limited-war strategy. There is no need to restate Hoag's arguments or the points made at the Princeton Conference. However, I want to make a few comments. Even if a superior case is made for a primarily conventional capability, it may not be compelling so long as the argument is accepted that the development of tactical nuclear equipment has reached the "point of no return." It would indeed go against the grain of military thinking to de-emphasize technically superior in favor of technically inferior arms. The question must be raised, therefore, whether or not tactical nuclear weapons are technically superior for the purpose of fighting limited war in Europe or whether, for this purpose, they are superior from the West's point of view. Hoag denies the latter assertion. He points

[15] Glenn H. Snyder points out that the probability of enemy aggression is essentially a function of four factors, as the enemy sees them: (1) the probabilities associated with various possible military responses to the aggression; (2) the expected severity of these possible responses; (3) the enemy's valuation of his objectives; and (4) the probability that he will succesfully gain the objective. Cf. his *Deterrence by Denial and Punishment*, *op.cit.*, p. 3.

out, furthermore, that, as a legacy of NATO's past, it has a substantial infrastructure for waging conventional war; that conventional weapons are capable of great technical improvement; and that, in fact, the West is now ill-prepared to fight anything but small wars either with conventional or with tactical nuclear armament. This means that we do have an option.

As reported by Healey, it is a British position that small forces equipped with tactical nuclear weapons are useful for ensuring American involvement on the level of strategic air power. This position is interesting for two reasons. For one, it is contradicted by the fear, sometimes expressed in Europe, that the United States and the USSR might fight a limited nuclear conflict restricted to Central and Western Europe (without attacks on one another's homelands).[16] Such a form of nuclear "disengagement" could be disastrous for Western Europe, and its anticipation denies the triggering effect assumed by the British position. This position is also in conflict with the assumption, sometimes made in favor of tactical nuclear forces, that a limited war fought with such forces is no more likely than conventional war to spiral to total war. If the West is or becomes serious about adopting a limited-war strategy at all, the spiraling problem is an obviously critical one. It seems convincing to me that conventional fighting is less likely to ascend to the undesired level than fighting with tactical nuclear weapons, and this especially if tactical nuclear weapons were delivered —by plane or missile—from points distant from the area of ground combat. The limits on weapons use are far more easily administered when nuclear armament is not resorted to. No doubt, it would be possible to minimize the spiraling danger in tactical nuclear war if we tried to regulate our and the prospective enemy's behavior beforehand. But, as Rear Admiral A. W. Buzzard has been stressing for years, this requires a great deal of advance planning on how and where to use tactical nuclear weapons, on what to do if any limits are violated, possibly by accident, and the prior communication of a set of rules. There is no evidence that the West has developed such an operational philosophy; and this despite the fact that, with its present strength, SHAPE would have no choice but to employ tactical nuclear arms if the Russians mounted any sizable limited attack.

Advocates of a limited-war strategy relying on primarily conventional forces usually prescribe a force of at least 30 full divisions. This target is certainly within the practicable range, provided France can

16 Cf. Wilhelm Wolfgang Schütz, *Das Gesetz des Handelns*, Frankfurt a.M., 1958, p. 101.

return from Algeria the troops withdrawn from SHAPE. The most favorable development in this respect has been the build-up of the West German forces, which are to provide 12 divisions by 1961 and, as Craig observes, seem to have excellent leadership, training, organization, and morale. The figure of 30 divisions, which General Norstad has requested and the NATO countries have agreed to furnish—though they have not done so yet—is related to the 22 Soviet divisions in Eastern Germany. Thirty NATO divisions should be able to stop a Soviet surprise attack on the ground. If the Russians proceeded with a more massive invasion, they could not deploy the necessary troops unobserved, and this would put SAC on alert. This conclusion raises a question about the future adequacy of the planned NATO shield. Thirty divisions seem enough so long as a full-scale Soviet ground attack is likely to bring SAC into play. But a SAC riposte is feasible only so long as the United States retains a counterforce capability on the strategic level—an assumption that should be realistic for some time to come, but not necessarily for a longer period. As Hilsman remarks, 30 divisions might be inadequate if, sometime in the future, it should happen that strategic forces everywhere were capable only of passive deterrence. In that event, the United States could not be expected to stop a massive Soviet invasion thrust and, for reasons given in the foregoing, it is at least doubtful that the threat of any counter-city forces in Western Europe would be credible enough to deter.

Depending on Soviet capabilities, as many as 60 divisions might then be required. To make such a large force feasible might demand increased contributions from the United States and the United Kingdom. It would also call for a reappraisal of the *kinds* of forces needed. With a total West European force of, say, 60 divisions, the deployment of most divisions would necessarily be along the common boundary with the Soviet bloc; only a relatively small number—perhaps on the order of 15 divisions—need be highly mobile. The frontier divisions could be given efficient weapons, but would not need the very expensive paraphernalia of high mobility, including a large "divisional slice."[17] Once reserve manpower has been trained and reserve weapons accumulated, these frontier divisions need not all be active forces. In large part, they could be a militia force. Such adaptations would greatly lighten the economic burden of a large limited-war capability.

The size of NATO's limited-war force also has an important bearing on the prospects of arms control. Provided such control ever be-

[17] Raymond Aron, *On War*, New York, 1959, p. 45.

came feasible, it would be hard for the West to accept a far-reaching regulation of strategic nuclear weapons unless NATO's limited-war forces were adequate to check those of the Communists, or a disproportionate reduction of Soviet forces brought these down roughly to the West's level. It would be difficult for the Soviets to agree to a rather one-sided reduction in this category; and it would therefore appear that a lesser imbalance of forces on this level might facilitate rather than obstruct agreements on arms control.

VI. THE FUTURE OF NATO?

The upshot of this book, it seems to me, is that—as Nitze demonstrates in his chapter—no reliable alternative to NATO is in sight although its form requires adaptation. As before, the military security of Western Europe will be critically dependent on American military power. If this power should fail the NATO countries of Western Europe, their safety would, under foreseeable circumstances, be grievously precarious at best. Should American air power slump to the extent of inviting defeat through overwhelming surprise attack and the Soviets accept the invitation, the extension of Communist military control over Western Europe, and the rest of the world, would be no more than a collecting operation. Should more sophisticated missiles, perhaps sometime during the mid-1960's, reduce *all* strategic air forces to the role of passive deterrence—the vaunted stable balance of power on which so many Western Europeans are setting their hopes—and should this condition be durable, SAC (by definition without a counterforce capability) could hardly be expected to come to Western Europe's aid, except possibly with a strategy of limited retaliation, which is a strategy, however, whose merits and demerits are as yet unclear. In that event, Western Europe would have two requirements. One is a substantial countercity force of its own, which could be provided best by a joint capability—though most difficult and perhaps impossible to organize—and by American help in the form of weapons or at least weapons know-how. The other requirement is for a substantial limited-war capability—a requirement which it would be impossible for each country to meet separately and which, even by an allied effort, could be met more easily with American participation than without.

But a review of the past would make one skeptical about the expectation of only passive deterrents all around as an enduring condition. Unless checked by effective disarmament, it seems more probable that the headlong technological arms race will continue and that, on the strategic level as well, security will continue to go to those who earn it the hard way—again a condition which, given the West's political and economic systems, and its preference for the enjoyment of material comfort, the NATO countries would find onerous to meet, except perhaps as an effective coalition including the United States. The alternative of dependable arms control is a satisfactory alternative to NATO; and NATO should certainly be a working coalition for seeking this alternative as well as for defense. But, for reasons which have been lucidly analyzed by Raymond Aron,[18] we are entitled to no more than the slimmest hopes, and any success in this direction would seem again to call for a very close concert of the NATO countries.

The security of Western Europe is, of course, crucially affected not only by what happens to the American military posture but also by American intentions or, more specifically, by the value which the United States places on keeping Western Europe free from Soviet domination. If this country gave this value an overriding priority, Western Europe might even nurse hopes of enjoying American protection while going formally "neutral" or, though remaining in the alliance, making no more than token contributions to it. However, not only does European behavior impinge on American intentions; it is also necessary to view intention and capability in their interdependence. For the reasons stated at the beginning of this chapter, the military capabilities of the United States may well fail to measure up to this role.

Regarding the uncertain future, NATO's need is for a *more* rather than *less* centralized alliance. Now that Russia has greatly gained in military strength vis-à-vis the NATO coalition, Hoag rightly questions whether national military independence is feasible.[19] The military probabilities seem to argue compellingly against going it alone. When someone at the Princeton Conference asked, "Where can the European NATO countries go if they come to find the alliance too onerous?" another participant replied, not wholly facetiously: "To paraphrase the well-known American bestseller, 'Where would you go?' 'Out!' 'What would you do?' 'Nothing!' " The visible military facts of life do not make this a mature solution. In fact, the cost problem alone may leave no feasible alternative to collective arrangements. What is clearly desirable, in an uncertain future, is a wide spectrum of capabilities in order to give sufficient choices of response. But only increased NATO interdependence would permit the desirable to be

---

[18] *Ibid., passim.*
[19] For a confirming opinion, see *ibid.,* pp. 75-76.

financed. Efficient interdependence would mean sharing of weapons, of their development and production, and it would also mean largely complementary forces.

A high degree of interdependence is impossible without federation and this is not, at least now, a practical proposition. Even the prospects for a moderate increase in interdependence appear to be dim at this moment. British hesitations, and the growth of an embittered nationalism in France, represent serious barriers; and there are few encouraging signs of American readiness to underwrite the genuine participation in decision-making on which, in the West, increased interdependence must rest. At present, the political trends favor a relative disintegration rather than a reintegration of the alliance. Unless corrective action is taken soon, European preoccupation with independent retaliatory forces—though they are unlikely to give individual countries the ability to go it alone—will make NATO's future bleak indeed. And if a serious missile gap should develop between the strategic forces of Soviet Russia and the United States, the effect on our European allies will not only be demoralizing but also lower their attachment to the alliance, even though their true military position calls for exactly the opposite response.

What can the United States do? A policy of drift may be fatal. A policy of merely painting over the cracks in the structure of the alliance is not enough when the need is for initiative to rebuild the structure. We need to think through the problems, innovate, and act boldly. The United States should do so in the knowledge that American leadership in this matter is crucial, that there are no ideal choices, and that today's solution may be obsolete tomorrow. As Alastair Buchan reminds us, we should do so also in the knowledge that an integrated defense system imposes a "steady sacrifice of national independence" on America's allies.[20] If we know this, we will also know that American independence cannot remain sacrosanct. And if the United States is unable to set itself on an innovating course, it could still do better than merely let things drift. As a member of the Princeton Conference put it: "We must keep working, even if only by small measures, at strengthening the alliance, including its political foundation, whenever and wherever we can. There is no alternative to NATO. We should keep bases and troops in Europe. We must keep involved. The more involved we are, the less is the danger of independent action and independent failure."

[20] "Their Bomb and Ours," loc.cit., p. 14.

Yet any American initiative would have an excellent chance of meeting with an unconstructive response unless the Western European countries also thought through the problem facing us all without too much wishfulness and with a curbed appetite for security "on the cheap." Above all, they should re-examine their stand on the need for sizable limited-war forces and the disadvantages as well as the possible benefits of independent strategic capabilities. Like the United States, they should stop parroting the syllogism that a joint strategic force is impossible without federation, that federation is impossible, and that a joint nuclear force is therefore impossible. The first premise may not be true.

Of course, the main factor underlying the West's security is not material but moral resources. At bottom, the problem is one of motivation, not of manpower and industrial capacity. One participant at the Princeton Conference said: "To deter Soviet aggression, we need force and fortitude." Nothing could be more true, and if we muster the fortitude, we will have the force.

ASPECTS OF NATO STRATEGY:
A CONFERENCE REPORT

BY KLAUS KNORR

IN January 1958, the problems of NATO strategy were discussed at two successive conferences held in Princeton. At the first conference, attended by about 80 persons, four of the papers in this volume—those by Hoag, Black and Yeager, Healey, and Nitze—were presented and discussed. The 25 participants at the second conference had read all the papers prior to the conference and subjected the most acute problems of NATO strategy to a searching examination. All chapters in the book were revised to some extent after these meetings.

At the meetings, most of the assumptions, analyses, and conclusions found in the preceding chapters were confirmed, qualified, or rejected, and many additional thoughts were offered. No attempt was made to arrive at group agreement; and, though there was substantial concurrence on many points, agreement was rarely complete and, on many issues, the group remained divided. Yet the discussion was so productive of thought that this report will shed much additional light on the problems raised in the preceding chapters.

Rapporteurs recorded the statements made at both conferences, and it is on these records that the following report is based. Since many participants had official connections with government, it was decided not to attribute particular statements to particular persons. Although only the author and editor is responsible for this report, its true authors are the participants at the conferences, and especially at the second and smaller conference. A list of the participants and further particulars about them and the conferences will be found at the end of this Appendix.

The Conference considered the familiar spectrum of military contingencies which the NATO coalition may have to face:

(1) All-out thermonuclear attack, or its threat, by the Soviet Union, with or without surprise, against all, or only one, or several NATO countries.

(2) Limited attack or its threat, with conventional or tactical nuclear

weapons, on either a massive or a probing scale, against all, or one, or several of the European NATO countries.

The Conference discussed the following military strategies to deter these threats, and to defend the West should deterrence fail:

(1) Massive strategic retaliation, or the threat thereof to deter all-out nuclear or limited attack.

(2) Limited strategic retaliation to deter or defeat a limited attack.

(3) A limited-war capability composed of tactical nuclear and/or conventional forces to deter or repel limited Communist aggression.

I. The American Capability for Strategic Deterrence

Over the last several years, as it is still, the official view has been that NATO is, as one Conference participant put it, "an all-out war alliance"—that is, an alliance primarily dependent on massive deterrence. The "shield" has been too thin to do more than cope with small probing actions or serve as a trip wire touching off massive retaliation. The "sword," which means SAC, has been the mainstay of the West's security. Whether or not, or under what circumstances, NATO can remain an "all-out war alliance" has been brought into doubt by the spectacular rise in Soviet strategic striking power and the presumption that Russia has a good "second strike" force.

One of the most critical questions is whether, during the next five to ten years, the United States can hope to retain a counterforce strategy, or whether instead it will have to make do with the mere capacity to strike back at Russian cities. To pursue a counterforce strategy, the United States must have the power for what has been called *active deterrence*—that is, power to hit the Russian strategic forces first, holding in reserve enough offensive capability to threaten heavy damage to Russian cities.[1] If it has only the capability for *passive deterrence*, the United States can merely hope to retain a "city-busting capability" after a possible first strike by Soviet Russia.

This question is a critical one because massive retaliation against a limited Russian attack or threat is credible only if the United States

[1] By means of "active deterrence" we would hope to deter highly provocative aggression, such as a Soviet attack on Western Europe. We would do so by threatening to hit Russia first with, of course, an alerted SAC. Under this assumption, the USSR would strike "second" with a damaged force, for in order to reduce damage to the United States, SAC's "first" strike would have been directed against the locations of Soviet offensive power; this is the mission requiring a counterforce capability. In the case of "passive deterrence," we assume a direct Russian attack on us, the United States striking back with a damaged force to bomb Russian cities—a mission requiring a "countercity" capability. Passive deterrence rests on Soviet expectations of the damage Russia is likely to receive from our retaliatory "second" strike.

commands a counterforce capability. So long as this country has counter-force power, and so long as there is an advantage in striking first, the USSR will hesitate to give the United States both opportunity and provocation for striking first by mounting more than a minor limited attack in Europe. In consequence, the Soviet Union could be expected to be deterred by SAC from such kinds of aggression. In contrast, to respond to lesser threats in Europe by *massively* using only a capability for passive deterrence would be inviting catastrophic damage in return. The most the United States could consider, under these circumstances, would be *limited* strategic retaliation (see below). The importance of this problem was stressed by one member of the Conference who said: "If the Russians deliver an all-out attack on the entire alliance, all would respond. This is an uninteresting question. The interesting question is posed when we assume the Soviets to attack or exert strong pressure on one NATO country. In that event, some allies may opt out rather than accept the risk of all-out attack."

A large number of Conference participants feared that, beginning in the early 1960's, the United States would find it impracticable to main-tain either a first-strike or a second-strike counterforce capability. For the latter, the United States would have to possess enough nuclear offensive power, after decimation by a Soviet surprise attack, to inflict decisive losses on Russia's offensive capabilities. This forecast was based on three considerations. First, Russia would retain an intelligence ad-vantage, in being much more able to identify the sites of American strategic air power than the United States would be able to identify Soviet sites. (This assumption was contested, however, on the grounds that technological advances in detection mechanisms would come to nullify or greatly reduce the present Soviet intelligence advantage.) Second, the anticipated hardening of missile sites would render it more difficult to destroy them. This particular development, of course, should also benefit American sites, and the hardening and mobility of launch-ing facilities would tend to make both strategic forces less vulnerable to surprise attack, and hence to a counterforce strategy. Third, a second-strike counterforce capability would be prohibitively expensive, espe-cially in view of the American reluctance to raise defense expenditures. To have a second-strike counterforce capability, this country would need a multiple of the missiles required for a first-strike capacity. The difference would be still greater between the capabilities for a second-strike active deterrent and for a second-strike passive deterrent. One participant placed this difference at a ratio of 10 to 1. Another stated that, while for a strictly countercity strategy we needed to protect only about 500 missiles, for a counterforce strategy we might eventually require as many as 30,000 or 40,000 missiles. Several participants also expressed the fear that, for the reasons mentioned, the United States might lose *any* counterforce capability.

Remarkably, only one member of the Conference professed to be unworried by this prospect. But several participants pointed to certain advantages which such a development might bring. The main advantage was seen to depend on the vital condition that the strategic air power of the United States, or of both the United States and Russia, would be protected by hardening, mobility, and dispersal to a degree making them largely invulnerable to an enemy attack. In that event, the two opposing forces need not react quickly and nervously to any signals that might indicate a hostile first strike. Relative invulnerability would permit each retaliatory system to postpone its reaction until enemy intentions had become unmistakable. Such a situation would render the "balance of terror" decidedly more stable and safe than it is at the present time. As one participant put it: "In that sense, it is in our interest that both the United States and Soviet Russia have invulnerable retaliatory forces." And another asked: "Is even an effective first-strike counterforce strategy worth pursuing if it increases the probability of all-out war touched off by accident? Is it not better if both sides have a secure second-strike countercity capability?"

Two other interesting points were made. If a counterforce strategy remained attractive in the future, and both Russia and the United States pursued it, a cumulative and extraordinarily expensive arms race would result. Furthermore, if the United States temporarily lost a counterforce capability but then undertook to rebuild it, the Russians would be tempted to attack before the rebuilding process was completed.

The above-mentioned advantages of a stable system of relatively invulnerable deterrent powers assume missile-site protection brought about by technological developments, shared by both sides, which would be reasonably cheap and unlikely to be upset by further scientific progress. On these assumptions, surprise attack would be relatively unimportant, and counterforce strategies would be dropped deliberately by both sides because they had become unattractive. It is, however, in some degree uncertain that this state of invulnerability will be actually achieved; and, since this development must await second- and third-generation missiles, it is in any case unlikely to materialize for several years, possibly not before the mid-1960's. During the intervening period a situation may well arise in which the United States—partly because of a lag in missile research and development and largely because it wishes to maintain a relatively low ceiling on defense expenditures—provides itself with far fewer operational ICBM's than Russia produces. In that case, the United States might possess no counterforce capability, while the USSR does. It is of course possible, as one Conference participant remarked, that Moscow also may be unable to afford a counterforce strategy. However, the Soviet Union is under less pressure to economize on defense; economic strain might cause it far greater concern if it followed a counterforce strategy under competitive conditions—while the United States did so, too.

The majority of Conference members were impressed by the appalling disadvantages and dangers of an unmatched counterforce capability in Soviet hands. Moreover, only so long as the Russians assume an American counterforce capability is it risky for them to mount any major action short of a direct attack on the United States. If the Russians try for a counterforce deterrent, while we do not, the resource requirements of a passive deterrent are greatly increased. The United States would have to produce far more missiles and planes than would be necessary if the USSR, too, had only a city-busting capability. Otherwise, as one participant said, the Russians might even be in a position to destroy our countercity capability, blasting our hard sites with multimegaton weapons and blasting larger areas to knock out mobile launching facilities. In that event, we would not even have a passive deterrent. Another discussant observed: "We can at best hope for a stalemate if the Soviets have a counterforce capability and we do not. The best response left to a Soviet strike would be *limited* retaliation with a few weapons only. But we could never hope for a 'win' in a thermonuclear exchange. Only counterforce capability makes such a 'win' possible." In addition, it was pointed out that the United States would remove a serious uncertainty from Soviet strategic planning and permit the Russians a great saving in defense resources, compared with a situation of competitive active deterrents. To concede all these advantages to the USSR would be an enormous price to pay for an American neglect of a counterforce capability. We would be moving to an entirely new order of possible and probable risks.

Indeed, most participants preferred an American capacity for active deterrence. One exclaimed boldly: "We absolutely require a counterforce capability!" Others agreed, but pointed out that to acquire a second-strike rather than first-strike capability would be extremely hard and expensive, though not beyond the resources of the United States. "We could afford it if we wanted to."

Another maintained that the actual problem is unlikely, except perhaps temporarily, to imply a stark contrast of either having or not having the capacity for active deterrence. It seemed to some participants improbable that the United States would stop *trying* to have the requisite forces. What might well emerge, and would be worth striving for, would be an intermediate capability—a *mixed* capability—there being in any case considerable, though limited, overlap between the weapons required for either pure strategy. A mixed or ambiguous capability, and an efficient strategy based thereon, might be confusing to Soviet Russia and exert substantial deterrent effect.

The Conference also addressed itself to the problem of the likely consequences of a continued "nuclear stalemate" or "balance of terror" between the two great powers. There was considerable support for the position made widely known by Albert Wohlstetter's article in the January 1959 issue of *Foreign Affairs*, according to which the balance of terror is not automatic, is very precarious at present, and will be hard to maintain in the future. This is so, it was pointed out, because in fact mutual annihilation is not as automatic as is often assumed. There is a great advantage in executing a first strike by surprise.

Not only might the Russians hope to cripple seriously American retaliatory capacity; they might also be capable of reducing counterdamage to an acceptable level. The USSR is reported to have made civil defense preparations far exceeding American efforts. Knowing in advance when it would strike, it could reduce blast and heat casualties by quick evacuation, and greatly cut the danger of fallout by relatively cheap countermeasures. It is conceivable then, as one discussant speculated, that—instead of having to face the risk of losing many tens of millions of people, and a substantial proportion of non-human resources—the risk might be reducible to a level of 20 million—the number of casualties actually suffered by Soviet Russia in World War II. This is not to say that the Kremlin would deliberately sacrifice 20 million Russians, but rather that it might, under certain conditions, accept the *possibility* or even the *probability* of suffering such a scale of destruction. According to this participant, a first strike is well within the range of Soviet policy. Once the Russians believe themselves to have achieved a substantial thermonuclear superiority over the United States, they could put heavy pressure on the West and they might decide that they did not want to continue living in a world in which the United States, Britain, and eventually France or even Turkey could threaten and blast Moscow or Kharkov.

However, several Conference participants were inclined to qualify or even to reject this representation of the Soviet threat. Thus it was pointed out that the Russian leaders would be loath to risk severe destruction of the ebullient Russia which they had created by dint of hard and unremitting effort; that they would not tolerate lightly the probability of 20 million casualties, especially since they attribute to themselves excellent chances of winning world leadership by non-military means. Before very long, one member added, China might become one serious factor deterring the Russians from a risky policy—that is, they might not want to run the risk of being hard hit themselves and, as a result, lose the direction of the world Communist movement to Peiping. Finally, it was doubted that Russian planners were able to calculate precisely enough to assure the Kremlin that 20 million casualties would be the upper limit if they started all-out war by a surprise attack. In fact, such planning would be confronted by many grave uncertainties; and uncertainty, as one Conference participant remarked, always works against the decision to attack. Another added: "Do not underestimate these uncertainties. They are far greater than suggested in most writing on the subject. And even if there were only a 15 per cent uncertainty of annihilation or the end of the Communist regime, this would cause the Russians to consider the possibility of disaster and the comparative merit of alternative courses of action."

II. Independent and Joint Nuclear Deterrents in Western Europe

As clearly explained by Healey in Chapter 9, the British decision to acquire an independent strategic deterrent was inspired by several factors. Mixed motivations—and not sheer vainglory—are now prompting the French in this direction, and this will hold true of other nations which may feel a need to join the nuclear Haves. Yet one central and rational factor—possibly the decisive factor in many instances—will be, as it has been, the diminished and diminishing credibility of United States willingness to accept the damage of all-out war in support of an ally.

Whether in fact this doubt is justified is largely immaterial. At the Princeton Conference, it was pointed out that the American record for honoring commitments is excellent, and recent American action over Quemoy and Berlin should be reassuring. Some participants expressed the feeling that a positive American response will remain more probable than many West Europeans assume; and they could have added that absolute certainty of such response—so long as the United States has the capability for it—is indeed unnecessary. For deterrent purposes, even a rather ambiguous commitment may well suffice. It is not, however, American estimates of future American responses which count in this matter. Rather, the threat of American reprisal must be thought *by Western Europe* to be credible to the Kremlin.

Whatever gloomy conclusions have resulted from European calculations, they have been mostly derived, thus far, from an analysis based on less pessimistic premises than the assumption, debated at the Princeton Conference, that it may be impracticable for the United States to continue a counterforce strategy even though the Soviets retain this advantage. As stated above, so long as the Russians know or suspect that we have a counterforce capability, they may well be deterred from initiating a major military action, unaccompanied by a first strike against SAC, for fear of conceding the opportunity for, and inciting, a first strike on themselves. Without a counterforce capability, the United States could rationally employ massive strategic retaliation only in the ultimate contingency of a direct Soviet attack; and our European allies feel that a Russian attack on them is not the ultimate contingency for us. Under these assumptions, it was pointed out at the Conference, the West would be in no position to adopt a limited-war strategy with conventional weapons, for we could not then use the threat of massive retaliation to keep the Russians from upping the ante and employing tactical nuclear armament. Even if the Soviet Union as well as the United States had no counterforce power, both retaliatory systems being well protected against a first strike, Moscow would obviously not be deterred from a limited but major attack in Europe for fear of losing the advantage of the first strike. The most the United States could consider under conditions of passive deterrents all around is a strategy of limited strategic reprisal.

The Princeton Conference extensively discussed the case for and against individual NATO countries in Europe acquiring a strategic nuclear deterrent of their own. The fact that France is following in Britain's footsteps, though with a vast lag, and the probability that other countries will do the same, were recognized as a development in NATO that might entail momentous consequences. Obviously, the independent capabilities in question would suffice for passive, not active, deterrence. It was also taken for granted that such capabilities could, for some time to come, only be highly vulnerable to a Russian surprise attack, and that relatively invulnerable systems of great hardness or mobility would not be available before the mid-1960's.

According to the common case made for independent deterrent power, our European allies need this capability in order to deter a direct Soviet attack on themselves, no matter whether the threatened attack involves all-out strategic or limited aggression. The case is based mainly on three possible premises. First, with the recent rise of Soviet thermonuclear striking power, an American reprisal is no longer regarded as automatic. In this respect, attention is drawn to the legal nature of the American commitment. Article V of the North Atlantic Treaty requires each member state to come to the aid of another member, who is subject to an armed attack, by taking "such action as it deems necessary." There is no written obligation which holds the United States to massive retaliation, and SAC is, after all, not under NATO control. In addition to the assumed American reluctance to accept the risk of devastation in order to protect a NATO ally, it has also been pointed out that, with the advent of ICBM's, the United States is becoming strategically less dependent on West European bases, that this development might lessen the American stake in the security of the area, and that this contingency is further eroding European confidence in American nuclear support.

Second, the stated case for independent national deterrents often rests on the further, but usually tacit, assumption that, for the very reasons which have made all-out American action less credible, every European NATO member is considered unlikely to come to the aid of any of its allies which is under heavy Soviet military pressure or attack, and that therefore only strategic deterrence by the hard-pressed country itself can be effective.

Third, independent deterrents are often deemed to be needed by each country not only to counter Soviet all-out threats but also to deter a major attack by Soviet surface forces on itself. "No aggressor will risk major conventional attack on any power which possesses strategic nuclear weapons." This rationale is supported by widespread feelings in Western Europe that such a limited attack, especially if it led to the use of tactical nuclear weapons, would entail enormous destruction in the invaded country and hence be as intolerable to it as a strategic nuclear assault. The better defense strategy, according to this view, would be to refuse limited war and rely entirely on strategic deterrent power. And, it is argued, even if a limited-war strategy involving conventional arms were not rejected, the threat of strategic reprisal would be needed to force the Russians to observe the limits; and, since the availability of American massive retaliation for this policing function was in doubt, independent nuclear deterrence would be required for this purpose also.

This case for independent strategic power drew lively criticism at the Princeton Conference. Much of the criticism revolved around three important questions.

Can the independent retaliatory power of European NATO countries really be effective in terms of surviving a first blow by the enemy and of being able to penetrate Soviet defenses? Possessing only a passive deterrence, each country must be able to hit the enemy heavily after it has been hit by him. None of these countries command the strength to have, compared with the United States and the USSR, more than a little capability. Over the next several years at least, it was generally recognized, the British capability, for instance, would remain highly vulnerable to a first strike although, even during this period, some protection would be technically possible—by air-borne alert—albeit only at high costs. Over the longer run, the achievement of a high degree of invulnerability was seen as a function of technological advance and costs. By about the mid-1960's, hard- and sea-based missiles would probably present the technological opportunity. Whether the costs of relative invulnerability would be high or not depended on several considerations, especially American policy, and was largely unpredictable. So was considered the penetrability of Soviet defenses, on which the size of the second-strike capability would in part have to depend.

Would not the development of independent reprisal capabilities by the NATO allies serve to reduce further the credibility of SAC's threat in support of an ally? One Conference participant doubted that the question should be answered in the affirmative; others, however, felt that whatever little independent deterrent power Western European countries would gain might be offset, and perhaps more than offset, by Russian calculations of a lesser chance of SAC intervention.

Will single European nations really muster enough fortitude in the face of massive Soviet threats to use their independent capability independently? Is their deterrent really credible? Is it credible, for example, in the event of a Soviet limited attack? Will the European country really threaten to commit suicide in order to stop such an attack?

Several additional criticisms were leveled against the trend toward independent national deterrents. Such a development, it was predicted, would encourage the Soviet Union to nibble NATO countries one by one by piecemeal attack and nuclear blackmail. Even if each country were able to put the Kremlin on notice that it was not worth to the USSR the damage which it could inflict on Russia, Moscow might not be deterred if it wanted to teach an object lesson by setting a precedent for future, more successful blackmail. It was also considered possible that the acquisition of independent retaliatory capabilities, especially if this happened in Germany, might frighten the Soviets into precipitous counteraction. The diffusion of deterrent power would also, in other ways, create more instability, and raise the danger of accidental outbreaks of war. Thus, the risk that a local conflict would touch off all-out nuclear war would be increased by the multiplication of independent deterrents. Whether in fact independent retaliatory capability would deter local war seemed uncertain. As one participant remarked, "A little big deterrent simply does not have total deterrent capabilities. Hence other responses are needed, especially to limited attack." And, in any case, an independent deterrent would be unable to deter local attacks which were not started deliberately. Exclusive reliance on this power was not therefore considered safe.

Cogent as these counterarguments are, they abstract from the possibility that, even if several West European countries acquired an independent nuclear force, the alliance would continue and, with it, the supportive threat of American reprisal, even though this had become less credible than it was some years ago. Consideration of this wider context led to some interesting countercriticisms. Until and unless advancing technology protected passive deterrent power against a first strike, it was admitted, independent European deterrents could not really be independent. Until this stage is reached, the main rational purpose of an independent capability would be to trigger off a massive American response. "The damage which a European nation with an independent nuclear capability could inflict on Soviet Russia might not be great for some time. But if the European nation had this capacity, and had a stronger ally behind it, its initial nuclear shot might trigger off the retaliatory force of the ally. No European nation could be sure that the United States would in fact intervene with SAC. But Russia could not be sure that this would not happen, and the risk would be likely to deter her." "The remaining uncertainty of the American response, moreover, would restrain European allies from acting imprudently." "The United States would retain the right not to be provoked into massive retaliation if an ally pulled the trigger irresponsibly."

Several further countercriticisms were made. The doubt that the independent reprisal threat of European nations would be credible even after the reprisal capacity were reasonably protected against a first Russian blow inspired the following rejoinder: "It is indeed possible that a non-nuclear attack by Russia might not touch off massive nuclear retaliation by a small power. But the Soviets must yet take this capability into account, whatever their speculation on the small country's intentions. They would face a risk. For instance, if they were to threaten or, by limited means, attack the United Kingdom, they could not be *sure* that the British would not respond with their strategic capability even though the response were suicidal and hence irrational."

Another point referred to the possibility of the West following a limited-war strategy to deter or defend limited attacks by the USSR. Discussions which favor a response with conventional armament to a Russian conventional attack have pointed to the need for a sanction which would deter the Russians from raising the original limits, should their limited operations prove unsuccessful. This sanction has been generally attributed to the threat of massive reprisal by SAC. However, as pointed out above, this attribution would be weakened if the United States were unable to maintain strategic counterforce capabilities. Hence the suggestion that limited, or graduated, reprisal or its threat—an intermediate-level threat—might be invoked as an effective sanction. In principle, of course, SAC could be called upon to execute limited reprisals. However, this role could also—and perhaps more advantageously—be assumed by independent retaliatory capabilities in Europe. One Conference discussant explained this possibility as follows: "There are two kinds of graduated deterrents in the event of limited conventional war. One is the ability to raise the ante on the ground—that is, proceed to the employment of tactical nuclear weapons. The other is to place retaliatory capability in the hands of NATO countries, although we should also consider less-than-massive retaliation by the United States." (The problems of such a strategy are discussed in the section on limited retaliation below.)

Finally, it was pointed out at the Conference—and this consideration, though highly imponderable, may be of great weight—that independent nuclear capabilities might play an important role with respect to Russian threats and blackmail even if the capabilities were vulnerable to a first strike. Over a wide range of threats and pressures, even marginal deterrents may stiffen the will to resist of the countries that possess them and thus prevent bloodless Soviet success.

Not all of these counterarguments in favor of independent passive deterrents in Europe remained unanswered. In reply to the idea that, at least for some time, the value of such deterrents would lie primarily in the ability of European NATO countries to involve SAC, it was stated repeatedly that the United States might be most reluctant to be tied in such a manner to Europe's "independent" nuclear capabilities;

that this might make "nuclear isolation" attractive in the United States; and that, in any case, the European allies could not hope to trigger off SAC retaliation if they acted *independently*. Furthermore, and most importantly, it was pointed out that this triggering idea was dependent on the United States having a counterforce capability—a condition which may not in fact obtain in the future.

A conference was patently not the place for weighing, however intuitively, all these pros and cons—with so many of them more or less hypothetical, speculative, and imponderable—and arriving at a net evaluation in terms of American or West European security. A few of the participants were undisturbed by the trend toward a diffusion of independent retaliatory capability through NATO. But others were not. These admitted that Britain and France had some valid excuses for their present course of action. It was, after all, the United States that first advocated massive retaliation against all Soviet threats; and the unwillingness of the United States to share its nuclear weapons with its allies gave the latter an incentive to develop such arms—once they were wanted—independently. According to the British experience, now confirmed by Congressional law, as one participant observed, the United States becomes willing to share only after a country has demonstrated its ability to make these weapons itself.

But such excuses cannot dissipate grave doubts that independent deterrents may well fail to redound to the security of Western Europe; and several implications of the projected trend must arouse serious misgivings in the United States. The idea that independent action by a NATO ally might involve the United States in all-out war with the USSR goes far beyond the autonomy which each ally is supposed to retain under the North Atlantic Treaty. There are, in addition, all the familiar anxieties about the nth-country problem, even if the fourth and fifth new nuclear powers are NATO allies. One member of the Conference stated: "The idea of ten countries sending out planes on alert, nervously fingering the trigger on missiles, and having submarines with Polaris-type missiles roaming the sea—this idea is intolerable." "There would be great difficulty in keeping independent nuclear power from leading to independent political or military action; and the possibilities of all-out war arising from accidents would be greatly enhanced." Indeed, the increased risks of being a member of such an alliance, it was felt, might well lead to the dissolution of the NATO coalition. One participant predicted flatly: "As the power to deter becomes general, the alliance will confer more risks on each partner than an independent stance would." The splintering of the coalition, however, could hardly be equated with increased security for its members.

Whether desirable or not, a good many participants in the Princeton Conference assumed that strategic nuclear diffusion was inevitable and only a question of time. On this view, the smaller allies might remain satisfied with inferior military capacities. But France could not be stopped from its determination to manage an atomic explosion and join the nuclear Haves. Eventually, Italy would follow suit. For the time being, Western Germany could hope for no more than receiving American IRBM's on the double-veto system at present used between the United States and Britain. In the longer run, however, Germany also was expected to demand nuclear "independence."

These assumptions did not remain unchallenged. It was emphasized that the interests of particular NATO countries would reflect their differing geographic location. In the case of Britain, the independent passive deterrent re-creates the English Channel, in some sense, by providing protection against the unlimited spread of ground fighting in Europe; and since the USSR would find it difficult to carry conventional war to the British Isles, an independent retaliatory capability seems to solve Britain's problem better than that of West Germany, Denmark, Norway, Greece, and Turkey—with France, Italy, and the Benelux countries occupying an intermediate position. The opinion was also expressed that the demand for independent deterrents in Europe was not as yet absolute; that the United States could demonstrate to aspiring countries the disadvantages of this solution, its special risks and expense, and the probability that these independent capabilities would be obsolete whenever they became operational; and that there were inter-allied alternative strategies of superior flexibility and deterrent power.

But what if the development toward a diffusion of nuclear retaliatory power were indeed irresistible? What should be the American policy on this assumption? Several Conference discussants felt that, *on this view*, the United States should consider two courses of action in order to manipulate events as much as possible in a way which would maintain NATO as a going concern and maximize the security of all its members.

One course would be for the United States to share its nuclear-weapons know-how with the allies, helping them to acquire independent passive deterrents (1) of the right kind, that is, weapons which are least provocative to the USSR and least vulnerable to a first strike—probably hard-based missiles; (2) at relatively low costs, that is, without the costs of independent research and development and possibly at the cost of American mass production; and (3) on certain conditions such as, for example, the condition proposed in Burns's chapter that the European NATO allies make a more determined effort to produce a sufficient limited-war capability. It was seen as a further advantage of deliberate and well-timed sharing that it would be revocable, at least in the sense that with rapid technological obsolescence continuing in the future, our NATO allies would depend on us to keep their capabilities up-to-date; this alone would confer on the United States a degree of control over the use of these weapons and over NATO policy.

The other course would be to offer our European allies a nuclear retaliatory capability, not on an independent national, but on a joint NATO, basis.

III. A Nuclear Retaliatory Capability Under Joint NATO Control

Mindful of the need many Western Europeans feel for a nuclear retaliatory capability which is available to them credibly—that is, automatically—most members of the Conference found a joint group capability in principle far preferable to the development of several independent national forces. Similarly, American sharing of nuclear forces, weapons, or weapon technology with a group was thought better than such sharing with individual NATO allies.

Yet, desirability granted, the striking difficulties of a joint capability and joint control over it were obvious to all. Indeed, several participants held firmly that this solution is unfeasible. The chief difficulty with unified control is, of course, that each country would be afraid of two things: first, that an ally or allies would want the joint capability employed when it did not want to be involved in the joint risk of employment; and, second, that it alone might demand employment of the joint force when its allies did not. As one participant at the Conference remarked: "Each country would want its fingers on both the trigger and the safety catch." Several members stated that institutions appropriate for the purpose, and safeguarding conflicting interests, could not be devised short of a fusion of national sovereignties; and that federation of the NATO countries was clearly not within the realm of practical politics.

Not all participants, however, accepted this negative conclusion as final. They agreed that the obstacles to designing a joint retaliatory system were formidable indeed. But they also thought that before a desirable solution is definitely rejected as unfeasible, the problem should receive much more study than it has so far attracted.

IV. STRATEGIES FOR MEETING LIMITED MILITARY AGGRESSION

In the past, so long as the United States was undisputably superior to Russia in thermonuclear air power, there was widespread support for the dominant Pentagon assumption that the risk of provoking a massive strategic riposte from SAC effectively limited Soviet behavior in attempting military gains by limited attacks—forms of aggression, that is, which may be limited in area and in the employment of weapons and must be limited in military objective. And if the Korean War was cited in criticism of this thesis, it could be replied that, in this instance, the Russians were mistaken about the real American interest in the area, that they were not directly involved in the fighting, and that they have not in fact started a limited war since 1949. However, as the Soviet Union was catching up with the United States in nuclear striking power and had acquired the means to inflict enormous damage on the United States itself, the massive-retaliation thesis was challenged increasingly on the grounds that, once a thermonuclear "stalemate" had come about between the two big antagonists, the Russians were bound to discount the risk that limited aggression by them would in fact be countered by American action initiating a mutually devastating war.

This assumption raises the question of whether limited Soviet attacks might not be staged in Europe, and of what should be the NATO strategy to deter such a move, or to stop it in the event deterrence failed. To be sure, Russian leaders and military publicists have stated frequently that a limited war in Europe is inconceivable. Yet such statements are not necessarily reassuring. They may reflect a time lag in Soviet military thinking, they may represent no more than peace-mongering, and they may be deliberately misleading for the purpose of preventing the West from making adequate preparations to meet this contingency. In any case, Russia, with her superiority in divisions, possesses ample means for launching limited attacks, and there can be no assurance that these means will not be used when opportunity beckons.

The Princeton Conference devoted a great deal of discussion to the dilemma posed by the suspicion that continued reliance on massive reprisal to deter limited aggression has become increasingly risky and possibly obsolete. Three Western responses to the danger of limited Soviet attack were considered: massive retaliation, limited strategic retaliation, and the establishment of a solid capability for fighting limited war with conventional and/or tactical nuclear forces. Most of the participants were disinclined to rule out completely any one of these possible counterstrategies, and did not see the need for now choosing one to the exclusion of the others. A few discussants indeed declared repeatedly that what the NATO coalition needs is the whole spectrum of responses "to be able to do whatever the situation calls for." But, as others rejoined, this is not entirely realistic advice, for—aside from a possible incompatibility of different strategies—the NATO countries cannot afford, or do not want to burden themselves with, ample means for every possible response. One discussant interjected that "the West also requires military preparations for conflict outside Europe, it needs plenty of resources for meeting the non-military offensive of the Sino-Soviet bloc, and economy in military preparations for countering Russian threats in Europe is therefore an important consideration." Economizing means choosing. But the wise choices might be choosing on the margin, so that choice does not require flat decisions on an either/or basis but rather on the basis of more or less reliance on several possible alternatives.

It was recognized at the Conference that massive retaliation to limited war has so far remained the preferred official strategy of the United Kingdom and, perhaps a shade less unambiguously, of the United States, and that—except for references to countering border incidents and minor probing operations—SHAPE also seems officially to prefer this solution. Some members at the Princeton Conference defended this preference mainly on three grounds. First, the adoption of a limited-war strategy would lower the credibility of the threat of massive reprisal. "If we build up a substantial limited-war capability, we invite limited attack by the USSR because we would be in fact declaring that we would not proceed immediately to the all-out war level if limited aggression occurred." Second, it was pointed out that most of the informed public in Western Europe distrusted and opposed a limited-war strategy for essentially the same reason. For many, if not most, or all, European NATO countries—which might become the battlefield in limited war—limited war seems to involve about as much destruction, and hence appears as unacceptable, as all-out war. Therefore they do not want *any* war in Europe, and the unlikelihood of any war seems best assured by the threat of massive retaliation. Beyond containing small incursions, the only worthwhile function of limited-war forces, on this view, is to act as a trip wire—that is, to ensure that massive retaliation would be touched off. Third, it was pointed out that, in any case, limited war in Europe probably could not be kept limited, that it would almost inevitably degenerate into all-out war. Several speakers expressed the conviction that a desire to minimize defense expenditures was another important reason why continued reliance on the threat of massive retaliation was being favored. When the Conservative Party came into office in Britain, it set out determinedly to pare the large defense budget adopted by the Labour government, and it was especially interested in abandoning the unpopular conscription of military manpower. For both reasons, the axe fell on limited-war forces and the emphasis was placed on strategic deterrence. In the United States likewise, the economy-minded Republican Administration had ordered substantial cuts in the forces that would be needed for waging limited war. Since nobody will argue that financial pressures should lead to economizing which would weaken SAC, budget considerations tend to support heavy reliance on strategic air power as a deterrent of *all* military threats. Nobody at the Conference defended the view that cost considerations should shape our strategy to the extent of putting excessive reliance on SAC.

The Conference supporters of the doctrine of massive retaliation also attacked a limited-war strategy on two grounds. For one, it was said, "Russia will launch a limited attack only if she is reasonably sure of being successful, and if she is successful, we have no choice but raising the ante, and that means falling back on the threat of massive retaliation." For another, should NATO be successful and beat back a Soviet limited attack, the Russians are likely to raise the ante and, again, we can prevent this only if we throw in the threat of massive retaliation. Hence, if the threat represented by SAC remains the main line of defense in limited war, why not use it to begin with? "Is the SAC threat more credible in defeating or policing limited aggression than in the immediate massive deterrence of limited attacks?"

This last argument drew prompt rejoinders. Regarding the question of what to do if the prospect of Soviet limited aggression were increased, it was pointed out that, as before, a *massive* Russian invasion of Western Europe should, and will, be deterred by the threat of massive reprisal; that we should provide limited-war forces to deter and, if necessary, stop an attack that is less than massive, even though substantial; and that the purpose for making such provision is to reserve only for unambiguously major attack the threat of SAC, which may now be neutralized by the Soviet counterthreat of devastating the United States. Similarly, the threat of massive retaliation "for policing the limits in limited war" would put SAC in a reserve position. A limited-war strategy would thus "put less weight on the immediate and risky use of massive retaliation."

The proponents of limited, as distinct from *massive*, nuclear reprisal averred that the threat of limited reprisal may not only be preferable to the threat of massive retaliation and a limited-war capability as a means to deter or defeat limited and local attacks, but could also be employed as a sanction which would keep the Soviets from raising the level of attack in the event that their limited aggression ran into effective opposition. As mentioned above, nuclear retaliatory forces under NATO or independent national control, as well as SAC, could be resorted to for this purpose. One Conference participant remarked: "The usual objection to this strategy is its alleged instability. If you attack the Russian homeland at all, it is said, the Soviets will be under heavy pressure to retaliate massively, and they are likely to yield to this pressure. But advancing weapons technology may remove this instability by providing each side with an effective strike-back capacity, thus discouraging a massive first blow. When this situation comes about, and neither side needs to rush into an immediate and all-out strike, there will be far less incentive to mount a full-scale strategic attack, or to assume that the other side will do so. It now seems implausible that, in response to an invasion of Europe, we would strike back by a limited strategic action, such as hitting the Russian Baltic or Black Sea fleet, and that the Russians, in return, would limit themselves to hitting one American target. But the comparative attractiveness of this strategy will become recognized as the stated technological conditions become clearly operational. Limited retaliation introduces the opportunity for bargaining as limited blows are exchanged. Neither big power will have to commit itself to all-out war too fast. Thus, limited reprisals will open up a new dimension of limited war—not limited local war, but nevertheless limited war. And it may also bring a new version of purely military war—that is, a series of actions confined to military targets."

V. Conventional or Tactical Nuclear Forces?

What kind of limited-war capability NATO would require, if the need for one were granted, was a question that evoked a spirited defense of primarily conventional forces—that is, forces equipped with modernized but non-atomic arms. In principle, this proposition was favored, perhaps surprisingly, by a strong majority of the Conference participants.

A substantial conventional-war capacity was seen to serve a twofold purpose. On the one hand, it would give NATO, in the event of a conventional attack by the Soviet bloc, a choice of responses and thus not force the coalition immediately to consider recourse to all-out nuclear hostilities. On the other hand, such a capability would deter a major conventional invasion by indicating to the Soviets a high probability that a conventional attack would end in defeat. By a "major invasion," the Conference meant more than border incidents or small probing actions but less than a full-scale attack involving a large proportion of the Communist divisions. The full-scale attack would, as before, have to be deterred by the threat of massive or limited nuclear reprisal. The deterrence value of the NATO force in question would lie in the fact that "to overcome it, the Russians would have to mobilize and deploy along the NATO boundaries a considerable number of divisions normally stationed in the Soviet Union." Russia could not therefore achieve surprise and, putting the West on notice, would give it time to consider appropriate responses to the threat.

The arguments favoring a conventional NATO force were mostly expressed as criticisms of a policy relying on forces equipped primarily with tactical nuclear weapons. First, why should NATO rely on tactical nuclear weapons which, if used for maximum military effect, would cause enormous damage in the NATO theater of war and which, if used in a way to minimize destruction of civilian population and assets—for example, by resort only to small-yield and "clean" weapons —would find their military effectiveness reduced and, moreover, could not prevent Soviet forces from employing high-yield bombs with large fallout? Second, the erstwhile argument that the West needed tactical nuclear forces in order to compensate for its inferiority in conventional troops no longer holds true, since the Russians have greatly increased their stockpile of bombs and have re-equipped many of their divisions with tactical nuclear armament. The West, therefore, cannot assume superiority in such arms and it may in fact be or become inferior to Soviet Russia in this respect also. One participant added: "If we resort to tactical nuclear weapons as an excuse for maintaining insufficient conventional forces, we are simply inviting defeat." Third, there is no evidence that the employment of tactical nuclear forces has the net effect of favoring defensive over offensive operations. Fourth, technological advance is by no means confined to nuclear weapons. While it is true that the past undue preference for nuclear arms has discouraged research and development in non-nuclear arms, there is every indication that modernization would make such weapons highly effective in future combat. However, for some time at least, we would probably lag behind Russia in this particular technological arms race. Finally, limited war with conventional arms is a great deal easier to keep limited than tactical nuclear war, which runs a greater risk of touching off resort to strategic nuclear forces. The greater stability of conventional limited war, in this respect, would provide the opponents with superior opportunities for negotiations designed to break off the limited conflict.

The proponents of tactical nuclear forces marshaled four counter-arguments. First, NATO cannot do without such forces in any case because the Soviets have them and might attack with such weapons rather than with conventional armament. Second, even if the Russians attacked conventionally, the West might be forced, if facing conventional defeat, to resort to tactical nuclear arms. Third, a conventional capability, therefore, would have to be *in addition to* an indispensable tactical nuclear capability, and this addition would be very expensive. Fourth, having been developed and made operational, tactical nuclear weapons are here to stay. Neither American nor West European forces would be satisfied with weapons less good than those in fact available to us and also possessed by the Russians. One Conference participant stated flatly: "The time will soon come when the U. S. Army will be equipped with nothing but tactical nuclear arms."

The proponents of a conventional capability replied as follows. Regarding the first point, they agreed that NATO needs some tactical nuclear armament and, hence, in some degree a dual capability. But they felt—and this was also in answer to the third argument of the tactical nuclear school of thought—that a *full* dual capability would be too costly to establish and maintain, and that the tactical nuclear capability, therefore, should be only marginal or modest. "A complete dual capability is not a matter of providing alternative sets of bomb racks for planes, and so on. A real dual capability calls for two entirely different kinds of major deployment in defense systems. Therefore, we should add only such elements of nuclear capability as are inexpensive and will not compromise the conventional capability." Another participant declared: "There should be no tactical nuclear capability at the expense of conventional capability."

Strong doubt was expressed about the proposition that, if NATO conventional forces were unable to repel a conventional attack, the West could readily raise the ante and shift to tactical nuclear weapons. For one thing, it was pointed out, the larger our conventional capability, the less need there will be to raise the technological level of fighting. For another, it would be very difficult for NATO countries to agree on when to shift from one level to the other. Different nations would have different interests in this matter and the "battlefield country" might prefer Soviet occupation to tactical nuclear destruction. Moreover, as one discussant observed, "The shift to tactical nuclear weapons may be disadvantageous because the West might end up with mixed forces and operations and unduly aggravate the difficulties of planning." Another added: "Once NATO is in a bad position conventionally, and is disorganized, it is also in a bad position to win with tactical nuclear armament." And if it looks as if the West were losing in a particular conventional conflict, NATO would have at its disposal other responses than "going tactical nuclear"—namely, enlargement of the conventional war, limited strategic reprisal, and the threat of massive strategic reprisal. The argument that tactical nuclear armament is in any case "here to stay" was accepted in the sense that "the military might encounter an insuperable psychological block if asked to forego what they consider the most 'modern' weapons. Yet a refusal to opt for a conventional force on this ground could obviously not be regarded as being based on sound strategic planning." Everything considered, one participant concluded: "A combination of adequate conventional and strategic reprisal forces would seem superior to a combination including a large and expensive tactical nuclear capability."[2]

On one point, it is worth reporting, the supporters of tactical nuclear weapons were clearly split. One of them denied that tactical nuclear conflict was more likely than conventional conflict to spiral to the level of all-out nuclear war. Another, however—obviously favoring massive deterrence over a limited-war strategy—disagreed sharply. According to him, it was the very danger of spiraling that would make a limited tactical nuclear capability invaluable as a mechanism for triggering off massive retaliation, thus making the latter more credible to Moscow than it might otherwise be and, in consequence, reinforcing deterrence of war.

There was nearly complete agreement on the size of the limited-war force which NATO should command. The 30 divisions demanded by SHAPE were held sufficient, provided these were full, effective divisions "on the line." To some extent, one participant observed, these divisions would and should be backed by reserves which could be speedily mobilized and deployed. Only one Conference member felt that

---

[2] The question of whether a tactical nuclear or a conventional capability would be the more expensive generated lively controversy, with different discussants arriving at opposite conclusions. On this matter, however, the available information was too scanty and vague to permit reasonably "educated guesses."

the force would probably have to be larger. A speaker who expressed the majority view concluded: "We are not discussing a revolutionary proposal. Indeed, once the 12 West German divisions are raised and France is able to return the bulk of its forces from Algeria, we will be close to the goal; and there is a great deal of NATO infrastructure which was built for conventional forces. The real question is one of choosing armament and strategy, not of numbers." And another added: "Neither are we proposing a return to World Wars I and II. We are not talking about long and massive conventional war."

VI. ARMS CONTROL

The Princeton Conference explored at great length the problem of disengagement in Central Europe. In this connection, a number of more or less passing remarks on various general aspects of arms control were made. A few of these seem worth recording.

Sentiment was favorable toward a test ban with effective control arrangements. One participant observed: "A ban on nuclear weapons testing would work against the acquisition by further NATO allies of independent strategic deterrents. It would instead rally support behind a joint NATO capability for strategic deterrence." Another speaker said: "A test ban would help to stop the dangerous drift toward more and more countries getting strategic nuclear forces. If more NATO countries build them, other countries, including Communist China, will follow suit. And, after all, our NATO allies would not give up much, for it is unlikely that they would come into possession of passive nuclear deterrents of much military worth." And a third advised: "If the United States and Russia can agree on a test ban, and President de Gaulle proves recalcitrant, we must remember that to be tough toward an ally is occasionally to the common good. In any case, if the two big powers are in agreement, it would be hard for a small or medium power to stand up against them."

Great value was also attributed to formal or tacit agreements designed to reduce the sort of uncertainty which might generate all-out war by mistake. "On some matters," one member stated, "we want to reduce Soviet uncertainty, and agreements to this effect would be mutually beneficial." Another participant explained: "One control task is to make advance preparations for reducing the possibility of accidental war. On this matter, both sides have a common interest. The question is whether we can discover ingenious ways of minimizing the rush to war if some accident does occur. The time available may be too short if we have to improvise in such a situation. Without advance preparation there may be nothing we can do, for example, to prevent accidental or misinterpreted moves in a limited war from touching off massive reprisal. Among the advance measures worth thinking about are arrangements for quick communications, in a crisis, between the heads of governments, or for verifying the persons who have authority to speak for the government. Or it might be to our advantage in a particular crisis to prove to the Russians that SAC is not on the way to bomb the Soviet Union, though it would also be to our advantage to furnish proof quickly without compromising SAC's security. Any inspection system, involving Russian inspectors in the United States— and American inspectors in the Soviet Union—might possibly be used for such purposes."

There was no doubt at the Princeton Conference that arms control, if feasible, would entail both invaluable benefits and grave risks. One participant stated: "Arms control agreements are enormously dangerous for the United States. If partial arms control brings a substantial relaxation of international tensions, the NATO countries—easily given to wishful thinking in this matter—might suffer the fatal disadvantage of a drop in defense budgets, a drop in military performance, a drop in alertness. And, unless control is airtight, such agreements might reduce for the Soviets strategic uncertainties which are holding them back at present. On the other hand, without effective arms control, the world will be so unstable militarily that it may not live to 1970 or 1980 without a catastrophic explosion."

Two other caveats were expressed. "In any arms control negotiations, we must be extremely careful that we do not condemn the West to military inferiority; we must be sure that there is an even trade-off in effective security." And what the Soviets may plan is, first, "a little agreement, satisfactory to all, and creating psychological relief to an extent that we are then softened up for a more important agreement which compromises our security."

On the other hand, it was remarked that arms control measures would seem "good for us if we are on the short end of the stick strategically—in either conventional, tactical nuclear, or even strategic nuclear capability. On this condition, arms control might complement our marginally inferior force structure." It was also pointed out that the West tends to be inferior to the Soviet bloc in military intelligence and in the ability to reinforce limited-war forces "on the line." Hence, arms control measures would favor us if they equalized military intelligence, if they equalized military capabilities, and if they made it harder for the other side to reinforce limited-war forces "on the line"—that is, to send additional divisions from Russia to East Germany.

VII. DISENGAGEMENT IN CENTRAL EUROPE

In the various forms in which disengagement has been proposed, it aims at an alteration of military and political arrangements in Central Europe. The pros and cons of disengagement received a great deal of attention at the Princeton Conference, but much of the discussion concerned political prerequisites, political objectives, and political consequences, for it was recognized that any appraisal of disengagement schemes called for a consideration of both political and military aspects. However, since this book is about military problems, only a minimum of the references to the politics of disengagement will be mentioned here.

There was a good deal of inconclusive discussion on the question of why the Russians favored, or pretended to favor, the Rapacki Plan or similar rearrangements in Central Europe. Were they motivated by their desire to break up NATO, or by the fear of a Germany eventually rearmed with nuclear weapons, or by both? While there was speculation on the political consequences of a Soviet military withdrawal from East Germany—could this lead to a political rollback of Communist rule or, at least, of Soviet control?—others doubted that the USSR would ever give up effective control over the Pankow regime —"if they gave up East Germany, this would be their first real postwar retreat." Apprehension was expressed lest the neutralization of Germany would deal a mortal blow to the integration movement in Western Europe. Several discussants felt that, even if the fear of a "nuclearized Germany" made the Kremlin want a scheme involving the neutralization of the two Germanies, and even if the United States and the Soviet Union could agree on a satisfactory scheme, there would be strong opposition from West Germany (unless she achieved real and democratic reunification with East Germany) and from France, "which does not want a change in the *status quo* of a divided Germany." The Conference participants were skeptical regarding the hope, expressed in some West European circles, that disengagement might or would be the first step toward a political rather than a military solution of the problem of Western security—a "move from conflict to cooperation with the Soviet Union." The general view was that "Soviet policy is one of implacable engagement; its disengagement policy is designed only to weaken NATO." Another discussant said: "You cannot disengage from a determined enemy."

One of the main inferences to be drawn from the Princeton discussion is that the benefit the West might derive from a disengagement accord would have to be political, for the military advantages mentioned were curiously few, minor, and hypothetical, unless such a scheme were only part of a larger general agreement involving effective and dependable controls on the production and employment of military forces. Disregarding this wider context, it was said that disengagement *might* somewhat reduce the danger of accidental war. It was also said that a mutual reduction of conventional forces *could* be useful to the West. (If there were an agreement stipulating a maximum Russian force of 20 divisions in East Germany, the USSR could not bring in an additional 20 divisions, ostensibly on maneuver, and thus confront the West with an increased threat of ground attack.) Perhaps the most solid advantage adduced was that a control scheme would lower the Russian advantage in military intelligence and that this would again limit the Soviet ability to launch a surprise attack on the ground. Finally, it was pointed out that, by agreeing to disengagement, "the West would not *give up* much militarily. If we agreed not to furnish West Germany with IRBM's, Western security would not be disadvantaged." "And if the West had a limited-war capability and strategy—especially with main reliance on conventional armament—the formal withdrawal of the West German divisions from NATO would not change the military equation very much. Disengagement would not make the West Germans less afraid of a possible Soviet ground thrust; and, in the event of such an attack, or the imminent threat of one, liaison could be quickly re-established between SHAPE and the West German army."

On the other hand, nobody had an answer to the question: "Exactly in what way would the Rapacki Plan lower the threat of war?" According to one participant, there was no evidence for supposing that local disengagement would diminish the threat of accidental war arising from political explosions in Eastern Europe. "We have had political explosions in East Germany and Hungary which did not result in war. And there is something nebulous about the very concept of accidental war. For an accident to lead to war, someone would have to decide that the time had come to start a war." It was also observed that denuclearization of a zone would not preclude tactical nuclear war in the area. "It would only mean that tactical nuclear weapons would not be deployed forward; and, especially with air-delivered weapons, the distance to the rear area would not be very significant." Another speaker replied: "Even if it were true that we would not give up much militarily, what can we reasonably expect to gain in our defense posture?"

A number of military disadvantages of disengagement were specified. The question was raised of whether, already extremely weak on the ground, NATO could safely cut its conventional forces in exchange for conventional cutbacks by the USSR. The familiar point was made that reduction of ground forces might lead to the retirement of American and British divisions from the Continent. One Conference participant, however, felt that there was a possibility—vigorously denied by others—of redeploying the Anglo-Saxon divisions in France. Another speaker maintained that NATO could lower its ground forces "if the West could match any Soviet build-up in forward areas by bringing in reserves." To this the familiar rejoinder was that the Russians could surely move in mobilized divisions much faster than SHAPE could mobilize or draw additional strength from overseas. One discussant replied that the West could lower its ground forces, since it could match a threat of additional Soviet divisions by its strategic retaliatory capacity. "Hence we need not match the Soviets division by division." According to one concluding statement on this particular problem, "It would be unsafe for the West to go further than the denuclearization of Germany." Yet even this statement was qualified by another discussant, who concluded that "the West would suffer a serious setback in defense if a regional regulation on the deployment and use of nuclear weapons were unaccompanied by a fair and reliable regulation of conventional forces."

Familiar doubts were expressed concerning the feasibility of "airtight" control mechanisms for ensuring compliance with military arrangements. What worried one Conference member even more—and this is a novel point—is that the West has a poor record of making our opponents observe agreements. Can we trust our own governments more than we can "trust" the Russians? "Our problem is that we cannot trust the governments of the United States and Great Britain to enforce agreements. Our governments might be weak and permit the Communists to cheat. And it is absolutely vital that, in important military matters, agreements are kept punctiliously. Too much is at stake in them." Several disquieting questions were broached in this connection. For example, "Exactly what could we expect the West to do in various contingencies after military forces have been thinned out in, or withdrawn from, certain areas in Europe? What would we do if there were a revolt against the government in Poland, and the Soviet

Army moved in?" "What would the Russians do, and what would we do, if a neutralized Germany were to manufacture nuclear arms? Would the hazards of a reoccupation of Germany not be very great?" "Would contingencies such as these not increase rather than decrease the danger of accidental war?"

Most participants appeared to agree with the concluding statement that, from the viewpoint of effective defense, "there is one great counter-argument against disengagement and the neutralization of Germany. It is that we would be taking a great risk without any firm expectation of getting compensatory gains." This warning was not necessily dispelled by the further remark, no doubt true, that "though disengagement involves us in dangers, there is nothing we can do that is not dangerous; the *present* situation in Central Europe is dangerous and, in any case, its continuation is unfeasible."

The Princeton Conference was far more hospitable to the possible benefits of disengagement than most Western governments have been in their official announcements. But, viewing the entire discussion, it seemed to this reporter that the defense considerations thus far advanced, pro and con, make disengagement schemes a matter of doubtful desirability; and that, if substantial political gains can be expected from such a move, it should not be forgotten that the substitutability of military and political advantages is definitely limited, that political benefits could be a poor compensation for military drawbacks.

Both conferences were organized by Professor Knorr. The first conference, held on January 13 and 14, 1959, was one in the series of Princeton University Conferences, which are designed to provide opportunity for joint discussion by members of the Princeton faculty and guests from other universities, organizations, and government, and especially from a number of business corporations which are members of the Princeton Conference.

The second conference, held on January 15 and 16, had more time for discussion than the first, and was confined to a smaller group of participants who were recognized experts on matters of military strategy. Its members were carefully selected to represent different approaches to, and views of, the subject at hand; for the purpose of the meetings was not to generate agreement but to be critical of all extant formulations of problems and solutions and, as much as possible, to be speculative, to be innovating, to come up with new questions and answers.

PARTICIPANTS IN THE SECOND CONFERENCE

CYRIL E. BLACK is Professor of History and Faculty Associate of the Center of International Studies at Princeton University. He is the author, with E. C. Helmreich, of *Twentieth Century Europe: A History* (2nd ed., 1959), and editor of *Challenge in Eastern Europe* (1954) and *Rewriting Russian History* (1956). He is also managing editor of *World Politics*.

A. L. BURNS, a Fellow of the Department of International Relations in the Australian National University at Canberra, A. C. T., is on leave during 1958-1959 as a Research Associate of the Center of International Studies, Princeton University. His publications include "From Balance to Deterrence: A Theoretical Analysis," *World Politics* (July 1957) and "The International Consequences of Expecting Surprise," *World Politics* (July 1958).

GORDON A. CRAIG is Professor of History and Faculty Associate of the Center of International Studies, Princeton University. He is the author of *The Politics of the Prussian Army, 1640-1945* (1955) and *From Bismarck to Adenauer: Aspects of German Statecraft* (1958).

Brigadier General SIDNEY F. GIFFIN, USAF, has been Director, Office of Armed Forces Information and Education, Department of Defense, since 1957. He previously served as Deputy J-3 for Plans of the U. S. European Command at Frankfurt, Germany, and at Germaine, France.

DENIS HEALEY has been Member of Parliament (Labour) for Leeds East since 1952. He is Vice Chairman of the Foreign Affairs Group of the Parliamentary Labour Party and served as Secretary of the International Department of the British Labour Party from 1946 to 1957. He was a delegate to the NATO Parliamentarians' Conference in 1955-1956 and to the Consultative Assembly of the Council of Europe in 1952-1954.

ROGER HILSMAN is Deputy Director for Research of the Legislative Reference Service, Library of Congress, and Research Associate of the Washington Center of Foreign Policy Research, The Johns Hopkins University. He is the author of *Strategic Intelligence and National Decisions* (1956) and co-author of *Military Policy and National Security* (1956).

MALCOLM W. HOAG has been a member of the Economics Division of The RAND Corporation since 1952. Among his publications are "Economic Problems of Alliance," *Journal of Political Economy* (December 1957), "NATO: Deterrent or Shield?" *Foreign Affairs* (January 1958), and "On NATO Pooling," *World Politics* (April 1958).

Colonel HENRY C. HUGLIN, USAF, served on the staff at SHAPE from 1953 to 1956. At the time of the Conference, he was Chief of Staff to the United States Representative to the NATO Military Committee and Standing Group.

PAUL H. JOHNSTONE has been a military analyst with the Weapons Systems Evaluation Group in the Pentagon since 1955. He was previously associated for six years with Air Force Strategic Intelligence.

HERMAN KAHN, a member of the Physics Division of The RAND Corporation since 1948, is the author of a RAND Report, "Major Implications of a Current Non-military Defense Study" (1958), and "How Many Can Be Saved?" *Bulletin of the Atomic Scientists* (January 1959). He has done work on the protection and composition of strategic forces.

MORTON A. KAPLAN, Assistant Professor of Political Science at the University of Chicago, is Visiting Research Associate at the Center of International Studies, Princeton University, during 1958-1959. He is co-author of *United States Foreign Policy: 1945-1955* (1956), and author of *System and Process in International Politics* (1957) and "Some Problems in the Strategic Analysis of International Politics" (Center of International Studies Research Monograph No. 2, 1959).

GEORGE F. KENNAN, a member of the Institute for Advanced Study at Princeton, N.J., was formerly U.S. Ambassador to the Soviet Union and head of the Policy Planning Staff of the Department of State. His recent publications include *Russia, the Atom and the West* (1958) and "Disengagement Revisited," *Foreign Affairs* (January 1959).

JAMES E. KING, JR., Research Associate of the Washington Center of Foreign Policy Research, was Executive Secretary in the Office of the U.S. High Commissioner for Germany in 1949-1952 and a military operations analyst with the Johns Hopkins University Operations Research Office in 1952-1957. Among his publications are "Nuclear Weapons and Limited War," *Foreign Affairs* (January 1957) and "Deterrence and Limited War," *Army* (August 1957).

KLAUS KNORR (Chairman) is Professor of Economics and Associate Director of the Center of International Studies, Princeton University. He is the author of *The War Potential of Nations* (1956) and other writings on defense problems.

ROBERT W. KOMER is a member of the Central Intelligence Agency.

FRANKLIN A. LINDSAY is a member of the firm of McKinsey & Company, Inc., management consultants. In 1955 he served as a White House consultant in the national security policy field and in 1957 was a member of the "Gaither Committee" on national security policy.

OSKAR MORGENSTERN is Professor of Political Economy and Director of the Economics Research Project at Princeton University. He is a member of the Advisory Panel to the Military Applications Subcommittee of the Joint Congressional Committee on Atomic Energy, and co-author, with John von

Neumann, of *Theory of Games and Economic Behavior* (rev. ed., 1955), and author of *International Financial Transactions and Business Cycles* (1959).

PAUL H. NITZE is President of the Foreign Service Educational Foundation, Washington, D.C., and Associate of the Washington Center of Foreign Policy Research. In 1950-1953 he served as Director of the Policy Planning Staff of the Department of State. His publications include "Atoms, Strategy and Policy," *Foreign Affairs* (January 1956), "Consultative Diplomacy in NATO," *Confluence* (Winter 1957), and "Symmetry and Intensity of Great Power Involvement in Limited Wars," in *Military Policy Papers* (Washington Center of Foreign Policy Research, December 1958).

ROBERT OPPENHEIMER, Director of the Institute for Advanced Study at Princeton, was Chairman of the General Advisory Committee of the Atomic Energy Commission from 1947 to 1953. His publications include *The Open Mind* (1955) and "An Inward Look," *Foreign Affairs* (January 1958).

Colonel FRANK R. PANCAKE, USAF, has been a member of the Plans and Policy Division of SHAPE since August 1955.

GEORGE W. RATHJENS was a member of the scientific staff of the Weapons Systems Evaluation Group, Office of the Secretary of Defense, during 1953-1958. Among his publications are "Notes on the Military Problems of Europe," *World Politics* (January 1958), and "Deterrence and Defense," *Bulletin of the Atomic Scientists* (June 1958).

Colonel EUGENE A. SALET, U.S. Army, has served as Secretary and Deputy Director of the NATO Standing Group in the Pentagon and, previous to that, was assigned to the planning staff of SHAPE.

THOMAS C. SCHELLING, Professor of Economics associated with the Center for International Affairs at Harvard University, is on leave at The RAND Corporation in 1958-1959. He is an editor of the *American Economic Review* and of the *Journal of Conflict Resolution*. Among his publications are *National Income Behavior* (1951) and *International Economics* (1958).

JOSEPH R. STRAYER is Professor and Chairman of the Department of History at Princeton University.

FREDERICK J. YEAGER.

The *rapporteurs* were:

BERNARD C. COHEN, Assistant Professor, Woodrow Wilson School, and Research Associate, Center of International Studies, Princeton University.

GLENN H. SNYDER, Research Associate, Center of International Studies, Princeton University.

SIDNEY VERBA, Research Assistant, Center of International Studies, Princeton University.

It may be interesting to note that the authors of the chapters and the discussants at the second conference represent a meeting of military and government as well as academic *expertise*. Four of the participants were currently members of the military profession, three from the Air Force, one from the Army, and three of these four had current duties connected with NATO. Eight other participants were currently with government or with The RAND Corporation, a private research organization engaged in research for the U.S. Air Force. Six of these eight were professionally concerned with defense matters. Of the remaining twelve participants, all but three had seen extended government service and many were currently consultants of various government agencies. About two-thirds of the group had a substantial record of publications on military problems.

INDEX

accidental total war, 70f., 74, 81f., 86, 94, 95f., 113, 191, 198ff., 284, 295, 296, 316, 319

Acheson, Secretary of State Dean, 18, 68, 71, 120, 210

Adenauer, Chancellor Konrad, 237, 239, 240, 242, 243ff., 253ff., 259

air defense, 123; Soviet policy of, 46; passive and civil, 71, 74, 75, 105, 108f.; active, 110

arms control, 7, 94ff., 162, 170, 172, 189, 245, 279, 302ff., 329ff.; Soviet policy toward, 58f.; measures to safeguard against surprise attack, 95, 176ff.; as alternative to new independent nuclear deterrents, 152, 168; open-skies proposal, 176, 191f.; conflict between arms control and measures against surprise attack, 180f., 183ff.; problems of inspection, 191ff., 195ff., 200ff.; and dispersal of nuclear systems, 295, 296

arms race, 75f., 186ff., 189, 286f., 303f., 310, 312f., 326f.

Aron, Raymond, 304

balance of terror, as condition of mutual deterrence, 178ff., 184f., 188f., 281ff.; and relative numbers of strategic weapons, 183ff.; and accuracy of strategic weapons, 185f., 285ff.; and invulnerability of weapons, 186ff., 285f., 291f., 310; and fear of surprise attack, 195f., 197ff., 205f.; uncertainties concerning, 279ff.; instability of, 286f., 303f., 312f.

Benelux, 166f., 320

Berlin dispute, 57, 149, 210, 254, 313

Blackett, Prof. P. M. S., 216f.

Blank, Defense Minister Theodor, 242; *Dienststelle Blank*, 236, 239

Brentano, Foreign Minister Heinrich, 254, 255ff.

Brodie, Bernard, 179n., 188, 284f.

Brucker, Secretary of the Army Wilber M., 52n., 67, 78n.

Buchan, Alastair, 279, 305

Bulganin, Foreign Minister Nikolai, 254f.

Buzzard, Rear Admiral A. W., RN (Ret.), 301

China, Communist, 38, 51, 53, 72, 84, 172, 263, 313, 329

Churchill, Sir Winston, 26, 214, 217

Common Market, *see* European Economic Community

Community of Six, 4, 263, 266, 274

Cyprus dispute, 3, 230, 263

Czechoslovakia, 51, 53, 57, 254, 257

de Gaulle, Gen. Charles, 133, 166, 231, 232, 329

Denmark, 19, 22, 166f., 320

deterrence, *see* independent nuclear deterrents *and* joint system of nuclear deterrence

disarmament, *see* arms control

disengagement from Central Europe, 267ff., 331ff.; Soviet views of, 56f.; British views of, 232ff.; German views of, 254ff.

Dulles, Secretary of State John Foster, 26f., 72, 85n., 218, 245, 259

Eden, Prime Minister Anthony, 212, 233

Eisenhower, Dwight D., as Supreme Commander, NATO, 20f., 211, 214; as President, 26, 72

Eisenhower Administration, defense policy of, 20, 26, 280, 281f., 324

Erler, Fritz, 241, 244, 254, 256

Eschenburg, Theodor, 245

European Atomic Energy Community (Euratom), 4, 263

European Coal and Steel Community, 4, 263

European Defense Community (EDC), 23, 212, 236, 238

European Economic Community, 4, 263, 274

Exercise *Carte Blanche*, 11, 26, 240

"forward strategy," *see* NATO

France, and Algerian dispute, 3, 100, 133, 263; and Suez crisis, 3, 56, 221; desire for independent nuclear deterrent, 7, 133, 160f., 164f., 229ff., 231, 288, 313, 314, 319, 320; and EDC, 23, 212; attitude toward Germany, 238, 263; and limited war strategy, 300, 301f.

Gaitskell, Hugh, 233, 257

Gale, Gen. Sir Richard, 280

Garthoff, Raymond L., 68n., 73n., 77n., 211

German reunification, 57f., 233, 257f., 271, 331

Germany, East, 51, 57, 85, 173, 256, 258, 332; Soviet forces in, 22, 23, 25, 31, 302, 332; neutralization of, 268ff., 331f.

Germany, West, decision to rearm, 17f., 20, 212f., 236ff.; Russian policy toward, 57f., 331; question of independent nuclear weapons development, 165, 167, 229, 320; growth of *Bundeswehr*, 236ff.,